O9-CFS-935

Smoke and Mirrors

Smoke and Mirrors

Violence,

Television,

and

Other

American

Cultures

John Leonard

THE NEW PRESS · NEW YORK

Library of Congress Cataloging-in-Publication Data

Leonard, John.
    Smoke and mirrors: violence, television, and other American cultures /
John Leonard.
    P. CM.
    ISBN 1-56584-226-X
  1. Television broadcasting—Social aspects—United States. I. Title.
PN 1992.6.L46   1997
302.23'45'0973—DC20   96-29421
                                       CIP

Published in the United States by The New Press, New York
Distributed by W. W. Norton & Company, Inc., New York

Established in 1990 as a major alternative to the large commercial publishing
houses, The New Press is a nonprofit American book publisher. The Press
is operated editorially in the public interest, rather than for private gain; it is
committed to publishing, in innovative ways, works of educational, cultural,
and community value that, despite their intellectual merits, might not normally
be commercially viable. The New Press's editorial offices are located at the City
University of New York.

Book design by [sic]

Production management by Kim Waymer, The New Press
Printed in the United States of America

9 8 7 6 5 4 3 2 1

In Memory of Richard Ashcraft and Walter Clemons

When I got my first television set,
I stopped caring so much about
personal relationships.

Andy Warhol

Countin' flowers on the wall,
That don't bother me at all,
Playin' solitaire till dawn
With a deck of fifty-one,
Smokin' cigarettes and watchin'
Captain Kangaroo.
Now don't tell me
I've got nothin' to do.

Statler Brothers, *Flowers on the Wall*

Come, children, let us shut up the box and the puppets, for our play is played out.

William Makepeace Thackeray, *Vanity Fair*

Contents

Introduction:
Why Are We Meeting
Like This?

In the summer and fall of 1993, like Sumer warrior kings, daubed with sesame oil, gorged on scapegoat, hefting swords and hurling anathemas, the attorney general of the United States, a tripleheader of headline-hungry senators and a noisy cohort of underemployed busybodies in the private sector—social scientists, tabloid columnists, antidefamation pressure groupies, religious sectarians—stormed Burbank, California, as if it were Waco, Texas. According to Janet Reno, Ernest "Fritz" Hollings, Daniel Inouye, Paul Simon and the moralizing coalitions to which they pandered, we hurt one another because of…television! From a ziggurat in fabled Ur, Fritz warned readers of *The New York Times*: "If the TV and cable industries have no sense of shame, we must take it upon ourselves to stop licensing their violence-saturated programming."

Hollings and Inouye were co-sponsors in the Senate of a bill to ban *any* act of violence on television before midnight. Never mind whether this was constitutional, nor what it would do to the local news. Never mind that Fritz himself voted against the Brady Bill to restrict the sale of handguns. (Guns don't kill people; television does.) Never mind, either, that in Los Angeles that August, at the Beverly Hilton Hotel, in front of six-hundred industry executives and a live CNN audience, the talking heads—a professor here, a producer there, a child psychologist and a network veep for program standards—couldn't even agree on what they meant by "violence." (Is it only bad if it hurts or kills?) Nor on which was worse, a "happy" violence that sugar-coats aggressive behavior or a "graphic" violence that at least suggests there are consequences. (How, anyway, does TV manage somehow simultaneously to *desensitize* but also *exacerbate;* to *sedate* but also *incite?*) Nor were they really sure what goes on in the dreamy heads of our cabbage-patch children as they crouch in the dark to commune with the tube, while their parents, if they have any, aren't around. (*Roadrunner? Beep beep.*) Nor does a "viewer discretion" advisory apply to cartoons and soaps, pro hockey (white men beating up on one another), pro basketball (black men beating up on one another), Sarajevo or Oklahoma City.

Momentarily, after the election of a guns-and-God Republican Congress in 1994—a Keystone Khmer Rouge pledged in its slash-and-burn Contract on America to cleanse Phnom Penh of every pointy-headed intellectual with a tutu in his closet, every parasitic lowlife painter who ever suckered a dime from the National Endowment, every third-world wetback here to steal a job and every child who was ever "difficult," not to mention their welfare mothers, crackhead fathers, shyster lawyers and other inconvenient codependents who ought instead to be growing rice and eating fish paste in the boondocks—the focus of tube-bashing switched from networks and cable, where "hidden persuaders" were accused of exploiting our vulgar appetite for blood and semen, to the Corporation for Public Broadcasting, where "liberal elitists" were alleged to promote their ulterior agenda of multiculti/feminazi/gay-pride/socialized-medicine/performance art. But by late spring 1995, Bill Clinton had recovered enough initiative to endorse a "V" chip with which worried parents could zap their children prior to unhealthy programming, and, that summer, language actually mandating such *zap* technology when the manufacture of new TV sets was inserted into the Telecommunications Bill by both houses of Congress. By August, Fritz and friends were in full cry again about the "family hour." That fall, warming up for the presidential politics of 1996, Bob Dole jumped on the sex-and-violence ban wagon with an attack on the vampire media elite, and William Bennett, former secretary of virtue in Ronald Reagan's Caligari cabinet, assigned himself to trash patrol among the blabbermouth Geraldos. Upon the signing into law of the 1996 Telecommunications Bill just in time for Valentine's Day, the front page of *The New York Times* reported an agreement among the four major networks to establish their very own ratings system, since PG, R and X seemed to work so wonderfully well for the Motion Picture Association of America. Simultaneously, without a single hearing to educate itself on the intricacies and intimacies of Internet, Congress voted in the Communications Decency Act to ban from cyberspace speech that was otherwise publishable in books, magazines and newspapers. Off-color? Not on *our* line. Hardcore? Not in *our* software.

Those of us who suspect that a V chip will be about as helpful in reducing violence in the society as student uniforms are likely to be in reversing the decline of the public schools find ourselves in a strident minority. Everybody else seems to agree that watching television causes antisocial behavior, especially among the children of the poor. That there is more violent programming over the air now than there ever was before. That *Beavis and Butt-head* inspired an Ohio five-year-old to burn down his family trailer. That in the crepuscular blue gray cathode glow we have spawned affectless toadstools, serial triffids, and cannibalistic rapist-killers.

In fact, except for hospital shows, there is less violence on network TV than there used to be. Because of ratings, sitcoms predominate. And the worst stuff is Hollywood splatter flicks on premium cable, which the poor are less likely to watch. Everywhere else on cable, not counting Court TV, home shopping and the perpetual-motion loop of Ted Turner's westerns, and not even to think about blood sports or Pat Robertson, the fare is wholesome to the verge of stupefaction: Disney, Discovery, Learning, Family, History, Nashville, Nickelodeon. Since his Ohio trailer wasn't even wired for cable, the littlest firebird must have got his MTV elsewhere in the dangerous neighborhood. Besides, kids have played with matches since at least Prometheus. (I burned down my own bedroom when I was five years old. The fire department had to tell my mother.) And far from sitting at home like lumps of Spam, "narcotized by hegemonic manipulations of symbolic reality," as an academician put it, more Americans than ever before go out to eat in restaurants, see films, plays, and baseball games, visit museums, travel abroad, even jog. Even when we *are* watching TV, we do something else at the same time. While our kids play with their Quicktime software, Adobe Illustrators, Vidicraft CCU 120 Commercial Cutters and Domark Virtual Reality Toolkits, the rest of us eat, knit, smoke, dream, read magazines, sign checks, feel sorry for ourselves, think about Hillary and plot shrewd career moves or revenge.

Actually watching TV, unless it's C-SPAN, is usually more interesting than the proceedings of Congress—or what we read in hysterical books like Jerry Mander's *Four Arguments for the Elimination of Television*, George Gilder's *Life After Television*, Marie Winn's *The Plug-in Drug*, Neal Postman's *Amusing Ourselves to Death* and Bill McKibben's *The Age of Missing Information*. Or what we'll hear at panel discussions on censorship, where rightwingers worry about sex and leftwingers worry about violence. Or at symposia on "The Apocalypse Trope in Television News" and seminars on "Postmodern Transgressions, Gender-Bending and Unkindness to Small Animals in Heavy Metal Music Videos." Or lolling around the academic deep-think tank, trading mantras like "frame analysis" (Erving Goffman), "fake realism," (T.W. Adorno), "processed culture" (Richard Hoggart), "waning of affect" (Fredric Jameson), "social facsimile" (Kenneth Gergen), "violence profiles" (George Gerbner), "iconography of rooms" (Horace Newcomb), "narcoleptic joy" (Michael Sorkin), "glass teat" (Harlan Ellison), "thalidomide" (Robert Bly) and "masturbation" (Michael Arlen, Allan Bloom, David Mamet). Down among the mad hatters of critical theory, you'd think the looking glass was somehow entropic, a heat-death of the culture.

Of course, *something* happens to us when we watch television. Networks couldn't sell their millions of pairs of eyes to advertising agencies (at an amazing $40,000 for every *second* of the 1996 Super Bowl) nor would those agencies buy more than $150 billion worth of ad space and commercial time per annum if speech did not somehow modify behavior. But *what* happens is usually fuzzy, and won't be greatly clarified by lab studies, however longitudinal, of habits and behaviors isolated from the larger feedback loop and echo chamber of a culture full of gaudy contradictions. We are at least as imprecise in front of our talking furniture as Heisenberg was uncertain contemplating quanta. It is as preposterous to believe that all entertainment is hypodermic, directly injecting bad ideas into the innocent bloodstream of the passive masses, as it is to pretend that all behavior is mimetic and that our only models are Eliot Ness or Dirty Harry. What about Mr. Rogers and Jessica Fletcher? Every fifties sitcom celebrated the two-parent nuclear family, and the divorce rate soared. The most popular program in the eighties was *The Cosby Show*, and race relations have never been worse. Until 1996, every television movie and every episode of a dramatic series that ever contemplated capital punishment ended up opposing the death penalty, yet a bloodlust rose throughout the nation and we're happily back dispensing divine justice. Why, after so much M*A*S*H every week for seven years in prime time and every night in reruns ever since, aren't all of us tree-hugging wiseguy pacifists?

And while the brief of this book is less than imperial, it's worth noting a few discrepancies abroad. Japan is the only country in the world where they watch more television than we do (and you should also see their snuff movies and pornographic comic books), but their per capita rate for murder and rape is little league compared to ours. Some Indian critics earlier this decade sought to blame the surge in communal violence on a state-run television series dramatizing the *Mahabharata*. But many of the same critics had earlier blamed a *fatwa*-afflicted Salman Rushdie for subcontinental bloodletting, as in Bangladesh they recently sought to pin the rap on novelist Taslima Nasrin. (Since Mahatma Gandhi was assassinated by a Hindu, and Indira by her Sikh bodyguards, and Rajiv by Tamil separatists, maybe organized religion causes violence, in Belfast as well as East Timor.) No one blames German TV for neo-Nazi skinhead violence against Turkish migrant workers. Nor does anyone blame Lucille Ball for what Idi Amin did to Uganda, even when an entire video library of her sitcoms was discovered in the palace vault after he was deposed. Czech TV deserves partial credit for the Velvet Revolution, but not as much as Havel or Gorbachev. Though the mullahs in Iran complain about *Baywatch* by jiggle relay from the Great Satan, and the Ministry of Culture in Vietnam has banned videotapes of American TV programs as well as copies of *Paris Match* containing a photograph of model Naomi Campbell's bare breasts, Teheran and Hanoi are no more fun now than they were in the days of SAVAK and Ho. (There is, as a matter of fact, more pornography and less violence against women in Holland than anywhere else in the western world, while the exact opposite is true in Thailand.) And while Yugoslavia's disintegration may have been encouraged by hate television in several of the republics, we also know from the remarkable novels of Milorad Pavic that behind the eyes of every Serb there has been, for seven centuries, a rerun of the Battle of Kosovo, where the Ottomans died in Lazar.

But nobody normal watches TV the way attorneys general, congressmen, symposiasts and McKibbens do. McKibben and his friends taped 1,700 hours of television, on a single 24-hour day, on all 93 channels of a Maryland cable system. He spent six months watching all this tape, after which he took an Adirondacks hike. And then he wrote his book, explaining that television dumbs the Republic. What a guy. The rest of us must be less thrilling.

For instance: In a March, 1993, episode of *Homicide*, written by Tom Fontana and directed by Martin Campbell, Baltimore police detectives Bayliss (Kyle Secor) and Pembleton (Andre Braugher) had twelve hours to wring a confession out of "Arab" Tucker (Moses Gunn), for the strangulation and disembowelling of an eleven-year-old girl. In the dirty light and appalling intimacy of a single claustrophobic room, with a whoosh of wind-sound like some dread blowing in from empty Gobi spaces, among maps, library books, diaries, junkfood, pornographic crime scene snapshots and a single, black, overflowing ashtray, these three men were as nervous as the hand-held cameras, as if their black coffee were full of amphetamines and spiders; as if God Himself were jerking them around. Pembleton, who is black, played Good Cop. Bayliss, who is white, played Bad Cop. Then, according to cop torque, they reversed themselves. This bearded "Arab," a fruit peddler whose fiancée dumped him, whose barn burned down, whose horse died, was attacked for his alcoholism, his polygraph readings, his lapsed Baptist church-going and his sexuality. About to crack, he struck back. To Pembleton: "You hate niggers like me 'cuz you hate the inner nigger...you hate being who you really are." To Bayliss: "You got your dark side and it terrifies you...You look into the mirror and all you see is an *amateur*." Finally, the cops got a confession, but not to the murder of the girl to whom "Arab," as if from the prodigal riches of Africa, had given peaches and pomegranates and an avocado: "I never touched her, not once." Yet this Adena was indeed "the one great love" of an old man's otherwise wasted life.

You may think the culture doesn't really need another cop show. I would personally prefer a weekly series in which social problems are solved through creative nonviolence after a Quaker meeting by a collective of vegetarian carpenters. But in a single hour that March, for which Tom Fontana eventually won the Emmy he deserved, I learned more about the behavior of fearful men in small rooms than I had from any number of better-known movies and serious plays and modern highbrow novels by the likes of Don DeLillo, Mary McCarthy, Alberto Moravia, Nadine Gordimer, Heinrich Böll and Doris Lessing.

This was an accident, as it usually is when those of us who watch TV like normal people are startled in our cool. We leave home expecting for a lot of money to be exalted, and almost never are. But staying put, wishing merely for a chortle or a pipe dream, suspecting that our cable box is just another bad-faith credit card enabling us to multiply our disappointments, we are ambushed into sentience. And not so much by "event" television, like Bergman's *Scenes from a Marriage*, originally a six-hour miniseries for Swedish TV; or Zeffirelli's 1984 Easter mass in Rome for Italian TV; or Marcel Ophuls's *The Sorrow and the Pity*, conceived for French TV; or Werner Fassbinder's *Berlin Alexanderplatz*, commissioned by German TV; or from Britain *The Singing Detective* and *The Jewel in the Crown*. On the contrary, we have stayed home on certain nights to watch TV, the way on other nights we will go out to a neighborhood restaurant, as if on Mondays we ordered in for laughs, whereas, on Fridays, we'd rather eat Italian.

And suddenly Napoleon shows up on *Northern Exposure* frozen like a Popsicle, while Chris reads Proust on the radio. Or *Law & Order* decides to mix up the World Trade Center bombing and the Branch Davidian firestorm, to suggest that not all terrorism is fundamentally Islamic. Or *Roseanne* is about joblessness and lesbianism as well as bowling. Or *Picket Fences* has moved on from elephant abuse and gay-bashing to euthanasia and the Supreme Court. Or, on *Mystery*, there is enough static cling between Inspector Morse and Zoë Wanamaker to hydroelectrify the Yangtze. On *The Young Indiana Jones Chronicles*, no sooner has Indy finished consorting with Bolsheviks and Hemingways than he is being advised on his sexual confusions in Vienna by Dr. Freud and Dr. Jung. Kurt Vonnegut Jr. on Showtime! David "Masturbation" Mamet on TNT! Norman Mailer wrote the teleplay for *The Executioner's Song*, and Gore Vidal gave us *Lincoln* with Mary Tyler Moore as Mary Todd. In just the last decade, if I hadn't been watching TV, I'd have missed *Tanner '88*, in which Robert Altman and Garry Trudeau ran Michael Murphy for president; *A Very British Coup*, during which socialists and Mozart took over England; *My Name Is Bill W.* with James Woods as a founding father of Alcoholics Anonymous; *Roe v. Wade* with Holly Hunter as a Supreme Court case; *The Final Days* with Theodore Bikel as Henry

Kissinger; *Common Threads* on the AIDS quilt; *No Place Like Home*, where there wasn't one for Jeff Daniels and Christine Lahti, as there hadn't been for Jane Fonda in *The Dollmaker* or Mare Winningham in *God Bless the Child*; those two home movies on America's second Civil War, *Eyes on the Prize*; *Sensibility and Sense*, with the astonishing Elaine Stritch in Richard Nelson's post mortem on Mary McCarthy, Lillian Hellman and Diana Trilling; *Separate but Equal*, with Sidney Poitier as Thurgood Marshall; *Seize the Day*, the Robin Williams riff on Saul Bellow; *Mother Love*, with Diana Rigg warming up for the Medea she'd bring to Broadway; *High Crimes & Misdemeanors*, Bill Moyers' special on Irangate and the scandal of our intelligence agencies; *Sessions*, in which Billy Crystal used Elliott Gould to bite psychoanalysis in its pineal gland; not only *Mastergate*, Larry Gelbart's deconstruction of the Reagan-Babar text, but also *Barbarians at the Gate*, his sendup of vulture capitalism; *Daughters of the Dust*, Julie Dash's painterly meditation on Gullah culture off the Carolina coast; *The Boys of St. Vincent*, about the sexual abuse by Roman Catholic priests of Canadian orphans; a *Caine Mutiny Court Martial* set by Robert Altman on a basketball court; a half-dozen *Prime Suspect*s; plus Evelyn Waugh's *Scoop*, Bette Midler's *Gypsy*, Graham Greene, Philip Roth, John Updike, Gloria Naylor, George Eliot, Arthur Miller, Gabriel García Márquez, Paul Simon and Stephen Sondheim. Not to mention those hoots without which any pop culture is as tedious as Anaïs Nin—like Liz Taylor in *Sweet Bird of Youth*, the Redgrave sisters in a remake of *Whatever Happened to Baby Jane?*, and the loony episode of *The X-Files* in which a turbanned cult of vegetarians was blamed for kidnapping and terrorizing farm-town teenagers who turned out to have been doped with alien DNA disguised as bovine growth hormone.

What all this television has in common is narrative. Even network news—which used to be better than most newspapers before the bean counters started closing down overseas bureaus and the red camera lights went out all over Europe and Asia and Africa—is in the story-telling business. And what do we know about narrative? Well, we know what German novelist Christa Wolf told us in *Cassandra*. "Only the advent of property, hierarchy, and patriarchy extracts a blood-red thread from the fabric of human life...and this thread is amplified at the expense of the web as a whole, at the expense of its uniformity. The blood-red thread is the narrative and struggle and victory of the heroes, or their doom. The plot is born." And we also know what Don DeLillo told us in *Libra*: "There is a tendency of plots to move toward death.... the idea of death is woven into the nature of every plot. A narrative plot no less than a conspiracy of armed men. The tighter the plot of the story, the more likely it will come to death."

In other words, either the Old Testament or the *Iliad* was the first western and the *Mahabharata* was no less bloody-minded. Think of Troy and Masada as warm-ups for the Alamo. This frontier sex and violence stuff runs deep—from Hannibal, to Attila, to El Cid, to Sergio Leone. What all westerns have always been about is clout, turf, sexual property rights and how to look good dying. So, too, can the typical movie-of-the-week and miniseries be said to derive comfortably from the worldview of antiquity: from Ovid or Sophocles. At least since the marriage of Cadmus to Harmony, abduction and rape were not only what gods did constantly to mortals, but also the principal form of East-West cultural exchange in the ancient world, with Europa and Io and Medea and the Argonauts, poor Helen stolen, first by Theseus and later on by Paris of Troy, Ariadne in Argos and Naxos and Persephone in the underworld. But so far nobody in Congress or the Justice Department has suggested a Brady Ban on myth and legend.

Because I watch all those despised network TV movies, I know more about racism, ecology, homelessness, gun control, child abuse, AIDS, gender confusion and rape than is dreamed of by, say, Katie Roiphe, the Joyce Maynard of Generation X, or than Hollywood ever bothered to tell me, especially about AIDS. Because I've followed many of my favorite series over months, years and even, in reruns, decades, I have a lively sense of just what television has been trying to tell us about common decency, civil discourse and social justice. I am not one of those newspaper or magazine critics who think they're *better* than TV and should really be writing about something more important—the theater, say, or foreign policy—and who bring to their drudge a condescension like a prophylactic. Nor am I one of those swinging postmodernists who wear Heidegger safari jackets, Foucault platform heels, Lacan epaulets and a Walter Benjamin boutonniere to every faculty meeting as if it were a Paris Commune, for whom TV is a convenient opportunity to assert that the Enlightenment was a lie; that causality, continuity, history and morality are delusions; that such "master-narratives" as scientific progress, class struggle and the Oedipus complex are bankrupt; that books, films, comic strips, advertisements, TV programs and even authors themselves are "socially constructed" compost heaps of previous texts, at best unwilling stooges and at worst bad-faith purveyors of a "dominant discourse"; and that the rest of us, readers and watchers, are likewise each the helpless vector of forces we can't even locate much less modify, stuck in spectacle and juxtaposition, "life-styles" and language games, allegory and aesthetics. In my opinion, long before postmodernism, there had always been the blues. And on retro television, the Enlightenment is far from dead. Like the parent of any child, TV behaves as if we could assuage those blues. This book is about what we actually see on television, how we go about seeing it, why we'd want to and whether the meanings we attach so feverishly to our spectatorship are accurate, much less interesting. I argue that TV, however much a creature of the fast-buck media monopolies and quarterly-dividend greedhead crowd, is full of surprising gravity and grace; that where it departs in any significant way from the tenacious norms of the pop culture that long ago preceded it and still today surrounds it, those departures have been open of mind and generous of heart if also wishful and naive; and that we'd actually be a kinder, gentler, healthier nation if in fact we embraced the scruples and imitated the behaviors recommended by most entertainment programs—more welcoming of diversity and difference, more impatient with the routine brutalities of a master class and a mass society, more of a community than an agglomeration of market segments and seething sects.

We were a violent culture before TV, from Wounded Knee to lynching bees, with a bloodier labor history than most any other nation in the industrialized world. Slave rebellions, railroad strikes, mountain blood feuds, night riders, vigilantes, and, from 1830 on, urban mobs rioting against Negroes, Catholics, Jews, Chinese, abolitionists and the draft...the Knights of Labor and the Ku Klux Klan...the Haymarket riot, the Homestead strike, Harlan County and the Black Hole of Ludlow...Rangers, Pinkertons, Jayhawks, Blacklegs, Flatheads and Slickers...Liberty Boys, Molly Maguires, Regulators, White Caps, Bald Knobbers, Know Nothings, Copperheads...Tulsa, East St. Louis, Cincinnati, Detroit, Harlem, Newark and Watts...the Ghost Dance Wars and the Mountain Meadows Massacre...Hell's Angels and Black Panthers...

Attica and Altamont. Before television, we blamed our public schools for what went wrong with the little people, back when classrooms weren't overcrowded, in buildings that weren't falling down, in neighborhoods that didn't resemble Beirut, and whose fault is that? *The A-Team?* We can't control guns, or drugs; and two million American women are annually assaulted by their male partners, usually in an alcoholic rage; and three million children under the age of three, one quarter of our infants and toddlers, grow up each year in poverty without adequate adult supervision, intellectual stimulation, a decent diet or health care. Whose fault is that, *Miami Vice?* The gangbangers menacing our city streets aren't home watching Cinemax. Neither are the psychopaths who make bonfires in our parks of our homeless, of whom there are another million, a supply-side migratory tide of the deindustrialized and dispossessed, angry beggars, refugee children and catatonic nomads, none of them traumatized by *Twin Peaks.* (They were traumatized instead by down-sizing light manufacters and utilities companies, by the flight of capital to third-world sweatshops and by baby tycoons in the real estate racket who wanted their neighborhoods for condo conversion.) So cut Medicare and kick around the Brady Bill; sacrifice music appreciation, arts education, chess clubs and computer classes at P.S. 69, so that property taxes will never go up on those summer homes from which, in letters to Janet and Fritz, we animadvert TV movies about Amy Fisher and commercials for killer sneakers. But children who were loved and protected long enough to grow up liking themselves as adolescents and young adults, in a society where schools prepared them to find jobs with a particle of meaning, wouldn't riot in the streets. Ours is a buck-grubbing, status-grabbing, commodity-obsessed tantrum-yoga culture that measures everyone by his or her ability to produce wealth, and morally condemns anyone who fails to prosper, and blames its own angry incoherence on the very medium that faithfully reflects these appalling values. Why not wrathful gods, recessive genes or Arab terrorists? The Mafia, the zodiac or the elders of Zion? Probability theory, demonic possession, original sin? Alien abduction! Madonna! Tofu! And, of course, the Designated Hitter in American League baseball.

In the Great Depression year of 1933, there were 9.7 homicides per 100,000 Americans, an all-time high until the 1990s, when—

after a doubling in two decades of teen joblessness—the murder rate reached 10 per 100,000. Can it be that poverty contributes to violence? TV certainly thinks so. It's suspicious too of war, since the far-off killing fields are such excellent training for the unlicensed violence of everyday life. How odd that while the rest of the popular culture still loves war, in comic books, country music and Rambo movies, on series television since the late-sixties demise of *Combat* and *Rat Patrol*, what war has looked like is *M*A*S*H* and *China Beach*. When a reporter like Michael Herr went to Vietnam, as if Dante had gone to hell with a cassette recording of Jimi Hendrix and a pocket full of pills, he found our first rock-and-roll war, some "speeding brilliance" and "all the dread ever known." A black paratrooper told him, "I been *scaled,* man, I'm *smooth* now." "Disgust," wrote Herr, "was only one color in the whole mandala, gentleness and pity were other colors, there wasn't a color left out. I think Vietnam was what we had instead of happy childhoods." When a novelist like Robert Stone went to Vietnam, he found "cooking oil, excrement, incense, death...the green places of the world on fire...a kind of moral fascination." One character explained: "When I decide what happened, I'll decide to live with it." When moviemakers Michael Cimino, Francis Ford Coppola, Oliver Stone and Brian De Palma went to Vietnam, they found a splatter-painted Jackson Pollock mandala—streaks of brilliance, trickles of dread, childhood, hell and Joseph Conrad. And when network television went to Vietnam, what it found was *China Beach*—a dream ward where the wounded went after the jungle. In the jungle were the ghosts: unknowable history. On the beach, if the wounded were lucky, there was music and booze and they would be patched up by the black Irish nurse McMurphy (Dana Delany). Or they would buy the services of K.C. (Marg Helgenberger). If they weren't so lucky, they met Beckett (Michael Boatman), a dark prince of body-bags. On China Beach, as in any community beseeching an absent God, they had learned to live with what happened through pagan ritual. When Miss America refused to visit them, they staged their own mock beauty pageant. When Dr. Richards's stateside ex-wife remarried, they staged a "black unwedding," part Templar mystification, part Viking burial and part Wagnernian bonfire. When McMurphy was captured by the Viet Cong and forced to operate on the enemy, in a candlelit underground tunnel, we saw suddenly in those catacombs something like a sacrament. And they took the war with them wherever they went after Vietnam, to biker bars and Republican conventions and an Indian reservation, where McMurphy stopped drinking; to Hong Kong, where K.C. disappeared into her money, after the fall of Saigon and the parcel-posting of her child; to Montana, where Dodger found God in a converted school bus; and finally, all of them, after a reunion to mourn the loss of their innocence, their youth, faith, purpose, intensity of feeling and vanished community, after circling and staring and stuttering their emotions, after posing for snapshots and hiding in lavatories and singing a strange anthem and fighting off flashbacks that arrived like seizures, color-saturated, as if the past were modern art and the future merely television—to the black marble wall of the Vietnam Memorial in Washington, D.C.

A medium capable of *China Beach*, *M*A*S*H*, *St. Elsewhere*, *Northern Exposure*, *Homicide* and *The X-Files* has less to be ashamed of than many of its critics do, and most of its competition. Nor has it taught us how to hurt each other.

Violence, television, culture and America are all lots more complicated. A friend of mine, a professional musician, attributes the recent quadrupling of young females who have chosen in our schools to learn to play the saxophone to the fact that the cartoon character Lisa plays one on *The Simpsons*. After more than a quarter century of writing about the medium, it is my strong feeling that—except by accident, and in conjunction with various other fevers of the swampy moment, complicated by the vessel of desires and desperations we bring to our watching as individuals and social subsets, compounded and confounded by power relationships and interlocking monopolies in the commodity culture that *X-Files* FBI agent Fox Mulder has so memorably called a "military-industrial-entertainment complex" and in the larger society of which that complex is a nervous component, a dependent ward and a fax machine—television is not a Pandora's box, an hallucinogen, an erogenous zone, a Leninist plot, Prozac or the dark side. Partly a window and partly a mirror, and allowing for the messy software in our own systems as we sit down to process what we see, TV more resembles a household pet, like a loyal retriever, or a kitchen appliance, like a microwave oven, a vacuum cleaner, an Exercycle or a night-light, as well as a department store and amusement park. We gather like Druids to partake of blue magnetic light, in various states of readiness. We are at times just curious: an Oscar or a Super Bowl. We are at times compelled: a Watergate or Berlin Wall. We may hope, at exalted moments like a moonshot, and on dreadful occasions like an assassination, to experience some virtual community as a nation—message center, mission control, Big Neighbor and electronic Elmer's Glue-All. But more often we go to television because we're hungry, angry, lonely or tired. And TV will always be there for us, a twenty-four-hour user-friendly magic muffinmaker, grinding out narrative, novelty, *empathy* and distraction; news and laughs; snippets of high culture, remedial seriousness and vulgar celebrity; a place to celebrate and a place to mourn; a circus and a wishing well.

Ed Sullivan
Died for Our Sins

Each week since October, 1988, I've delivered myself of a five-minute "media criticism," a sort of sermonette, on *CBS Sunday Morning*. A dozen times in those eight years a stranger has stopped me on the street, at a movie, or waiting in line for a glimpse of Matisse to ask: "Do you write your own stuff?" To which I have learned to reply, passively-aggressively, "Well, they didn't hire me for my looks." But at least it's a human question. More often and more mystifying is the suspicious stare, the abrupt nod, the pointed finger and the accusation: "I saw *you* on television." After which, *nothing.* Not "I liked what you said," or "You're full of crap," or "How much do they pay you?" Just "I...*saw you.*" And then the usual New York vanishing act, like Shane. This used to bother me a lot, as if the medium lacked substance, or I did, or the spectral street, maybe even Matisse. Lately, though, I've begun to wonder whether what such strangers really seek on the surprising street is assurance. The problem is epistemological. *They saw me on television. I am real. Television might also be.* After almost half a century of looking at the ghosts in our machines, we are agnostics about reality itself.

Never mind docudramas, re-creations, staged news, creative editing, trick photography, computer enhancements, or commercials that sell us cars by promising adventure and sell us beer by promising friendship. Our *dubiety* about television probably started with the quiz show scandals in 1959. Oh how they wept, like *Little Mermaids*. That's one of the things I remember most about television in the fifties. Nixon cried in his Checkers speech. Jack Paar cried about his daughter. And Charles Van Doren cried because he'd been caught. So did Dave Garroway cry on the *Today* show because he was upset about Van Doren, the English instructor-son of a famous poet-professor, who'd parlayed his *21* winnings into a job as a "guest host" on Garroway's very own program. And because Dave was upset, so was his chimp, J. Fred Muggs. Who says men don't have feelings? "A terrible thing to do to the American public," cried Dwight D. Eisenhower on finding out that Van Doren, Patty Duke, Dr. Joyce Brothers and even Major John Glenn, before he ascended into space and the Senate, had all been fakes. This was some months before Ike lied to us himself about those U-2 overflights. Nor had Ike been exactly above-aboard about the CIA in Guatemala and Iran. But big government and big business have always been more creative than big TV, e.g., Watergate, Abscam, Chappaquiddick, Iranamok, BCCI, S & L, Whitewater and the Gulf of Tonkin. As Reagan apparatchik Elliott Abrams once told Congress: "I never said I had no idea about most of the things you said I said I had no idea about."

Enough fifties nostalgia. As much as we may have loved Lucy, what we did to our children was Howdy Doody and Captain Video. When John Cameron Swayze died recently, we ought to have been reminded of how bad TV news used to be back when his *Camel News Caravan* was "hopscotching the world for headlines," before he went on to pitch Timex ("takes a licking and keeps on ticking"). Even the Golden Age of TV drama was full of home-shopping Ibsens like Paddy Chayevsky and greeting-card Kafkas like Rod Serling, of bargain-basement Italian neorealism and kitchen-sink Sigmund Freud, where everybody explained too much in expository gusts, yet all were simultaneously inarticulate, as if a want of eloquence were a proof of sincerity and an excess of sincerity guaranteed nobility of sentiment, like a bunch of clean old Tolstoy peasants. And how clean were they, really? So clean, you never saw a black face, not even on a railroad porter. So clean, that Chayevsky's own family in *The Catered Affair* had to be Irish instead of Jewish, as the butcher in *Marty* was somehow Italian. So clean, that when Serling wanted to tell the story of Emmett Till, a black Chicago teenager lynched for whistling at a Mississippi white woman, *U.S. Steel Hour* turned it into a pawnbroker's murder in a Thornton Wilder sort of *Our Town*. So clean, that the Mars candy-bar company would not allow a single reference on *Circus Boy* to competitive sweets like cookies or ice cream, and *The Alcoa Hour* was so solicitous of a good opinion about aluminum it wouldn't let Reginald Rose set a grim teleplay in a trailer park, and, most famously, the American Gas Company insisted on removing any mention of "gas chambers" from a Playhouse 90 production of *Judgment at Nuremberg*.

A better beginning for any discussion of American television's childhood and prolonged adolescence in the Age of Faith is the original Mr. Ed. They didn't hire him for his looks.

To think that you're gonna be on television with Ed Sullivan was comparable to a nightclub comedian in those days to playing the epitome of a nightclub like the Copacabana. Or an opera singer being at the Met. Or, if a guy is an architect that makes the Empire State Building. Or it was a guy that was a Nazi to be Adolph Hitler. This was the biggest.

Jackie Mason

This "biggest" lasted twenty-three years. From 1948 to 1971, every Sunday night at 8 o'clock, a man who couldn't sing, or dance or spin a plate entertained fifty million Americans. Never before and never again in the history of the republic would so many gather so loyally, for so long, in the thrall of one man's taste. As if by magic, we were one big family. And what a lot of magic there was, as well as animals and acrobats, ventriloquists and marching bands, David Ben-Gurion, Brigitte Bardot and the Singing Nun. All by himself on CBS, handpicking every act, Ed Sullivan was a one-man cable television system with wrestling, BRAVO and comedy channels, Broadway, Hollywood and C-SPAN, sports and music video. We turned to him once a week in our living rooms for everything we now expect from an entire industry every minute of our semi-conscious lives. Such was his Vulcan mindmeld with his audience, one thinks of Chairman Mao.

Tiresome as the Boomers are, celebrating from their electronic nursery the nitwitticisms of *Leave It to Beaver, Gilligan's Island, The Brady Bunch, The Partridge Family* and *Happy Days*, they have intuited a truth about television as a timeline in our secret lives. It's as if this reservoir of images, consumed since childhood, stored on memory tape, amounts to something like the "pottery clock" of the archeologists, like clam-bed fossils and dinosaur teeth, Irish peat bog and California bristlecones, rings of trees, layers of acid, caps of ice and the residue of volcanic ash. We carbon-date ourselves. I was 10 years old when I first saw Sullivan, in 1949, talking to Jackie Robinson on a tiny flickering screen in my uncle's Long Beach, California, rumpus room. I was 12 when I realized that he'd be around forever, or at least a lot longer than your average stepfather. We were living then—after the rooms above a bowling alley in Washington, D.C., a ranch in New Mexico, a northern Wisconsin fishing lodge and a southern California Cubist sort of pillbox through whose portholes blew breezes of orange rind, petroleum and cow dung—in Queens, New York, behind a tavern, lullabied to sleep each night by Johnny Ray on a juke-box, singing "The Little White Cloud That Cried." On the portable Zenith my mother really couldn't afford, except that her latchkey children needed something warm to come home to after P.S. 69, there was Ed, chatting up Margot Fonteyn before she became a dame. As the following year he'd chat up Audrey Hepburn, before or after, I can't remember which, he laughed out loud when an automat ate Jackie Gleason. I was probably too busy to sit still for longer than *Crusader Rabbit*. I had my socialist newspaper, *The Daily Compass*, and my toy telescope to look at Sagittarius at night from the apartment house rooftop for signs of Velikovsky's multiple catastrophisms. At least a mock-heroic *Crusader Rabbit* made fun of the internal contradictions of the ruling class. Ed on the other hand...how could he have been back there in California and right here in Queens? And around, too, later on with Elvis in 1956, when I was flunking volleyball and puberty rites in high school? As, like the F.B.I., he'd find me wherever I went, in Cambridge, Berkeley, even Greenwich Village, chatting up Buddy Holly, Ernie Kovacs, Noël Coward, Stevie Wonder, Sonny and Cher, Cassius Clay, Eskimos and Beatles. Ed was my first inkling that henceforth all of us everywhere would simultaneously experience everything that is shameful or heroic about our country on one big headset;

as if, in a nomadic culture, the TV screen were the windshield of our mobile home, and all America a motor lodge.

There were only three channels to turn to at the start, duking it out for the most desirable hour of the television week. Ed's prime-time competition took the high road (*Philco Playhouse*, and Steve Allen) and the low (*Bowling Stars* and *The Tab Hunter Show*). Jimmy Durante, Perry Como, Eddie Cantor, Bob Hope, and Dean Martin and Jerry Lewis, *Sir Francis Drake*, *Bill Dana*, *Dragnet*, *National Velvet*, *Jamie McPheeters*, *Broadside*, *Buckskin* and *Wagon Train*, came and went while Ed stayed put. James Garner in *Maverick* beat him two years running in the ratings, then collapsed from nervous exhaustion. Back in the days when corporations owned entertainers like trademarks or tropical fish—when Arthur Godfrey belonged to Lipton Tea, Milton Berle to Texaco, Bob Hope to Pepsodent, Dinah Shore to Chevrolet, and Jack Benny to Jell-O; when Kraft, Lux, Revlon, G.E., Westinghouse, Magnavox, Budweiser, Armstrong Circle and Johnson Wax all had *Theaters;* Bell Telephone, Twentieth-Century Fox and U.S. Steel had *Hours;* Philco, Schlitz and Prudential had *Playhouses,* Geritol an *Adventure Show Case,* DuPont its *Show of the Month,* Hallmark a *Hall of Fame,* Twin Toni a *Time,* Firestone a *Voice* and Pabst Blue Ribbon *Bouts*—Colgate Palmolive spent $50 million on a *Comedy Hour* to knock Ed out of his Lincoln-Mercury. But he won his time period every week until Colgate bought a slice of him themselves.

Like Eddie Lopat, the crafty Yankees southpaw, Sullivan seemed to throw nothing but junk, and still they couldn't hit him. How did he do it, this spinning of the public like a plate?

They were making up TV as they went along, by accident and some sort of bat sonar, without focus groups, market surveys, "Q" ratings or Betsy Frank at Saatchi & Saatchi. "A door closing, heard over the air," wrote E. B. White at television's dawn, "a face contorted seen in a panel of light, these will emerge as the real and true. And when we bang the door of our own cell or look into another's face, the impression will be of mere artifice."

Imagine at any moment in those primetime years a six-room suite on the eleventh floor of Manhattan's Delmonico Hotel, where Ed and his wife, Sylvia, seem to have lived forever, with a Renoir landscape, a small Gauguin, autographed snaps of Cardinal Spellman and Ella Fitzgerald, and an original Disney cartoon in which Ed plays golf with Donald Duck. He gets up at 11 AM; breakfasts invariably on artificially sweetened pears, iced tea and a room-service lamb chop; reads the papers and makes hundreds of telephone calls, dialing them himself. He puts on one of his Dunhill suits—numbered like his shirts and ties, so that he can tape a new introduction to an old rerun without looking as though he'd dropped in on his own program for a surprise visit from Kurdistan—and a pair of buckled loafers. (His favorite shoes were a gift from George Hamilton whose feet he once admired.) He lunches invariably between 3:30 and 4 PM at Gino's on Lexington Avenue on roast chicken from which he detaches and pockets a drumstick, which he'll nibble later on. (From a childhood bout with scarlet fever and a high-school football injury, he developed permanent sinus trouble: America's tastemaker can't smell or savor his own food.) He hasn't a manager, an agent, a chauffeur for his limo or even a limo. He likes to talk to cabbies about his show and to Lincoln-Mercury dealers. On his way to the studio, he will carry his own change of clothes on a wire hanger in a garment bag. After a movie screening or a Broadway play, he'll supper with Sylvia at the Colony, Le Pavillon or Le Grenouille. They order sweet wine, which Ed improves with hoarded packets of Sweet 'n' Low. And then they are off to the Yonkers harness races and the frantic nightlife of the clubs.

We aren't talking about a Rupert Murdoch, a Michael Eisner, a Ted Turner, a Barry Diller, a John Malone, an Aaron Spelling or any other morning star pedalling his epicycle in a Ptolemaic universe of hype according to which the very heavens buzz in eccentric orbits around the need of a vacuous public for gas. Ed is a regular guy. Except...he's made somehow of air.

Almost from their first date, a heavyweight prizefight, Ed and Sylvia were self-sufficient, a mollusk of a marriage. They never ate in. Nobody cooked. The only domestic help they needed was the hotel maid. Isn't this odd? Not just the single chop for breakfast, the drumstick in the Dunhill pocket, the Sweet 'n' Low for wine, but this peculiar weightlessness, as if the Delmonico were an aquarium: artificial sweetening; artificial light. As in a Hollywood movie or TV action-adventure series or experimental novel, nobody had to wash a dish or make a bed. Till she was 12 their daughter, Betty, never ate with them; she ate at Child's with a paid companion. Days and nights always had this *floating* quality, like the dream-life of athletes and gangsters, actors and comics, show girls and sports, hustlers and swells; of songwriters, gagwriters and ragtime piano players; of men who gambled and women who smoked; guys and dolls. Ed and Sylvia were children of the roaring jazz-age twenties, that nervy post-war adrenaline-addicted Charleston state of mind confabulated in New York by admen, poets and promoters, and then nationally syndicated by Broadway columnists like Damon Runyon, Walter Winchell, Louis Sobol and Ed himself—men who had gone to newspapers instead of college.

Newspapers and Broadway: together as Ed came of age, they were inventing twentieth-century American popular culture. Though vaudeville had been around since the 1880s, its heyday began on Broadway with the Olympia Theatre in 1895; the Victoria, the Loew's American and the Palace in 1913; the Ziegfeld Follies in 1915. Schubert Alley with all its *legit* theaters was just a couple of blocks from Tin Pan Alley in the Brill Building at Forty-ninth and Broadway where the pop music got composed and published. Nearby bloomed every variety of cabaret and lobster palace. In Prohibition's speakeasy years, bootleggers might come and go but the nightlife never stopped. To the north, Madison Square Garden and Fifty-second Street jazz clubs. To the south, the Metropolitan Opera and the garment district. In between, wigmakers, costume cutters, set designers, booking agents and burlesque. And just a cab ride away for the after-hours thrill-seeker, Harlem's Cotton Club. In this same neon-and-billboards Broadway entertainment zone, the new radio networks located themselves, the movie studios established New York offices, and TV with its cumbersome machinery scrummaged for space. Mass communications, by trial and error, formed a mass taste. Whatever else might go on behind the shades of a Puritan-genteel New England, a Calvinist-Victorian Heartland, a Pentecostal small-town South or the desert-western wastes—and probably a lot more *did* go on than anybody guessed, except the expatriate novelists— Broadway was the big time and the hot ticket, where they dreamed for us all those imperial city dreams of license, celebrity and scandal; of crossing race, class and gender boundaries into the demimonde and the forbidden; a floating operetta; a rilly big shew.

Or so we were told by the columnists. Because the newspapers moved to Broadway, too, and magazines like *Vanity Fair*, *Smart Set* and *The New Yorker*. Broadway was invented by *Variety*, the show biz daily, and by Runyons and Winchells who covered the theater, nightclubs and crime waves the way they covered sports. The columnists had all been sportswriters, anyway, before they went to Broadway; they reported the neon night as if it were one big game, in a permanent present tense, with its own peculiar slanguage of ballpark lingo, stage idiom, underworld argot, immigrant English, fanspeak, black-talk, promoter hype and pastrami sandwich. That's about all they reported, too. They certainly didn't report the political corruption and the racism that have always been the big city's biggest stories, not even the real-estate swindles attending the construction of the IRT subway that brought those crowds to Times Square to begin with. What they wrote, in a Broadway Babel pastiche of "suckers," "bogus," "lowdown," "scoop" and "who sez?" were press releases for a saloon society of singers like Caruso, fighters like Dempsey and mobsters like Lansky; a fictitious twenties where the long legs of the chorus girls went on forever and all the gangsters were as cute as Gatsby.

If not from novels like *The Big Money* and *Ragtime*, then surely from biographies like Neal Gabler's *Winchell: Gossip, Power, and the Culture of Celebrity* and Jimmy Breslin's *Damon Runyon*, or such dazzling social histories as Jackson Lears's *Fables of Abundance* (on advertising as the "folklore," "iconography" and "symbolic universe" of market exchange) and Ann Douglas's *Terrible Honesty: Mongrel Manhattan in the 1920s* (on the convergence of "formalism" and the hard sell, of "avant-garde innovation and media smarts" to create "an egalitarian popular and mass culture"), we ought by now to suspect that some of this was fantasy: the raffish flipside of Tin Pan Alley songs about Easter bonnets and grand old flags and of Hollywood films about home towns full of nuclear families. While the ad agencies that gave us Aunt Jemima for pancake mix and Rastus for Cream of Wheat may have been entirely WASP, the songs were composed and the movies produced mostly by the children of immigrants, who marketed these American myths as a form of wish-fulfillment—as if the melting pot were a centrifuge for spinning cotton candy, from which we'd all emerge uniformly pink and squeaky clean. Later, after a twist of the color-adjustment knob to achieve the perfect Aryan fleshtone, TV sitcoms would be pink fables too. As much as the popular culture craves velocity and sensation, it's also a state of longing.

But everybody drank too much and wrote fiction or ad copy

(what Jackson Lears, wittily, calls "Capitalist Realism"). In the era of photojournalism and jazz-age novels, Edward Steichen and J.P. Marquand worked for J. Walter Thompson, and F. Scott Fitzgerald for Bannion, Collier. Sherwood Anderson was a copywriter before *Winesburg;* Dorothy Parker wrote underwear ads for *Vogue;* Maxfield Parrish painted General Electric calendars and Jell-O ads; Joseph Cornell designed perfume double-spreads for *Harper's Bazaar* and *House & Garden*; Alexander Woollcott plugged Muriel cigars; Georgia O'Keefe pushed Dole pineapples, and Rockwell Kent, Steinway pianos. (Dr. Seuss and Jim Henson also got their start in advertising. So did Philip Rahv, in southern California, before coming east to co-edit the *Partisan Review.* Allen Ginsberg was in market research correlating supermarket sales of toiletries with the money spent on ads by his toothpaste and baby-powder clients when he wrote *Howl.* For that matter, George Bernard Shaw, Arnold Bennett and H.G. Wells all flacked for Harrod's department store, James Joyce sold ad space for a Dublin newspaper—"What is home without Plumtree's Meat? Incomplete!" recalled Leopold Bloom in *Ulysses*—and Bertolt Brecht wrote radio jingles for a German car company.) Even reportage of the time verged on the fictitious. From Breslin, we learn that while Damon Runyon's father, in a wild American West, had reported the truth about that gloryhound, George Custer, his son *didn't* report it about such gloryhounds as Pershing in Mexico and Patton in Europe. Runyon's famous and shameless rules for the journalism of *his* time were: Never bite the hand that feeds you, and Go along to get along. Pistol-packing Winchell hardly stirred from his reserved table at the Stork Club, except to tool around town in a squad car listening to cop radio. Most of what he needed for the columns that let him bed down with showgirls and ruin the careers of homosexuals got leaked to him by eager publicists or confided to him by that matched pair of sinister buddies, J. Edgar Hoover and Lucky Luciano.

This was Ed's gaudy, bouyant world—of the first book clubs, record charts, opinion polls, I.Q. tests, and birth-control clinics; a *Wasteland* with jumping beans—from 1922 at the New York *Evening Mail* to 1947, when he was discovered as a *Daily News* columnist who happened to be emceeing the annual Harvest Moon Ball, while a fledging CBS just happened to be trying out its primitive cameras. Serendipity! Like show biz, sports or war, like organized labor, organized crime and organized religion, tabloid journalism had been an agency of upward mobility. But TV would prove to be a trampoline...a flying carpet.

I think everything was wonderful and, look, here I go. It was a simpler era and we all knew who Ed was, and we knew who we were, and we knew what the country was and it was a wonderful time to be a part of it.

Joan Rivers

Ed was born, in 1901, in a Harlem that had been mostly Irish and Jewish but was changing fast when the Sullivans abandoned it five years later for Port Chester, New York, on Long Island Sound. A twin brother, Danny, died at nine months. One thinks of Elvis and the stillborn Jesse. Ed always felt that if Danny had been around, nobody would have beat up on him. Perhaps Danny was the one who had been intended to sing songs, tell jokes, tease cats and spin plates. Maybe Ed spent seventy-two years looking for him. This might also explain why, every Sunday night after the show was over, he always went to Danny's Hideaway.

His paternal grandfather fled County Cork in one of the nineteenth-century potato famines. Ed's father Peter was the oldest son in a family of eight. He had gone to work instead of finishing high school and resented a patronage job at the Customs House. Ed's mother Elizabeth was an amateur painter and had a green thumb in the garden, when they finally got one. On the top floor of the two-family Port Chester frame house, in a parlor with velveteen-upholstered furniture, an upright piano and an aspidistra, there was always music. Peter was partial to opera, especially Melba. Elizabeth loved John McCormack. And Port Chester was the sort of town in which an impresario of the democracies of performing talent should have grown up, a ragtime mix of Irish, Italians, Germans and Jews with a factory and a railway station but also a village blacksmith and watering troughs for the horses bought from Gypsies to draw the carriages that went to the medicine shows with the snake-oil salesmen. A young Ed stood on Boston Post Road and watched the Pierce Arrows and Packards chug their way to football games at Yale. He pumped the organ at Our Lady of Mercy for a nickel a mass. He caddied at the Apawanis Country Club in Rye for Nicholas Murray Butler, Columbia's insufferable president. He lettered in four varsity sports at St. Mary's, and ran away to Chicago at age 15. In Chicago, the Marines wouldn't have him, so he returned to his parochial school newspaper and wrote about sports instead.

Although an uncle offered to pay his way to college, the Port Chester *Daily Item* would pay him to go to games. Who wants more school when you can talk to Babe Ruth? From the ballpark he graduated to the police court and the undertaker's, the manly quick and the manly dead. From Port Chester, he graduated to New York in 1922, to two-finger type about college sports for the *Evening Mail*. On $75 a week, he lived over Duffy's Tavern, dated flappers and bought himself a Durant to drive to Flushing for a round of golf each dawn, after Ruby Keeler closed the Silver Slipper. Having sent him to Florida for winter sports in 1924, the *Mail* promptly folded. He'd spend the next three years bouncing from AP stringer to hotel PR man to the *Ledger* in Philadelphia to the *World* and *Bulletin* in New York; from the *Leader,* a socialist paper, to *The Morning Telegraph*, a racing paper. The *Graphic,* where Winchell invented the gossip column, hired him in 1927. Though sports editor Ed still cared more about fun and games than play acting, how he envied Winchell the column syndicated in so many papers and the radio show across the nation, not just for the money but also the inside hobnob and the mermaid splash. For four years they feuded, until Winchell was lured away by the *Mirror* and Louis Sobol by the *Journal-American*. Ed was suddenly out of the locker room and onto the Great White Way—as a writer instead of a sport. In his first column in 1931, he attacked all the other gossip columnists for dishing dirt. But dishing dirt was the reason for a column, and almost immediately Ed himself was Winchell-izing: "Jean Malin belted a heckler last night at one of the local clubs. All that twitters isn't pansy." The *Graphic* folded a year later. A week before it did, Ed was hired by the *Daily News*, where his "Little Old New York" column would appear for the rest of his life.

The rules for the column were: Lead with Your Scoop; Speed It

Up; an Item for Everybody. The rules for CBS would become: Open Big; Keep It Clean; Stick in Something the Kids Will Like. In the lifetime of Ed's career, the popular arts devolved from something vital but dangerous to something safe and consoling, until rock came along to rattle the cage. But on Sullivision, there was to be no sex, not even cleavage, nor an unkind word about the people we were soon to meet. On TV everyone was always wonderful. Even the chimps were wonderful. So was Fidel Castro. A genuine journalist would not have gone so innocently to Cuba in January, 1959, and paid Castro to tell America, between a trained dog and Alan King, that "We are all Catholics! How could we be communists?" Nor would even a checkbook journalist, on being told by Cardinal Spellman that he'd made a mistake, then reneg on a promise to pay Fidel his $10,000 fee. But Ed was an impresario, not a journalist. He sought to give the public what the public wanted. Almost alone among early TV performers, he could hardly wait to consult his Trendex or, later, his Nielsens. If Elvis was socko on Steve Allen, Ed bought three of him. When an arrangement with the Metropolitan Opera cost him points, that was the end of opera on Ed. He had no personal use for rock, and still less for the hysterical teens it drew to his theater, but for an audience he'd track down Belial in an ashram or an opium den. In doing so, he perfectly anticipated the market-research geeks who decided in 1971 that his day was done. But what a very long day it had been.

He had taken a pay cut, from $375 to $200 a week, to go to the *Daily News.* He scrambled off his beat to compensate, working double-shifts on short-lived radio interview programs for CBS and NBC, from a table at "21," with sponsors like Adams Hats and American Safety Razor, introducing George M. Cohan, Irving Berlin and Flo Ziegfeld; or, on stage at the Paramount and Loew's State Theaters, as an emcee working five hour-long vaudeville shows a day. At Loew's State, he also emceed something called Dawn Light Revue. A glance at the typical program—Peg Leg Bates, the one-legged acrobat and tapper; Rita Rio, a singer "in the accepted hotcha fashion"; Dave Vine, "one of the most observant of Jewish dialect comics"—tells us all we need to know about where the television program came from, besides Port Chester. And when not on the stage at Loew's State, he ran benefits and dance contests for the League of Catholic Charities, the B'nai Br'th, the Poor Richard Society and a war-bond drive. At one such benefit, the 1947 Harvest Moon Ball, he was discovered, at the awkward age of 46, by adman Marlo Lewis.

It's instructive if not surprising to note how many pioneers of early television, as of early radio, came directly out of advertising, just like the jazz-age novelists: "Pat" Weaver, father not only of Sigourney but of the *Today* and *Tonight* shows; Grant Tinker, who invented MTM; and the wonderful folks who gave us the quiz show scandals, after which the networks took the programming away from the ad agencies. William S. Paley bought CBS to begin with, in 1928, because radio advertising had doubled his cigar company sales. No other nation in the world had turned over its airwaves to advertisers, in a tidy-wrap package of mass production and mass persuasion. These men didn't know exactly what to do with their new toy except to make it spin and sizzle so that the public would sit still staring at it long enough to be stupefied into desiring all the goodies a feverish market might disgorge. Like Mickey Rooney and Judy Garland, like a Mad Avenue Crusader Rabbit, they wanted to put on a show in their garage. Ed already did so.

Ohh, my! That Ed is just the greatest. He's—well he's like Howard Johnson's. Do you know what I mean? Wherever you are, there'll always be good food and clean restrooms.
Member of Sullivan's studio audience

Except with critics and sponsors, *Toast of the Town* was a hit from its get-go on June 20, 1948. Nobody knew why, nor did they credit Ed. Emerson Radio hated him and CBS shopped the show, with or without the host, to anybody who'd take it. (When, after three months, Emerson bailed out and Lincoln-Mercury took over, Ed was so grateful to the Ford Motor Company that he would log more than a quarter million miles in the next five years as its "ambassador," landing on Boston Common in a chopper, floating down the Mississippi on a Royal Barge to the Memphis Cotton Festival. From Paris, he sent picture postcards to every Ford dealer in the nation.) But that first Sunday, from a firetrap studio on Broadway, was the prototype for the next 1,087—Dean Martin and Jerry Lewis, headliners; Rodgers and Hammerstein, volunteer guests; pianist Eugene List; ballerina Kathryn Lee; singing fireman John Kokoman; boxing ref Ruby Goldstein; Ray Bloch and six of June Taylor's neediest dancers, calling themselves Toastettes.

And like every other Sunday to come, Ed had decided how many minutes each of them got at the morning dress rehearsal, after which one audience was chased out of the studio, and another seated for the real thing. Over two decades much changed in the technical production of the hour—it was the first show with a permanent chorus line, the first to introduce celebrity guests from the audience, the first with overhead cams and rear-screen projection, the first to hit the road for remote telecasts and the first to play with high-resolution cameras, a zoom lens and videotape—but not the dreaded rehearsal, which was Ed's initial look at the lineup. As quick as his temper, so too was his judgment snappy. If a rehearsal audience didn't laugh, a wiseguy was gone, and the singer got an extra song. Add a mime; lose the hippo. Ed agreed with George Arliss: when crowds assemble together "their mass instinct is perilously close to intelligence." Public opinion, he said, "is the voice of God." What's amazing in retrospect is how seldom God, Ed and the mass intelligence missed the Royal Barge to Memphis. If Nat "King" Cole and Dinah Shore got booted off the show because they wanted to plug their *new* songs instead of singing Ed's hit parade favorites, well Pearl Bailey rose from a sickbed-fever of 103° to perform, and Alan King could be counted on to fill any other sudden holes. King was so reliable he didn't even have to rehearse, and refused to appear on any program with a rock group.

Nothing pleased his critics. Fred Allen: "Sullivan will be a success as long as other people have talent." Joe E. Lewis: "The only man who brightens up a room by leaving it." Jack Paar: "NBC has its peacock, and CBS has its cuckoo...Who else can bring to a simple English sentence such suspense and mystery and drama?" Even Alan King: "Ed does nothing, but he does it better than anyone else on television." But when Fred Allen came back to shoot the wounded—"What does Sullivan do? He points at people. Rub meat on actors and dogs will do the same"—Ed was stung to reply, and did so tellingly: "Maybe Fred should rub some meat on a sponsor."

So he looked funny. Even his best friends called him Rock of Ages, the Great Stone Face, the Cardiff Giant, Easter Island and Toast of the Tomb. He had been, in fact, a handsome man, before an auto accident in 1956 knocked out his teeth and staved in his ribs. In his early days he'd been often mistaken for Bogart. But after the crash there was always about him a shadowy wince, like Richard Nixon's, or Jack Nicholson's in the *Batman* movie, playing the Joker *as* Nixon. An ulcer didn't help, despite which he drank and smoked. (Like his old enemy Runyon, he would die from cancer.) Nor did the belladonna he took in his dressing room help while it expanded the duodenal canal, it also dilated the eyes. Later, hearing problems and arteriosclerosis accounted for some forgetfulness and those famous malapropisms. Introducing singer Dolores Gray: "Now starving on Broadway…" Or forgetting Sergio Franchi's name: "Let's hear it for *Ave Maria!*" Mixing up Antipodes: "the fierce Maori tribe from New England…" Right here in our audience: "the late Irving Berlin!" Once: "I'd like to *prevent* Robert Merrill." On another occasion: "Let's hear it reeelly big fer singer Jose Feliciano! He's blind—and he's Puerto Rican!" On a third, Ray Bloch was asked to strike up the band for Andres Segovia, whose act was solo guitar.

Yet the public loved him, the stars showed up, and his critics couldn't really attribute the success of the show to his column. Maybe, in the first few years, Sullivan did bully guests into appearing, as Winchell and Louella Parsons and Elsa Maxwell had bullied them onto their radio programs with the promise (or threat) of syndicated clout. But it quickly became obvious that appearing on TV was more of a career-maker than getting mentioned in any newspaper column. This was good news for CBS, and bad news for print journalism.

And his success isn't so very complicated. He was the best producer of his era. Television is a producer's medium, as movies used to be a director's medium, before the bankers took over, which is why all the best writers for the medium, in order to have some control over their own material and some of the profit as well, turn into executive producers whose names alone are all we see frozen on the screen after each episode of a series program like the sign of Zorro: *Steven Bochco*. It is also why the writing so often declines in the second or third season of even the best series. The executive producer has gone off to dream up another pilot and to executive-produce another series. But all Ed cared about was Sunday night on CBS, forever, reinventing his show each new season for a tribe of ghostly millions. His other talent was the transparent kick he got out of it, as pleased to be exactly where he was as we'd have been. Like Upton Sinclair's Lanny Budd, Woody Allen's Zelig or Tom Hanks's Gump, Ed made every crucial scene, and didn't put on airs about it. If he had to leave town, he brought back something he knew we'd like because *he* did: a bicycle, a puppet, a Blarney Stone. From France, Edith Piaf. From Scandinavia, Sonja Henie. From Mexico, Cantinflas. From Italy, Gina Lollobrigida. From the moon, astronauts.

In *Fables of Abundance*, Jackson Lears ends his history of advertising shortly after World War II, with a dot of Vance Packard (*The Hidden Persuaders*) and a dash of David Riesman (*The Lonely Crowd*), skipping television almost entirely. In *Terrible Honesty*, Ann Douglas sticks to the 1920s, when "New York's essential product was attention itself" and the popular arts were "a dispatch from the frontlines concocted of adrenaline, bravado, and cultural ESP." But Lears and Douglas might have been writing Sullivan's subtext. What else was such an hour, if not an electronic amalgam of Douglas's "cultural ESP" and Lears's Wild West patent-medicine show; of magic and minstrels, menageries and midgets, mummery and mime, a cult of the transitory and a celebration of "empty signifiers of status ascent" in a new economy of installment buying and planned obsolescence? P.T. Barnum and Señor Wences…

Doc Hashalew's Elixir of Life! Dr. Wrightman's Sovereign Balm of Life! Dr. Raphael's Cordial Invigorant! Dr. Chase's Nerve Pills! Ho Ang-Nan's Great Chinese Herb Remedy! Bumstead's Worm Syrup!

There used to be more high culture on television because there was less television, and we would watch almost anything, and middlebrows like Ed felt they had some dues to pay. Besides, Ed's father had loved grand opera and what the twenties had been about was a cross-pollinating of high arts and low: T.S. Eliot and Groucho Marx: Freud and *Krazy Kat*. Maybe as a byproduct of all those passionate nineteenth-century Italian tantrums, divas especially had the star quality prized by the celebrity culture Ed was helping to create, even if he had to wait a few years for a Maria Callas to glamorize opera the way Arnold Palmer had glamorized golf. Certainly Roberta Peters, "the little Cinderella from the Bronx," was a terrific front-page story after her walk-on triumph as Zerlina in *Don Giovanni*. As was Itzak Perlman, whom Ed discovered on the streets of Tel Aviv. And Van Cliburn, the surprise American winner of a Moscow piano-playing contest. And Rudolf Nureyev, just off the boat from the Evil Empire. Who will ever forget Jan Peerce, singing "Bluebird of Happiness"? Or Joan Sutherland, on stage with Tanya the Elephant?

Like the Broadway theater, the Metropolitan Opera House was just a couple of blocks away. In the mid-fifties Ed entered into a $100,000 deal with the Met's Rudolf Bing. To five different famous operas on five separate Sunday nights, Ed promised to devote eighteen minutes each. The first such Sunday, November 26, 1956, the first of the operas was *Tosca*, with Callas making her TV debut. This was Ed's best shot, and it cost him six points off his Trendex average. The second Sunday, January 27, 1957, with Dorothy Kirstin in *Madame Butterfly*, Ed actually *lost* his time period. Two equally matched imperial egos, Sullivan and Bing blamed each other for the fiasco. On March 10, the third Sunday, a desperate Ed cut *La Boheme* down to a four-minute duet by Renata Tebaldi and Richard Tucker. That was it for grand opera; Elvis had shown him another way. We hear a lot about what televion's done to the attention span of the American public. We never hear anything about what the attention span of the American public has done to television.

Still, unless you spent the fifties watching *The Voice of Firestone* and the sixties watching *The Bell Telephone Hour*, you weren't hearing much serious music anywhere else on commercial television. Ed cut a deal for first refusal rights on anything imported by Sol Hurok. Nobody else on network TV was ever better for serious dance. On no other show save *Omnibus* could we count on seeing any at all, from Agnes DeMille to Maya Plisetskaya. The Joffrey and the New York City Ballet were around the corner; Jerome Robbins was always available; San Francisco, Denmark, London, Florence, Hungary and Japan sent companies. The (overrated) Bolshoi was a smash hit. And when Ed went away, who'd step in to hold the middle of that brow? Except for an occasional White House gala, and Eugenia Zuckerman on *CBS Sunday Morning*, classical music has vanished from network television. Ballet only happens on BRAVO and PBS, though not ever during pledge week when they switch to folkies. Likewise opera, with the added insult of Peter Sellars tarting up Mozart. Symphony orchestras, like regional theaters, local dance troupes and jazz quartets, have to be subsidized by the oil companies and the feds. Even our libraries are closed after dark. Somewhere along the line to junk bonds, leveraged buyouts and hostile takeovers, middlebrows stopped trying harder and ad agencies decided that "elite" culture lacked a desirable demographic profile and America settled for, or maybe even turned into, a greedhead musical comedy.

Ed gave us Helen Hayes mourning her dead daughter, in a scene from *Victoria Regina*. And Joshua Logan confessing on stage, ad lib, to his own nervous breakdown. And Judith Anderson as the world's most difficult mother, *Medea*. And Oscar Hammerstein tinkling a plaintive rendition of "The Last Time I Saw Paris." And Richard Burton, when the Welsh vapors took him, declaiming Dylan Thomas. And Sophie Tucker, singing with the Ink Spots. Plus half the cast from *West Side Story* and the whole tribe of *Hair*. From the start, Ed and the legitimate theater he covered for his column were allies. As early as 1950, on back-to-back Sunday nights, he brought *Member of the Wedding* to television, black and white together, and a bit of the *Tobacco Road* revival. Selections followed from *Of Thee I Sing* and *Guys and Dolls*. By 1952, he was even saving shows like the musical comedy *Wish You Were Here* and the Pulitzer Prize–winning play *All the Way Home*. But if Ed was good for Broadway, Broadway was better for Ed; his ace in the hole competing with Colgate's *Comedy Hour* was all the talent down the block, young and able, tried and true, and almost always available for Sunday morning rehearsals of a little this and a little that from *Carousel*, *My Fair Lady* or *Mame*. It was on Sullivan's show that most of the country first heard of Cornelia Otis Skinner; where Yul Brynner visiting from *The King and I* became a pop-culture icon; where, before their musicals were turned into movies, the American public outside New York first saw Ethel Merman, Carol Channing and Gwen Verdon. After *Guys and Dolls*, as if at a benefit for one of the more popular diseases, all the best Broadway musicals showed up, from *Brigadoon* to *Pajama Game*, meaning that Gertrude Lawrence, Joel Grey, Elaine Stritch, Stanley Holloway and Mary Martin also sang and danced in our living rooms. So what if we never saw Beckett or Pinter? Ed just wanted us to clap our hands if we believed in Tinker Bell.

Hollywood hated TV before TV moved there. It was Ed's genius to convince a studio tinpot like Goldwyn that TV was free publicity, that clips of forthcoming films would entice millions to neighborhood theaters, that actors on Ed's stage could promote their careers without dissipating their mystery. Beginning in 1951, long before the rich and famous had "lifestyles," there were "biographies" of them on Ed. When he decided as a ratings gimmick to devote whole programs to Bea Lillie, Cole Porter, Walt Disney and Bert Lahr, he inadvertently invented the "spectacular," by which TV graduated from vaudeville, radio and Broadway into a humming ether all its own. The result was a steady stream of Bogarts, Grables, Hepburns and Pecks, a Liz Taylor and a John Wayne. Gloria Swanson appeared to tell an astonished nation that she did too believe in God.

Such intimacy! Such presumption! But celebrity is what a democratic society has instead of aristocrats. We may feel today that we're no longer safe anywhere from the stars and starlets so ubiquitous on *Good Morning America*, the *Today* show, Phil, Oprah, Joan, Geraldo, *Entertainment Tonight*, *Live at Five*, the late-night eye witless news and Letterman and Leno, who babble on forever about alcoholism, drug abuse, incest and liposuction in the weeks before, during and after their new film opens for the skeptical inspection of teenaged mutant ninja mall mice. But back then it *was* magic in our living rooms, as if the gods had come down from their pink clouds, the generals from their white pedestals, and the vamps from our fantasies, to schmooze, giggle and weep. And this same star-making machinery turned "unstar" Ed into an aristocrat himself. You will have noticed that TV news personalities like Edward R. Murrow, Walter Cronkite and David Brinkley, from a synopsizing of the quotidian on our small screen, get *heavier*, taking on the gravity of what they report. Their faces become front pages, etchings of all they have seen. History thickens them to a density that exerts a mighty pull on our frayed attention. Through their images we are accustomed to trafficking with the momentous.

So it was for Ed, too, case-hardened and at last secure in his celebrity, a glaze of so much pleasure rendered, so many heroes of the culture having been consorted with; an odd radiance of well-being; the kind of hum heard only in the higher spheres, as if he had levitated out of other people's talent into a gravity all his own. They sang hymns to him in *Bye Bye Birdie*, and almost made a movie of his life, and he did show up in the Hollywood version of *The Singing Nun*. Not bad for a boy from Port Chester. But there was a difference. Ed was not in his celebrityhood the least bit remote. He was one of us, not so special that we couldn't have been there too ourselves, singing along with Birgit Nilsson, hoofing with Gene Kelly, playing Jack Benny's straightman or a fourth McGuire Sister. That's why we forgave him when he found himself suspended in mid-air by the illusionist Richiardi, or landing on the deck of an aircraft carrier in a helicopter, or riding around in a chariot as if in ancient Rome, on the *Ben Hur* set. If it could happen to Ed, it could happen to anybody. That spinning plate was a flying saucer: I saw *you* on television.

Blood Purifier! Cholera Balm! Oriental Liniment! Omni-Balsamic Reinvigorator! Samaritan Pain Dissuader! Church's Kava-Kava Compound Kidney Cure! The Wild Girl From the Congo!

Julia Meade remembers a night Ed pulled the lion tamer aside just before he was supposed to go on camera. Look, said Ed, "we've got to cut you down to three minutes. Do you understand?" "Yeah," said the tamer, "I understand. But how am I going to explain it to the *lion*." The literature is rich with stories about what happened on live TV when they failed to explain whatever it was to lions, tigers, dancing horses, bears on bikes, chimps on motorcycles, elephants on water skis, pandas on rollerskates and dachshunds doing arithmetic; fire-eaters, ice jugglers, sword swallowers, sponge divers, limbo dancers, Swiss yodelers, Kuban Cossacks, Doodle-town Pipers, Polish glockenspielers, Kilgore College Rangerettes; Topo Gigio, Alvin's Chipmunks, Old Bill the Navy Goat and

Werner von Braun the Nazi rocketeer. As surprising as the fact that animals and people would actually do such things was that animals and people should want to. Ed needs an expanded definition of novelty. Leo Durocher *and* Bob Dylan on the same Sunday? Brigitte Bardot *and* Salvador Dali? We've a more pretentious word today for such radical juxtapositions of the silly and sublime, random conjunctures of blank incredulity and dreadful apprehension, campy romp (nostalgia laced with contempt) and absurd snippet (Rise Stevens singing "Cement Mixer, Putty-Putty"). Instead of novelty, we have postmodernism. But Ed already practiced what technology hadn't begun to preach—*channel surfing*. One Sunday when he didn't like an Allen and Rossi routine, the ever-obliging duo offered to substitute their always-reliable "Zulu" standby. "You can't," said Ed: "I have two hundred fifty Zulus in the basement." And so he did, for a big African dance number. Allen and Rossi went ahead and did their Zulus anyway, pretending they were Japanese instead. Like vaudeville and the jazz age, *the whole show was a novelty act.*

He could get any comic he wanted, from Will Jordan to Mort Sahl, stand-up or skit, Wayne and Schuster doing riffs on Shakespeare or Phil Silvers with a banana. They didn't have to adapt to a house style of humor; they weren't competing with their host, who wasn't a Milton Berle on Tuesday, a Jackie Gleason or Sid Caesar on Saturday. Ed was partial to the Catskills comics he'd grown up on, like Henny Youngman or Jackie Leonard, and to impressionists like Jack Carter or Frank Gorshin. His biggest favorites were Stiller and Meara (twenty-seven times), Myron Cohn and Alan King (thirty-nine each) and Wayne and Schuster (an astonishing sixty-seven appearances). We would have seen more of Berle, Gleason and Caesar, of Dean Martin and Jerry Lewis, Jack Benny, Bob Hope, Red Skelton, Jimmy Durante and Ernie Kovacs if they hadn't defected to their own variety shows, or if Woody Allen hadn't gone from writing for Sid Caesar to wanting to be Ingmar Bergman, or if Mort Sahl hadn't gotten odd about the Kennedy assassination...

But they all had to audition in advance: up the elevator at the Delmonico, into the Temple of Karnak. At home with a lamb chop, Ed insisted on hearing every word. As Jackie Mason proved, comics are dangerous. Mason was Ed's featured comic that infamous evening in October, 1964. They had been forewarned that L.B.J. would interrupt their show about halfway through, to say something about the war in Vietnam. They had expected him to be brief. He wasn't. And no one knew how long he'd go. By the time the show was back on "live," Jackie was in the middle of his monologue, and already annoyed at having been placed last on a program where he had to compete with a president. Ed began a frantic series of hand signals: *two minutes.* The audience, ignoring Jackie's punchlines, found Ed funnier. So Jackie began making fun of Ed's hand signals. This is when, according to Ed, Jackie gave him and the audience that storied middle finger. Although the judge ruled later in Jackie's favor, Ed's fury cost Mason $37,500 on a cancelled five-show contract. All the way back in 1964, Vietnam was already starting to ruin everybody's fun.

Ed was there to amuse, not to subvert, the republic. Comedy was supposed to make us feel better instead of worse. It was okay for comics to abuse themselves, and even, within limits, to abuse Ed (who so much wanted to be one of the boys, he once dressed up for Soupy Sales in drag), but he wasn't about to allow abuse of his audience, in the theater or at home. Don Rickles never worked his show, nor can one imagine Roseanne. Briefly, after Ed's son-in-law Bob Precht took over as producer in 1960, there were stabs at political satire. But social criticism never sat well. His female comics were not exactly on the cutting edge of the new feminism. If not clowns willing to die for us, like Carol Burnett, Totie Fields or Bea Lillie, they were full of a self-denigration amounting almost to self-hatred, like Phyllis Diller and Joan Rivers. And race wasn't any funnier than war. Ed was mystified at first by Richard Pryor, who made the Delmonico cut and appeared on the show a dozen times but was abruptly dropped after a rehearsal in which his wino routine gave Ed the creeps.

Jack Paar may have *discovered* more comics—including Diller and Burnett, Nichols and May, Shelley Berman and Bob Newhart—but they all went to the Delmonico, and thence to Ed's stage, to be *sanctioned.* Sullivan defined the permissible, as well as certifying celebrity in the velociraptor culture. When at last he went away, his role had already been assumed by Johnny Carson on the *Tonight* show, telling us when it was okay to laugh at Dick Nixon or Tammy Faye Bakker. But country and culture were both falling apart. After Carson, there was a hole in the ether where such sanctioning authority had once abided. Not even Letterman fills it, inside his ironizing "What, Me Worry?" blisterpack. Neither have the Comedy Channel, the improv programs, the locker-room jockstrap guy stuff of *Saturday Night Live* and those toothless sitcoms through which our erstwhile-outrageous standup comics grin, de-fanged and venom-challenged, telling O.J., Michael Jackson, Hillary and Bobbitt jokes. Amazing to think that these comedians only got to talk dirty on television four years after Ed left the air, with the first HBO premium-cable comedy special. Comedy appears to have disintegrated, like Yugoslavia. Like pop music, it lost the easy assumptions and lazy stereotypes that pass for coherence. On the other hand, Lily Tomlin: "I worry that drugs have forced us to be more creative than we really are."

We have, in fact, grown up and grown confused, from Sam Levenson to something ferocious. To see a Robin Williams, with Billy Crystal and Whoopi Goldberg in their annual telethon for the homeless, or alone on stage, beeping like a microwave, speaking to us as if in coded transmissions from a wormhole in some parallel universe or post-Ed Mork World Twilight Zone, is to see a brilliant mind unmade of equal parts of politics and paranoia, of music video and psychotherapy; at once exorcist and the possessed, a garbage disposal of high and low cultures, a scrambled egghead and a Jack-in-a-Pandora's-box. Robin Williams would not have been safe on Sunday nights in the fifties and sixties. And knowing what we do now, neither perhaps would we. Post-Ed, all the jokes seem to fly in our face, like toothpaste or fruit bats or hand grenades.

There are some pleasures that degrade a gentleman as much as some trades do. Sottish drinking, indiscriminate gluttony, driving coaches, rustic sports...
Lord Chesterfield

It was a guy thing, though Babe Didrikson and Sonja Henie did crash the party. Long before Ed had known or written about anything else in this world, before women or Renoir or Sweet 'n' Low, he had been a sport: athlete, reporter, fan and benefactor. His first big interview in high school was Babe Ruth. His first big interview in New York was Jack Dempsey. His first byline in journalism's big leagues was a dog-show story. His first philanthropic project was destitute boxer Johnny Dundee. And when he was no longer young enough to stay up all night and play golf at dawn, he bought horses of his own to race. He liked to hang out with the champs. So naturally he wanted them on his show, especially if they were down on their luck and could use a thousand bucks to take a bow. Baseball players: from Jackie Robinson and Ted Williams to Yaz and Henry Aaron. Boxers: all but Sugar Ray Robinson, heavy-weights. Golfers: Ben Hogan, Arnold Palmer, Chi-Chi Rodrigues, and Sam Snead. Not so many football players, if you don't count college all-star teams. Three jockeys: Eddie Arcaro, Billy Hartrack and Willie Shoemaker. One basketball player, excluding the Globetrotters: Wilt Chamberlain, who hadn't yet published his memoir of 20,000 one-night stands. At the billiards table, Willie Mosconi. On the ice, Dick Button. All-purpose: Jesse Owens and Jim Thorpe. All wet: Johnny Weismuller and Esther Williams.

What we saw was something refreshing: a startled, pleased, embarrassed, friendly, even grateful look, only no big deal. There was nothing about them of the celebrity glaze of the media brat to come in the age of too much sports on television; the crybaby arrogance, the pinched and antic fearfulness we'd later see in a Jimmy Connors or a Mark Spitz, as if they had to use up all their edge in the fifteen minutes before their fame was up or we'd cancel their product endorsement residuals; as if they're afraid they will be found out and deemed unworthy of all the money they are far too young to deserve; masked and puffy, with eyes as blank as the pips on dominoes.

Not so Ed's guys. I'm not into mythopoeia. Ed's guys probably included some wife-beaters, glue-sniffers, morons and kinks dependent on sportswriters to make up snappy quotes for them. But they had their wounds and their grace and the camaraderie of the battle-scarred, looking around for clues, yet otherwise comfortable with their own rhythms, acquainted with honor and shame, having lost a few; Ed's guys were before an age of jet pro-pelled sneakers and charging for autographs. There wasn't any baseball except on radio; nobody cared about pro football; not even public television carried tennis. Who could have imagined a Congress legislating the inalienable right of the American male to see *his* pro football team on TV *every* Sunday? Or a World Series played at night, in subfreezing mid-October temperatures, for the prime-time ratings? Or the natural rhythms of basketball and hockey interrupted for commercials? Or tiebreakers so that tennis won't go into the next regularly scheduled program? Or cable systems developed just to feed hometown athletic contests into bars and other bunkers of the betting action? Or franchises shifting cities in search of bigger TV markets or more lucrative pay-TV deals? Or whole leagues shutting down because they can't get a network contract?

Some sports, in fact, have been invented *just* for television: tennis challenge matches, the World Series of golf, punt-pass-and-kick and basketball-dunking contests. *ABC's Wide World of Sports* was, without a doubt, the Sweat Set's Sullivan show: demolition derbies, computerized prize fights, barrel jumping, kick boxing, ice boating and the annual Duke Kahanamoku surfing classic. TV at its most compelling promises that anything can happen next, and when it does, we will be the first to know. News and sports are the principal sources of these brutal and decisive moments. News though has a way of happening at inconvenient times and places without a warning to the camera crew. Even then, it is seldom decisive, nor visually dramatic. The nice thing about games is that you know in advance where and when, and at some point they will be over and somebody will be seen to have won or lost. Into the doldrums, morever, techies can insert their instant replays, slo-mos, split-screens and freeze-frames. And color analysts will elaborate on what we've seen as if it were as complicated as the astrophysics of anti-matter.

This is football's influence on sportscasting and TV news. The glorification of pigkick has made us conceive of our daily lives as station stops on an essentially brutish Great Trek, by way of a long bomb, a red dog blitz, a crackback block, a quarterback sack and sudden death in over-time unto that grandest of televised occasions on the calendar of the Garrison State, the Steroid Bowl, with SAC bomber/bimbo overflights and military oompah bands. Whereas in Ed's day, before the whole world turned into hectic television, a kinder gentler mush of metaphors obtained: baseball's. Nor had you to sit through eighteen hours of Ken Burns on public television to grasp these metaphors. While *Baseball* the miniseries was as slow, dolorous, cranky and obsessive as the pennant race, Burns seemed sometimes to forget that it was after all a *game* we suffered, not an epic poem of exile and return, not some compost heap of damp symbolic meanings, not a deconstruction from the French; a *game* about which grownup little boys who couldn't cut it like to gossip and to daydream, missing childhood and our dads, like Peter Pan with cleats. You need only listen for five minutes to George Carlin, speaking as if he prayed: *extra innings* instead of sudden death; a *slow curve* and a *no-hitter;* the *intentional walk* and the homerun *trot.* Consider *rain delay.* And most beautiful of all—*stealing home.*

What if Chubby Checker does not mean us well? What if Chubby Checker is up to no good?
Maxine Hong Kingston

A white man wrote "Bill Bailey, Won't You Please Come Home." As George Gershwin wrote "Swanee" and Al Jolson sang it. Irving Berlin, who was Jewish, wrote both "White Christmas" and "Easter Parade." As well as a New York neighborhood, Tin Pan Alley was a wiseguy state of mind. Whatever you wanted, they'd write it: sentimental ballads, comical immigrant medleys, Broadway show tunes, ragtime, even "coon songs." They also wrote the score for Ed's home movie of an innocent and consensual America. Creepy to remember, but no other singer appeared on his show as often as Connie Francis. Nor did we lack for Bing Crosby, Dinah Shore, Perry Como, Rosemary Clooney, Gordon MacRae, Patti Page, Wayne Newton, Vikki Carr, Liberace and Tiny Tim. For the longest time, even black entertainers like Nat "King" Cole and Leslie Uggams sounded as pink and squeaky clean as Pat Boone. It wasn't exactly elevator music. Ethel Merman and Pearl Bailey could blast through the wax in our ears. What Ella Fitzgerald or Sarah Vaughan did to standards was what alchemists had tried and failed to do to base metals. When they weren't stopping the show, Lena Horne and Nina Simone knew how to slow it down and make it think. At least Broadway musical comedies came with dancers like Fred Astaire, Cyd Charisse, Bojangles, and Chita Rivera. Not to mention a peppering of Copa Girls, can can and all those folk dancers who arrived, as if by cargohold and forklift, from Warsaw, Prague and Oslo, Mexico, Portugal and Ireland, Romania and Bali. But each appearance of a "mongrel" music, the distilled sound of an aggrieved subculture outside Ed's Dream Palace, had a fugitive quality, as if Dave Brubeck and Stan Kenton, Count Basie and Duke Ellington, Mahalia Jackson and Miriam Makeba, Johnny Cash and Odetta, were souvenirs, and Ravi Shankar a kind of curry. When Nashville and Motown learned at last how to plug their own songs on radio, they'd do terrible things to Tin Pan Alley. Rock, of course, would take elevator music down to hell, and Ed's show with it.

But without pop standards there would have been no show. They were more than the punctuation of the program; they were its sculptured space. Anything *might* happen, but someone *always* sang. And what got sung was the latest hit. Ed was *about* hits, and to make sure he had an uninterrupted flow of them, he had entered into a mutual assistance pact with Tin Pan Alley that amounted to a codependency. He needed the top ten. And, by appearing on his show, you *stayed* in the top ten, the way a book on *The New York Times* best-seller list will sell enough copies to remain there for months; it *must* be good. Besides, showing up twice a year on Ed guaranteed a singer year-round club dates, plus constant play on the radio and jukebox. This was less hanky-panky than a synergetic shakedown of mass-communications conglomerates. (If you *need* hanky-panky, look to CBS Records, with whom Ed had a cozy deal, which is why we heard so much *My Fair Lady* and so little Frank Sinatra, who belonged to Capitol.) As if to signify this codependence, Ed ordered fancy sets built for every singing act, and no set was ever used a second time. In other words, music video. But you had to go live and couldn't lipsync. Because Mary Tyler Moore insisted on syncing, she was banished from the show, a sort of premature Milli Vanilli.

Well then, rock. Ed passed on Elvis the first time around in 1955, at a loose-change price of $5,000. In July, 1956, however, a terrible thing happened to him on his way to the Trendex ratings. Elvis appeared on Steve Allen's brand-new Sunday show directly opposite Ed. The Monday news was Ed, 14.8; Elvis, 20.2. To reporters calling for his reaction Ed said, "I don't think Elvis Presley is fit for family viewing." But that afternoon he was on the phone to Tom Parker, striking a $50,000 deal for three spots. And, contrary to what you think you remember, when Elvis showed up for the first of these, in September, we saw all of him. Having been burned in effigy in St. Louis, hanged in effigy in Nashville, and banned, at least his lower body parts, in the state of Florida, the full-frontal Elvis didn't seem so awfully shocking. It was the second Elvis appearance that got shot from the waist up only, because producer Lewis had heard a rumor that a playful Elvis had taken to hanging a soda-pop bottle in the crotch of his trousers. Ed actually decided to like Elvis after a press conference in which a reporter asked if he were embarrassed when "silly little girls" kissed his white Cadillac. The King replied: "Well, ma'am, if it hadn't been for what you call those silly little girls I wouldn't have that white Cadillac." Like Trendex, this was something Ed could appreciate.

But did any of us appreciate what else was going on? With an Elvis, Ed not only opened the gates to the ravening chimeras and barbaric hordes of rock; he had also unlocked the doors to the attic, the bedroom and basement of the Ike culture. After a long sedation, all that sexual energy seemed to explode. It may have been acceptable to cross-pollinate the races and classes in Times Square. It was something else again when long-haired, poor white Southern trash insinuated a rockabilly/hubcap-outlaw variant of R&B and "dirty dancing" into the ears, hearts and glands of the Wonderbread children of a bored and horny suburban middle-class. What Elvis meant, along with Kerouac, Ginsberg and the motormouth Beats, was that the sixties were coming, an animal act that rattled everybody's cage and couldn't be contained on any consensus television program that doled out equal time to competing but acceptable subcultures in a median range of American taste. Some chairs were going to be broken, some categories, some heads and some hearts.

By the time rock got to Sullivan, the world was changing and so was television, and not, so far as he could see, exactly for the better. He *loved* Motown, especially the Supremes, in whom he seems to have found a dreamy mix of gospel and Tin Pan Alley. Rock, he merely put up with, because Bob Precht insisted: Even the Dave Clark Five (fifteen appearances) was no threat to Pearl Bailey (tweny-three), Theresa Brewer (twenty-seven) or, impossibly, Roberta Peters (forty). As for the Beatles, they were cute kids, if only they'd left their deranged teenyboppers back in Liverpool. The story goes that late in 1963 Ed and Sylvia, wandering through

Heathrow Airport, ran into 40,000 screaming nymphets. What was up? "Beatles," an airline employee said. Ed: "Well, can't you get some spray?" But as *The New York Times* once explained, "whatever Lolita wants, Sullivan gets." That Christmas he agreed with Brian Epstein on three shows at $4,000 each. The rest was more compelling as pop history than as network television. In oddly Edwardian suits, with freshly laundered moptops, on their very best behavior, the Beatles were looked at by 74 million Americans in a single squat. What frightened Ed were the shrieking groupies— including, in his own studio, the daughters of Leonard Bernstein and Jack Paar. After the Beatles, he refused to let anybody into the theater under age 18 without a parent or a guardian. Which didn't keep fans of the Stones from pushing Mick Jagger through a plate glass window in 1967, or the Doors from misbehaving after they had promised not to. (Told they'd never appear again on the show, Jim Morrison said: "Hey, man, we just worked the Sullivan show. Once a philosopher, twice a pervert.") And the worst sign of an approaching apocalypse was when Herman's Hermits came to town. A high-school student hung around backstage with a borrowed press pass, and then left by the stage door, where he was mistaken for a Hermit. The mob tore at his clothes. Fighting free into street traffic, he was killed by a passing car. To have died for Herman's Hermits—What was wrong with these people, that they couldn't behave themselves while Ed was *preventing* Robert Merrill?

What was wrong was that his audience, in the studio and at home, had gone to civil war. Parents and their children not only watched different TV programs on different sets in different rooms of a house divided, but these children seemed to live on different planets with alternative gravities, under bloody moons like Selma and Saigon. Pop music was no longer edifying, and not even harmless. For every Woodstock, there seemed, alas, an Altamont. Children of Ed Sullivan, flower-smoking media Apaches like Abbie Hoffman (a revolutionary Dennis the Menace who said that he'd prefer to overthrow the U.S. government by means of bubble gum, "but I'm beginning to have my doubts") and Jerry Rubin (the poisoned Twinkie who announced, "Sirhan Sirhan is a Yippie!") took over campuses and parks, the Stock Exchange and evening news. No wonder Ed looked tired, even sullen, towards the end: Where was the coherence?

Elvis, the Beatles and the Doors signified the confusion to come of politics and culture. The juvenile delinquents had their own tribal music, and it wasn't "Sentimental Journey." Rock was political—and hair, and sex; even whales. This confusion perceived itself to be in a profound opposition to a tone-deaf, anal-retentive, body-bag establishment. To a child of the sixties, Ed's last decade, *they* had the guns and *we* had the guitars. If the seventies belonged so depressingly to disco, just waiting for the eighties were Metalheads and Punks, shape changers and androgynous shamans who would scrawl graffiti and sometimes swastikas all over the walls of the malls. Rap and hip-hop would tell us things about the mythical America that Tin Pan Alley had done its best to cover up. By the end of the eighties, no less than Harvard University would publish a book on the Sex Pistols. We each listen now to our own musics, on wave-lengths designer-coded for age, color, class, sex, and sneer, through Sony Walkman headsets, on skateboards, Rollerblades and Harleys—when we aren't tuned in to hate radio. Do we miss Ed and his consensus? Sure we do, like Captain Kangaroo and Ferdinand the Bull and the Great Pumpkin and all the other imaginary friends of our vanished childhood.

All fixed, fast-frozen relations, with their train of ancient and venerable prejudices and opinions, are swept away, all new-formed ones become antiquated before they can ossify. All that is solid melts into air, all that is holy is profaned…
Karl Marx

Ed was a democrat and a *fan*. From Harlem, Port Chester and Broadway, from the ballpark, the saloon and the tabloid, all he cared about was talent, no matter what it looked like, where it came from, or how he pronounced it. Forget the feuds with Arthur Godfrey, Frank Sinatra, Jack Paar, Steve Allen, even Walter Winchell. What we saw on his screen was an encompassing, the peculiar sanction of the democratic culture. By being better at what they did than everyone else who did it, however odd or exotic, anyone could *achieve* his show, but nobody inherited the *right.* Ed's emblematic role was to confirm, validate and legitimize singularity, for so long as the culture knew what it wanted and valued, and as long as its taste was coherent.

During the Cold War, he was absolutely typical. When the blacklist hit the entertainment industry, he was as craven as the times and as his own network. (At CBS, the Ed Murrows were few and far between. They fired Joseph Papp as a stage manager because he refused to talk about his friends to a congressional committee.) Attacked in 1950 by Hearst columnist Cholly Knickerbocker for booking dancer Paul Draper and harmonica player Larry Adler, both of whom had been accused of unspecified "procommunist sympathies," Ed, through his sponsor's ad agency, apologized to the public: "You know how bitterly opposed I am to communism, and all it stands for.... If anybody has taken offense, it is the last thing I wanted or anticipated, and I am sorry." Draper and Adler had to leave the country to find work. When conductor Arthur Leif refused to tell the House Committee on Un-American Activities whether he had ever been a member of the Party, Ed dismissed him from the orchestra pit right before a performance of, ironically, the Moiseyev Dance Troupe, fresh from Moscow. Again in 1961, folksinger Leon Bibb was dropped from the show when he wouldn't apologize for his political past to American Legion Post No. 60 in Huntington, New York. Bibb, too, had to leave the country. Sean O'Casey was dumped from a St. Patrick's Day tribute in 1960, for leftwing anticlericalism. Bob Dylan dumped himself, in 1963, when he wasn't permitted to sing "The Talking John Birch Society Blues." Throughout a disgraceful blacklist period, Ed submitted performers' names for vetting to the crackpot Theodore Kirkpatrick, editor of *Counterattack* and author of *Red Channels: The Report of Communist Influence in Radio and Television,* a report slandering half of the entertainment industry, from Leonard Bernstein and Aaron Copeland to John Garfield, Uta Hagen, Lena Horne, Burl Ives, Zero Mostel, Dorothy Parker, Howard K. Smith and Orson Welles.

But then there was the other American obsession: race. At Harry Belafonte, Ed drew a line against the blacklist. From his earliest newspaper days Ed had been a brother. In his column he attacked New York University for agreeing to keep its one black basketball player on the bench in a game against the University of Georgia. When his friend Bojangles Robinson died, he paid anonymously for a funeral at the Abyssinian Baptist Church and organized a parade afterwards to the Evergreen Cemetery in Brooklyn with an all-star cast of foot soldiers that included Berle, Merman, Durante, Danny Kaye and W.C. Handy. When Walter Winchell savaged Josephine Baker, who had been refused service at his favorite Stork Club watering hole, Ed declared a war on the *Mirror* columnist that wouldn't end till a memorable night in 1952 at that same club, when Ed hustled Winchell into the men's room, pushed his head down a urinal and flushed him—as if to signify and celebrate the triumph of TV over Hearst. And, obliging though he had always been to his sponsor, Ed was contemptuous of those Ford dealers in the South who objected to his hugging of Ella Fitzgerald on camera, his kissing of Diana Ross and Pearl Bailey. With Louis Armstrong, he'd go anywhere in the world: Guantanamo, Spoleto. From Duke Ellington to Ethel Waters there wasn't an important black artist who didn't appear on Ed's show, just like famous white folks.

But as television expanded—let a hundred channels bloom!—the culture fell apart. It was as if the magic once so concentrated in a handful of choices had managed somehow to dissipate itself, like an expanding universe after the Big Bang, into chaos, heat death and fractals. By the end of the sixties there were twenty variety shows on TV, and that wasn't counting the bloody circus of Chicago 1968, the porn movies from Vietnam and *Götterdämmerung* in Watts. Instead of Irving Berlin, Joan Baez; instead of Broadway, Newark. *None of this was Ed's fault.* For more than two decades he had not only kept the faith but he had every week renewed it, telling us what was funny, who was important, and how we were supposed to feel about the world he monitored on our behalf. But that world had detonated, concussing even our own homes, where we went in separate furious sects to separate electric altars, alien dreamscapes and bloody creepshows.

Where's the coherence, much less the consensus, when the people who watch *The X-Files* on Fox and the people who watch ice hockey on Sports Channel and the people who watch the *News Hour* on PBS don't even speak to the people who watch Guns 'n' Roses on MTV? Of the nation's 95.4 million TV households, 70 percent have more than one set and 11 per cent have four or more. Who needs Ed when we can become famous for nothing more compelling than having already been on television? How amazing that such a show ever existed at all: such innocent bonds, such agreeable community, so much Broadway, Tin Pan Alley and Port Chester. Can you imagine a prime-time variety hour like Ed's trying to make the nation feel more like a family, seeking some gentle like-mindedness in, say, fin-de-siècle Vienna, the world capital of dessert and alienation? Freud! Herzl! Schnitzler! In our studio audience, take a bow: Ludwig Wittgenstein! Instead of June Taylor Dancers, Gustav Klimt's witchy women, combing their Secessionist nerve-strings, whipping us with their hair. After too many Strauss waltzes, twelve-tone music. After too much operetta, psychoanalysis. After an overmuch of puffy pastry, blood in the Sacher torte. History *mit Schlag*! Or, more daunting yet—a *Toast of the Town* for the Weimar Republic with Kurt Weill and Lotte Lenya singing Hindemith golden oldies, Thomas Mann in a bully pulpit and Rosa Luxemburg battered to death with a revolver butt on her way to prison, dumped in a canal. Behold the poet-*dompteur*. Wearing his signature steel-rimmed spectacles and his cute little leather cap, direct from the Black Forest where he ate Rilke like a mushroom—Bertolt Brecht. Let's hear it for the Reichstag fire! Not to mention Adolf and his laughing gas.

Ed had Liza Minnelli on his show—he even had her mother!— and held out as Joel Grey for twenty-three years, but life stopped being a cabaret.

Sometimes late at night, in the rinse cycle of sitcom reruns, cross-torching evangelicals, holistic chiropodists, yak-show yogis and gay-porn cable, surfing the infomercials with burning leaves in my food-hole, I think there must be millions like me out there, all of us remote as our controls, trying to bring back Ed, as if by switching channels fast enough in a pre-Oedipal blur, we hope to re-enact some Neolithic origin myth and from the death of this primeval giant, our father and our Fisher King, water with blood a bountiful harvest and civility.

Family Values,
Like the House of Atreus

Or the Brothers Karamazov.

You will remember the scandalous goings-on of the best known family in the glory that was Greece, adultery being the least of it for Agamemnon and Clytemnestra, Aegisthus and Cassandra, Orestes and Elektra. Incest, infanticide, patricide, matricide, cannibalism and other gaudy dysfunctions were almost all that Aeschylus ever wrote about, as if to hype his ratings. Nor do the soaps have anything on Sophocles. I mean, Oedipus murdered his father and married his mother, after which he was visually challenged. These are behaviors as lurid as Caligula's, who tried to marry his sister. Or Claudius, who, when it didn't work out with Messalina, had her tried for treason. Or Nero, who wasted his mom. Byzantine family life specialized in stranglings of heirs apparent in their bubbly baths, as well as many lopped-off hands. The best of their emperors, Justinian, married Theodora, the daughter of a bear-keeper and a circus acrobat, who, before she showed up in Ravenna mosaics, is said by Procopius in his *Secret History* to have indulged in "bestial practices [and] unnatural traffic of the body," afterwards complaining that Nature had short-changed her with only three apertures for intercourse. (Moreover, as if for pay-cable: "Often in the theatre, in full view of all the people, she would spread herself out, and lie on her back on the ground. And certain slaves, whose special task it was, would sprinkle grains of barley over her private parts; and geese trained for the

{49}

purpose would pick them off one by one with their beaks...")
Richard III! Borgias! Romanovs! Medea and Catherine the Great
were both Mommie Dearests. St. Augustine deserted a wife and
two mistresses. Rousseau dropped off each of his five children by
Thérèse at a foundling hospital. To get on with physics when times
were tough, Einstein abandoned his baby daughter and never gave
her another thought unless we count the theory of relativity as a
sublimation. What Susano-o did in the cave of his Japanese Sun-
Goddess sister Amaterasu was not only unspeakable but also bad
for matriarchy. The Bible is a how-to manual on abusive sex and
crazy violence in a sun-stunned, goat-munched desert.

Or the Mafia. There was an episode of *The Rockford Files* on
NBC in 1977 called "Requiem for a Funny Box." Like many *Rock-
fords*, it involved the Mob. It took James Garner most of the hour to
figure out that the Mob had been responsible for the murder of a
comedian because the comedian had been conducting a homosex-
ual affair with the son of a Mob boss. Confronted by his outraged
capo father, the son with chilling dignity explained that he had
felt this way about men since age 17 and had even tried to talk
about it to a father who refused to listen. This son also pointed out
that, considering the deplorable nature of the family business,
putting on high moral airs about *anything* was a bit thick. So the
father ordered the son shot, too.

As old as any family value is the family curse. Most of our violence, like most of our sex, is domestic. But we *think* about both
more than we *do* either, which is why we've got novelists, play-
wrights, poets, movies and television. Naturally, gathered around
the burning storyteller log in our home-entertainment centers,
there is a part of us—kind, dutiful, thrifty, hygienic, repressed—
that we'd like to see affirmed. But there is another part that is
trapped, sad and furious. This part seems to enjoy seeing all the
bad stuff acted-out by somebody else in public, as if the bloody
fate of kings and queens were a caution; and the bad luck and
hurtful sex of the undeserving rich, unfairly talented and cal-
lously handsome were a comfort; and the punishment of the bor-
ing and the blameless by random evil and dreadful chance were
somehow emancipating, an opportunity to start over after decks
are cleared and worlds collapse—*as if we were fans of excessive
behavior.* Who knows which kind of television is better for the
domestic tranquility? Or what it means that TV itself, that sleek

console full of contorted faces, is the most domestic of our distractions? Perhaps how families present themselves *to* the box is as important to think about as how those families are presented *on* the box. We are since the fifties more *fluid* in our homes, floating in and out of rooms like ghosts, according to the rhythms of spectacle on demand; more *episodic* and *discontinuous*, like impatient vagabonds, choosing to tune in to fictitious lives and counterfeit experiences on the shape-shifting menu at the electric Automat; *deritualized*, as if no longer grounded in our kitchens, dining rooms, front porch, backyard or stoop, as casual about eating as we are about relationships, zapping emotions in a microwave for a quick thaw or a loud pop; *vertiginous*, from a lightness of being. At a dinner party in Manhattan several years ago, a friendly female psychiatrist told me that, in her opinion, TV cuts down on child abuse: the little kid in the dark corner, watching his superheroes sell him sugar bombs, is out of the way of the big fists and the big feet of the angry adults in the shameful house.

What is it that we think we need in our fantasy lives, and why do we blame Burbank when we don't get it? First, the laughter; then such a weeping of eyes behind tinted contacts and such a gnashing of teeth that are capped, you'd imagine that Akbar the Great had died all over again, and the carrion birds had come down on the ghostly ramparts of Fatehpur Sikri.

I've never been to jail, Mr. Grant! I never even had to stay after school!
Mary Tyler Moore

Though situation comedies are now and always have been mostly about families, they didn't start out as socializing agencies. That was what parents were for, and schools, churches, synagogues, armies, therapists and jail. From our bygone radio days through the first two decades of network television, the best we could hope for from a sitcom, chugging along like a choo-choo on its laugh-track, was a certain rueful wisdom. As in the slightest of John Cheever's short stories, perfectly nice people, who played golf and raised flowers and never forgot to stock seed in their bird-feeding stations, might cry "at the death of a cat, a broken shoelace, a wild pitch," but real pain and genuine suffering were "a principality, lying somewhere beyond the legitimate borders of western Europe." Of course, in almost every Cheever story, something happens to darken the screen. Men drown and fall off mountains. Fifteen-year-old boys commit suicide. A wife shoots her husband as he is about to hurdle the living room couch. Someone is arrested for confusing a young woman with a Lucky Strike cigarette. Someone else is devoured by his own dogs. A killer sings commercial jingles. Innocents incinerate when a can of charcoal igniter explodes at a barbecue party. In the swimming pool: an undertow. In the liquor closet: skeletons. In the tossed green salad: lighter fluid instead of vinegar. In the snow: wolves.

But not on TV. Sitcoms hardly daring to do more than suggest coping mechanisms for such routine domestic crises as incompetence and mischief were not about to explore the mysteries of intimacy, much less promote a secret social agenda in favor of working women, class war, teen sex, racial justice, secular humanism, gay rights and spotted owls. We aren't talking about art *or* politics. Can you really imagine gag writers in New York or Hollywood trying to come up with two jokes a minute, forty-four jokes for every half-hour sitcom, with time out for commercial breaks, while simultaneously sneaking in subversive snippets from Adorno or Wilhelm Reich? Then, as now, gag writers were trying to sell a fail-safe concept to network programmers, who were selling audiences in the tens of millions to ad agency account executives, who were selling floor wax and reek to a benumbed republic and themselves to greedy clients. Then as now these gag writers read the same magazines and newspapers, saw the same movies, listened to the same music and skimmed the same reviews of the same bestselling books as everyone else. They also stole from each other. Yes, *if* a concept survived pilot-testing, *and* the public liked the actors, *and* the series lasted a couple of seasons, *and* the nation in its living room was ready to tolerate a Nutrasweet version of the ideological fevers that already raged on the streets outside, then and only then, and even then only maybe, would the private pain, politics and passion of the writer surface in a pointed wisecrack, a problematic new character or a surprising ambiguity. And always *after* the culture already knew that it had major trouble on the event horizon, after the zeitgeist had already sneezed that sneeze.

For instance, the sixties: In a decade of civil-rights turmoil, the *only* lead character on a network sitcom who happened to be black was a high-school teacher on *Room 222*. In a decade of rioting on city streets, we sat down to watch *The Beverly Hillbillies, Green Acres* and *Petticoat Junction*. In a decade of consciousness-raising and militant feminism, the small screen seethed with dreamy genies, kitchen witches, magical nannies and flying nuns. In a decade of youthful opposition to war in Vietnam we got Gilligan, Dobie, Beaver, Dennis the Menace, *Hogan's Heroes*, Batman and Martians, *My Mother the Car* and a spy who talked to his shoe. When, in the sixties, the angry and the disaffected petitioned the media for redress of grievance, we heard about it not on sitcoms but on the evening news with those images of water cannons and police dogs, or on *The Smothers Brothers Comedy Hour*, from Pat Paulsen and Pete Seeger, before they were cancelled in favor of *Hee Haw*. Only after the election of Richard Nixon did sitcoms take a turn towards the subversive, as only after the abdication of Ronald Reagan would westerns make a comeback. Does this mean that television is a *counter*-culture?

But I can shuffle these concepts like a pack of cards and deal out almost any hand I want to. I can toss the cards in the air and assign arbitrary meaning to a random scatter. Why did black Americans disappear from sitcom television in the sixties? (After *Amos 'n' Andy* and *Beulah* in the fifties, it was perhaps a mercy.) Why did urban working-class Americans likewise vanish, after *The Life of Riley* (aircraft factory), unless we count *The Honeymooners* (buses, sewers), till *Alice* (diner), *All in the Family* (tool and die), *Laverne & Shirley* (brewery) and *Taxi* (garage) in the seventies, after which of course *Roseanne* (plastics)? (We know they're working-class because they go *bowling*.) Why are so many sitcoms set in TV newsrooms or on talk shows or at radio stations or in ad agencies, even once at a talent agent's, and why have so many of the male leads been newspaper columnists, usually covering sports? (Write what you know, like Herman Melville and Jackie Collins.) Once sitcoms moved out of the kitchen and into the living room, how come we always saw the same couch, directly facing the camera, as if the characters were laughing at us instead of the TV set *they* never seemed to look at, while *we* did little else? (Think of the screen as a looking-glass, with Alice on one side and Narcissus on the other, both thinking about Heidegger: in one sense obviously "being-there" [*Dasein*] but in another sense, just as obviously, "not-at-home" [*Unheimlichkeit, Nicht-zuhause-sein.*]) What was it about the eighties that caused so many dreadful sitcoms to succeed, while the best of them (*Frank's Place*) failed, and the hour-long dramatic series went into one of its cyclic tailspins? (I would blame it on King Babar and Queen Celeste in the White House and Ollie North in Neverland. What was Iran-Contra but a high-concept Tom Clancy-S.J. Perelman sitcom?)

We need a nation closer to The Waltons *than* The Simpsons.

George Bush

Hey, we're just like the Waltons. Both families spend a lot of time praying for the end of the Depression.

Bart Simpson

I was a big, huge Partridge Family *fan. When I was a kid, I tried to kill my dad so my mom would take us out on tour.*

Paula Poundstone

Late in the seventies, a New York know-it-all with a flashy line in psychic yardgoods, for whom TV criticism was merely a part-time indulgence, a kind of avuncular moonlighting between serious books on loftier subjects, I flew coach to California to present a paper at a conference on "Television and Human Sexuality" (Was it good for you? More taste! Less filling!) sponsored by a foundation that felt there was room for improvement. A car awaited me at LAX. This is because it's necessary in California to drive for two hours whether you want breakfast or transcendence. In my case, it was two hours north to Ojai, where golf links lay like a rug in a lap of little hills and swimming pools shivered like sheets of undulant tin. We slept at night in bungalows carved out of pastel chalk and candle-wax, and rose at dawn to put on leopard-spotted Bermuda shorts and troop to tape-recorded T-group sessions. Among psychologists, sociologists, network veeps and by-the-numbers tele-playwrights, I was the only media smarty-pants. In Wilfrid Sheed's savvy novel about a critic, *Max Jamison*, we were told:

> He was in love with the way his mind worked, and he was sick of the way his mind worked. The first thing that struck you about it…was the blinding clarity, like a Spanish town at high noon. No shade any-where. Yet not altogether lacking in subtlety. Very nice filigree work in the church. This was the mind they were asking him to blow.

You've heard such riffs. I was clever at the expense of those nuclear-family sitcoms of the fifties wherein it was permissible to cry but never to divorce and certainly not to die, not on *I Love Lucy*, *The Life of Riley*, *Mama*, *The Goldbergs*, *The Aldrich Family*, *Father Knows Best*, *The Trouble with Father*, *The Adventures of Ozzie and Harriet*, *December Bride*, *I Married Joan*, *My Little Margie*, *Blondie*, *Leave It to Beaver*, and *Make Room for Daddy*. Several exceptions proved semi-contagious. In *Mr. Peepers* and *Our Miss Brooks*, Wally Cox and Eve Arden found families in the schools where they taught. And in *You'll Never Get Rich*, Phil Silvers, as Sergeant Bilko, found one in an army platoon. The idea that you could enlist or be drafted into a family led in the sixties to sitcom families on ships at sea (*McHale's Navy*, *Mister Roberts*), in marine barracks (*Gomer Pyle*), in prison camps (*Hogan's Heroes*), cavalry forts (*F Troop*), high schools (*Room 222*), a convent (*The Flying Nun*) and a spy agency (*Get Smart*). The nuclear family nevertheless kept on trucking in the sixties, from *Dick Van Dyke* to *Peyton Place*, missing the occasional parent (*Doris Day*, *Julia*, *The Courtship of Eddie's Father* and *The Partridge Family*), adding the occasional ani-mal (*Mister Ed*, *Gentle Ben*, *Flipper* and *The Monkees*) and the occa-sional monster (*The Munsters*, *The Addams Family*). But nobody on the small screen smoked pot, dropped acid, seized a college build-ing, burned down a ghetto, or fragged a Bilko in 'Nam.

As Wally and Phil were exceptions in the fifties, *That Girl* was the exception of the sixties, with Marlo Thomas as a wage-earning alter-native to Donna Reed, Anne Southern and *Gidget*. *That Girl* made it possible in the seventies for a mysteriously single Mary Tyler Moore to have a career and even sex; for Diana Rigg, briefly, to be divorced; and for Bea Arthur's Maude to have the first and the last abortion on a prime-time series till *Picket Fences* in 1994. (Even so, marriage and childbirth still goosed ratings. As it had been for a raucous Lucy and a bewitched Samantha, delivering babies in the fifties and the sixties, so it was for Rhoda's wedding in 1974, and so it would be for Murphy Brown's baby Avery in 1992.) Mary, Valerie Harper, Linda Lavin, Cloris Leachman, Karen Valentine, Sandy Duncan, Loni Anderson, Penny Marshall and Cindy Williams found surrogate families in the seventies on radio and at TV stations, in dress shops, ad agencies, law firms, acting studios, beer halls and consumer groups, as did Hal Linden at a police station, Gabe Kaplan at a high school, Dick Van Dyke on a soap, Bob Newhart in group therapy and Alan Alda in Korea. Not that the family burden didn't remain primarily nuclear: *All in the Family*, *Good Times*, *Happy Days*, *Benson*, *The Jeffersons* and *Mork & Mindy*. Briefly, even Don Rickles came home from *his* ad agency to a wife and child who pretended to want him. But there were at least more working women, more black faces, and some fallout. As *Maude* faced up to abortion, and *M*A*S*H* to war, and *Good Times* to heroin, *All in the Family* sought to "cauterize" bigotry with taboo-busting incantations of "spic," "coon," "dago," "hebe" and "fairy."

So, I said, television is catching up with America. And because everybody in Ojai is afraid of our keynote speaker, Germaine Greer, all we have talked about, so far, is what this means for women. And certainly—if we duck our heads in order not to see the network movies whose only premise is a female menaced, in a lonely bedroom late at night in an empty suburban house, in a stalled car on the deserted road in a surprise monsoon, in a telephone booth on a mean city street in a problematic neighborhood, in a high-rise elevator or, especially, the underground parking garage—the women we see on TV more closely resemble the women we meet in the world than they used to: Instead of Harriet Nelson, Jane Wyatt, Barbara Billingsley, Betty Furness, Grandma Moses, the Miltown tranquilizer or a White Tornado, they remind us of Annie Oakley, Amelia Earhart, Margaret Sanger and Eleanor Roosevelt. Next year in Burbank: Antigone.

But what about men? Why is it on sitcom television, between, say, Robert Young and *The Waltons*, that the American father is so generally a mishap, such a Dagwood Bumstead anti-hero sandwich? From Desi Arnez in *I Love Lucy*, Stu Erwin in *The Trouble with Father*, Ozzie Nelson in *The Adventures of Ozzie and Harriet*, William Bendix in *The Life of Riley*, Charles Farrell in *My Little Margie*, and Danny Thomas in *Make Room for Daddy*, to Carroll

O'Connor in *All in the Family*, Tom Bosley in *Happy Days*, John Amos in *Good Times*, Sherman Hemsley in *The Jeffersons*, and Redd Foxx in *Sanford and Son*, the Sitcom Dad can't lace up the shoe on the foot in his mouth without falling off his rocker, into contumely.

According to the theater, we are James Tyrone in *Long Day's Journey Into Night* and Willy Loman in *Death of a Salesman*. According to the movies, we have devolved from Gregory Peck in *To Kill a Mockingbird* to Charles Bronson in *Death Wish*. According to the men among our novelists, well, from Melville and Twain and Henry James to Malamud, Mailer and Vonnegut, they've been either silent or evasive. Faulkner violently engaged the generations, but his children were flowering curses, clocks wired to bombs. Fitzgerald and Hemingway were bright little boys to the bitter end, waving wooden swords. (Who knew from *Gatsby* or *Tender Is the Night* that Scott was writing such splendid letters to his daughter? Only after Papa ate a gun would he worry, in a posthumous novel, about what fathers do to sons.) In Updike, a child is for feeling guilty about after a father commits adultery. Bellow's no help. Both Eliot Nailles, in Cheever's *Bullet Park*, and Robert Slocum, in Joseph Heller's *Something Happened*, commute to dispiriting jobs in New York from homes in exurban Connecticut to which they've removed their families to spare them the frightful city. Slocum's boy stops talking to him: "He used to have dreams, he said, in which the door to our room was closed and he could not get in to see us. Now I have dreams that the door to his room is closed, and I can't get in to see him." Tony Nailles goes to bed and won't get up: "I just feel terribly sad." Neither father can protect either son—from what, exactly? From Dad, perhaps: so fearful of failure that he secretes it. Failure is his homespun art.

Should genetic engineers and radical feminists conspire, we'll no longer be needed, period. After all, Dr. Danielle Petrucci kept *something* alive for twenty-nine days in a jar. When they reach the point where life can be cloned or synthesized in labs, asexually from single cells, on a petri dish or in a centrifuge, what happens to Oedipus? Who takes the rap? Sperm banks on every block like nail salons! Day-old frozen embryos, like packets of flower seeds! What a sitcom: no blood, no birth, no love, no death, no sweat. And no wonder our own children look up at us so startled and wary when we interrupt them in their music, their recreational drug-taking and their dreams of vengeance, as if we couldn't be trusted to go to a grocery store without a nametag or a stamped self-addressed envelope; as if our clumsiness might kill them.

This leaves Ralph Waite. Say good night, John-Boy.

Well, at Ojai, they were hard put to sit through this persiflage, so anxious was everybody for the flamboyant sexuality of Greer, her ferocious grin. It had been a decade since she pounced on us in *The Female Eunuch* from Cambridge and the Outback by way of Shakespeare, disdaining Freud: Down with marriage, morality and the state! Pleasure had seemed to be her only principle, and she knew how to put on a show, and if I can't now remember a single word she said from the podium, I do recall a chat we had, at dinner beforehand, about fathers. Hers had been a mystery to her. He'd looked like Basil Rathbone. He'd hated carrots and priests. Ten years later she would publish *Daddy, We Hardly Knew You* and it turned out that Reg Greer, who sold advertising space for a Melbourne newspaper, had lied to his wife and daughter about almost everything. He hadn't been born a gentleman in South Africa and somehow fallen out of social grace. Nor was he secretly Jewish. Nor had he suffered in the war any romantic wounding, shellshock, brainwash. Rather than descending from Scottish kings, Reg seems to have been the bastard son of a servant girl; to have been raised in a loving foster home in Tasmania; to have abandoned that home without a backward glance; to have shirked in the war his duties as a cipher clerk at an underground decoding machine in Malta; to have been at the newspaper office a "masher" and a "bounder"; and to have never known his own real name, although Germaine now does. But in finding this father, the daughter lost an excuse. At her own decoding machine, she can no longer see why she should have been forced to grow up, in Melbourne, in a house without music, books, flowers, cheese or love. His alibi wounds were phony, like his advertising.

This, too, is a digression, but one that speaks to empty spaces, variable gravities, floating identities, the blank check. About all I know of my own father is that he could have been another Dennis Day, singing on the radio, except that in his teens, by leaping through a window to save a child from a burning house, he so scarred his left leg that he gave himself permission ever after to sing tenor only in the shower, to drink rye round the clock, to die young like a Romantic poet, and to be remembered by his son as a wholly imaginary being, a flaming seraph who fell out of the sky and into a bottle. These are the TV movies, the reruns, in our heads.

Anyway, the next morning at Ojai, we were asked in our T-group by the "facilitator" with the kindly voice and the gentle beard to close our eyes and talk about our sex lives. What? Yes. Well: very nice filigree work in the church. After which, three of the very best writers in the sitcom business, James L. Brooks, Allan Burns and Ed Weinberger, fresh from *The Mary Tyler Moore Show*, *Maude*, *Lou Grant* and *Taxi*, on their way to *The Cosby Show*, *Alf*, *The Simpsons* and *The Critic*, ganged up on an NBC vice-president for broadcast standards (a censor). Brooks had heard that any script submitted to NBC touching in any way on the subject of homosexuality was sent by the net for vetting to *a gay dentist in New Jersey*. Could that possibly be true? *Not* true, the veep replied: In New Jersey, he may once upon a time have been a dentist, but he was now a *psychotherapist*. We stared for awhile at the clouds in our coffee. Then Weinberger waggled a hand. "You mean," he said, "you mean…there really *is* a Tooth Fairy?"

The point here is not to stamp one's foot at a wisecrack that may be offensive to gays, or to dentists, or to New Jersey. When push comes to shove, at Stonewall or on Rodeo Drive, Brooks, Burns and Weinberger are likely more liberal than the rest of us NIMBYs and certainly more fun to talk to, even in a T-group, than most of the people you meet at a New York literary cocktail party, obsessing about real estate. The point is, this is what sitcom writers do. They turn everything, even censorship, into wisecracks. It should not surprise us that Diane English and Jerry Seinfeld turned O.J.'s white Ford Bronco into a sight gag in the fall of 1994. Can you imagine what the gang at Sid Caesar's *Your Show of Shows*—Carl Reiner, Mel Brooks, Neil Simon, Larry Gelbart, Woody Allen— would have done to O.J.? To Michael Jackson? To a John Wayne Bobbitt? Or, for that matter, to Woody, Mia and Soon-yi? *That's what they get those big bucks for and why Chekhov doesn't.* From *Cheers* did you really expect the loneliness of the long-distance runner or a goalie's anxiety at the penalty kick? From *Home Improvement*, a class-action suit against the Ford Motor Company for exploding Pinto gas tanks? The surprise ought not to be that nothing under our sun is safe from the trivializing one-liner. The surprise is that, every once in a sitcom while, there is actually something new under that sun, like Hawkeye's nervous breakdown in an episode of *M*A*S*H*; or Judd Hirsch on *Taxi* falling in love with the radio voice of an obese dispatcher and learning just how thin our culture is, how starved for sympathy; or Jane Curtin's discovering late in *Kate & Allie*'s run what it felt like to be homeless; or Tim Reid on *Frank's Place* taking the paper bag test to see if his skin color was light enough for membership in the New Orleans men's club; or Dixie Carter on *Designing Women* opening her mouth to deliver an impassioned aria on Anita Hill and Clarence Thomas; or Roseanne opening *her* mouth to kiss Mariel Hemingway.

> [The Aliens Show] *was a situation comedy about a group of extraterrestrials ranging from cute to psycho, from animal to vegetable and also mineral, because it featured an artistic space-rock that could quarry itself for its raw material and then regenerate itself in time for next week's episode; this rock was named Pygmalien, and owing to the stunted sense of humor of the producers there was also a coarse, belching creature like a puking cactus that came from a desert planet at the end of time: this was Matilda the Australien, and there were the three grotesquely pneumatic singing space sirens known as the Alien Korns, maybe because you could lie down among them, and there was a team of Venusian hip-hoppers and subway spray-painters and soul-brothers who called themselves the Alien Nation, and under a bed in the spaceship that was the program's main location there lived Bugsy, the giant dung-beetle from the Crab Nebula who had run away from his father, and in a fish tank you could find Brains, a superintelligent giant abalone who liked eating Chinese, and then there was Ridley, the most terrifying of the regular cast, who looked like a Francis Bacon painting of a mouthful of teeth waving at the end of a sightless pod, and who had an obsession with the actress Sigourney Weaver. (Salman Rushdie,* The Satanic Verses*)*

A decade passed before I dared again to leave the house for another conference, this time at Brown University in Providence on "The Changing American Family." There's no reason why I couldn't have repeated the same growl about dumb dads—Know-It-Alls are invited to summit meetings in order to repeat themselves and secure a niche; it's like performance art—updated, maybe, with a new emphasis on "the single father epidemic." While single fathers have always been around on network television, more often widowed than divorced, from *My Little Margie*, *The Rifleman* and *Brave Eagle* in the fifties, to *My Three Sons*, *Bonanza* and *The Andy Griffith Show* in the sixties, to *Nanny and the Professor*, *The Courtship of Eddie's Father*, *Sanford and Son* and *Hello Larry* in the seventies, they had seemed in the eighties to undergo a fruit-fly proliferation—*Benson*, *Coach*, *Empty Nest*, *Silver Spoons*,

You Again, Rags to Riches, Dads, My Two Dads, Paradise, Free Spirit,
Raising Miranda, I Married Dora, and *First Impressions.* (The odd
trend would spill over into the nineties with *Blossom, City, Uncle*
Buck, American Dreamer, Sunday Dinner, It Had To Be You, Second
Half, Me and the Boys, Daddy's Girls and *The Critic*). What could this
possibly mean? Although divorce was catching up to death as an
excuse for single fatherhood, and many of these dads at least had
rudimentary nurturing skills, the facts were out of whack. According to the U.S. Census Bureau, 25 percent of all children in the
Real America lived with single parents in 1989. But in this same
Real America *89 percent* of all those single parents were *women.*
Moreover, 57 percent of the children who lived with single parents
were black and 32 percent Hispanic. Whereas, in TV America,
more than 90 percent of all the Little People with just a single Big
One in the backyard bomb shelter seemed to be yogurt-colored.

It would also have been necessary to face up to the two most
important television fathers of the eighties, neither bearing much
resemblance to reality for the rest of us. One, of course, was Bill
Cosby. Cosby had originally proposed a blue-collar sitcom. ABC
turned him down. He then upwardly mobilized the concept to
white-collar professional, starring himself as Dr. Heathcliff
Huxtable, an obstetrician practicing out of his Brooklyn Heights
brownstone; Phylicia Rashad as Clair, his lawyer wife who left that
home to toil nobly every day for Legal Aid; and five children for
whom a wise, if sarcastic, dad would always be there, whether they
wanted him or not. ABC turned *that* down, too. NBC was shrewder.

The other important father of the eighties was Edward Woodward as Robert McCall, in *The Equalizer:* a retired intelligence
agent who set up shop, in a Manhattan apartment to die for, as a
last-resort detective, bodyguard and avenging angel, doing good as
a way of doing penance for his nasty past in Latin America, Southeast Asia and the Middle East. While McCall's relations with his
own son, Scott, were strained, it was amazing how often the children of strangers in trouble happened on his classified newspaper
ad and left desperate messages on his answering machine. To
which messages he invariably responded. This was post-Freudian
and deeply satisfying: the mythic father all children wish for and
none of us has ever had, *or ever will have*, who promises to protect
us from the Dark Side—exactly like Ronald Reagan.

But not many of us work at home in such agreeable neighborhoods as Brooklyn Heights with friends like Stevie Wonder, B.B. King and the Count Basie Band to drop in. Even fewer of us are guilt-stricken intelligence operatives, any more than we are a Captain Ahab or the Lone Ranger, which is why we watch television instead of leading insurrections. We don't even work for ad agencies. We are, like an Al Bundy and a Homer Simpson, less thrilling. Not old enough yet for a reptilian retirement in Florida, we seem never to have been as young as the demographically desirable NYPNS (Neat Young People in Neat Situations), DINKS (Double Income, No Kids), or what the mystery novelist David Handler calls YUSHIES (Young Urban Shitheads). Did I really have to think about Yup instead of fatherhood? Of course I did. As a professional critic, it was my zeitgeist duty to think about *whatever* the crybaby-boomers were thinking about, which was always their conflicted, Y-person selves. As a guy said to a gal in the TV movie *Bare Essentials*: "The only food-gathering you've ever done is at a salad bar."

For instance: *thirtysomething*. Sensitive Jewish Michael and supermom Hope and bearded Elliot and blonde Nancy and red-haired Melissa and long-haired Gary and careerist Ellyn felt bad every Tuesday night from 1987 to 1991 about children, adultery, Thanksgiving, computers and the sixties. Growing up hurts so much you want to suck your big toe. They rode their anxieties, like Melissa's Exercycle. Or wore them, like Hope's Princeton T-shirt. They played parent the way they played mud volleyball or Lazer-Tag. For all the smart talk, their frontal lobes seemed full of video rentals instead of books or politics; medium tepid instead of *Big Chill*. They were as lukewarm and secondhand in their erotic fantasies as in their attitudinizing, as if they'd bought the whole Xerox package of other people's prefab experiences already market-tested by Michael and Elliot at, of course, their ad agency. There was no true north in them, nor any bravery.

Who needed this in my living room? I could leave the house, and go to the corner, and find an overmuch of such people in my own yupscale neighborhood: sun dried as if in extra-virgin olive oil, crouched to consume their minimalist bistro meals of cilantro leaves, medallions of goat cheese and half a scallop on a bed of money; gaudy balloons of avarice and ego tethered by their red suspenders to all that's trendiest, waiting with twenty-four-carat coke spoons for Tom Wolfe or Dave Letterman. By day this block belonged to barbers, dry cleaners, shoemakers and locksmiths. But at night, in the sports bars, pubs and ethnic restaurants, the Y-people bloomed like henbane or belladonna and you heard their wounded wail: "Gimme, gimme." For their many sins, they had been punished on a Black Monday with the stock market crash of October 1987. But they'd forgiven themselves and promptly risen, almost the very next night, with an hour of prime-time television of their very own, like a platinum American Express card.

Why was *thirtysomething* such a popular success and *The Days and Nights of Molly Dodd* a network flop, shuffled off to cult status on Lifetime cable? Wasn't Blair Brown a boomer, too, eating Chinese, teaching piano, listening to rockabilly in a West Side apartment building where the elevator never quite properly stopped to meet the floor, as Molly never quite met life at the proper angle? But Molly was a poet, divorced from a jazz musician. And worked in a bookshop, where D.H. Lawrence was actually spoken. And then at a publishing house, where she wasn't on the best-seller fast track. And dated, instead of an account executive or a pork-belly future, a black cop, whose name was Nathaniel Hawthorne. And was lusted after by her own psychiatrist, who happened also to be female. And went out after work to night school and museums instead of sports bars. A brave and baffled Molly made her own experiences. You'd never catch *her* in silk jacquards, tapered Lord & Taylor tunics, tobacco-suede Euforia boots, and Lady Datejust Oyster Perpetuals, eating steamed skate and pumpkin seeds on Columbus Avenue, smelling like the guts of a sperm whale. And yet the television culture disdained her almost as much as it had disdained Geena Davis and Alfre Woodard as storefront lawyers in *Sara*, or the Linda Kelsey who had quit the rat race to teach preschoolers in *Day by Day*.

However, by the time I got to Providence I was a humbler and chastened Know-Only-Some-of-It. In Kyoto, in front of Takanobu's "Portrait of Taira no Shigemori," a Japanese scholar told André Malraux that "You want to be *in* the painting, whereas we want to be outside it. European painting has always wanted to catch the butterflies, eat the flowers and sleep with the dancers." As if television were my European painting, I had spent a good portion of the eighties alone in my house, wanting to catch, eat and dance with those butterflies, flowers and dancers. I was hitting bottom, and then in the beginning stages of a recovery from alcoholism. Never mind the horror stories about hospitals and estrangement. You have already seen their equivalent, if not in your own lives, then certainly in the TV movies: a wife hiding out in a West Side loft, with her spices and her afghan; the children in exile in Madison, Prague and Taipei; the X-rays, EKGs and CAT scans; the old people who seemed, in their tatty bathrobes, to be practicing a martial art on the lawn each morning and the young people of the adolescent wing who roamed in packs at night in their fluted Ionian deathgowns; the withdrawal dreams of basilisks, scorpions and ravens' heads, of peacock tails and Pontic rhubarb. In Saul Bellow's *More Die of Heartbreak* one character asks another: "Uncle, how do you picture your death—what's your worst case scenario for death?" Uncle replies: "Well, from the very beginning there have been pictures—inside and outside. And for me the worst that can happen is that those pictures will stop."

When I came back from the hospital to an empty house, television no longer seemed an upstart medium, amusing in its presumption, about which to sermonize and smarty-pant. There were, to be sure, the video cassettes that arrived now by messenger and express mail, the same size and as self-important as the books I spent the other half of my professional life reviewing. I no longer had to leave the house and visit the networks and wait around in darkened anterooms for a member of the appropriate craft union to replace a cartridge and punch up a preview tape. I had only to consult the clock of my convenience, settle my fragile self in front of the VCR, and, like a car alarm, anticipate being burgled. But tape was not enough, nor was there enough tape, to fill all the holes in my apprehension. I needed TV in a different way. And it was like looking through the window of a washing machine during a spin-dry cycle, at tumbles of bras and socks, at twisted arms and severed heads. I was, suddenly, watching TV as a civilian. I fell into it, as if to waterbed. After a decade of passing out and coming to, I couldn't sleep at all. Like some Aztec Mother Serpent, my metabolism was shucking skins. There are only so many books and tapes a pair of eyes can read or watch, so many words a pair of hands can process, so many walks a pair of feet can plod, around the block or to a meeting. At those amazing meetings, in an underground network of church basements, over the cardboard cups of lousy coffee in a blue smog of cigarette smoke, we told each other stories to get us through the night. These many stories—of joblessness and paranoia; smashed cars and nights in jail; wife-beating, child abuse, loony bins, AIDS; hallucinations and attempted suicides; disconnection and the end of love—were really merely one, about a lost child in a black forest of bad chemicals.

None of this was television's fault. But enough of it showed up on television to suggest to a disordered mind, if not coincidence or causality, at least an eerie series of correspondences, a hanging-together of related metaphors as the metaphors had bunched up in, say, Nahuatl poetry, or Roman and Gothic world views, among Mings and Renaissance Florentines. So I watched *Hill Street Blues* not only because it was the best TV series of the eighties and not even because Daniel J. Travanti as Frank Furillo and Joe Spano as Henry Goldblume had assumed the Alan Alda Hawkeye role model of the New Man Who Has Non-Predatory Feelings, but because Furillo was a recovering alcoholic, and when Kiel Martin's LaRue finally got himself to an A.A. meeting, there was Frank already in The Rooms. I watched *Cagney & Lacey*, not only because such a part-nership of class-conscious fast-talking street-smart feminists was so singular as to have become Gloria Steinem's favorite show, nor because anyone could have guessed that Sharon Gless and Tyne Daly in New York would make Thelma and Louise imaginable in Hollywood, but because Chris Cagney so obviously had a drinking problem, and when she finally got around to doing something about it after her father's death, the series dogged her every step of the diffi-cult way, all twelve of them. Toward the end of the decade, while I liked everything else about *Murphy Brown*, its breezy nonchalance on the matter of Murphy's drinking ticked me off, as if alcoholism were another of her quirks or cranks. In the pilot, Murphy was just back from Betty Ford. Thereafter at Phil's she drank designer water. One New Year's Eve, subtracting scotch, she was minus a sense of humor. Otherwise the flagrant behaviors of her drinking days were recalled by her officemates as comic romps. So much for recovery. It's as easy as having a baby, if you forget about both for weeks at a time. And having a baby, of course, was another half-baked, unbright idea that occurred to *Murphy*'s writers and shouldn't have, not for fear of ruffling Dan Quayle's indignant feathers but because even the sleepiest of us knows a real-world Murphy would have aborted. Compare such glibness to the gallows-humor sitcom fashioned for the nineties by John Larroquette—*Under the Volcano* with *Barney Miller*'s laughtrack—from his own experience of bottoms and recov-ery, which partook of memory, process and duration.

On the other trembling hand it was hard for me to watch either *Cheers* or *St. Elsewhere*. I needed never again to be in bars or hospitals: those dream-like Easter Islands, with their long-eared priest-kings, their birdman cults, their ancestor worship, their megalithic petroglyphs, those great stone faces under black-rock top hats on Cubist penguins with their goofy, abstract, Bob Hope look. For the only time in my life, I sounded even to myself like Goethe: "How dare a man have a sense of humor when he considers his immense burden of responsibilities toward himself and others? I have no wish to pass censure on the humorists. After all, does one have to have a conscience? Who says so?" But whatever a Jackie Gleason drank on stage in the fifties and a Dean Martin in the sixties and seventies, it wasn't funny, as Sid Caesar, Carol Burnett, Dick Van Dyke, Susan Saint James and Don Johnson had strobe-lit reason to know.

Obviously, this is no way to review television. You have to watch *St. Elsewhere* so that you will be prepared when some of the same writers come up with *Homicide: Life on the Streets*, as you have to watch *A Year in the Life* to understand where *Northern Exposure* and *I'll Fly Away* came from. But it is also an important way that civilians *do* watch television, as if by periscope under the heavy water of our own vagrant needs and monomaniacal compulsions, down where we are bottom-feeding like octopods on the fluffy bacteria and tube worms of everything we feel bad about, all those thermal vents in a problematic self. While I was reading and reviewing Gabriel García Márquez, Salman Rushdie, Toni Morrison, Milan Kundera, Nadine Gordimer, Don DeLillo, Günter Grass, Christa Wolf, Kōbō Abe and Cynthia Ozick, I was afraid of *Cheers*. What if I were coming home from teaching English as a second language in an overcrowded public school, or an assembly line factory job, or milking cows and greasing tractors? What if after a hostile take-over, leveraged buyout or obsolesence, I hadn't a job at all? Or grew up uncertain of my sexual identity? Or was running out my string in a geriatric gulag where, like a rhododendron, I was misted twice a day? Or were poor, black, gay, Inuit, Rosicrucian or a mixed grill of the above? What then would I require of television? How would it, all unwitting, muddle with *that* mind?

*We've got some footage from the show last night, I would
like you to watch the way Murphy Brown handles a baby,
she supposedly loves this baby, this baby is supposedly one of
the highlights of her life, you watch how she handles baby
Brown, look at her, acting like it's a bomb, look at her,
where's the nearest trash can, what can I do with this thing?
Would you hold your baby that way? Look at the poor
baby's arms, that baby can't possibly be loved and happy. I
mean that kid, Murphy, if you don't start handling that kid
right you're going to end up with a serial murderer on your
hands, that kid is not going to be loved.*
Rush Limbaugh

Every time you hurt a small animal, a clown dies.
Brett Butler

Years ago, when my daughter was five, together we watched *The
Littlest Angel*, a Christmas special about a shepherd boy who dies,
goes to heaven, returns briefly to earth to collect his box of favorite
things, and then gives that box to God (E.G. Marshall) as a birthday gift for the Christ child. While I remember objecting to the
idea of all that polishing and vacuuming in heaven (the Protestant
ethic of drudgery even unto afterlife), *The Littlest Angel* seemed
otherwise harmless. Not so to my daughter. First, when the shepherd boy looked around at the other angelic gifts, he was so
ashamed of his, he tried to hide it. God, of course, noticed. "God is
sneaky," my daughter said. "He can see around corners. He'd *never*
lose at hide-and-seek." Next, after the program, she burst into tears
and couldn't sleep. It took me an hour to find out what upset her
so. She had noticed that when the little boy returns to retrieve his
box of favorite things, his parents can't see or hear him. That must
be what death is.

We hadn't watched the same program. I couldn't protect her
from *The Littlest Angel*; no one protected me from *The Yearling*.
Childhood isn't *Sesame Street*, nor adulthood sitcoms. Suppose
Amy hadn't eventually graduated from *The Brady Bunch*, *The Par-*

tridge Family and the afternoon soaps she taped all through college, to trade in her prurient preoccupation with Jim Morrison of the Doors for an equally obsessive crush on Martin Luther and become a doctoral candidate in Reformation history? Suppose, instead, she had turned into a professor of American Studies at Hampshire College, like Susan J. Douglas. Douglas published in 1994 a remarkable meditation on growing up female with the mass media, *Where the Girls Are*, in which she watched the same TV programs, went to the same films, read the same magazines and listened to the same music as every other alert munchkin. Through her eyes, what sort of television culture do we see? She had to wait a long time, from Molly Goldberg and Alice Kramden, for a Joyce Davenport. Why did Stephanie Zimbalist need a "Remington Steele" in the first place? What is a young girl being told by *Queen for a Day*, *The Newlywed Game*, June Cleaver, Elly May Clampett and Lily Munster? By Connie Stevens as Cricket in *Hawaiian Eye* and Diane McBain as Daphne in *Surfside Six*? By *Police Woman* and *Wonder Woman* and *Bionic Woman*? There's nothing *abstract* about Douglas's gratitude to NBC News for Liz Trotta, Norma Quarles, and Aline Saarinen, nor her celebration of *Kate & Allie*, *Cagney & Lacey*, *China Beach* and *Designing Women*. While I saw *The Equalizer* as a Superdad, Douglas resented him as a collector of wounded women. While I was admiring a bionic Lindsay Wagner for her lioness graces, the violin string of restless intelligence that refined the shadows and planes of her good-bones face, Douglas deplored the dumbing-down of "liberation" into narcissism: Buns of Steel! On the other hand, while I disdained *Charlie's Angels* as a harem fantasy (except for Kate Jackson, the Thinking Angel with a whiskey rasp of a voice, the Lauren Bacall-Blythe Danner erotic croak), Douglas identified with a trio of adventurous and resourceful young women who saved themselves and each other while occasionally crossdressing.

Periscopes! Like God and television, we see around corners. In the popular culture, we all play hide-and-go-seek. We find our models in the oddest places: a glint here, a shadow there, a scruple, a qualm, some style and attitude. Douglas reminds us that pop culture is more than TV. She found an abundance of possible selves in music: in the Shirelles and Cyndi Lauper, in Joan Baez, Diana Ross and Janis Joplin; in Aretha Franklin, Bette Midler and Madonna. But also at the movies with Joan Crawford and the Hepburns (Kate in *Pat and Mike*, Audrey as Holly Golightly); in books by Pearl Buck, Simone de Beauvoir, Betty Friedan and Susan Brownmiller; in sports, with Billie Jean King, and in politics with Shirley Chisholm. And so was the enemy everywhere. To save her own sanity, Douglas had to swim out from under magazines like *Cosmo, Seventeen, Glamour* and *Redbook*; from Revlon and Victoria's Secret; from *Mary Poppins*, James Bond and biker movies; from Norman Mailer, Hugh Hefner, liposuction and Ultra Slim-Fast.

To which we might add a *Whole Earth Catalog* of other shadows on our blameless childhoods. As much as the fifties were *I Love Lucy*, Howdy Doody and Davy Crockett's coonskin cap, or Dick Nixon and Charles Van Doren in prime-time tears, they were also Korea and *Peanuts*, Marilyn Monroe and Rosa Parks, Joe Stalin and atom-bomb air-raid drills, Joe McCarthy and polio, hula hoops and Grace Kelly, Levittown and Ralph Ellison, Edsels *and* Sputniks, Castros and Barbies. (From M.G. Lord's 1994 "unauthorized biography" of that doll, *Forever Barbie*, we would learn that Mattel Corporation practically invented the advertising of children's toys on television in 1955, committing most of its entire net worth of $500,000 to commercials for a jack-in-a-box, a Burp Gun and a Uke-Doodle on *The Mickey Mouse Club*, paving the way for Mortal Kombat.) Instead of Barbie, I had a Lone Ranger atomic bomb ring with a color snapshot of the mushroom cloud, available in the late forties from General Mills for a couple of Kix cereal box tops. I also loved those horror comics that so alarmed congressional committees and psychiatrists like Dr. Frederic Wertham in the early fifties, as if they'd never heard of Grimm's fairy tales. Nowadays, we only pay attention to cartoons if they show up on TV, like *The Simpsons* on Fox or *Beavis and Butt-head* on MTV. We haven't noticed, at the candy store or the headshop, Swamp Things, Freak Brothers, the Flaming Carrot, Reid Fleming (World's Toughest Milkman), Elektrassassin (Cold War Beast), Dr. Manhattan (the Princeton physicist who fusions himself into a human hydrogen bomb) or *Love & Rockets* (lesbians who wear combat boots and speak barrio Spanish). Plus any number of musclebound acidheads into the superheroics for the money, the sex, the violence, the publicity and the chance to dress up in their underwear.

For that matter, as much as the sixties may have been about Dylan and Joplin and Vietnam, they were also about *Blow Up*, Kurt Vonnegut and Twiggy. As the seventies were about disco and the eighties about AIDS. Think of jet planes and birth control pills, of drive-ins and drive-bys, of transistors and malls. As Billy Joel once explained: "We Didn't Start the Fire."

Consumption of beer leads to military behavior…One day you're going to read about some scientist discovering that hops, in conjunction with certain strains of "yeast creatures," have a mysterious effect on some newly discovered region of the brain, making people want to kill—but only in groups. With whiskey, you might want to murder your girlfriend—but beer makes you want to do it with your buddies watching.

Frank Zappa

But even this assumes a coherence I didn't bring to my TV set, nor find there either, in the wastes of recovery. Imagine turning to the dream box when all else has failed—after you have met deadlines, paid bills, closed down a computer, tied up a green sack of garbage, left the house to save the world, gone to a twelve-step meeting at the nearest Angkor Wat with the golden Buddha, the Rainbow Bridge and the batsqueak in the banyan trees, come home again to microwave a rush past food (no longer a ceremony of fire and ice), phoned a friend, disdained an author-God and curled your lip at the latest English uppityness in the *New York Review of Books*— only to discover at the last resort of the small screen, surfing an electromagnetic junk-mail wave, that all the old boundaries between genres are dissolved, that it is no longer possible to differentiate a sitcom from a disease movie, news from docudrama, science from sci-fi, music from jingles, the dysfunctional soap from the pop-therapeutic freakshow or anthropology from archaeology. Wanting to kill time, you drop instead by wormhole into a different kind of space.

Did it matter if eighties television tried to do a better job on, say, gender typing than TV in the seventies, sixties and fifties, when eighties television consisted as much of seventies, sixties and fifties reruns as it did of original programs? In TV deep space, all those decades co-existed simultaneously, jabbering at one another in a warp of white noise. Just as every character in a nineteenth-century English industrial novel who felt bad about dark satanic mills had to depend for his or her deliverance on a fortuitous marriage, a miraculous inheritance, sudden death or immigration to Australia, so the afternoon soaps depended on amnesia and the evil twin. This same psychic stuff, gussied up by the roboshrinks for whom amnesia was a repressed memory syndrome and evil twinship a multiple-personality disorder, moved across the dial from soaps to yakkies, speaking bitterness in an endless Chinese struggle meeting, with Oprah, Phil, Sally and Geraldo, on its way to a TV movie, a "trauma drama." (No wonder Oprah and Phil prefer to stand off-stage among members of the studio audience, to distance themselves from guest freaks. To Donahue, in a program on incest, someone actually said: "I'm a decent man. I provide for my family. I don't run around on my wife, and I've never slept with anyone except my wife and my daughters.") If soaps were industrial novels, prime time was penny dreadfuls, shilling shockers and the gothic. What occurred to women on cable was worse than anything done to Erendira by García Márquez, and shouldn't have happened to Candide's Cunegonde. (As Isabel said to Tristao in John Updike's *Brazil*: "Use me. Whip me if it pleases you. Beat me, even. Only, do not break my teeth.") What happened to us all on the late-night local news was a Newgate Calendar. And what happened to sexuality itself in music video was a crossover gender-bending so extravagant, so RuPauling, that it might have brought a blush to Rama and Sita in the ancient Bengali texts, to Qamar al-Zaman in the *Arabian Nights*, to Viola in *Twelfth Night*, to Yentl and Tootsie.

*I cannot listen to other people blaming their mothers for
another year. I have to move on.*

Oprah Winfrey

By the time I got to Providence, I hadn't guessed the half of it. The
TV movie is the sitcom's evil twin—a Polaroid of Dorian Gray
syphilitic in the attic. *This* is how families behave when they aren't
watching *The Brady Bunch*. To be sure, from Hallmark or Disney,
we can still count on comfort food to lukewarm and uplift the
feel-good heart: remakes of *Heidi* and *The Computer Wore Tennis
Shoes*; holiday reunions of *The Waltons*; Jean Smart as a teacher or
Yarn Princess when she isn't cast against type as a serial killer; Kirk
Douglas learning to read; Frank Sinatra singing to Olympia
Dukakis; Alan Arkin achieving Cooperstown; Glenn Close pio-
neering (twice) as Sarah, plain and tall; Jason Robards getting Julie
Harris for his Christmas present; Charles Bronson writing the
editorial that advised Virginia, "Yes, there is a Santa Claus"; Lloyd
Bridges *playing* Santa Claus; the Ted Turner biblicals in which
Richard Harris as Abraham, the tough-love father of three religions, and Matthew Modine as Jacob, who practiced for fourteen
years with sheep before getting to sleep with Lara Flynn Boyle,
saw more sand than a hot camel; any TV movie with Jessica
Tandy, Hume Cronyn, Angela Lansbury, Kris Kristofferson, Betty
White, Barnard Hughes or Rue McClanahan; any TV movie with
either insufferable Olsen twin, Ashley or Mary-Kate; and, alas, any
one of the high-concept/lite-beer ratings busters in which a game
but palsied Katharine Hepburn is prevailed upon to embarrass
herself, as if in the bare ruined choirs of what she once was, she
should have to put up with a Jason Bateman or a Ryan O'Neal, as if
the mass-marketing of such ravaged beauty weren't a scandal, and
maybe even a sin.

Most of the time, however, the *function* of the TV movie is to *dys*;
it's an Hieronymus Bosch of martyrs and victims. Alcoholism, for
example, has been a genre of its own since 1962, with Jack Lemmon
and Lee Remick in J.P. Miller's *Days of Wine and Roses*. Among

many other actors who began their careers as perfectly healthy adults, Donna Mills, from *Knots Landing*, devolved into a TV movie drunk. Meredith Baxter, late of *Family Ties*, came back from bottled journalism in one film to star in another as a pill-popping alcoholic nurse who falls in love, at a methadone clinic, with a heroin-addicted Stephen Lang. Even Piper Laurie ended up after *Twin Peaks* as an alcoholic mother of a coke-head, Susan Dey, whom we'd prefer to remember from *The Partridge Family*. And this is not to mention, yet, any of the TV movies about women and children abused by men who stoked their rage with booze. Which is why, in 1989, the culture really needed *My Name Is Bill W.*, with James Woods as Bill Wilson and James Garner as Dr. Bob, the co–founding fathers of Alcoholics Anonymous. While this otherwise scrupulous TV version of the A.A. origin myth omitted a few of Bill's flaws (even sober, he womanized compulsively, dropped acid, gobbled niacin by megadose and was never sure himself if his famous conversion experience was the sight of God in a blaze of "indescribably white light" or the hot flash of a toxic psychosis), what millions saw on ABC and would see again two years later on PBS in *Circle of Recovery* was the embodiment of sanctuary, a place where the wounded were not only safe from ambush, but also assisted by others like them at inventing braver selves. Magazine journalists and TV comedians make fun of twelve-step programs for their bumper-sticker slogans, their retro-therapeutic baby talk and their apolitical self-absorption—as if we'd all be better off on the barricades, in loony bins or reading Derrida. But such programs seem to some of us a whole lot healthier than the communitarian alternative of a Michigan or Montana militia. Whether God shows up at an A.A. meeting is problematic. But somehow, in the collective wisdom, witness and example of these friends of your affliction, there falls a kind of grace. You are less a stranger to yourself, and so go to bed, one midnight at a time, having chosen not to drink.

Likewise its very own genre is the disease-of-the week movie, at least since *Brian's Song* (1970), with Billy Dee Williams, James Caan and Michel Legrand making music out of cancer. In the past eight years alone Anne Archer, Bernadette Peters, Maureen Stapleton, Lindsay Wagner, Kathleen Turner, Susan Dey and Jacqueline Bisset have all had TV tumors. Mel Harris has suffered leukemia; Fred Savage, muscular dystrophy; Nicolette Sheridan, a paralyzing stroke; and Raquel Welch, Lou Gehrig's disease (amyotrophic lateral sclerosis). Kirstie Alley, Patty Duke, Melissa Gilbert, Angelica Huston and Kelsey Grammer have each had to cope with autistic children. Down's syndrome has been so popular in the TV families of Tyne Daly, Richard Crenna, JoBeth Williams, Jeff De Munn and, again, Patty Duke, that it got its own network series, *Life Goes On*, which also faced up to AIDS. There was even a TV movie, *A Child's Cry for Help* (NBC 1994), that introduced us to a disease we'd never heard of, Munchausen-by-proxy syndrome, requiring hysterically overprotective mothers like Pam Dawber to hurt their own children so they could spend quality time in a hospital with a doctor like Veronica Hamel. It probably did less harm than *Leap of Faith*, a 1988 CBS movie encouraging us to believe that, by "guided imagery," we could love ourselves back to health from modular lymphona. *Leap of Faith* was Burbank's equivalent of the Fig Newtonians in our recent Congress solving the crisis in health care by sticking pins in Hillary. In fact, with four new weekly hospital series in 1995, prime-time television may be America's only hope for comprehensive medical coverage.

Abuse, too, has its own archive, with overlapping cross-references to battery, rape, child molestation, female madness and an eighties emphasis on incest. Since Farrah Fawcett, in *The Burning Bed* (1984), a battered spouse like Michelle Lee or Annette O'Toole has shown up on TV more often than the Witness Protection Program. Though we usually meet her as a subplot on a cop show, recent TV movie examples include Pamela Reed, beaten up in *Shameful Secrets* by Tim Matheson after which she was hospitalized, and then again in *Woman with a Past* after which she was jailed; Susan Dey in *Beyond Betrayal*, who has no sooner started a new life with bearded and sensitive Dennis Boutsikaris than her sadofascistic ex-husband Richard Dean Anderson arrives to torpedo their boat; Jennie Garth, who is treated by Gregory Harrison in *Lies of the Heart* a lot like the yearlings he stalks and skins, until her girlfriends gang up to kill him; Kellie Martin in *If Someone Had Known*, beaten by Ivan Sergei like a gong, and sometimes with a golf club, before she blows him away with a shotgun; JoBeth Williams, so tired in *Final Appeal* of being pounded on by a speed-freak-pediatrician husband that she stabs him with a Gurkha knife and hires Brian Dennehy, her alcoholic lawyer-brother, to get her off; and Valerie Bertinelli in the miniseries *In a Child's Name*, determined to avenge her sister's bludgeoning-to-death by Michael Ontkean, a weight-lifting, coke-addled *dentist* in the Laurence Olivier–Steve Martin mode (*Marathon Man, Little Shop of Horrors*). As often as shelters, this abuse leads to madness.

Never mind that most TV rape movies manage, simultaneously, to exploit and to deplore, to be smutty-minded and to moralize. Look instead at the variety: date-, marital-, gang- and dad. Recent examples range from the heroic (*e.g.*, Patricia Wettig as Nancy Ziegenmeyer, who went public in the Des Moines *Register*) to the preposterous (*e.g.*, Jaclyn Smith as a surgeon who gets to stick her scalpel in the brain of the creep who hurt her). See also Annabeth Gish, a pre-med from the wrong side of the Brooklyn tracks, who goes all the way to California to meet in college the dimpled and predatory football quarterback who won't take no for an answer; Judith Light as a nightclub singer raped by her own psychiatrist; Carrie Hamilton as the folkie guitarist whose angry mother, Meredith Baxter, spends more time tracking down the rapist than comforting his victim; Missy Crider, whose equally furious mother, Lesley Ann Warren, guns down her rapist in court after he escapes conviction on a technicality; and Cynthia Gibb who unwittingly *marries* her rapist, Richard Grieco, without catching on until she needs a tissue-matching kidney donor for the child she insisted on carrying to term. In addition to Cheryl Ladd, Donna Mills, Elizabeth Peña, Melissa Gilbert, Madeline Stowe and Tiffani-Amber Thiessen in TV movies, as if to up the ante on gratuitous living-room dread, continuing female characters that we cared about on such network *series* programs as *St. Elsewhere*, *Hunter* and *Law & Order* were also raped.

In real life, according to figures gathered by the National Center for Missing and Exploited Children in 1988 and confirmed in a 1990 study Congress commissioned from the Department of Justice, as many as 350,000 children are abducted *every year* by a parent or another family member—whereas only 200 to 300 are abducted by "nonfamily members where the children were gone for long periods of time or were murdered." On TV, too, children are kidnapped by fathers who lose custody battles and by mothers who suspect those fathers of sexual abuse. But more often the kidnappers are strangers: pedophiles who were themselves abused as kids; or Veronica Hamel, to pep up her marriage to an Air Force captain; even Mary Tyler Moore, who specialized in *Stolen Babies*

(1993) in auctioning off the blue-eyed newlyborns of the rural poor (a blood proletariat) to the barren well-to-do (their decorator told them they needed a toddler). Or they are snatched away from helpless mothers like Marg Helgenberger, Pamela Reed, Kate Jackson, Sara Jessica Parker, Meg Tilley, Tess Harper, Bonnie Bedelia, Bernadette Peters, Beverly D'Angelo, Lori Loughlin, Lisa Hartman, Mare Winningham, Valerie Bertinelli and Mariel Hemingway—by overworked cops, busybody nurses, family-court judges who hold such mothers in contempt and welfare, foster-care and social-services bureaucrats who deem them incompetent; even, in Mariel Hemingway's case, by a chauvinist-piggy Arab. It could be worse—like the Dionne quintuplets, in *Million Dollar Babies* (CBS, 1994), they might have become a theme park and a circus act—but what is TV really telling us when Mary Tyler Moore is the wicked witch of the Romper Room? And in the real world, of course, abused children are returned like lost luggage or stolen stereos to their abusive parents, to be abused all over again until, at last, it's fatal.

Of mad and/or murderous mothers, there has been an astonishing TV-movie amplitude, as though the producers had something to prove to themselves and their shrinks. (It only seemed that half of these movies starred Meredith Baxter, who sought, after *Family Ties*, to change her gentle image and managed perhaps to overdo it: a Medusa facelift. But television, with its continuing call for so many mothers as victims or monsters or both, is at least a source of gainful employment for actresses over the age of 30. On the small screen, Patty Duke, Melissa Gilbert and Susan Saint James grew up before our indulgent eyes. Jessica Lange, Tyne Daly, Kate Nelligan and Kate Mulgrew had a place to go with their adulthood.) While most of these misbehaving mother movies explained away their gruesome behavior with an equally gruesome family secret from the repressed past, two of the recent best offered no excuses at all.

In *Mother Love*, for instance—a British production, based on Domini Taylor's novel, that showed up here in 1990 as a three-part *Mystery!* miniseries—Diana Rigg came on less like Mother Russia or Mother Courage than Medea, famous for killing her children in the weepie by Euripedes. For middle-aged men like me, who loved her in leather as Mrs. Peel in *The Avengers*, the idea that Rigg would punish us for the bohemian happiness of our second marriages came as a terrible shock to the fantasy life.

Whereas Wanda Holloway derived as a pop-culture icon from newspaper headlines instead of a novel. When her klutzy daughter was beaten out for the high-school cheerleading pep squad by another woman's child, Wanda down in Texas put out a contract. For which, like the Menendez brothers, she got *two* TV movies. In ABC's so-so 1992 version, Lesley Ann Warren was the killer mom and Tess Harper her target. The subtext seemed to be that Texans take football far too seriously. As Molly Ivins, the nonpareil Fort Worth newspaper columnist, has elucidated:

> One of the more brain-spraining aspects of Texas culture is Baptist sex. As we all know, Baptists...are agin sex, which they define as drinkin', dancin', and carryin' on. Carryin' on is the worst. That Baptists see nothing wrong with the Dallas Cowboy Cheerleaders, who are indisputably open-air coochie girls, is one of those anomalies we all live with here. Because football requires the suspension of rational thought, just as theater requires the suspension of disblief, we see nothing odd in such phenomena as the Kilgore Rangerettes, the Apache Belles, and other noted practitioners of the close-order drill and baton-twirling arts [even though, objectively] what these girls do is dress up in costumes that would do credit to a striptease artist and then prance about in front of thousands of people, shaking their bums and jiggling their tits.

But the second Wanda, for HBO in 1993, was the crackerjack. In Michael Richie's version of her story, *The Positively True Adventures of the Alleged Texas Cheerleader Murdering Mom*, Holly Hunter played her as a speedfreak media monster, half delusional, half giggly. With Beau Bridges as the ex-brother-in-law Wanda turned to for her hitman (low rent, affably sinister), Swoosie Kurtz as Beau's wife (a scene-stealing Drano fetishist), Matt Frewer (Max Headroom himself) as a bemused lawyer, and Gary Grubbs as an incredulous F.B.I. agent ("God, I miss drug busts!"), it was a commotion-causing cast. And to this commotion director Richie added not only a spacey script by playwright Jane Anderson, plus cameo walk-on roles for his producer, James Manos Jr., a real-life Houston TV reporter and *Inside Edition*'s Mike Waitkiss, but also his own lyrics to a bunch of country-and-western songs composed by Lucy Simon (*The Secret Garden*) and making fun—while we looked at white skulls and black spiders, red fingernails and orange explosions—of church-going, baton-twirling, mother love and oil refineries. The flimflam went further. Holly as Wanda appeared on *A Current Affair*, watched "herself" on *Donahue*, and critiqued ABC's movie about "her." The subtext here was postmodern slumming: There wasn't really *any* Wanda, nor any football, not even any pep, only culturally-constructed hype.

More usually, though, mother mayhem is blamed on one or another girlhood trauma. Take three especially lurid examples: In *Small Sacrifices* (1989), a miniseries based on the Ann Rule true-crime best-seller, Farrah Fawcett played Diane Downs, accused of murdering one of her three children and of the attempted murder of the other two, one of whom would testify in court against her. Not only was Farrah, with her hoarse cracked voice and torn blonde hair, her miniskirts and mythomania, on trial for killing a child and yet again hugely pregnant, the embodiment of a narcissism so extravagant it amounted to either a cosmology or Mariah Carey, but it is hard to imagine another TV movie pushing so many hot buttons on the pulp-mind console: from *incest* (besides raping her, her father shot her dog) to *infanticide* (she wanted a man who didn't want children, so she sought to simplify herself); from *battery* (an ex-husband beat her up) to *abortion* (her boyfriend insisted); from *Baby M.* (after making "beautiful babies," she tends to lose interest) to *Fatal Attraction* (the high price of one-night stands); from *gun control* (she had three of them) to *tattoos* (his and hers wormy roses). For literary critics who need symbolism, there was even a *unicorn*; and, for sociologists who need paradigms, a *U.S. post office*. In Idaho and Oregon, in a uniform with kneesocks to cry for, our Farrah carried letters. Except for the televised example of *Small Sacrifices*, how else explain an epidemic ever since of multiple murders by "disgruntled" postal workers? Like Eve, Circe and Salome, a black-widow spider of female sexuality, *Farrah delivered the angry white mail*. "I'm a Twinkie," she told the court; "inside I'm soft." In fact, the real-life Diane in Ann Rule's book was peculiar beyond even Farrah's powers to convey. On the stand, she named many lovers and read a poem on masturbation. The court cartoonist sketched her very pregnant, trying to escape from prison. She held a pistol to her own belly, warning: "Stop or I'll shoot." But, of course, her daddy made her do it.

Daddies, too, were to blame for Truddi Chase and Candy Morrison, who showed up back-to-back on network television in May 1990. In *Voices Within: The Lives of Truddi Chase*, Shelley Long as Truddi "acted out." From age two on, Truddi had been a lonely crowd. In a cornfield, in a barn, in a chicken coop, at the bottom of a well with a bucket of snakes, her stepfather pursued and abused her, when he wasn't chaining dogs to starve to death beneath her bedroom window or killing her pet rabbits. From these "games" of terror, the only place for her to hide was inside her mind, in a multiplication of protective personalities like Mean Jo and Sister Mary Catherine, Twelve and Rabbit, Miss Wonderful and Ean the Ancient Irish Philosopher. These teeth on a slipping ratchet wheel, these shards of a smashed self, Truddi called her "Troops." At her therapist's suggestion, these Troops would write the book, *When the Rabbit Howls*, that inspired the ABC movie in which Long played all the parts. Truddi eventually confronts her stepfather with a pair of airport scissors, but not until her Troops have seen her through girlhood, motherhood, a career and more disjunctures than a Picasso. "Do I know you?" her stepfather asks. "We are a lot of people," she replies; "you never knew any of us."

From Picasso to Grant Wood's *American Gothic:* in *Killing in a Small Town*, instead of acting out, Barbara Hershey's Candy was altogether inward, sealed up tight like her Tupperware. Like the empty Texas sky, the broad brown land, the flat affectless chatter and the peppermint communion wafers, Tupperware signified. Behind the Sunday-school granny glasses, emotions had been refrigerated. But a neighbor is found hacked to death with an axe. There on the icebox door are Candy's bloody paw prints. A shrink hired by the defense discovers, through hypnosis, a crippled inner child, a four-year-old so full of hate her fugue state is a sort of mercy. On the stand at her murder trial, as if to deliver herself from a pregnancy of dreadful rage, this child will *hiss* through the clenched teeth of an adult who really needs to primal-scream.

Tom Conti and Hal Holbrook played the sympathetic shrinks who assisted Truddi and Candy to their deliverance. So much satirized and reviled in novels and movies, psychologists, psychiatrists and psychoanalysts are surprisingly often good guys on television, from Bob Newhart in the seventies to Elliott Gould in Billy Crystal's *Sessions* to Carolyn McCormick on *Law & Order* to Kelsey Grammar on *Frasier* to *Dr. Katz* on the Comedy Channel. It is an intimate medium, and so predisposed, like the Freudians, to believe that most of our ogres live at home as members of the family, under the bed instead of outside in politics or history. (Shrinks may also benefit from the medium's traditional hero worship of doctors generally. Except on *St. Elsewhere*, TV doctors from Robert Young and Richard Chamberlain and Vince Edwards to Alan Alda and Mike Farrell to George Clooney and Hector Elizondo, whether godlike, or merely avuncular, or shockingly sexy with their scapels and stethoscopes, are invariably nicer than, say, lawyers. Not for television any of those profound suspicions of the medical profession we see elsewhere in western culture, in Shakespeare, Molière, Dickens, Flaubert and Shaw, as Dr. Frankenstein and Dr. Jekyll, Dr. Caligari and Dr. Strangelove, Dr. Mengele and Dr. No; mad scientists and black magicians.) You will have also noticed TV scripts are almost always reductive and determinist. (Existentialism, according to which we choose new and feistier selves by thinking against our family origins and class interests, by acting *as if* we were free, is reserved for commercials.) The TV *experience*, however, is more ambiguous, complicated by the pathos and skepticism we bring to our watching and our personal neediness at the smorgasbord and trough: a face-off of competing gestalts.

Meanwhile, not even counting Roseanne Barr, LaToya Jackson and Suzanne Somers, prime time has been chockablock with adult women who were sexually abused as children. In just the last five years, in TV movies derived from newspaper accounts, trial transcripts and as-told-to tell-all books, besides a Fawcett, a Long and a Hershey, these women have been portrayed on the small screen by Kathryn Dowling, Melissa Gilbert, Shelley Hack, Carrie Hamilton, Mel Harris, Joanna Kerns, Michelle Lee, Marlo Thomas, Ally Sheedy and a dozen others—all of them white and many of them blonde, as if, for every WASP, there had to be a sting—with rich semiotic references to such props as a toy horse, a wind-up ballerina, a rocking-chair, a toilet bowl, a cold leather couch and surgical gloves. These TV movies vary, of course, in quality. While an actress like Hershey can astound us, the based-on-a-true-story format practically ordains a want of surprise, much less transcendence. And yet, to the tens of millions who tune in, again and again, as though television were itself an A.A. meeting and these were the tales we told each other to get us through the night, intimacy speaks to intimacy. It can't be an accident that Melissa Gilbert in *Shattered Trust* compares child abusers to war criminals, nor that Marlo Thomas's father in *Ultimate Bretrayal*, a police consultant who likes to strut in uniform in front of a "line-up" of his daughters, is an American "Nazi," and their home is "a concentration camp," and Marlo herself, groping her way through a chamber of clouds to touch her own repressed experience, worries that she may have been, like her mother, a "collaborator."

*God help all the children as they move into a time of life
they do not understand and must struggle through with
precepts they have picked up from the garbage can of other
people, clinging with the passion of the lost to odds and ends
that will mess them up for all time, or hating the trash so
much they will waste their future on hatred.*

Lillian Hellman

This much can still be said for our troubled culture: the sexual abuse of children not only turns the stomach and breaks the heart; it wounds the soul as well. It can't be figured according to any ordinary moral arithmetic. The violation of a child also violates our fundamental notions of ourselves as guardians, what we owe to the innocent and defenseless, how we feel about family and authority, who we want and need to be. Faced with such violation, our helplessness is both a personal nightmare and a subversion of the social fabric. We want to avert our eyes. No wonder Dostoyevsky's *The Possessed* was published for decades without Stavrogin's confession.

Something About Amelia started it on television, in 1984, with Glenn Close as the incredulous mother, Roxanne Zal as the abused daughter and Ted Danson, already two years into *Cheers*, as the father who promised never, ever, to do it again. But between *Something About Amelia* and the close of the 1980s an odd thing happened. In spite of facts we knew perfectly well—acts of domestic violence occur every fifteen seconds; four percent of American families are abusive to children; almost three million cases of suspected child abuse were reported in 1992; more than a third of American girls are sexually molested, *usually by men they trust*—the focus on television somehow shifted from family to strangers. And so did the blame except insofar as parents were at fault for entrusting their children to these strangers. Especially culpable were moms who insisted on punching a clock or playing tennis when they should have been home with their angelfood cupcakes—unless of course they were *welfare* mothers, who didn't *deserve* children. (Although we can't ever *prove* anything about pop culture and the zeitgeist, we can at least point to a *correspondence* between this new network emphasis and the great porn scare, the Christian fundamentalist backlash, homophobia, "victimology," and a Reagan-Bush antifeminist agenda.) *Amelia*'s own Ted Danson was part of the shift, when he coproduced a 1986 TV version of Jonathan Kellerman's novel *When the Bough Breaks*, starring himself as the child psychologist who tracked down and smashed a ring of well-heeled, politically-connected pedophiles. Suddenly, as in *I Know My First Name Is Steven*, kidnapping made a comeback. Or, in *Judgment* (1990), the Roman Catholic Church was accused in court of covering up for a Louisiana priest who'd seduced altar boys ("We're going to sue God!" exulted Jack Warden), as the mother church and Canadian provincial government itself would go on trial in *The Boys of St. Vincent* miniseries (1994). Worst of all in these paranoia sweepstakes, in both *Do You Know the Muffin Man?* (1989) and *Unspeakable Acts* (1990), preschool day-care centers were nests of pedophilic vipers. Behind Tiny Tot's locked doors at afternoon naptime...

This is not to say that incest, having used up its fifteen minutes of prime time, disappeared from the small screen. On the contrary, we continued to meet more Truddis and Candys than we wanted to, even, in *A Deadly Silence* (1989), a Cheryl Pierson, the Long Island teen who hired a high-school classmate to gun down her abusive father, after which she spent several months in jail. (Omitted from the TV film was the problematic note that ended the Dena Kleiman book from which the movie had been adapted: Having done her time, Cheryl was met at the jailhouse door by her boyfriend and her brother, in a stretch limosine with a backseat bar and a TV set.) More troubling was *Child of Rage*, an appalling story that showed up first on HBO cable in a half-hour documentary (1990), and then again on network television as a CBS movie of the week (1992). On HBO we saw a real-life 6-year-old Beth, abused and abandoned by her "birth father," taking it out on pet animals, a baby brother and her adoptive parents, a "monster" without conscience or the capacity to trust or love who had to be locked up in her room at night like the Neanderthal baby in Doris Lessing's *The Fifth Child.* Her talks with a therapist were videotaped, and so was her commitment to a special "home," a "controlled environment" for children with "attachment disorders." And that therapist permitted these tapes to be televised: America's nightmare home videos. On CBS, Ashley Peldon played the child; Mel Harris and Dwight Schultz, the bewildered foster parents; and Mariette Hartley, the therapist—a production not so much to be reviewed, from any sort of aesthetic distance, as to be winced at. We were asked to acknowledge how often the abused turn into abusers; to wonder how many of our missing children are runaways fleeing abusive relatives instead of kidnap victims; and to worry whether the face on the milk carton at the supermarket might actually be *hiding* from us.

But the revised emphasis elsewhere was on the barbarians who cruised outside the gates. *I Know My First Name Is Steven*, the 1989 NBC miniseries, was a very Grimm fairy tale at the end of which everybody was eaten up by guilt instead of wolves. (What are fairy tales, anyway, if not coded fables of child abuse?) In real life, a dreamy and troubled seven-year-old Steven Stayner was kidnapped in 1972, on his way home from school in Merced, California. In real life, in motels and shacks all over northern California, he was sexually abused. In real life, he escaped *seven years later* and only when his captor stole another little boy. And in real life, he couldn't go home again. He wasn't the same boy, his family wasn't the same family, and the very idea of "home" had been violated. TV told this savage story without a fabric softener. As Steven's father, John Ashton was all but destroyed by bewilderment. As Steven's mother Cindy Pickett found you can't love somebody back to health. As Parnell, the horn-rimmed, chain-smoking kidnapper, Arliss Howard was a soft-spoken monster with delusions of divine afflatus. As teen-aged Steven, Corin Nemec came back to Merced a self-blaming wild boy. By devoting as much time to what happened after his homecoming as to the abduction, *I Know My First Name Is Steven* did the uncompromising work of art. It was as if Spielberg's *Empire of the Sun* had gone on to tell us the future of the blank-eyed boy who survived the war. Steven's kidnapping seems to have corrupted everybody. They didn't know how to feel about what they would rather not imagine. It's not just that the Brothers Grimm taught us to fear Black Forests, nor that we have always been fascinated by tales of wild boys raised by wolves, as we've been fascinated since the start of our country by the captivity narratives of children stolen by Indians and of slaves in the Middle Passage; and, since late in the nineteenth century, by Freud's seduction theory; and, since the middle of the twentieth, by death-camp horrors. Family itself is a kind of ecology, an interdependence of organisms in an environment. No matter how arbitrary that environment is, the organism adjusts or dies. *People*, unfortunately, can adjust to almost anything, and yet hate our own adaptations. Like Steven, we may not forgive ourselves. It's one thing to tell our children not to talk to strangers. It's another if the *child* is a stranger, to us and to himself.

Even scarier, because more artful, was *The Boys of St. Vincent*. Just minutes into the first hour of a nightmare miniseries about an orphanage in Newfoundland in the 1970s, the janitor tells the superintendent: "There are things in life that are broken and can't be fixed." Halfway through, what's broken beyond fixing has come to include the little boys abused by the All Saints Brothers *and* the very idea of accountability. The police suppress a report of their investigation. The church and the Ministry of Justice conspire at a cover-up. Brother Lavin, who insisted that his "special boy" call him "Mother," is permitted to leave both the church and Newfoundland for Montreal where he will father children of his own. When I first saw *The Boys of St. Vincent*, at a screening of Banff Television Festival prize-winners, most Canadians hadn't. Its broadcast up north had been delayed until the conclusion of the trial in the case that inspired director John N. Smith, who cowrote the script with producer Sam Grana and poet Des Welsh. More than a legal nicety, this delay seemed a scruple. So powerful was the film, trapped in dream-speed, drugged with menace, painterly yet visceral, you wanted to lay about you with an ax. So mesmerizing was Henry Czerny as Lavin, handsome, even dashing, princely but satanic, that you saw him in your cutthroat mirror like an evil eye. So corrupt were the agencies charged with protecting these abandoned boys, for whom there was neither appeal nor meaning, that you felt orphaned yourself: bereft. Part I was medieval: Never mind the telephone or the swimming pool where a 10-year-old discovered what being Brother Lavin's special boy really meant. At St. Vincent's, 1975 could be 1275, all passion and agony in a gothic vault of skeletal shafts, stained glass and morbid candles; gargoyles and Gregorian chants. With a crucifix slung in the belt like a cudgel, in cassocks like black sails, the brothers patrolled corridors and tucked-in barracks beds as if they were cowboy Templars. Obedience had nothing whatever to do with God; power was sickly erotic; the only gravity was despair. Part II jumped to 1990: We met the damaged boys grown up around their wounds, and their corruptors at bay in the headlines. The modern imagination tried to come to grips with age-old evil in the distinctively modern manner, with a courtroom trial, a royal commission, a psychiatrist and a call-in radio talk show. But the mind fell down like a torn black kite. So much for *Boys Town*.

No such art, but similar fears, applied to *Do You Know the Muffin Man?* and *Unspeakable Acts*. Until *Muffin Man*, we had not seen on television so many children so vilely used, so numb and inward, so trapped in shame, so disbelieved by so many adults, so tormented by their peers, so ridiculed on cross-examination by a hateful defense attorney. Nor had we experienced to such an excruciating degree the corresponding powerlessness of parents unequipped to make "the bad thing" all right, cancel it out, even to exact revenge. At a *pre-school,* of all places…the hooded figures, burning candles, and pornographic Polaroids. About the "satanic" component of *Muffin Man*—the magic names (Virgo, Isis) and murdered rabbits, the bloody altars and black-mass pentagrams—I expressed some reservations in a magazine article in October, 1989. But this was the lazy agnosticism of the armchair critic. You make reservations, but never actually go anywhere. Besides, had not *Muffin Man* been "inspired" by a "true" story? Hadn't we already read in the papers about similar cases of "ritual abuse" in Los Angeles, El Paso and the Bronx?

Three months after the murdered bunny rabbits in *Muffin Man* on CBS came a dead chicken in *Unspeakable Acts* on ABC. As chickens go, this dead one was a red herring, introduced early in a TV movie "based on" accusations of child abuse at a daycare center in Dade County, Florida, and then dropped before the trial, as if a Chicken Little in Burbank were having second thoughts. I certainly was. We were asked to believe the children, which ought to have been easy. After all, they accused Gregory Sierra, who had brought with him to the TV movie all those bad vibes from his many lowlife roles on *Miami Vice*. But looking at the therapists who coached the children in their testimony, the screen got smaller. It was impossible not to suspect the therapists themselves of something ulterior: Brad Davis, with his self-righteous little blond ponytail, and Jill Clayburgh, on some sort of Simone Weil starvation diet, seemed almost to slither, in thrall to an extraterrestrial music. Their eyes glistened, as if from esoteric rite. They were…creepy.

We've come to an interesting intersection of television and other American cultures. The Movie of the Week (MOW) had not, of course, invented alcoholism, cancer, wife-beating, child abuse, madness, murder or rape. On the other hand, although we lack the helpful statistics, it's hard not to imagine that a steady diet of such movies encouraged more Americans to report intimate crimes, leave abusive homes, go into therapy and twelve-step programs, petition courts, legislatures and the media for redress of grievance, feel anxious and speak bitterness and sue. Because MOWs as a genre tend to emphasize the vulnerability of women and children, they also doubtless contributed by feedback loop to what critics came to characterize as a "victim psychology" and "political correctness." (Amazing really that sensitivity to other people's pain should somehow turn into a whole new rhetoric of ridicule, as if empathy and old-fashioned "knee-jerk liberalism" were any threat to the paychecks, perks and power games of a muscular patriarchy; as if feeling bad on behalf of the aggrieved were simultaneously lily-livered and totalitarian. Or even worse: un-hip; less than way-cool.) But in the related hysterias about incest and satanic ritual abuse, television was far behind the cultural curve, so late it was out of any loop.

We first heard about ritual child abuse in February, 1984, when newspapers, radio and TV excitedly reported accusations that for two decades teachers at the McMartin Preschool in Manhattan Beach had tortured and raped small children and killed their bunny rabbits. (Bunnies were to ritual abuse scenarios of the 1980s what black helicopters would become for rightwing militia fantasies in the 1990s.) That spring, in Jordan, Minnesota, there were twenty-four arrests for membership in a kiddie-porn sex ring said to murder babies, drink their blood and toss their corpses into a river. In April, a janitor and three teachers at Chicago's Rogers Park Day Care Center were accused of boiling and eating babies. In May, in Reno, a Montessori day school was shut down on account of satanic rites and a "naked movie star game." In Memphis in June, a teacher's aide and a Baptist minister at the Georgian

Hills Early Childhood Center were brought up on charges of sexual assault and animal sacrifice. All that summer, from Malden, Massachusetts, to Sacramento, California, from West Point to Miami, hysteria spread. According to *Satan's Silence*, an angry account of "the Making of a Modern American Witch-Hunt" by Debbie Nathan and Michael Snedeker (Basic Books, 1995), accusations of ritual abuse triggered criminal cases in more than a hundred communities between 1983 and 1987. On the one hand, forks, spoons, screwdrivers, Lego blocks, monster masks, mind-altering drugs, feces-eating and urine-drinking; on the other, battered-child syndrome, rape-trauma syndrome, child-sexual-abuse-accommodation syndrome and post-traumatic stress disorder. Janet Reno prosecuted the Country Walk case in Dade County, Florida. When Kelly Michaels' conviction was overturned in 1995, the aspiring actress and part-time worker at the Wee Care Day Nursery in Maplewood, New Jersey, had already served seven years in prison, with another forty to go, for atrocities that supposedly ranged from licking peanut butter off children's genitals to playing piano in the nude. As for the case that started it all, after seven years in court and $15 million in expenses, nobody associated with the McMartin Preschool was ever convicted on a single count of anything—not of sodomy, rape, group sex, satanism or even excessive fondling; not of "Goatman," the Alligator Game, the ritual murder of a horse with a baseball bat or the cutting off of the floppy ears of bunny rabbits and making munchkins drink their blood, much less membership in what the media had called "a nationwide conspiracy of pedophiles in day-care centers."

The counterattack actually began on television. In 1990, in the church-going community of Edenton, North Carolina (population 5,000), seven defendants at the Little Rascals day-care center were charged on 429 separate counts of abusing children with knives, forks, scissors, needles and hammers. Public-TV producer Ofra Bikel went to Edenton and talked, on camera, to almost everybody—accused, accusers, relatives, neighbors, lawyers, therapists, even many of the children named in the indictments—and the result was a 1991 *Frontline* documentary, "Innocence Lost," that won not only an Emmy and the Columbia University-Alfred I. duPont Silver Baton but also scared the hell out of those of us who had been predisposed throughout the eighties to believe whatever children said or whatever their therapists had coached them to say. After a mixed bag of guilty verdicts in 1993, Bikel returned to Edenton for another batch of interviews and to *Frontline* with a four-hour reconstruction, overview and cry of rage. After the first program, it's amazing anyone in North Carolina would talk to her again, but most just couldn't help themselves, including a judge with hindsight doubts and five troubled members of the jury that sent Bob Kelly, the co-owner of Little Rascals, to prison for twelve consecutive life sentences.

Like a coin toss or a veto, the television camera image makes us choose up sides. This was what a whole nation would be up to during O.J.'s trauma drama, deciding for or against Judge Ito and Hertz rent-a-car, pulling for Marcia Clark or F. Lee Bailey, groaning at Kato, hissing Mark Fuhrman, fingering the DNA and the bloody gloves and the Johnnie Cochrane race card as if they were Lotto numbers or Yoruba fetishes. In a way that is no less credible merely *because* it is more persuasive than print journalism, *television messes with epistemology.*

Because of Ofra Bikel, We the Jury know more than the actual jury did about Edenton as a frazzled community, about social-service agencies with their own agendas, about cops wanting to close an ugly case, about psychiatrists with ego investments, about similar cases falling apart in other states and even about jury irregularities in Edenton itself. To our watching, we bring some history and respond (again, not ignobly) with a visceral rush. We start taking everything personally. For instance, I didn't much care for the shifty-eyed Kelly. His wife, Betsy, seemed nicer, although she grew old before our eyes. And Betsy's passionate younger sister, Nancy, was immensely appealing. Whereas Bob's principal accuser, Jane Mabry, was somehow operatic and ulterior. And many of the parents who turned against the Kellys, including Bob's lawyer once he was told that his own child might have been a victim, were clearly hysterical. (Well, wouldn't you be, if you thought for a minute…?) After which electronic personalizing, we all turn into advocates: No way, looking at such Little Rascals caretakers as Robin Bynum and Dawn Wilson, could we believe either capable of such devil-worship horrors. Hadn't they been offered a plea bargain, even *after* the verdict on Bob Kelly? Knowing she was innocent, Wilson rejected such a bargain, and was sentenced to the max. How come? Jurors told Bikel they hadn't trusted what little there was of medical evidence. (Of physical evidence, there was none.) Nor did they credit certain details of the children's testimony. (Like Bob shooting babies.) But they took into their deliberations the lurid reports of the therapists, and these had apparently been decisive. Bloodlust, besides, has its own momentum, and so does bad faith. (If Bob was guilty, didn't Dawn have to be?) And now everybody felt bad.

No one felt worse than Bikel, who refused to let go of her subject. Two years later in April, 1995, she returned to *Frontline* with four more hours on "Divided Memories." She interviewed dozens of adult "victims" who, after years of "repressing" memories of childhood sexual trauma, "recovered" these memories in therapy. She interviewed members of the families of these "victims." She quizzed the therapists themselves, careful to sort out differences between hypnosis and "reparenting," between "reparenting" and "age regression." She talked to psychologists who blame Freud for having abandoned his seduction theory and to lawyers who are suing everybody, including, to their indignant surprise, the therapists themselves. It turns out that some of these patients "recovered" memories of ritual abuse in *previous lives*. It also turns out that, if any of these therapists had the slightest doubt whatsoever about the nightmare tales to which they had given such color and shape, they didn't think factual accuracy really mattered. What the patient felt was all that counted. "Confabulation," defined by the dictionary in its strictly psychiatric sense as "replacement of a gap in memory by a falsification that the subject accepts as correct," seems to be contagious—as it had been among teenaged girls in Salem, Massachusetts, in 1692, and was again among goat-faced Bolsheviks at Stalin's show trials in the 1930s.

There hadn't been a more depressing program on television since Edward R. Murrow's *Harvest of Shame*. Until, that is, May, 1995, the very next month, when HBO aired its McMartin docudrama, *Indictment*. Enter Oliver Stone, executive producer. And Abby and Myra Mann, who wrote an angry script in the best tradition of TV agitprop. And Mick Jackson, directing in the slambang take-no-prisoners style of Stone himself. And James Woods as Danny Davis, a lowlife lawyer more accustomed to defending "drug dealers and other scumbags," who would seem to have ennobled himself by representing three generations of McMartins. And Mercedes Ruehl, as the prosecutor who would do anything to advance the political ambitions of her D.A. boss. Not to mention a strong supporting cast that included Lolita Davidovich as a therapist who coached the children at their confabulations; Chelsea Field as a member of Ruehl's team who began to have doubts; Sada Thompson as the grandmother; Virginia McMartin, and Shirley Knight as her daughter Peggy, and Henry Thomas as her grandson Ray, who forgot sometimes to put on his underwear and was caught with a skin-mag centerfold.

Well, they *looked* guilty: "Perfect typecasting," said a prosecutor; "they could be Buchenwald guards." So what if their accuser was an hysterical alcoholic who may have been covering up for her own abusive husband? So what if the prosecutors neglected to screen the unlicensed therapist's videotaped interviews with the kids? So what if that therapist misrepresented the contents of those interviews besides sleeping with a tabloid-TV reporter and feeding him pillow talk scoops? And so what if sad-sack Ray spent five years in jail before getting bail? "A client's a client," explained Woods in his *Salvador/True Believer* raw-meat mode, before he saw beyond the lizard eye of law as usual to the light of a just cause like a moral corona. No medical evidence of any variety of abuse at the McMartin Preschool was ever produced in court, not a single porn Polaroid, not a single sighting of an underground satanic cavern, nor the least residue of hot wax and singed fur. And who was to blame for these witch hunts? According to *Indictment*: parents, cops, prosecutors, therapists and the vampire media.

To which list, according to Frederick Crews in two long articles in the *New York Review of Books* in 1994, we must add Sigmund Freud. An emeritus professor of English at the University of California, Berkeley, Crews had been hounding in hot pursuit after Freud for years, to punish him for the many sins of a subdivision of literary criticism bent out of shape by psychoanalytic concepts. To be sure, Crews was equally disdainful of Marxist, feminist, structuralist and post-modern literary criticism—those kaleidoscopic lenses through which the trendier academics are accustomed to peering at every artifact of the culture in order to find it guilty of something. But the "recovered memory" controversy was a chance to up the animus ante. Feminists had an investment in the incidence of incest. Fundamentalist Christians had an investment in the existence of satanic ritual. And therapists had an investment in vulgarized Viennese voodoo. In this conspiracy of true believers, the victims weren't texts; the victims were families and careers and human rights and common sense—all because of "recovered memory" techniques based on a theory of repression for which, like psychoanalysis as a whole, there was no empirical evidence and, thus, no scientific validation.

We would seem to have strayed from two-dimensional television into a swamp. Well, you can't watch television, raise children, think about Freud and fend off Frederick Crews, all at the same time, without starting to suspect that the culture's constituents connect, collide and ramify in messy ways, and that interrelatedness may be the normal respiration of intelligence. In May 1996 *The New York Times Magazine* devoted an entire issue to swatches of wounding memoirs by writers like Susan Cheever, Mary Gordon, Mary Karr, Chang-rae Lee, Leonard Michaels, Joyce Carol Oates, Luc Sante and Art Spiegelman. The editor of this special issue, James Atlas, seemed mildly susprised to find so much emphasis on dysfunction, alcoholism, incest and mental illness. He seemed also to blame the contemporary novel, for no longer "delivering the news." He simply hadn't been watching much television. He might also have been reading the wrong novels.

While watching Ofra Bikel and skimming *The New York Times*, I was also reading the novels of Peter Hoeg. And what should I find in Hoeg's Denmark but Hans Christian Andersen and Søren Kierkegaard, a Little Mermaid, an Ugly Duckling and a sacrifice of Isaac, incest and orphans and reform schools, feral children on the run and little lost boys like Adonis, "the forsaken youngest son of the fairy tales who must now set off into the world alone." In Denmark, that goody-goody welfare state! Hoeg's heroine in *Smilla's Sense of Snow* is the daughter of a Danish doctor and an Inuit huntress, torn from her childhood village in Greenland after her mother's disappearance, and shipped off by an indifferent and embarrassed father to be "civilized" by foster homes and private schools and racial prejudice. Fleeing a father who never really wanted her, she'll spend the novel using everything she knows—about auks, meteors, fossils, mummies, parasites, forensic medicine, marine biology, dead bodies in the frozen Arctic, corrupt science and corporate huggermugger in surprising Copenhagen, and the creation myths and space-time continuum of the Eskimos—to solve the murder of a six-year-old Eskimo boy who was the only child she had ever really cared about. Ice and snow are mother's milk. In *Borderliners*, a 12-year-old Peter has spent his orphaned childhood in Christian missions, outpatient clinics, assessment centers and reform schools before a surprise scholarship sends him to the elite Biehl's Academy, where an emphasis on science masks an experiment in social control gone murderously awry. As if in a Norse myth from an Elder Edda, or a fairy tale about penal colonies and panopticons, Peter is trapped: in "utter time and utter stillness." Held too tight, children crack. In *The History of Danish Dreams*, Hoeg's last novel to be published here but the first he wrote—contemptuous of journalism and organized religion; the bourgeoisie and the welfare state; the army, the police, the civil service and the legal profession; investment bankers, arms manufacturers, chemical plants and western culture since Voltaire—we will meet children in cages, hospitals, water closets, military schools, lunatic asylums and jail, among circus dwarfs and religious fanatics, as bastards, prostitutes and incest victims. When Child Services bureaucrats look at delinquent Maria, through their kaleidoscope they see a Little Red Ridinghood, a Little Match Girl, a little lost lamb or baby Jesus: "Gretel without Hansel, the dream of the Innocent Child." No wonder, wearing her stolen police helmet, she makes a getaway on skis. She will grow up to be a Smilla, to fly through dreaming ice to a true-north reckoning in a Winter Palace.

You don't have to be postmodern in black leather with a nipple ring to recognize in such a literature of disenchantment and subversive subjectivity some of the kinky stuff Foucault was onto, with inscripted bodies and disciplinary technologies and transgressive subtexts. The lost child—coveted, abused, eroticized, abandoned, "missing," homeless, inner, emblematic, mode of production, consumer and commodity, Little Mermaid and Ugly Duckling—is both a product of the culture, like nylon or plywood or microchips, and a magic slate on which we scrawl ourselves, like the pulpy page or the TV screen—or a milk carton.

When Crews at last published his essays in a book, *The Memory Wars*, in the fall of 1995, I put on another of my hats, as coeditor of the literary pages of *The Nation*, and shipped it out for review, along with *Satan's Silence*, to an anthropologist at the University of Washington. What we got back from Marilyn Ivy and published that December still strikes me as the sanest take on the topic so far. After synopsizing both books, Ivy used them as booster rockets. So psychoanalysis isn't scientific? Well, we have known for years "about the tension in Freud between his interpretive modalities and his scientism…" Nevertheless:

Crews' Popperian valorization of science makes him uncomfortable indeed with ambiguity, not to mention undecidability. He can only imagine two alternatives: that there is real sexual abuse, or that psychotherapists plant false memories of abuse in children's (or "recovering" adults') minds. Having foresworn the murky depths of interpretation in favor of the transparent verifiability of science, he has no way to think about phenomena that don't readily resolve themselves into the stable objects of real science but that remain unstable para-objects: memory, sexuality, desire and terror. It's true that we wouldn't have recovered memory therapy as it is today if Freud hadn't theorized repression... [But] we also wouldn't have had a body of thought, with its still discomfiting assertions of child sexuality and the reality of fantasy, that directly disputes the primitive premises on which that therapy is based.

As Nathan and Snedeker suggest in *Satan's Silence*, what is also going on is "the systematic, class-based scapegoating of people who represent the intersection of the public sphere with the (ideally) privatized, sacrosanct sphere of the family: caretakers in day-care centers. In a nation in which an increasing number of women work, with the ongoing fragmentation of the nuclear family...the obsession with the sexual abuse of children in public places reflects widespread moral panic about the breakdown of gendered and generational boundaries." Ivy continues:

> What is clear from the record is that such moral panic could not have occurred without the intense investment in the pristine innocence of the "child" in late twentieth-century America. Recovered memories or no, the insistence on a wholly pure, sexually innocent child—and the terror that the potential defilement of that purity provokes—remains at the very heart of the ritual abuse panic (as well as the adult recovered memory movement). What makes this insistence even more revealing is that it occurs under the immense sexualization of children within consumer capitalism: There is no more charged figure for the seductive and the seducible than the child. The effect of mass media and consumption on children's sexuality seems rarely remarked in the analysis of abuse cases, and not surprisingly. For to think about the child as a sexual object in capitalism is already to have violated the pristine space that the child must occupy to guarantee the crumbling social order...

Freud, of course, taught us that children are sexual beings. And memories are narrative reconstructions, artful mixtures of event and fantasy. Put into language, they can be deceptive. But equally deceiving are the "rococo paranoia" and "socio-sexual fantasies" of parents, child support services personnel, therapists, law-enforcement officials, district attorneys and doctors, who so easily imagine midnight masses, devil masks and rape orgies:

> And along with those fantasies, an even stranger and stronger one: that of the untouched child, pristine and unaffected by the capitalized sexuality all around her. It is Nathan and Snedeker's book that powerfully unmasks this world of specifically American phantasms, in which the terrors of day-care abuse appear as fabulous, perverse displacements of the systematic—satanic?—societal abuse and neglect of millions of real kids.

In March, 1996, unattended by any sort of fanfare, in an otherwise routine MOW on ABC called *Forgotten Sins*, network television came full circle after only six years. John Shea, who had starred as a tough cop convinced his son had been molested at a pre-school in the 1989 TV movie that started the whole prime-time craze for ritual abuse, *Do You Know the Muffin Man?*, also starred in *Forgotten Sins*, once again as a cop, who this time out was somehow persuaded that he himself had abused his own daughters, and so had half of his buddies on the force, all of them belonging to a satanic cult into goats and swords, dolls and pitchforks, Viking helmets and sacrificial infanticide. Shea was encouraged in this delusion, unto prison, by religious nuts, crazed prosecutors, bullying therapists and, of course, the vampire media. But "sociologist" William Devane had bearded doubts. Bess Armstrong, playing Shea's wife, only pretended to go along with the witch-hunt so she could keep custody of her little boy. *You* wouldn't have believed one of these accusers, Lisa Dean Ryan, if she told you she'd gone to the bathroom. And while the ABC movie had nothing to say about a psychology that insists on the sexual innocence of children, an economy that sexualizes them, our need for Satan now that Stalin's gone, the perverse displacement of our fear of our own families onto surrogates like day care, or Little Red Ridinghood and the seduction theory, *Forgotten Sins* at least felt bad in all the right places.

Masks, mirrors, psychoanalysis, family values, consumer capitalism, the succubus media, and spectator sports...all show up on television because *everything* shows up on television because television can't help itself. In both directions, sending or receiving, it's always on: "The cat eats the bird; Picasso eats the cat; painting eats Picasso." Before the lost child on American television, there was the lost child in American culture, from the captivity narratives of

New England Puritans kidnapped by Indians to Huck Finn, Little Orphan Annie and Holden Caulfield. ("Though I have done other things through the years," we are told by the surprise parent in Anne Beattie's *Picturing Will*, "I still think of myself as the person who knelt so many times to tie your shoelaces. Who needed to see them double-knotted and to know that you were safe, again, from tripping. I could have identified your feet, and still could, I see them so clearly, in a lineup of a hundred children.") Before Freud, there was Kaspar Hauser, the Wolf Boy of Aveyron and the punitive Brothers Grimm. (In *Absence*, Peter Handke remembers "how in childhood we had often hidden from others because we wanted them to look for us." Kafka's first novel, lost to us, alas, was called *The Child and the City*.) And previous to these Black Forests there was Goethe's Gretchen, who drowned her newborn before killing herself, not to mention the slaughter of the innocents and the sacrifice of Isaac in the Bible, or the ritual infanticide of the mother cults of the ancient Middle East, or a classical literature full of dreadful fantasies of mothers losing or killing their children and of maidens dragged by their fathers to sacrificial altars, dying of despair at abandonment, stoned because they were raped; of Niobes, Medeas, Iphigenias, Ariadnes and Didos. Don't let's get started on Claude Lévi-Strauss and his embroidery of the Amazonian Tucuna myth about the baby-snatching frog and the honey-gathering cycle. TV, like fairy tales and structuralism, is how we dream out loud about ourselves. Sitting down to watch, we are also projecting. In *Possessing the Secret of Joy*, her scary novel about female genital mutilation in Africa, Alice Walker took as her epigraph what she described as a "bumper sticker": *When the ax came into the forest, the trees said the handle is one of us.*

Pulp Fiction

So the sexual politics of television is more female-friendly than what we usually get from, say, big-screen Hollywood, pulp-machismo detective fiction, wild boy sci-fi or gangsta rap and industrial noise. Part of the explanation is surely situational. A living-room medium is bound to emphasize problems at home, while selling us something to relieve or escape those problems. And part of the explanation may be economic. It costs a lot more to pander to men in an "action-adventure" than to pander to women in a domestic exacerbation—all that machinery, all those explosions, so many extra dead bodies and riven landscapes and fascist uniforms. But production budgets don't explain the rest of TV's social agenda, which is simultaneously populist, meliorist, escapist, nostalgic, therapeutic, paranoid and sort of liberal-humanist wishy-washy.

You are shaking your head. We seem always to be shaking our heads at the entertainments of the masses, and what those masses make of them in spite of us.

Incapable of sustained attention, assertive memory, logical inference, or that range of consciousness which groups many incidents into a harmonious whole, they abhor the drama and adore burlesque—for its very fault's sake.

The Atlantic Monthly, 1909

Just as a donkey with a hard mouth can only be guided by violent jerks upon the reins, so a dull literary sensibility can only be awakened by the harshest literary appeal.

The North American Review, 1913

Pure trash, pure vulgarity, if you will, but—pure. Here are stories that are all plot, snap, ginger, and wish-fulfillment; cheap fairytales of business and adventure, turned out as if by machinery. The product, though multitudinous, is uniform: and one can buy one's magazine by the color of the eyes of the girl on the cover. Here is illustration that carries rubber-stamp beauty and heroism.

Seven Arts, 1916

Plutocratic, feudal America, made up of cockney, white-collar slaves, sordid, golf-playing, spruce overseers, and the Masters, speak through this school. The writers are amazingly expert technicians who perform a definite function in the industrial dynasty. They feed the masses the opium of cheap romanticism, and turn their thoughts from the concrete to the impossible. They gild the filth in which we live; they make heroes out of slave drivers and saints out of vultures. But they cannot create great art.

Liberator, 1921

That last quote was from Mike Gold, professional proletarian, self-appointed commissar of U.S. culture in the 1930s and Soviet social-ist-realist scribbler. Neither could Mike, of course, create great art. Changing your name from Irwin Granich doesn't automatically do the difficult trick. *All* the above quotations are wrenched from their persuasive context in Paul R. Gorman's nifty backwards look at *Left Intellectuals and Popular Culture in Twentieth-Century America* (North Carolina, 1996), which isn't to say that *Atlantic Monthly, North American Review* and *Seven Arts* were leftwing magazines. One of Gorman's points is that intellectuals of the conservative right and the radical left were equally offended by popular culture and equally fearful of its epidermal and testaceous effect on a lumpish and susceptible mass public:

> From the early decades of the twentieth century most attacks on popular literature, music, motion pictures, and modern dance styles were based on a implicit assumption that the messages or meanings contained in these forms had direct effects on the public's behavior. The stimulus provided by an entertainment was believed to cause an immediate, direct response. Thus, sexually suggestive literature was cited as causing promiscuity, films depicting robberies were reviled for driving young men into crime, and the emotional freedom of ragtime and jazz was equated with general moral decay. This "hypodermic" theory of the effects of communication media, suggesting the direct injection of ideas into intellectually passive audiences, began to be employed formally in the 1920s.

My guess is they were jealous too—of all that vulgar energy and spontaneous hullabaloo—the way those of us who are getting on are jealous of the young, on whom so much sex is wasted. Gorman goes on to assert that diverse publics will respond variously to a range of stimulations, depending on which "interpretive communities" we may belong to, which local "opinion leaders" we happen to respect, where in theory we find ourselves in a "two-step flow of communication" and, of course, our own neediness and cussedness. Gorman borrows from Clifford Geertz an anthropological conception of "mass entertainments" as "something good to think with"—not to be taken literally, but "narrative vehicles designed for making the world intelligible and providing emotional pleasures." I wish he had specified with some examples and how we use them—media "texts" are surprisingly rich in "oppositions"—but no single book can do everything, not even mine. What *is* fun is to read these outraged critics, animadverting magazine fiction, Hollywood cinema and jazz bands as if they were bullfights, gladiator games or public hangings. How comforting to be reminded that long before trash television, and the trashing of it by a Bill Bennett, the *National Police Gazette* ran a regular column called

"Murder and Suicide: A Gush of Gore and Shattering Brains All Around the Horizon." To hear Jane Addams, from her besieged Hull House, deplore "nickel madness": "We need only look about us to perceive that quite as one set of men have organized the young people into industrial enterprises to profit from their toil, so another set of men...have entered the neglected field of recreation and have organized enterprises which make profit out of their invincible love of pleasure." To listen to the music critic for *The New Masses* complain that if "Mozart composed for a romantic bourgeoisie," a jazz artist "composes for a bastard capitalist civilization." To learn that, in the brave new world of the Soviet Union, Maxim Gorky himself called jazz "the music of the gross," and leaders of the proletarian culture movement tried to ban the saxophone. To be told in *Partisan Review* by a Dwight Macdonald, who himself loved Krazy Kat and jazz, that pop culture "manipulates the cultural needs of the masses in order to make a profit for their rulers." And then to be told by Clement Greenberg in the very same journal not to make such a big fuss about it: "In the West, if not everywhere else as well, the ruling class has always to some extent imposed a crude version of its own cultural bias upon those it ruled, if only in the matter of choosing diversions. Chromotypes, popular music and magazine fiction reflect and take their sustenance from the academized simulacra of the genuine art of the past. There is a constant seepage from top to bottom, and kitsch (a wonderful German word that covers all this crap) is the common sewer." But to be warned again, by Irving Howe in *Politics*, that "amusement without insight and pleasure without disturbance" are bad for us.

Yet Dwight Macdonald finished up as a movie critic for *Esquire* magazine. And I know from personal experience that Irving Howe watched Yankee games on television. Even Edmund Wilson, the highest of our literary brows, who had dismissed detective fiction as "rubbish," nonetheless admired the hero in James M. Cain, "who carries his precipice with him like Pascal."

Television docudrama abhors what it considers polemic, didacticism, speechifying. Convention clamps a tight frame around the story. It doesn't want the larger public world leaking in. The soapbox is forbidden furniture. This convention of the small, restricted, realistic story has ideological consequences. It has the effect of keeping the show compact, narrow, simplified. Indeed, coherence is defined as narrowness, and not just in the thinking of the writers but audiences too. It is the dramatic aesthetic that prevails in this culture. Such conventions are shared, not imposed. When they are shared long enough and deeply enough, they harden into the collective second nature of a cultural style.
                                        Todd Gitlin, *Inside Prime Time*

Well...sometimes. But hardly always. Gitlin's generalization, like every other about the medium, invites contradiction. (After *Gunsmoke*, Westerns were finished on television—until *Lonesome Dove*. Science fiction was likewise a prime-time loser—except for three different *Star Trek* derivatives, *Babylon 5* and of course *The X-Files*. The hour-long dramatic series can no longer compete with sitcoms and newsmagazine shows—unless they turn out to be *N.Y.P.D. Blue* and *ER*. No generalization is safe from programs people *like*.) There have been polemical, didactic and speechifying docudramas on Auschwitz and Attica and Kent State; on Agent Orange, Love Canal and whales; on blacklists in Hollywood and apartheid in South Africa; on James Brady and gun control, Oppenheimer at Los Alamos and the integration with Joanne Woodward's help of Central High in Little Rock; on Yalta, Watergate, Ruby Ridge and Tailhook. Nor has the soapbox been missing from Norman Lear, Larry Gelbart, Linda Bloodworth-Thomason and Diane English sitcoms. Or from Steven Bochco, Barney Rosenzweig, John Sacret Young, David E. Kelley, Barry Levinson and John Falsey/Joshua Brand dramatic series. There is so much on TV, so often at the same time, we forget what we saw last month in our irritation with what we must sit still for tonight while ignoring what we failed to see last week because we were out to lunch or comatose. Many TV movies are better than their capsule descriptions in the consumer guides and many are worse, like books and jackets or candidates and promises. Nor do TV critics see the programs we review, from preview cassettes in the comfort of our communications command modules, in the context of the commercial package thrust upon the general public between promos and hurricane advisories, baseball scores and car alarms, with all its crazy juxtaposing, cognitive dissonance, ectopic insinuation and inversive ironizing. In the same psychic space—even if we aren't with our remote control jitterbugging through the many channels in the chambered nautilus—serial murder and a Hair Club for Men...toxic waste and singing raisins.

But there is a proximate television cosmology, with probabilities of space, time, causality and randomness, inertia and entropy, variable gravities and surprising grace. Seeking to please or distract as many as possible, to assemble and divert multitudes while selling them something they may not want and do not need, it is famously inclusive. Whereas hate radio, exploiting one or another fervent niche, sounds like a flat shriek, a competing snarl, a bullyboy and a sword in the ear, network TV, building audiences instead of making politics or art, has an enormous stake in consensus and civility of discourse. And so as a registry of symbols, a bulletin board of types and a harmonium that seeks by repetitions to flatten the discords of its market segments, it will broker social differences, mediate political conflict and soften lines and edges to make a prettier picture. But it's also weirdly democratic, multicultural, utopian and quixotic. Even as it seems to glorify and glamorize white-collar middle-class professionals, for example, it also subverts them with anti-social archetypes like cowboys and gangsters. I have been in this business long enough to realize that assigning fixed meanings to entertainment products is at least as tricky, and usually as ludicrous, as imagining the symbolic significance of, say, Aztec cannibalism. We used to believe that Aztecs ate human flesh for religious reasons—something to do with the local creation myth. Then we thought it was psychosexual—when they weren't eating their enemies, didn't they favor virgins' hearts? Then came a revisionist view that cannibalism was a typical first-world bad rap on a vanished third-world empire. Which was followed by a protein deficiency theory: they ate people because they ran out of dogs. It has been recently argued that this diet was, for Aztec aristocrats, a status symbol, like truffles.

With such a caveat very much in mind, I'd still suggest that television movies and serials have put on the game face and behaved a lot like traditional nineteenth-century novels. They are anthropologies of the way we live now, representations of the least powerful and most aggrieved among us, constructions of empathy and compassion, criticisms of social policy or indifference, and road maps for citizenship. They seek to generalize from the particularity of an individual's predicament to a universality of common need and human plight—almost as if the modern novel hadn't already gotten all morbid about the inadequacy of language to convey meaning, and as if the postmodern novel hadn't lampooned narratology, ideology and symbolic production itself. Television lets its cameras do the talking. To be sure, empathetic identification is no guarantee of a will to change. But without it, we wouldn't even know anything needed changing. "'Value,'" as Michael Berube points out in *Life As We Know It*, his brilliant book on his Down's syndrome son James, "may be something that can only be determined socially, by collective and chaotic human deliberation; but individual humans like James are compelling us daily to determine what *kind* of 'individuality' we will value, on what terms, and why." Berube is no more certain than I am "why it is that we possess the capacity to imagine others, let alone to imagine that we might have *obligations* to others," but a moral index has to start somewhere. Let us look in this chapter at television's take on big business, the wild west and deep space; in the next, at crime and punishment; and after that, at social diseases, in the body politic and the electric republic.

The group which calls itself Society is composed of symbolic figures. Each of its members represents an abstraction. It is necessary that all the powers of this world should somewhere meet together; that money should converse with beauty, and politics become familiar with elegance; that

*letters and birth grow friendly and serve each other
tea.... Just as a banknote is only a slip of paper, so the
member of society is a sort of fiduciary money made of living
flesh. This combination is extremely favorable to the designs
of a subtle novelist.*

                                    Paul Valéry on Marcel Proust

Fox cancelled *Profit*—what a wonderfully unambiguous name for
a dramatic series about unbridled greed, like Warhol's *Sleep,* Glad-
kov's *Cement* or Michener's *Hawaii*—after only four episodes in
April, 1996. Maybe Rupert Murdoch thought he was looking into a
funhouse mirror and smashed the glass before too many of us
caught a glimpse of him. Which would be sad-making, because
not since *Empire,* the short-lived 1984 sitcom with Patrick McNee
as the loony-tunes chairman of a multinational conglomerate, has
a weekly program cut closer to the bone of the commercial culture, while simultaneously making fun of the very landlord it had
to suffer. Like Ian Richardson's Francis Urquhart, Adrian Pasdar's
Jim Profit talked to the camera as if he were his own color analyst.
But instead of Tory politics on the way to 10 Downing Street, the
greasy pole Jim climbed in *Profit* for a month of Mondays was corporate hugger-mugger, on his way to CEO at Gracen & Gracen, a
Fortune 500 giant squid. He was Sun Tzu writing on war while
waging it, or Machiavelli with a PowerBook. But he was also a
character out of Samuel Beckett, with the usual Beckett womb
fixation. Instead of a mound or an urn or a rubbish bin, he found
himself in a cardboard box. I will explain in a minute.

First you should know that Profit was the new man in acquisi-
tions at Gracen & Gracen, the "Family Company." The old man
died of a very surprising heart attack. At the Company funeral—
one almost expected a Company anthem and Company beanie—
our Jim was already suborning his predecessor's secretary. His previous post had been in auditing and if he didn't know everybody's
dirty little secret, he would simulate it on his computer screen,
which glowed in the dark like his tank of tropical fish. So Chaz
Gracen, CEO, was a "wantonly cruel and endlessly greedy" philan-
derer; and the younger Gracen brother, Pete, an impotent alcoholic; and Jim's immediate boss was over his head in debt while
playing footsie with the chief of corporate security who had her
own traumatic, sibling-rivalry secret. With forgery here, blackmail

there, deleted files, a babyfood scandal, rumors of lesbianism and a frame for murder, Jim would cut his way through wormwood to the top. Nothing was beneath his eager good looks. He pretended, in the pilot, to be vegetarian, and the following week, at a twelve-step meeting, posed as a recovering rummie.

But Jim had secrets too—including a heroin-addicted step-mother, a father in a burn ward, an off-shore banker who might be laundering money for Mideast terrorists, and a Tulsa, Oklahoma, warrant for his arrest. Which brings us back to Beckett. In the opening credits of the *Profit* pilot and in the concluding shot we saw Jim crouched, naked in a fetal position in a cardboard box. He had been raised in a such a box in Tulsa. Literally. His abusive father dumped an infant Jim in a brown cardboard movers' box with Gracen & Gracen's corporate logo, "The Family Company," stamped on its side and a hole for the kid to look out at a television set, which was *always* on. "Do you believe in the life to come?" asked Beckett in *Endgame*, adding: "Mine was always that." Or, as Malone observed while dying, "If I had the use of my body I would throw it out of the window." As you'd expect from executive producers like David Greenwalt (*Shannon's Deal*), John McNamara (*Lois & Cark*) and Stephen J. Cannell (the P.T. Barnum and Carl Jung of pulp dreams), *Profit* had a lot of motives—Beckett again: "I have enough trouble as it is in trying to say what I think I know"—but there can be no question that its principal conceit was the representation of upward corporate mobility as a form of symbolic patricide.

Accuracy in Media, the American Enterprise Institute, *Forbes* magazine, *Commentary*, *The Wall Street Journal*, *National Review*, Ben Stein and other capitalist tool-bags are always complaining about the lousy image of big business on TV, taking out ads like Mobil on the Op-Ed page of *The New York Times*, blaming a "new class of intellectuals...rooted in the nonprofit sector" of our thriving economy for emphasizing storylines about bribery, pollution, corporate tax write-offs and exploding Pinto gas tanks and making cruel fun of, say, Exxon *Valdez* and its (oops!) oil slick or the $50 billion savings-and-loan scandal. They probably didn't like *Profit*, either. And they have a point. Daddy Warbucks has been disapproved of on television at least since Rod Serling and *Patterns* in 1956. Miniseries like Irwin Shaw's *Rich Man, Poor Man* (immigrant turned entrepreneur), Taylor Caldwell's *Captains and the Kings* (big oil), Arthur Hailey's *Wheels* (big cars) and Norman Bogner's *Seventh Avenue* (the garment industry) did nothing to improve this Warbucks rep, nor did prime-time soaps like *Dallas* (also oil), *Dynasty* (even more oil), *The Colbys* (oil, shipping, real estate, aerospace) and *Falcon Crest* (wine-making), whose increasingly berserko plots, in the Reagan–jodhpur–class–war–deficit-spending–Star Wars-a-go-go eighties, perhaps reflected a time-lag confusion of purpose and failure of nerve. It was one thing to be left wondering at the end of the 1979–80 season who shot J.R.; it was quite another to be told that Pamela had only dreamed the entire 1985–86 season of *Dallas*, meaning Patrick Duffy would be back as Bobby as if he'd never been hit by a car, wounded by an assassin or broken up with Jenna, before she murdered Marchetta. We also had to waste the entire summer of 1985 worrying which of *Dynasty*'s Carringtons survived the royal wedding in Moldavia after revolutionaries burst into the palace and machine-gunned everybody. You may not recall that the first season of *The Colbys* ended with Charlton Heston thrown into jail for wife beating and attempted murder, and the second with the abduction of Emma Samms by aliens. As though exhausted from this frenzy, TV stopped fantasizing for awhile about the filthy rich, whose money, anyway, had never really been interesting except to license their bad behavior, until a Democrat got back in the White House. In this interim maybe it forgot how. While two new soaps in the fall of 1995, *Central Park West* on CBS and *The Monroes* on ABC, seemed to have oodles of all the right stuff—money, power, sex, furniture, Kennedy envy, deep-pore cleansing, a sense of entitlement and lots of transportation, from horses to helicopters—the public disdained them. I'd like to think that this was Larry Gelbart's fault.

You will recall 1988, a gone-gone year when everybody on Wall Street sought to gobble up R.J.R. Nabisco, the crackers-cigarette conglomerate. Nabisco's Atlanta directors were besieged by American Express, Shearson-Lehman, Henry Kravis, Forstmann Little and First Boston, all waving tender offers. We are talking about billions of dollars in leveraged buyouts for an outfit whose stock was going nowhere. And none of those billions had anything to do with a better product or an improved service. It was voodoo bungee-jumping. Bryan Burrough and John Helyar wrote a blood-curdling book about it, *Barbarians at the Gate*. Ray Stark bought the movie rights. After what Hollywood did to Tom Wolfe's stock-market novel, there was every reason to expect yet another big-screen bomb. But a funny thing happened to *Barbarians* on its way to the gate. Larry Gelbart wrote a screenplay playing it for laughs, as if Nabisco's buyout were Restoration comedy or French farce, as if capitalism were a kindergarten snit. And that's the *Barbarians* we got on HBO in 1993—a Karl Marx Brothers slapstick; a *Food Fight of the Vanities*.

James Garner starred as F. Ross Johnson, Nabisco's good ol' boy CEO. He'd counted on a new smokeless cigarette, Premieres, to boost his stock, but the end result was "a filtered Edsel." He sought advice from Henry Kravis, played by Jonathan Pryce like a Mafia don pretending to be a Renaissance prince. While they ate rabbit under Renoirs, Kravis explained vulture capitalism. Fearing Kravis wouldn't let him keep his bicoastal perks and personal jet, Johnson enlisted his good buddy at American Express, James Robinson (Fred Dalton Thompson). Robinson brought in not only his social-climbing Exercycle of a wife, Linda (Joanna Cassidy), but also his Shearson-Lehman pitbull, Peter Cohen (Peter Riegert). Before long the good ol' boy couldn't even go to the men's room at a Republican Party hootenanny and be safe from an attack of bankers in his toilet stall. While all this went on, we kept seeing *poor* people—beggars and bag ladies, the homeless and wasted—wandering in and out of camera range, like some mute Greek refugee chorus. From Johnson, for whom we rooted in spite of our-selves because, after all, he was Maverick and Rockford, there was a stirring coda: "They make money the old-fashioned way. They *steal* it."

Watching these barbarians so variously indisposed or over-wrought, like Nuremberg maidens or Disney dwarves, it seemed to me that *greed glows in the dark,* like Chernobyl. Given how much money they already had, why should they want any more? Bar-bara Ehrenreich, one of my favorite social critics, wrote of these bungee years: "They did not sow, neither did they reap, but rather sat around pushing money through their modems." But Ehrenre-ich, like most of us, has never essayed a hostile takeover. A bumper sticker on her four-cylinder car reads: "I'D RATHER BE PER-FORMING ACTS OF KINDNESS." And she says that she's always being passed, in the fast lane, by a turbo-charged Porsche 944, with a gonzo at the wheel who enjoys taking out vanloads of nuns at 180 miles an hour. On the bumper of this killer-car there is another sort of sticker: "HE WHO DIES WITH THE MOST TOYS WINS."

So television—with heavy-breathing movies of the week and indignant episodes of continuing dramatic series on kickbacks, chemical dumping, medical malpractice and crooked nursing homes, insurance and investment scams, rapacious real estate moguls, pharmaceutical research fraud, tainted meat and spoiled milk, unsafe airplanes, space shuttles and basinettes, landlords who hire arsonists, lobbyists who buy legislators, corrupt construction firms and amoral arms dealers and nuclear energy meltdown cover-uppers—is unkind to big business, in spite of the fact that HE WHO DIES WITH THE MOST TOYS WINS has been the medium's message since General Sarnoff issued his first marching order at RCA, and though television itself is the hyperkinetic child of one of the biggest businesses of them all, an entertainment industry so interlocking and oligopolistic that it makes Gracen & Gracen look less like a giant squid than a ruptured duck. It is not just that General Motors and Walt Disney and Westinghouse make money on each broadcast and every rerun of an anti-business drama, as Time Warner rakes it in marketing the anger of gangsta rap and the alienation of punk and grunge; it's also that we swim as we watch in a sea of seductive supplications for getting and spending; for better sex through shinier Jeeps and mental health through personal hygiene. What more can the business community reasonably expect from the dream factory than this deliverance of the docile to its golden gates? It's not as if they hadn't their own TV channel, CNN Financial News, and their own apologists on PBS, from Adam Smith to Louis Rukeyser, and a portion of every newscast devoted to the superstitious magic of their trading on our futures, and the craven deference of blow-dried journalists at every spin of an expensive suit, behind their lines of credit, inside the enclaves of their hush money.

Early in the summer of 1996, cable-TV's History Channel abandoned plans for *The Spirit of Enterprise*, a series of programs purporting to look inside our major American corporations, with unique access to each company's archives and its executives. When questions were raised, even in industry-friendly periodicals like *Advertising Age*, about the historical and journalistic objectivity of a series whose corporate subjects not only underwrote production and sponsored broadcast, but also exercised editorial control over their own profiles, everybody jumped ship. This seemed overly fastidious. Who needs respect if you've got liquidity? After all, the History Channel is a subsidiary of the Arts & Entertainment Network. A&E is jointly owned by Hearst, NBC and ABC. ABC is a subsidiary of Cap Cities. Cap Cities is wholly owned by Disney. For all of these people, flying business-class with their laptops open like pencil boxes or Ouija boards, the rest of us are Tiddly-winks on a credit grid. As Horace wrote in a hot epistle in 25 B.C., "The populace may hiss me, but when I go home and think of my money, I applaud myself."

Moreover, from the point of view of the American Enterprise Institute, it could be a whole lot worse. Big business could be organized labor, organized religion, the federal government, the judicial system or the media, to all of which TV is much unkinder than it's ever been to General Motors or a Donald. Mob-connected thugs, hypocrites or nuts, faceless or sinister bureaucrats, criminal-coddling ambulance chasers, journalistic succubi—they're all of them beat up on like rugs or gongs. Television, like the low culture for which it is a machine intelligence, specializes in the politics of resentment. Populist and punchy, deep-down in its seething unconscious it is suspicious of institutions, leery of technology, offended by discipline, relishing flashpoints and the quick fix, yet underdogged and little-guyed, loving mainly loners and losers.

And when in this culture or any other in the West did money-makers get respect? Not since the Renaissance. Until Florence came along, status in Europe depended on class. Class depended on blood and dirt, both of them inherited. We are talking aristocracy. But besides inventing the bill of exchange and personal checks, Florentine bankers like Lorenzo de Medici invested heavily in the arts. Florentine artists were so grateful that they wouldn't even let landowners into their guilds: merit, not land; money, not blood. Behold the bourgeoisie. After Florence though, it was mostly downhill image-wise for businessmen, give or take a Rembrandt portrait of a rich Dutch burgher and his well-fed wife, no matter how hard Peter the Great tried to make manufacturers as respectable as estate-holders. Since most European writers were themselves the children of a new middle-class, you'd think they would have appreciated money as a social or psychic blank check, the very antihistamines of creativity and progress. But they chose instead to be Oedipally revolting. The capitalist lesson—that a redistribution of rewards and status perks could liberate new energies into culture as well as commerce—was lost on writers and the rest of Europe for another four centuries. France, until the Revolution of 1789, punished any nobleman who went into trade by stripping him of his titles. That nothing of the sort ever occurred to anybody in England perhaps explains why the British got a head start on the Industrial Revolution.

Not that they enjoyed it. If Brits bothered to notice the motions of machine-made money, it was usually to run in the other direction, like Byron, Keats and Shelley. Or to deplore them, in "industrial novels" like Harriet Martineau's *Manchester Strike* and Frances Trollope's *Michael Armstrong: The Factory Boy;* like Dickens on Coketown and Kingsley in sweatshops and even Disraeli, in *Conningsby* and *Sybil*. If Elizabeth Gaskell, in *Mary Barton*, had been terrified of Chartists under the bed, and Charlotte Brontë in *Shirley* sided with the mill owners against those dirty lowlife Luddites, there was this wonderful passage in George Eliot's *The Mill on the Floss*:

> But good society, floated on gossamer wings of light irony, is of very expensive production; requiring nothing less than a wide and arduous national life condensed in unfragrant, deafening factories, cramping itself in mines, sweating at furnaces, grinding, hammering, weaving under more or less oppression of carbonic acid—or else, spread over sheepwalks, and scattered in lonely houses and huts on the clayey or chalky corn-lands, where the rainy days look dreary. This wide national life is based entirely on emphasis—the emphasis of want, which urges it into all the activities necessary for the maintenance of good society and light irony...

Jane Austen, in her father's parsonage, chose not to notice. The resurgent vogue for Austen in the winter of 1995–96—the novels reissued in handsome hardcover and paperback editions by Modern Library and Penguin; Roger Mitchell's oddly morose *Persuasion*, Emma Thompson's ultraslim rewrite of *Sense and Sensibility* and Alicia Silverstone's Valley Girl version of *Emma* in *Clueless* on big screens simultaneously, followed closely by Gwynth Paltrow's *Emma* according to the canonical text; calendars and cookbooks (ragoo of celery, harrico of mutton, jaune mange and solid syllabubs) and home-video boxed sets of the six-hour BBC *Pride and Prejudice* mini-series that most of us were already watching on A&E cable—was one of those mysteries of contagious enthusiasm a critic's better off not thinking about too strenuously, like the Burger King tie-in to Disney knockoffs of *Toy Story* characters, or Hootie and the Blowfish. We *knew* Lizzie would get married in the sixth hour of *P&P*, so would her sister, and so had every other heroine of an Austen novel after many aphorisms and lots of putting on hats, piling into coaches, going to balls and shooting birds, like Cinderella or Sabrina. To be sure, inside her courtship rituals and Oedipal conniptions, Austen had mounted a moral critique of the Georgian gentry, but with so much ironic wit, to such a terse and tapered point, that subsidiary characters seemed to bleed to death from paper cuts and dimples.

I thought I'd understood the *Victorian* revival, from the wishful thinking of Gertrude Himmelfarb to the cyberpunk fantasies of Neal Stephenson: We had made a mess of it. Somehow, the longing for a bygone civic virtue shaded over or leaked into nostalgia for Empire. After eighties greed, nineties hypocrisy...the concurrent vampire craze could even have been a part of it, the soft erotic underbelly behind those respectable vests, that secret nineteenth-century bond with grand opera, Romantic poetry, psychoanalysis and bassoons. But could we possibly be nostalgic for *Regency* England; for arranged marriage and primogeniture? *Sense and Sensibility* was published in 1811; *Pride and Prejudice* in 1813. In that unmerry England, unions were unlawful. The first owner of the first machine-driven mill was also the first to enslave children from age five on, six days a week, on fourteen-hour shifts. Men were hanged for poaching rabbits; women for stealing a shilling's worth of shoes. If Austen had looked out her window at Mansfield Park, which depended for its maintenance on slave-labor revenues from sugar plantations in Antigua, she'd have seen bad harvests, rising prices, food shortages, landlessness, mass unemployment and a ragtag King Ludd army of colliers with picks, fishmongers with knives, masons with hammers and weavers with sickles, smashing power looms and spinning jennies. But she didn't.

A century later, Kafka looked into his mirror and what he saw was the modern corporation. He also invented workmen's comp.

Do you look at television this way? I mean, there is sardonic Darcy, on the screen, at the ball, with the noisy poor outside in the rain, and I'm thinking that as the landed Georgian gentry developed their taste for leisurely rituals of hunting and shooting, squirearchs like Darcy also intensified their prosecution of the

Game Laws. I am reading E.P. Thompson and Eric Hobsbawm instead of Gertrude Himmelfarb. You probably are thinking about, and reading, something else. But you *are* thinking something, reading something, remembering or forgetting or promising or denying something. To Jane Austen or *The Nanny* or *Roseanne*, you bring your own monocle and morbidity, whether you are Terry Rakolta, Peggy Charen, Rev. Donald Wildmon or an editor of *Social Text*; you cut or paste, underline or italicize, delete or dump a day's worth of brave deeds and shameful secrets, a lifetime's compost of compunctions and regrets. These condition how we see what we see and whether or not we want to shoot a fox. "And that's how we are," wrote Pablo Neruda, "forever falling/ into the deep well of other beings." Anyway:

It should have been different here, a nation of bad blood and shopkeepers from the start, whose manifest destiny it was to landgrab from Indians, swap whales and rum for slaves, build railroads and peddle patent medicine. Emerson is on record saying, "Money, which represents the prose of life, and which is hardly spoken of in parlors without an apology, is, in its effects and laws, as beautiful as roses." Thoreau did time in a pencil factory. But our hearts belonged, with a Whitmanesque barbaric yawp, to Natty Bumppo, Captain Ahab, Huck Finn, Neal Cassady and Rabbit Angstrom, as if American literature were hiding out or on the lam not only from the civilizing schoolmarm, but also from Jim Fisk, Jay Gould, John D. Rockefeller and Mary Baker Eddy. Even Henry James decamped to England. ("What was it?" asked Mary McCarthy about "the small, unmentionable article" that made the Newsomes wealthy in *The Ambassadors*: "Garters? Safety pins?" A dirty secret.) William Dean Howells, Theodore Dreiser, Frank Norris, Upton Sinclair and Sinclair Lewis were as shocked by what they saw when they looked at a Haymarket riot, a stock exchange, railroads, stockyards and Babbit, as William Blake had been by England's dark satanic mills. According to F. Scott Fitzgerald, money broke Gatsby's heart. From a Cuban fishing boat, Hemingway explained that the rich were always "either busy studying how to get more wealth, or horses, or what is wrong with themselves, with psychoanalysis, or horses, or how not to lose what wealth they have, or horses, or the moving picture business, or horses, or all of these things together, and, possibly, horses." Nathanael West made fun of Horatio Alger. Arthur Miller's salesman had to die before we paid attention. While Saul Bellow, E.L. Doctorow and William Kennedy have all explored the American romance with money, they've done so from a gangster perspective: the urban outlaw as pop icon. That leaves Louis Auchincloss, practicing law, and John Updike, selling Toyota Corollas, unless you count Ayn Rand. The high point of any rapprochement between American business and American literature was probably 1916, when that pretty face on the newly minted silver dime belonged to Elsie Stevens, who just happened to be married to the poet Wallace Stevens, who worked for a Hartford insurance agency.

This literary bias against businessmen—in favor of deerslayers, whaling captains, river pirates, Pretty Boy Floyd, Calamity Jane and the Lone Ranger—is even more pronounced in riffraff genres like the pulp western, the dime detective novel, the gothic horror, science fiction, comic strips, radio serials, B movies and tiresomely reiterated variations on a theme of *noir*. Against such a buckling of swashes and donning of masks and punching out of dames, on high seas or mean streets, in forests primeval or badlands, the famous Steichen portrait of a J.P. Morgan with a paring knife and an endangered apple, the *Spruce Goose* of a Howard Hughes, the sled of a *Citizen Kane*, the death-in-the-saddle of a Nelson A. Rockefeller, the severed ear of a kidnapped Getty and the overexposure of a Donald and Ivana are not exactly the stuff of wet dreams. It's not as if any of our corporate-raiding buccaneers had lived a miniseries sort of life—unlike, say, John Jacob Astor, who slaughtered all of Hawaii's otters; or Daniel Guggenheim, who was cutting silver deals with Porfirio Diaz and helping out King Leopold II of Belgium with a spot of trouble in his Congo before it ever occurred to him to endow a museum; or Andrew Carnegie who, before he brought us a music hall, also brought us a Homestead Strike. Never mind "Papa" Hemingway. What would Sam Spade have said about an adult activity whose notion of grace under pressure is baying like a hound at the spiderspeak in green decimals of international currency speculation?

And these riffraff genres are, of course, where television came from.

We shot a few Mexican bandits, drank a lot of whisky.
Robert Duvall, *Lonesome Dove*

Life's a knife. Sooner or later a man slips and gets cut.
James Garner, *Streets of Laredo*

A man's gotta do what a man's gotta do, no matter how hard Boot Hill is on pretty misseys, because the rest of the townfolk are sheep dip, unless they are Native Americans, in which case they are followed around by a missionary and an anthropologist and an F.B.I. agent, and make big mystical deals out of pan pipes and buffalo skulls, and speak in Zen koans about The Great Tree.

I did not mourn the passing of the western. With the demise of *Gunsmoke,* in 1975, after twenty years on CBS, there was no more lemon to be sucked. They had used up Kit Carson (Bill Williams), Wild Bill Hickock (Guy Madison), Bat Masterson (Gene Barry), Daniel Boone (Fess Parker), Hopalong Cassidy (William Boyd), the Cisco Kid (Duncan Renaldo), Wyatt Earp (Hugh O'Brian), Jesse James (Christopher Jones) and the Lone Ranger (Clayton Moore). They got all the way to Zorro (Guy Williams) and even included Cochise (Michael Ansara). For Henry Fonda, Clint Eastwood, Steve McQueen, Dale Robertson, Richard Boone, Walter Brennan, Lorne Greene, Ward Bond, Neville Brand, Nick Adams, Clint Walker and Ronald Reagan, they had dreamed up a whole new motorcade of iron horses and wagon trains, ponderosas and paladins, bounty hunters and confederates, laredos and death valleys. They pointed their six-guns at the railroad owners, cattle barons, mortgage-foreclosers, rustlers, card sharps, Bible nuts, dancehall girls, Geronimos and half-breed sociopaths, and for decades they horsed around.

For awhile, everything worked. Then, after awhile, nothing did, not even an anti-western like *Maverick.* Mockery is the last refuge of a bankrupt genre, after which it will end up on the Cultural Studies curriculum at a major university. (In *The Empire's New Clothes*, his Marxist analysis of mass-market fairy tales, the

Chilean playwright, novelist and critic Ariel Dorfman asked himself "Who *was* that masked man?"; and then decided that the Lone Ranger only "apparently" suffered from an identity crisis, brought about by what mod philosophers would call his "boundary situation." He's actually a "mythic reincarnation" of advanced capitalism, an "industrial product of fiction," whose mission it is to police a frontier that seethes with internal contradictions. If you like this sort of thing, and I do, be advised that Dorfman looks into World of Disney and sees Mickey in the sky as Logos, with white ducks propagandizing for the Protestant work ethic; that he reads the Babar series of children's books and declares that the elephant king wears panties like a lamb chop because of French colonial condescension to black Africa. And so on, though he inexplicably omits any mention of Dr. Doolittle, surely the smarmiest printout of imperial condescension since *Little Black Sambo*.) We are only amused until we realize that we are laughing at ourselves. Self-loathing is another way for an exhausted genre to go, as in Clint Eastwood's *The Unforgiven*. But it's also a one-shot. Only advanced novelists can make a career out of hating what they do; a TV series would be insufferable.

We got along without a western until 1989, when what happened to television was Larry McMurtry. And this is what we saw that February on CBS: Weary on the Rio Grande of stealing horses and raising pigs, ex-Texas Rangers Woodrow Call (Tommy Lee Jones) and Gus McCrae (Robert Duvall) left civilization and its discontents for an eight-hour, 2,500-mile mosey to Montana, taking with them the obligatory whore-with-a-heart-of-gold (Diane Lane), the token black (Danny Glover), the hot-tempered ne'er-do-well (Robert Urich) and the fatherless pubescent (Ricky Schroder), not to mention many head of cattle and the evil half-breed Blue Duck (Frederic Forrest), through sandstorms and saddlesores, savage whoops and enormous Nielsens, during which, with time out for a Nebraska rest-stop schmooze with Anjelica Huston, men were hanged and women raped and children perished in rivers full of water moccasins. If most of us rooted for Duvall's Gus, who took time off from empire-building to play poker, poke women and chase buffalo, it was because *Lonesome Dove* seemed to suggest that fanatics like Call just might be *crazy*. Nevertheless, the fun-lover first lost his leg and then his life, while the crazy hauled him home again, in a coffin passage out of Faulkner, to a stand of pecan trees in Texas.

Call made the same run from Montana back to Texas in a seven-hour 1993 sequel, *Return to Lonesome Dove*, this time with William Petersen as the designated buddy, with New Age *feelings* instead of Gus's gusto; Louis Gossett Jr. as the designated African-American cowboy; Dennis Haysbert as the designated half-breed, Cherokee Jack, more mindlessly malign than Blue Duck; Will Scott as Pea Eye, the designated Old Coot; Oliver Reed as the designated cattle baron, doing his King Lear-King Tut with a self-indulgent brogue; and Ricky Schroder back again as fatherless Newt—fifteen hours and he still hadn't come of age. But *not* back were Larry McMurtry (writing his own sequel), Duvall and Urich (dead), and Jones and Huston (making big-screen movies). Which meant that John Voight had to take over as Woodrow Call, whose vatic utterance through biblical beard correspondingly deteriorated from phlegmy-gnomic to obtuse-comatose. It should have been a disaster. That it wasn't was owing mostly to the women: Barbara Hershey, waiting around with her Arabian horses and her weathered rawhide-pioneer look for Woodrow or a prairie fire, under a nifty cap; C.C.H. Pounder stirring pots, whipping wagons and pointing rifles on the cross-country mustang drive, with some humor mixed in her loam; Nia Peeples, a fiery dish and Gus's daughter from a south-of-the-border saunter, rounding up vacqueros for the mustang drive and blowing away the cavalry troopers who tried to do to her what everyone did to Diane Lane in the orginal *Dove*; and Reese Witherspoon as the cattle baron's spoiled sulky teeny-bopper child-bride. We cared about the men because their women seemed to.

But what do we say, as critics, after we've already said, as I did in the introduction to this book, that all Westerns from the Bible on are the same story about turf, clout, sexual property rights and how to look good dying? Well, try this on for size: Call was nursed back to health by a Cherokee woman, who then followed him around with mute devotion. And Chris Cooper as July Johnson, the former Arkansas sheriff, had an obvious crush on Nia Peeples, the spicy Latina. *Suppose Woodrow's dream of breeding wild mustangs with Barbara's Arabians was meant metaphorically?* For that matter, what if Cherokee Jack represented primitive accumulation; and Oliver Reed monopoly capitalism; and John Voight the Last of the Zapatas? This Big Sky-Ariel Dorfman fantasy of miscegenation lasted until November, 1995, and the next miniseries, *Larry*

McMurtry's Streets of Laredo. To be sure, while *Laredo*'s baby-faced killer Joey Garza (Alexis Cruz) was supposed to be Mexican, he was also blond and blue eyed, which would seem to suggest that he emblematized racial paranoia, like the equally evil half-breeds Blue Duck and Cherokee Jack. But there was otherwise not a hint in *Laredo* of *Return to*'s crossbreeding multicultural agenda. And with Sissy Spacek taking over Diane Lane's Lorena role—the former-whore-with-heart-of-gold turned, of course, into a *teacher*, thus amalgamating the two cliches of womanhood in classic westerns, schoolmarm and pop tart—there wasn't a chance of trashing the genre, not even with anti-cowboy Jim Garner as the third Call in as many mini-series, certainly not with Sam Shepard as Pea Eye, Wes Studi as a Kickapoo tracker, Randy Quaid as John Wesley Hardin and Ned Beatty as Judge Roy Bean, hanging from his own rafter. In the way that Kurt Waldheim had a skin so thick he didn't need a spine, *Laredo* was so straight it didn't need a point.

Which left me like George Carlin (yes, George Carlin was in *Laredo*) with nothing to think about except Sonia Braga who played the killer's mother as if she were half Frida Kahlo and half Antigone. I will say this about Sonia Braga: Wow. Like most of the women in *Laredo*, she would be raped, but that wasn't the only reason for her to worry about eugenics. Of her three children from four marriages, one was blind, another so feeble-minded he carried around a baby goat and baaa-ed like a baby lamb and the third, Joey, less a bad seed than an entire lousy ecology. There was a powerful scene near the end with the dead bodies of Sonia and Joey side by side on the same bed, suggesting that either McMurtry or director Joseph Sargent had been reading Greek tragedy through a Freudian pince-nez. But the rest of *Laredo* for all its sandstorms and choochoos, wind mills and lynchings, cacti and rattlers, burning dogs and bird chirp, a severed leg and a shot-off ear and a symbolic invasion of Mexico (sort of like NAFTA), was oddly Buddhist—as if fatalism and reciprocity were codependents. When, in the spring of 1996, cassettes arrived of a Larry McMurtry *prequel* to all these *Lonesomes*, I decided to give it a rest.

Each subsequent *Lonesome* did worse in the ratings than the last. And while many certainly tried, nobody managed to cash in on what was perceived in 1989 as a revival of the genre—Rick Schroder himself in John Carpenter's *Blood River*; a pudged-up James Arness in two *Gunsmoke* retreads; *Ned Blessing* and *The New*

Adventures of Brisco County as TV movies and as series both; Judge Reinhold, M. Emmett Walsh and a delicious Patricia Clarkson in *Four Eyes and Six Guns*; Kenny Rogers and Stacy Keach in *Rio Diablo*; Jimmy Smits as *The Cisco Kid*; Charlton Heston as Brigham Young in *The Avenging Angel*; Tommy Lee Jones and Sam Shepard in *The Gold Old Boys*; Richard Dean Anderson as a *Legend*; Anjelica Huston as Calamity Jane in *Buffalo Girls*; Sidney Poitier in *Children of the Dust*, gunslinging on behalf of black homesteaders; and *Bonanza: The Return*. While most of these programs did better than the big-screen Hollywood *Maverick* and *Earp* remakes of the same period—I can't explain that either, unless we prefer to be intimate with hoary genres in the privacy and safety of our own homes—none mounted much of a ratings challenge to the regular recycling of old westerns on the Turner super-channels: niche broadcasting for obsessive niche-wits. It may be that once Kevin Costner, like Lawrence of Arabia, cross-dressed to prove his sincerity to the Lakota Sioux in *Dances with Wolves*, the western had used up all its empty space and had nothing more to say to us. David Carradine must have known what he was doing when he decided to come back in *Kung Fu: The Legend Continues* as his own grandson, Kwai Chang Caine. And where and when he came back *to*, instead of the Old West, was of course modern-day Los Angeles. And *his* son, no surprise, was a cop.

Where have all the cowboys gone? Probably to outer space. But not before they'd left behind two important spurs on the Achilles heel of American popular culture: lynching and genocide.

So ninety percent of science fiction is bullshit. Ninety percent of everything is bullshit.
                                                    Theodore Sturgeon

To my own surprise, as a civilian, I liked *Alien Nation* enough to tape it Monday nights in 1989 on Fox, the upstart network, and watch it after *Murphy Brown*. The surprise was because I thought I'd outgrown the science fiction of my youth (the Bradburys, Heinleins, Asimovs and Sturgeons), and of my young adulthood (the Herberts and Ballards), and had never much cared for it on television—from Captain Zero and Johnny Jupiter and Tom Corbett, Space Cadet, with tin-can-and-flashlight robots, kiddie-car time travel, wavy-gravy other dimensions, fright-mask nightmare worlds and extraterrestrials made of thumbtacks and Spam, up to and including *Star Trek*, which in my dissenting opinion deteriorated after its first two seasons into an inter-galactic spaghetti western, trying to get by on personality instead of strangeness. The best sci-fi is either about strangeness, or it's subversive social criticism. The social criticism looks at who we are through the eyes of the Other—alternative histories, religions, ecologies, technologies and black arts—and finds us woefully wanting. The strangeness imagines that Other: since we can't even talk to a dolphin, how would we chat up an alien reptile or insect, a thinking crystal, a mental enzyme, a virus from a distant star? It might be blind and see the world through smell, temperature or pressure; communicate in math or music; exhale cyanide gas or excrete radioactive waste or give off bone-shattering sound vibrations. It might have only one dimension and slip by us (or more than three and overlap). Like single-cell bacteria it might even be immortal. Poison-tipped mandibles! Breeding triads! Mind-body transfer! Technicolored dream hunters! Giant sandworms! Robots who want a piece of the action! *What if we can't kill it?*

Except for *Max Headroom*, which lasted just long enough on ABC for the network to figure out that this was a series that made savage fun of television itself—the watching of it compulsory, the ratings for it calculated by nanosecond, the frenzied trading on the ad exchange, trial by electronic plesbescite, stealing a minicam a capital offense, distribution of emergency video recorders during social disturbances, guerrilla media terrorists, and, of course, the computer-generated nonexistence of Max himself—sci-fi on TV tended to be action comics like *Superman, Batman, Wonder Woman* and *Flash Gordon*, or soaps in another solar system, like *Lost in Space* and *Land of the Giants*, or woo-woo creepie-crawlies, like *Twilight Zone* and *The Outer Limits*, or standard-issue paranoid fantasies, like *Logan's Run* and *Man from Atlantis* and *The Invaders*, or hardware and mysticism (H&M), like *The Six-Million Dollar Man, The Bionic Woman* and *Their Hard-Wired Dachshund. V.*, a popular miniseries but rejected weekly series, was a good example. Not only did our "visitors" turn out to be humongous lizards, but they also ate us.

Alien Nation was social criticism, and also strange, and also

{119}

funny. It was about two cops. One of them was one of us, and the other wasn't. Matt, played by Gary Graham, was, inevitably, "streetwise." George, played by Eric Pierpoint, was, ah, spacey. We were supposed to be living in 1995, five years after Newcomers like George had arrived on Earth by a saucer from another star. They had two hearts, and funny-looking spotted heads like designer bowling balls. They boozed on sour milk, and ate beaver sushi. Most of them moved to Los Angeles where you'd think they'd fit right in. But even though the American Civil Liberties Union won them their rights as citizens (and the baseball Dodgers signed one up as a pitcher), try telling L.A. to like a bunch of earless two-hearted milk-drinking telepathic beaver-eaters who are smarter than we are and breed faster and hum to one another prior to sex. Since Newcomers were called "slags" (if not "spongeheads") and lived in "slagtowns" and were reviled by "Purists," we were made to think about ghettos and racial riots. Because each had been arbitrarily assigned an Earth-type name, like Thomas Jefferson, Albert Einstein or Jean-Paul Sartre, we saw Ellis Island. And because the saucer they had crashed in turned out to be a slave ship, with brutal overseers who subdued them with gas, we saw again the middle passage from Africa and antebellum plantation life and, with amazing delicacy, even the Holocaust.

This overview barely suggests the filigree. It was a cop show, so Matt and George were always cracking wisecracks and crashing cars and busting perps, but with time out for gender-bending George to bring his fetus to term. And the murderer they were looking for had probably killed somebody like the astronomer who just happened to discover a radio signal on the original trajectory of the defunct saucer, which meant that the writers were thinking about Dred Scott and the Fugitive Slave Acts. And George, the eager autodidact, always got our colloquialisms just a little bit wrong, as when he fumed, with his wife in a coma: "I can't just sit around in a hospital with Moby Dick in my hand." And the look of the show was postapocalyptic shabby-genteel, like *Max Headroom* and *Brazil* and the Mel Gibson *Road Warrior* movies, as if the foggy future were a junkyard of all our killer toys. *Alien Nation* had a social conscience and a sense of humor and it made me grin as well as think—and Rupert Murdoch killed it after a single shining season, just in time to miss the sudden resurgence of science fiction all over the rest of television.

Four years later, maybe remorseful, they brought it back as a two-hour TV movie, *Dark Horizon*. George's wife Susan (Michelle Scarabelli) and his daughter Emily (Lauren Woodland) are attacked by a virus fatal only to Newcomers. At Susan's hospital bedside, George and Matt have to sing her favorite song, which is "Do You Know the Way to San José?" The killer virus will prove to have been cooked up by slag-bashing Purists under the dictatorial direction of a fanatic whose name is Phyllis Bryant. Meanwhile, above our spongeheads, another space ship full of Elite Overseer Commandos has been surfing the electromagnetic waves in search of their lost slaves. They will send down Ahpossno (Scott Peterson) to scout about undercover as a sort of scientist-musician-interior-decorator-ninja. Will Ahpossno save the Newcomers from the virus and the Purists, only to ship them back to slavery? Will Matt learn to hum, or miss his chance at alien sex? Is it possible that "Phyllis Bryant" was intended to remind us of Phyllis Schafley and Anita Bryant? Which would perhaps also mean that *Dark Horizon* had something to say about separatism, identity politics, AIDS and genocide, which would be pretty cheeky for a TV show whose writers—Andrew Schneider and Diana Frolov—had been hiding out at *Northern Exposure* ever since Murdoch snuffed their series.

Alien Nation made me pay more attention to TV sci-fi just when there was more of it to pay attention to. Even as *The X-Files* would legitimize UFOs, alien abductions, vampire possession fantasies, conspiracy theories of government cover-ups and rightwing paranoia about black helicopters full of Jewish bankers, USA, the cable network for *noir* and wrestling, spun off the Sci-Fi Channel with reruns of everything woo-woo plus its own Planetary Premieres of made-for-TV movies like *Official Denial*, in which Parker Stevenson was not only abducted by other-worldly creeps who sucked out his sperm but abducted as well by government agents Chad Everett and Dirk Benedict, who, in a tit-for-tat worthy of Checkpoint Charlie and a Middle East hostage crisis, also abducted one of the sperm-suckers; and *The Lifeforce Experiment*, in which the CIA sent, of all people, Mimi Kuzyk, to of all places Canada to find out whether mad scientist Donald Sutherland at his computer console behind his beard was really stealing souls and stocking them like urine samples; and *Deep Red*, a futuristic *noir* in which low-rent gumshoes Michael Biehn and Joanna Pacula foiled a plot to corner the market in "virus protein microchips" that enabled the rich to live forever if they wanted to. (I especially admired *Deep Red*'s satanic milk wagon. It could have been an *hommage* to the Paris laundry truck that killed Roland Barthes or the Barcelona trolley that ran down Antonio Gaudi.)

Meanwhile, on the respectable networks we got movies like *Murder by Moonlight*, in which Brigitte Nielsen with her lovely smile and scary shoulders is sent by NASA to the moon in 2015 A.D. to head off thermonuclear war by mining the lunar rock for telltale deposits of Julian Sands. And *Dark Avenger*, in which Leigh Lawson as the incorruptible Judge Cain, though thought to be dead from fire and acid, lives on disfigured behind a metal mask in a high-tech crime lab from which he is determined to revenge himself on Robert Vaughn and/or Hector Elizondo, while resolving such issues from his nightmare past as kidnapped children, serial killers, corrupt psychiatry, drug induced paranoid schizophrenia and coded references to Zorro. And *Not Of This World*, in which Lisa Hartman, a single-mother electrical enginer in a drop-dead miniskirt, is building a power plant for some nervous Japanese investors when meteors fall down on everybody, and from the cosmic rubble and radioactive waste emerges a sort of big lizardly bat-like biomechanical spore from outer space that leaves with its laser-drill teeth a hieroglyphic pattern of burn marks on the pigs, dogs, computers, public-relations spin doctors and Pat Hingles it gobbles up on its way to the power plant, like a vacuum cleaner the size of a Hobbesian Leviathan. As well as weekly series like *Quantum Leap,* with Scott Bakula and Dean Stockwell crossing timelines and going around the gender bend, and *Mantis*, with Carl Lumbly as a millionaire paraplegic biophysicist who fights violent crime and political corruption in Ocean City by wearing a masklike virtual-reality superpower "harness" while riding in a 1957 Cadillac that turns into a helicopter with rocketship accessories, blazing away with a gun that shoots freezing darts. Or the series spinoff from the TV movie *Something Is Out There*, with a *Mad Max-Robocop-Terminator 2* feel to it that was arty enough to frighten the French, in which streetwise L.A. cop Joe Cortese and his mind-reading starchild partner Maryam d'Abo made Arnold Schwarzenegger jokes while dodging laser rays from vengeful baddies in kryptonite flak jackets. Or *Mann and Machine* in which in a not-so-distant future—the baseball Giants have moved to

Tokyo—David Andrews is the streetwise cop, Bobby Mann, and Yancy Butler his inhuman partner Eve, dishy but deep down full of semiconductors and mic-rochips, a female cyborg from a Silicon Valley whiz kid's toy store, who dreams of being human and cracks safes by removing eyeballs. I also had to catch up with *Beauty and the Beast.*

By December 1989 the relationship in *Beauty and the Beast* between Catherine, the yuppie lawyer, and Vincent, the lion-faced warrior-poet from "a secret place," had progressed, please don't ask how, to parturition. Linda Hamilton, about to leave the series for her Rambimbo role in *Terminator 2*, was clearly preggers. (So much for the famous taboo: CANNOT BE TOGETHER.) *Something* had happened during her long nights in a Black Hole nursing Vincent back to life from the previous season's visit to his dark side. Vincent had paid a terrible price for resolving his Oedipal conflict. He'd lost his "empathic connection" with Catherine—that extrasensory bond that warned him whenever she was in danger, thus activating the weekly rescue fantasy. And it was the worst possible time for Ron Leibman's psychic beeper to be on the blink. Not only was Catherine pregnant. She was also *abducted*, by a criminal conspiracy bigger than anything ever dreamt of by *Indiana Umberto and the Templars of Doom*, masterminded by a guy named Gabriel (Stephen McHattie) with so many of his own sexual problems that he was always quoting Schopenhauer. While the assistant district attorney (Jay Acovone), the lovelorn architect (Edward Arnold) and the high-priced private eye (Richard Roundtree) looked everywhere for Catherine, Vincent in his subterranean kingdom whimpered like a Hamlet, raged like a Lear and looked not a whole lot beastlier than your average death-metal rocker with bad British teeth. Most of the scary stuff was obstetrics. (Nothing like stirrups to make you think: medieval.) Most of the chitchat was *ur*-Joseph Campbell, As Told To Bill Moyers. (Catherine and Vincent, for instance, listening to music: "How do you feel?" "There are no words." "Try one." "Bliss.") Symbolic resonance abounded, not just eclectic but promiscuous, as if Ron Koslow, who created the series and wrote this script, had yanked on Frazer's *Golden Bough* and all of mythology fell down on him. Besides death and resurrection, Christ the Lion, and the usual Jungian caves, we were also reminded of Michelangelo's Sistine Chapel, William Blake's "O Rose thou art sick," the golden apples of Hesperides and the curse of the wandering Jew, not to mention

Catherine the Great, horsing around, and Casper the Friendly Ghost. I'll admit that I used to tune in to *Beauty and the Beast* for the occasional geopolitics—there was one episode on the witch-hunting of atomic scientists in the fifties and another having to do with IRA terrorists—whereas its loyal followers were all watching to find out, of course, if Rapunzel made it with Rumpelstiltskin, and couldn't care less if Vincent was really Parsifal, or, if so, did that make Catherine the Nibelungen Hoard or a Holy Grail? But you have to say it was a lot more interesting than a western, and Vincent's tunnel gave a whole new meaning to the concept of the closet.

The real action, however, was in syndication. As *Star Trek: The Next Generation* wound down, *Star Trek: Deep Space Nine* was revving up. Jean-Luc Picard himself (Patrick Stewart) put in a special guest appearance on the pilot of the new series, to set the twenty-fourth century stage for Avery Brooks as the Federation's watchdog, from a space station, on the development of war-ravaged Bajora, as the rippled-nosed Bajorans, newly liberated from their iguana-faced Cardassian oppressors, fiddled with an intergalactic "wormhole" wherein might dwell a super-species to whom ideas like "sex" and "time" and "baseball" were as strange as Gene Roddenberry. Brooks, who had been Hawk on the *Spenser* detective show and Paul Robeson off-Broadway, was a splendid choice to succeed Stewart, as Stewart had been a revelation upon succeeding William Shatner. Even better was Nana Visitor as the Bajoran Kira Nerys, an excitable woman warrior. Bajora itself seemed vaguely Moorish, with mosque-like domes and a magic door called the Tear of the Prophet on the other side of which was the last remaining Teaching Orb. Thanks to cyberpunk executive-producers Michael Piller and Rick Berman, we also heard about plasma fields, resonance waves, neutrino disruptions and, rather wonderfully, a "nonlinear" *grief*. "Are we," asked Avery Brooks, "reduced to chasing metaphors?" We certainly were, at warp factor 9.

It would take another two years to launch the third *Star Trek* derivative, *Voyager*, with the very first female captain of an *Enterprise* derivative. Never mind why the *Voyager*, with all its twenty-fourth century bioneural circuitry, should suffer a "Badlands" plasma storm and end up 70,000 light years off course, on the wrong side of whichever galaxy, where Kate Mulgrew and her multiculti crew find themselves in the clutches of a heavy-metal "array," inside of which a dying alien, sort of like Howard Hughes,

had been playing God with the desert planet below. I'll report a resonance trace in my private warp core because of Mulgrew as Captain Kathryn Janeway. We saw her mind watch itself think, in split
seconds, as if hesitation were a form of sloth. She was born to command, with her hair swept up like Edith Wharton's, her eyes narrowed like a basilisk's, the best jaw on television this side of Karen
Sillas, so crisp that she crackled like a graviton particle and so
svelte in her Federation woolens she seemed to chuck herself into
action like a spear. Would the faithful beam her up, as they came to
embrace Picard—and, with her, the first Native American in outer
space (Robert Beltran as Chakotay, who had visions), a black Vulcan (Tim Ross), a half-Klingon (Roxann Biggs-Dawson), the thug-
gish Kazons, the subterranean Ocampa and Robert Picardo from
China Beach as a fussbudget medical hologram? Probably. These
primally-directed would have to finesse their long way back to Federation space without any help from Starfleet, like those Greek soldiers in Xenophon's *Anabasis* who fought their way back from
Babylon. Or, perhaps more to the point considering Mulgrew, like
Dorothy and her friends trying to get home from Oz.

What did it mean—so many cowboys and Indians in outer space,
so many SWAT teams and drug-busters, and such a foam and froth
of humanoid diversity? It was hard to tell, just sitting there trying
to sort out the Minbaris from the Centauris from the Vorlons from
the Narns, all of them gathered on *Babylon 5*, the "Interspecies Station in Neutral Space," with mind-scanners, changeling nets, customized atmospheres, variable gravities and Claudia Christian, that
started out its series life in 1993 as "the last best hope for peace," but
had become, by 1996, "the last best hope for victory" instead, as well
as changing captains. Here today, gone next month: *Space Rangers*,
with Linda Hunt bossing around her ragtag band of deep-space
troubleshooters, mostly human but one of them a biochip mobile
unit, which coed lonesome rangers seemed to be chasing a one-man
crime syndicate wormhole whose name, if I heard it correctly,
seemed to be Istiqlal. (Since *Istiqlal* is Arabic for "freedom," this
would amount to grievous Western-imperialist wog bashing in a
network series.) I'd no sooner focused on some nice Puff the Magic
Dragon/*Terminator 2* F/X pyrotechnics than this *Dirty Dozen* in virtual reality had vanished, to be replaced by *TekWars*, with Greg Evi-
gan as a twenty-first century ex-cop employed by William Shatner's
private detective agency to sneak into cyberspace, with the help of

some friendly hackers, and morph up the druglord baddies in a future as acrylic as Russian Constructivism. Which hardly left time for *Earth 2*, a promising Swiss Family Robinson Stranded on Mars sort of show, with three different alien species plus Debra Farentino, yanked almost immediately to make room for *SeaQuest*, where Roy Scheider talked to dolphins, underwater, in his nuclear submarine, which wasn't nearly as interesting as Dale Midkoff, the twenty-second century cop who had been "tele-transported" in *Time Trax* back to 1993 to apprehend criminal masterminds from his own era who were hiding in the past, in places like the CIA and the nuclear power industry.

None of these series was anywhere near as good as *VR.5*, another show that Fox killed after only half a season, with Lori Singer as a computer hacker who had gone to hell. Never mind her nightmares of traumatic childhood. Nor the weird green eyes, the gangster movies, the nameless "committee," the virtual sex and the consumer-culture dread she met in cyberspace, which was also her unconscious. Ignore those techno-weenies who complained on the Net that *VR.5* was untrue to the mysteries of their meat/machine interface. Somehow, changing her clothes as often as an operatic diva, Singer tapped into primal psychic stuff. As you'd expect from an executive producer like John Sacret Young, whose previous network series was *China Beach*, it was stunning to look at. It was also paranoid-playful, like Patrick McGoohan in *The Prisoner* and Alice in her Wonderland. Making fun of Bogart movies, *Thelma & Louise*, *La Femme Nikita*, Sigmund Freud, *Max Headroom*, the Rosicrucians and *The Avengers*, it had something slick to say as well about sinister elites, hacker chic, survivor guilt and the fetishism of commodities. This is what the inside of a digithead probably looks like: pixels gently falling on a mother board of designer drugs, machine dreams and junkyard culture, a pop cryptogram of crossed wires, secret signs and Lori Singer dipped in sky. Unlike the retro *Sliders* that replaced it, *VR.5* was sci-fi's future—the hacker as cowboy-private eye-flying nun: Samantha Spade, cyberspace samurai.

Cyberspace itself had of course already been cartographed, not in movies or on television, but in novels by William Gibson like *Neuromancer* (1984), *Count Zero* (1986) and *Mona Lisa Overdrive* (1988). It was a dream of "meat" emancipated—into a "consensual hallucination" of the glowing cores, burning grids, neon clouds, crystal nerves and singing spheres of a universe of information; pyramids and shopping malls of data; havens of the matrix. All Gibson's heroes are computer hackers, who project their "disembodied consciousness" into this 3-D chessboard "nonspace of the mind." Usually, they are thieves, doing mercenary work "for other, wealthier thieves," employers who provide the exotic software needed to penetrate the bright walls of corporate systems, opening windows into rich fields of data. But what they find beyond the "green cubes" of Mitsubishi banks and the logarithmic "spiral arms" of military intelligence agencies, in the middle of their "fluid neon origami trick" of levitation, is the *rush* of warp velocity.

Understand this is all imaginary. Other science-fiction writers, before and after Gibson's trilogy, also dreamed their way into what they called the grid, net, web or matrix, but none so lyrically. It's no longer possible to imagine computer space at all, *embodied* data, on any but his terms. Except for Pat Cadigan in *Synners* (1991) and Neal Stephenson in *Snow Crash* (1992), hardly anybody bothers. TV sci-fi, trying to picture ripples of the net, would be a blank screen without Gibson. From him, too, derived the whole idea of cyberspace as the ultimate frontier for guys who couldn't get a date in high school and *cyberpunk* as an outlaw culture, pitting the grace of hip against late capitalism and its marketing of commodified emotions. As in the fifties we got rock-and-roll bikers, and in the nineties Angry White Males, so in the eighties the buying and selling of Mac hackers, crash clubbers and postmodern critics on a high-concept stock exchange got parlayed into a *Time* mag cover story. It was an attitude: alienation and chaos theory; hard science and pop dreams; reality-hacking and new wave rock; blown minds and blown fuses. And it was a fashion statement: leather jackets, mirror shades, nose studs, nipple rings and tattoos.

This is not perhaps the place to think about cyberpunk, either as an intellectual take on the meat/machine interface (the kiss of the killer cyborg) or as a performance art of video games, leather bars, trash culture, designer drugs, hip-hop, film noir, *Max Headroom* and John Cage, crystal meth and gangster chic, Sex Pistols and Robocops, Yamaha TX81Z FM tone generators and RX5 digital rhythm programmers. To go on about Mike Saenz's "adult" computer adventure *Virtual Valerie*, Pepe Moreno's Batman computer comic *Digital Justice*, the photoscan sequence in Ridley Scott's *Blade Runner*, the vector graphics in Disney's *Tron*, the industrial noise of SPK and Skinny Puppy, Kraftwerk's "cyberpop" Robo Rock, Steve Wilson's Buffalo River Grain Elevators, Mark Pauline's ram cars and robot scorpions or David Therrien's Crucifixion and Fetal Cage crash machines is to frighten the horses of coherent argument. But they'll all show up on television after it has exhausted its current vein of evil aliens. And by that time, a new bunch of outlaws will have disappeared, by eyephone, dataglove, bodysuit, feedback loop and neural jack, into a world of computer-generated simulations of everything from "smart" bombs to protein molecules, from cadavers and solar systems (virtual surgery and virtual astronomy) to "tele-dildonics" (the great wet dream of virtual sex), and worried congressmen will be writing Telecommunications Bills forbidding any and all of it unless they sell advertising at the tollbooths.

But if cyberspace is a trope, the ground zero of all its post-apocalyptic posturing—Gibson's "Sprawl," Cadigan's "Mimosa," Stephenson's "Burbclaves," "Franculates," "Sacrifice Zones" and "Shantytowns"—is remarkably familiar: a third world like Mexico City or Delhi or Sarajevo; a blasted heath, like Mad Max on his way to Tina Turner's Thunderdome; a refugee black market fire sale of drugs, information, computer viruses, shuriken dagger-stars and spare body parts; an inner city of gangbanger cults and "nihilistic technofetishists"; a media-pacified populace of Pynchonian "tubal abuser" image-addicts, and a government of gangster cartels... against whose cyborg armies our only hope is the samurai hackers (whose credo may as well be Cadigan's: "If you can't fuck it and it doesn't dance, eat it or throw it away"). I am not making fun of cyberlit. I am inclined to agree with Bruce McHale—"We can think of science fiction as postmodernism's noncanonized or 'low art' double, its sister-genre in the same sense that the popular detective thriller is modernist fiction's sister-genre"—even if it means having to hear too much about "imbrications" and "diagetics" from various assistant professors of Problematizing Ontologies in Transgressive Subtexts (POTS). Like TV serials, cyberlit belongs to the noblest tradition of pulp. The villains are greedy s.o.b.'s. The heroes are cowboys and private eyes, in future drag. Language-jazzed, they propel themselves to mythic grandeur. This is how pop culture *thinks*, in primary colors with lots of noise. It's no weirder than, say, Scientology, which, not so coincidentally, shows up a lot in cyberlit. There are passing references in Gibson and Cadigan and the nastiest character in *Snow Crash*, who seeks with a systems virus to explode the pixel gridwork and destroy the deep neurolinguistic structures of the hacker brain itself, seems an amalgam of L. Ron Hubbard and H. Ross Perot. And the Bruce Wagner cyberpunk comic for *Details* magazine that inspired Oliver Stone's *Wild Palms* miniseries on ABC may also have had Hubbard, Scientology and Dianetics in mind, with its portrait of Tony Kreutzer, the weathly industrialist (and former sci-fi novelist) who has his own TV network, with its VR sitcom, his own religion, the Church of Synthiotics, his own cult parishioners, the New Realists, and his own fascistic paramilitaries, called Fathers because they kidnap the children of their many enemies.

Meanwhile, on television as we know it before it becomes something else, *TekWars*, *Time Trax*, *SeaQuest* and *Earth 2* have come briefly and gone forever. About the sci-fi's that remain, can anything be generalized? A big-screen paranoid possession flick, *The Arrival*, showed up in neighborhood theaters in June 1996, with Charlie Sheen as the radio-astronomer nerd whose love life with Teri Polo, and whose career at NASA, both suffer because he has to save the arctic ice cap from global warming and the planet itself from toadstool-spotted chameleonic creatures from Out There Somewhere, with sectional parts and wrong-way knees, who hide out in third world countries plotting to do to us what the scorpions had already done to geobotanist Lindsay Crouse. I preferred it to *Independence Day*. I am worried about global warming, too. And the idea of radio astronomy as a deep regression, a sort of hypnotherapy, is appealing: we listen at the satellite dish to our own worst fears. But you will have noticed that *evil* aliens have made a comeback. On the small screen, no more Morks, Alfs or Favorite Martians, though we can't be sure about John Lithgow. And on the big screen no more namby-pamby E.T.'s. No more wishy-washy liberal humanist feel-good close encounters with fancy harmonicas from outer space. Whoever they are, they're out to get us. Like the Shadow Empire, waging war on Babylon 5. And those Kazons with the bad complexions who seized control of *Voyager* and dumped Kate Mulgrew on a prehistoric pile of lava, among subverbalizing ape people, without Federation technology. And those gaseous insects called CHIGs against whom the marine cadets of *Space: Above & Beyond* waged total war every Sunday night on Fox. Not even to think about the alien usurpation of our very own

Social Security Administration by dozens of replicas of Roy Thinnes, an invader this time instead of an invadee, in the 1996 season finale of *The X-Files*. For awhile there TV sci-fi, like the rest of television, had seemed to preach some respect for difference—as if aliens were poor people, avant-garde artists, African-Americans or even gays. But we regressed in a hurry from Ray Bradbury to William S. Burroughs, from the chronicles of dreamy Martians to pulp-paranoid cosmologies according to which, one hundred thousand years ago in the Gobi desert, we had been attacked in our DNA by a black hole of red-haired Venusians, causing such mutations as monotheism, the Industrial Revolution, Communism, the CIA, hydrogen bombs and of course that "parasitic Other Half," *adult women*—the corrupters of Natural Man, creatures of the vampire Lilith as well as Ixtab, "the goddess of ropes and snares and sexual hanging."

The obvious explanation for the return of the bad-seed alien—of Triffids, Pods, Blobs and Body Snatchers—is that after the end of the Cold War we needed a brand-new implacable enemy and another Evil Empire on which to project our fearful fantasies. And, as always, the popular culture provided: man-eating dandelions, meteoric slimeballs, blood-sucking carrots, collectivized Bolshevik killer ants. We rely on sci-fi to extrapolate from the personal anxiety of *noir* to the generalized paranoia of dark satanic forces and species-devouring systems. But I wonder whether the bad news from outer space isn't also a variant of the current vogue for immigrant-bashing. After all: *illegal aliens*. From, of course: *third worlds*. Black holes and wet backs…The other day, before they suspended her again, Marge Schott, the owner of the Cincinnati Reds baseball team, was quoted as saying about Asian-Americans, "Well, I don't like when they come here, and stay so long, and then outdo our kids. That's not right." Nor is it liberal-humanist. The fault, dear Brutus, is not in ourselves, but in the stars, that we are underlings.

Crime and Punishment

Or CLOP, for Crime, Law, Order and Punishment. Never mind *noir*, which is basically a hairy situation you got your own self into more or less by accident or maybe for the easy money and the desktop sex with color-coded silk panties in a USA cable movie, but you always end up in a *noir* hurting so much you realize what Saul Bellow knew all along: women eat green salads and drink human blood. *Assume the position!*

After 30 years it makes no difference to our enjoyment of the great sagas by Chandler, Ross Macdonald, and others that the eternal Robin Hood should have got mixed up with Marx's angry young men and Tennyson's Galahad, and wound up in self-contradiction.
                                                    Jacques Barzun

One of these days, Hammer, I'm going to bust your gum-ball machine.
                        Special Prosecutor Barrington to Mike Hammer

> *It would have been grand if I could have waited for Beam
> to say, "Okay, kill him now," as my cue to move. But that only
> happens on the TV, where they also play a musical warning
> before you die.*
>
> Walter Mosley, *A Little Yellow Dog*

About what Americans did to the English language, Raymond Chandler was quoted as saying: "They've knocked over tombs and sneered at the dead, which is as it should be." He was English himself, a public-school boy educated in the classics, full of a schoolboy's ideals of good sportsmanship and Christian duty and the schoolboy's fear of women. How he ended up in Los Angeles—married to a woman seventeen years his senior—wearing white gloves, smoking a pipe and drinking himself to death at the portable typewriter where he invented Philip Marlowe as the template from which succeeding generations of hardboiled American private eyes, cracking wise and feeling mushy, would be minted, was the engaging subject of a cable television documentary, *Raymond Chandler: Murder He Wrote*, in 1995. Chandler was yakked about by Frank McShane, his intelligent biographer; and Robert Mitchum, one of several movie Marlowes; and James Ellroy and George V. Higgins, two of his hundreds of epigones. He was even impersonated by Robert Stephens, reading from the many letters he wrote at night after his invalid wife had gone to bed. And then there were the movie snippets, from *The Big Sleep*, *Farewell My Lovely* and *The Long Goodbye*, with Bogart, Mitchum, Dick Powell, James Garner and even Elliott Gould as Marlowe loners on the film *noir* range. We were spared any clips from the single-season ABC series, in which Philip Carey had been far too gussied up, and I was grateful. But also contemplative...

From the admiralty to the apricot ranch to the oil business to *Black Mask* to Billy Wilder, Marlowe was Chandler's alter ego—the man of action with "a coat, a hat, and a gun," pledged to "protect the innocent, guard the helpless, and destroy the wicked." What he said about Dashiell Hammett applied at least as much to Chandler himself: "Hammett gave murder back to the kind of people who commit it for reasons, not just to provide a corpse; and with the means at hand, not with hand-wrought dueling pistols, curare, and tropical fish." This was the Declaration of Independence of American detective fiction from the English jigsaw puzzle. But it also spoke to downward mobility, a lowering of class from Poe's declassed aristocrat Dupin, and Conan Doyle's coke-addicted scientist-fiddler Holmes, and such titled gentry as Wimsey, Appleby and Allyn, through genteel Father Browns, Hercule Poirots and Miss Marples, to the world-weariness of European bureaucrat cops like Maigret, Van der Valk and Martin Beck, unto revolutionary consciousness— the detective as stormbird (Hammett's Continental Op), or as St. Francis of Assisi (Chandler's Marlowe), or as shrink (Ross Macdonald's Lew Archer). "Democracy," wrote Ross Macdonald, "is as much a language as it is a place. If a man has suffered under a society of privilege, the American vernacular can serve him as a kind of passport to freedom and equality."

Macdonald's Archer novels got themselves adapted into a couple of Paul Newman movies, in which for some reason the detective was renamed "Harper," and an NBC series with Brian Keith so low on blood sugar that it lasted only six weeks in 1975. Actually, the best thing to happen to Macdonald on any screen was an ABC TV-movie in 1992, *Criminal Behavior*, based on his 1960 non-Archer novel *The Ferguson Affair*. A Mexican-American nurse from the Los Angeles barrio, on trial for the murder of a pawnbroker, is defended by an attorney whose investigation leads to the usual Macdonald mansion, occupied by the usual Macdonald multimillionaire, with the usual incest secret. (On television, defense attorneys, like newspaper reporters, have always been indistingishable from private eyes, whether they do their own legwork and intricate scams, or farm the sleuthing out to eager young investigators who are either hunky, as in *Perry Mason*, or African-American, as in *Matlock*.) The salient difference between novel and movie was that, in the novel, the defense attorney was a man; in the movie, she is Farrah Fawcett. And she gets off the second best line in TV-movie annals: *"At least your daughter didn't get pregnant while you were sleeping with her."* (The all-time best belongs to Phoebe Cates in *Lace: "Which one of you bitches is my mother?"*) Although I felt there were more than enough triple-cross plot twists, class-conflict overtones, race-related subtexts and bedpan revelations in these two hours alone to float three seasons of a feisty series, the public obviously disagreed.

As we speak, in the summer of 1996, there is not a single private-eye or defense attorney show anywhere on prime-time network television. Naturally, on cable or in syndication, we can get our fill of Rockford, Spenser, Magnum and Hammer reruns. On public TV, there are always Sherlock, Hercule and Joan Hickson; and, on A&E, Anna Lee and Cracker. But it still astonishes that the most popular and enduring mythic figure of America's pulp imagination is temporarily missing from the airwaves. (Temporarily, because new models are tooling up for the fall schedule.) From Boston Blackie through Richard Diamond to Martin Kane and Johnny Staccato, from Nero Wolfe through Charlie Chan to Barnaby Jones and Banacek, from Hardy Boys through Snoop Sisters to Thin Men, Saints and Equalizers, we have counted on some variation of the same smart-mouth gumshoe on the same mean streets, the last romantic in a corrupt world—an omelette of St. Francis, St. George and sweet-and-sour Parsifal; a mixed grill of Quixote, Galahad and Robin Hood; a submarine sandwich of vigilante, psychotherapist, John Rawls and killing machine.

Cop shows, we have to beat off with a billy club. This might worry me more if I imagined for a minute that a frightened nation so longs for a reassertion of authority that it has fallen in love with uniforms and handcuffs. But in one new cop show, *Pacific Blue*, they wear short pants and sissy helmets and ride around on bicycles, blowing whistles at baddies on the beach. A more likely explanation is that there hasn't been a smash-success private-eye series since *Murder, She Wrote*, which means there haven't been any copy cats, either. Perhaps, and this is my usual stretch, we no longer credit an individual's capacity to rectify so much that's so radically wrong with reality. (The paradigmatic mystery begins with a murder which is then reimagined backwards. Consequently, old scores are settled, satisfying eighteenth-century Enlightenment ideas about rationality and progress, by a hero who's sad, brave and eloquent on the subject of his own deductive powers, satisfying a nineteenth century need for romantic geniuses and long-winded arias like Tolstoy and Wagner, whose explications of why and how are twentieth-century empirical-positivist and whose transgressive behaviors are either existential or postmodern.) Or maybe we no longer believe in innocence, and so prefer the cops, because they always think that everybody's guilty, whereas private eyes and defense attorneys are paid to think the opposite.

Whatever: to take in some of the culture's dirty laundry and mythic slack, cop shows have incorporated and internalized many norms of the hardboiled and soft-hearted shamus, like class hatred, a consorting too gladly with lowlifes in the Alley of Temptation and, especially, a disdain for civil liberties. Contemporary cops are as scornful of legal niceties as the most impatient of traditional freelance dicks-for-hire. To a repertoire that already included a derisory attitude toward "reasonable cause," "excessive force" and the Miranda warning, they have added the P.I.'s encysted contempt for statutes on breaking and entering, in order to search and seize, as well as his sneerful take on the Bill of Rights as a manual for nitpicking.

Missing, alas, is the indignant heart.

Imagine—and what could be more serendipitous, democratic and postmodern than alphabet soup?—this: Ralph Bellamy, Brian Dennehy, John Cassavetes, Shaun Cassidy, William Conrad, Troy Donahue, Buddy Ebsen, Jeff Goldblum. Louis Gossett Jr., James Earl Jones, Stacy Keach, Brian Keith, Peter Lawford, Robert Loggia, Frank Lovejoy, Ray Milland, J. Carrol Naish, Robert Preston, Burt Reynolds, Wayne Rogers, Cesar Romero, Richard Roundtree, Ben Vereen, Robert Wagner, Jack Warden and Efrem Zimbalist Jr. have all been private eyes on TV series. While the list of female shamuses is much shorter, it includes the most wildly successful crime-stopping busybody in American TV history, Angela Lansbury, as well as Anne Francis as *Honey West*, Pamela Sue Martin as *Nancy Drew*, Helen Hayes, Kate Mulgrew, Mildred Natwick, Cybill Shepherd, Efrem's daughter Stephanie and half a dozen Charlie's Angels. Not all of these actors have impersonated people who *describe* themselves as gumshoes. Besides defense attorneys and newspaper reporters, as if fronting for the CIA, they have been mystery novelists, boat captains, insurance investigators, jazz musicians, diplomatic couriers, anthropologists, restaurateurs, professional gamblers, billionaires, bounty hunters, burglars and beach bums. And while most have pretended to sleuth in New York or L.A., they aren't strangers to Beacon Hill, Miami Beach, Bourbon Street, Atlantic City, San Francisco, San Diego, Chicago, Houston and Hawaii. Nor are they always fleet of foot, lean of limb, bright-eyed and bushy-browed: As *Cannon*, for instance, William Conrad was fat; as *Longstreet*, James Franciscus was blind; as *Ironside*, Raymond Burr was wheelchair-bound; as *Mike Hammer*, Stacy Keach ran like Roseanne Barr; as *Harry-O*, David Janssen couldn't smile. They're better dressed than they used to be back in the *Black Mask* days when peepers were presumed to descend from Philoctetes, the Greek warrior-hero who smelled so bad from a festering wound that they only let him off his island into polite company when they needed his bow and arrows to stick their many enemies. This gentrification of genre *does* worry me. One of *Moonlighting*'s ingratiating attributes was the seediness of Bruce Willis. *English* detectives are dandies. An *American* shamus should be downwardly mobile. Only *pimps* dress up.

But the job, usually a mission, sometimes a hobby, remains the same. Unless his client is a beautiful broad, in which case she is the predator and he's the prey, the P.I. is a social worker with a code of honor and a gun. The poor and the weak, or maybe a relative, need help against the rich and violent—neighborhood bullies, organized criminals, corporate goons, ministries of fear, drug cartels, death squads and global conspiracies of unrepentant Nazis, renegade KGB or Syrian-sponsored terrorists—and the cops are unbelieving, or too busy, or hamstrung by constitutional quibbles. Tenants vs. landlords and sheep vs. wolves: It is necessary for our huddled masses to have Archers and Spades to rely on so that they won't band together, start a book club or a union or a revolution and lean themselves on their oppressors. By definition, little people are *amateurs*. If you've ever wondered why our urban oppressed, standing dispirited or jobless on a sidewalk of an inclement evening, don't stone the smoky windows and slash the radial tires and the thick throats of the chauffeurs at the steering wheels of the stretch limos of the resting classes out for an air-conditioned slum, it's because they are waiting for Peter Gunn or Father Dowling, for Remington Steele or a Shaft. The public may avert its gaze; a private eye will weep for you. Usually, he comes equipped with a gum-snapping secretary from the ranks of the proletariat, devoted and earthy. Almost always, at least on television, he's got a buddy on the local police force, to run a license plate or interference for him. Like a country-and-western song, he's been there. Like a mutt, he is loyal to who feeds him. Like a nineteenth-century novelist, he is also *curious*, and will bring back the grubby tidings of the silent family, the stonewalling organization, the clever racket, the ingenious frame and the guilty cover-up—and name names before he shoots them.

Of course, Rockford kept his gun in a cookie jar, and only used it when he absolutely had to. Whereas Hammer never went anywhere without his "Betsy," an odd name for a phallic symbol unless you're into gender-bending, which Mike wasn't, though Betsy might have been. I mention these golden oldies not only because both came back for TV movies in the nineties, after the new P.I. shows all crapped out, but because they represent extremes of *strapped*. All dicks are, like cops and cowboys, whereas reporters and lawyers behaving like dicks generally aren't. I see no point in discussing Steve McQueen's sawed-off carbine or William Shatner's phaser set to stun.

Private Eye, a 1987 Anthony Yerkovich series on Friday nights on NBC, ought to have been a genre classic. Creator-writer-executive-producer Yerkovich, who learned his crime and punishment from Jesuits at Georgetown before writing thirty-five episodes of *Hill Street Blues* and the super-slick two-hour pilot for *Miami Vice*, had the tools, the pedigree and the concept. His year was 1956, in a corrupt and dreamy paranoid-mindscape Los Angeles, back when Elvis was frightening American mothers, speed-freak disk jockeys demanded payola, the mob had moved in on the recording industry and most cops were on the take. One cop not taking was Jack Cleary, though everybody thought he was, which was why he was off the force and deep in the bottle: "I used to feel at home in the world, surrounded by things I believed in. Now—I don't know what I feel anymore." When his private-eye big brother, Nick, was blown away in the pilot, Jack got mad and even. With the help of a duck-tailed muscle-boy (Josh Brolin), a baby-doll secretary (Lisa Jane Persky) and a small arsenal, he wasted Sunset Strip. It didn't make him feel better, but the former flatfoot decided to fill his brother's gumshoes anyway.

To these basics *Private Eye* added a gloss of Joe Jackson's cool, almost cryogenic jazz score, with time out for hophead rock and Patti Page jokes; slo-mo deadfalls, silhouette sex, close-ups of nostrils, "Ask me if I care" bombastics and a generally overripe atmosphere as if plums were rotting in the smog bowl. "Film *noir* and German Expressionism," Yerkovich explained, at least laughing when he said it. These TV young gun hotshots—Steven Bochco, Michael Mann, David E. Kelley—all talk a glib grad-school patter. For years, they've read treatments instead of novels, but they remember how. For a nightmare episode in a red-light zone, Tony Yerkovich built a Fritz Lang set: "forced perspective—two-dimensional chiaroscuro." He'd bury a dead rocker in a '57 Chevy, while Duane Eddy played guitar. Other installments were devoted to Hollywood's ripping off of black R&B artists; corrupt entertainment unions; the usual southern California landgrab; managers of mob-controlled nightclubs who wound up drinking toxic waste; scandal-and-slander magazines like *Confidential* and the whole fifties blackmail scene. "It's different now," said Yerkovich. "You go on Donahue and tell everybody you're a heroin addict and a child molester." He wanted, through his private eye, to film the fifties as a seedbed of changes: Ike's torpor, the start of the civil rights movement, teenagers with their own music finding power as "a consumer identity group," the Hula Hoop and Bomb. He was after "a city of the imagination—the Los Angeles of Nathanael West and Joan Didion." *Private Eye* should have worked. It lasted four months. The public hated it. Especially, the public hated Michael Woods as Jack Cleary, so stiff he could have been a '57 Chevy. By blaming an actor instead of questioning the concept, TV would waste another decade trying to confect a private eye, *any* private eye, the masses might *like*: priests (Tom Bosley in *Father Dowling*), bounty hunters (John Schneider and Paul Rodriguez in *Grand Slam*), ex-cons (James Earl Jones in *Gabriel's Fire* and D.W. Moffett in *Palace Guard*), ex-cops turned radio talk-show hosts (Gary Cole in *Midnight Caller*), ex-rock stars playing former studio security chiefs (Glenn Frey in *South of Sunset*), ex-gangbangers turned martial-arts vigilantes (*Knightwatch*), ex-surfers become U.S. congressmen in time to thwart a coup d'etats in a Latin countries with nose candy problems (William Katt in *Top of the Hill*), jive ass quick-change artists (Mario Van Peebles in *Sonny Spoon*), psychiatrists (Brian Dennehy in *Birdland*, who solved murders by interpreting dreams), psychologists (Tim Matheson in *Mood Indigo*, who blamed himself for his wife's violent death), anthropologists (Louis Gossett Jr. in *Gideon Oliver*, taking on Son of Sam satanists and Chinatown tongs), loafing-around-the-house-boat Travis McGee wannabees (Burt Reynolds in *B.L. Stryker*), bankrupt Palm Beach playboys (Larry J.R. Ewing Hagman in *Staying Afloat*), professional gamblers (Kenny Rogers) and professional adolescents (Richard Grieco).

So desperate were they that they even tried some more women: Ex-*Angel* Jaclyn Smith as a Harvard-educated San Francisco investment counsellor whose *Christine Cromwell* was forever stumbling over corpses that had to be explained by one or another of her three stepfathers, the cop (Richard Bradford), the shrink

(Theodore Bikel) or the sawbones (Mel Ferrer); ex-*Moonlighter* Cybill Shepherd searching in *Stormy Weathers* for an Italian count last seen in 1976 in a black revolutionary commune and finding instead high art, hard drugs, Doberman pinchers and mugger-nuns; ex-poster child for victimized womanhood in social-problem docudramas Mare Winningham, pretending in *Love and Lies* to be a honkytonk Houston good-time girl so she can undercover private-eyeball a creepy survivalist who hobbies in offing old folks; ex-witch Elizabeth Montgomery as Miami *Herald* crime reporter Edna Buchanan, in constant trouble with her computer, her cat, her cellular phone, her objectivity and love-life; and former vamp Victoria Principal as the mayor of Albuquerque, New Mexico, in *Sparks: The Price of Passion*, taking on macho cops, bought politicians, serial killers and mob-connected real-estate swindlers in a Sunbelt all the more implausible for the mystifying presence of a ziplipped Elaine Stritch.

Nothing worked, and maybe it shouldn't have, no matter how many brothel madams, Mafia dons, corrupt pols, child abusing serial killers and swinging poolsharp nuns we met in however many *Miami Vice*–Music Video–Post-Impressionist–Post-All Bran–Surreal Smear–Arty Deco Evil–Designer Void *mise en scenes*. It's not as if they looked terribly hard for a smart-mouth feminist gumshoe worthy of being serialized, or they would have discovered the detective novels of Linda Barnes, Susan Dunlap, Sue Grafton, Laurie R. King, Lia Matera, Marcia Muller, Sandra Scoppotone or Jill Smith. (After what Kathleen Turner did to V.I. Warshawski on the big screen, Sara Paretsky would probably die for a TV series with anybody else.) And if they were afraid of women, why not Jon Katz (the suburban detective), Tony Hillerman (the Navajo detective), or, gasp, Joseph Hansen (the gay detective), not to mention Lawrence Block, Ross Thomas and David Handler's Stewart Hoag, a ghostwriter around whom bodies fall like dominos. After what Denzel Washington did for Easy Rawlins on the big screen, Walter Mosley doesn't need TV, but Barbara Neeley's Blanche White novels would make a subversive series: she's a *maid*. Why hasn't there been an adaptation by anybody anywhere of the Burke novels by Andrew Vachs, each set in an urban underground as sordid as a sewer, "in the freak pipeline under the city," where children are pimped as prostitutes or chopped up and sold as spare parts, a kidney here and a liver there, in the hospital transplant racket? Or the Zen mysteries of Janwillem van de Wettering, in which the slave trade, the Holocaust, colonialism and psychoanalysis meet probability theory, uncertainty principle, random terrifying chance and a turtle? For that matter, steadfast stalwarts of modernism like Jorge Luis Borges, Italo Calvino and Stanislaw Lem all tried their sleight of hand at crime fiction sendups, riffs on causality. Many years ago, when I was an insolent pup at Pacifica radio in Berkeley, I informed Anthony Boucher: "Ross Macdonald married Freud to the detective novel!" Boucher, who for three decades had written the weekly "Criminals at Large" column for *The New York Times Book Review*, sighed back at me from his built-in precipice. "*The Brothers Karamazov?*" he suggested.

And during this same enduring mini-era of indifference and disdain for underdogs and those who care about them, defense attorneys were also a washout. It's a long and depressing casualty list, from a single season of *Against the Law* on Fox in 1990, with Michael O'Keefe as the furious maverick Simon MacHeath, bullying Boston judges on behalf of a stand-up comic arrested on obscenity, a young woman who had been date-raped, a college basketball player whose scholarship was revoked after a knee injury, and the victims of hospital negligence, to a single season of *The Client* on CBS in 1995, with JoBeth Williams as Reggie Love, an Atlanta family-court lawyer, a recovering alcoholic, a surrogate mother with the need to nurture, and an avenging angel of lost children everywhere. Not even the executive producer Steven Bochco's magic could save *Murder One* from disastrous ratings in its first semester and we will see if it survives without the bald-is-beautiful Daniel Benzali, whose scruple and pride it was to defend *anybody*: "It civilizes *us*," he explained, "to treat them as innocent." In retrospect—the safest perspective from which to slap meanings on a TV series like adhesive plasters—it seems clear that Bochco's *L.A. Law* succeeded for close to a decade because of its Moog synthesizing of big money, hard bodies and soap shenanigans, its dwarf tossing and Venus butterfly sex jokes, almost in spite of courtroom deliberations on race quotas, "outing" and AIDS. It is also possible that by the end of *L.A. Law*'s long and lurid run, most of America held most private-practice lawyers in contempt.

Shannon's Deal seemed to have everything going for it in April 1990: Jamie Sheridan as a downwardly mobile Philadelphia lawyer with a gambling problem; Elizabeth Peña as the client who couldn't pay him and so signed on as his secretary; original scripts by John Sayles; original music by Wynton Marsalis; Alan Dershowitz as a legal consultant; and a rip-snorting two-hour pilot involving—I mean, how fanciful can TV get?—a rightwing movement called the Guardians of Liberty in bed with various unnamed clandestine government agencies to finance the purchase of guns and bombs for various unnamed Latin American freedom-fighters, by the sale of cocaine. Shannon later took on cases to do with anything from country-and-western music to corporate smoothies who had bankrupted a dockworkers' pension fund. NBC at first refused to pick up the series that fall, then rushed it back into production the following spring, then lost it somewhere during the summer. Even so, it lasted longer than *Eddie Dodd*, a series spin-off on ABC from the James Woods *True Believer* movie, with Treat Williams as a sixties radical lawyer still trying to win impossible cases in the nineties. And longer than *The Wright Verdicts* on CBS, with Tom Conti as a British-born and Shakespeare-quoting New York criminal lawyer who found himself, with his gambling-addicted private investigator Margaret Colin, in the middle of cases involving female law students, gay Columbia professors, sexual harassment, animal rights, stolen sperm and synthetic heroin. And longer than *The Antagonists* with Lauren Holly for the prosecution and David Andrews for the defense, who were more interested in each other than they were in getting a conviction or a fee. With Sharon Gless as a public defender, talking to her therapist about her midlife crises and worrying in and out of court about rape, abortion, homelessness, due process, perjury and the privileges of her own socioeconomic class, *The Trials of Rosie O'Neill* limped along for parts of two different TV seasons, in the spring of 1990 and the fall of 1991, before it got the unforgiving ax. *Sweet Justice* lasted longest, one whole season spread over two, with Cicely Tyson as the senior partner in a public interest legal commune and Melissa Gilbert as her newest recruit to unpopular causes like a black ballplayer who sues a college for failing to teach him how to read, a young white woman who sues a military academy for refusing to admit her, and a wrong-side-of-the-tracks mother who wants custody of her child returned to her from an abusive father's "fine Southern family."

We seemed more sympathetic to claims of innocence and lawyers who chose to believe them if both claims and lawyers were transferred to the distant past and some other America safely hazy in the recollection. A couple of made-for-TV movies starring Walter Matthau as Harmon Cobb, an underemployed and down-at-the-heels Colorado lawyer in the 1940s, were relatively popular in spite of the fact that, for Cobb, considerations of individual rights and social justice were less a vestigial twitch of the nostalgia gland than the normal respiration of intelligence. In *The Incident* (1990), Harry Morgan as a visiting federal judge first found Walter conveniently next-door to a German prisoners-of-war camp in Lincoln Bluff in 1943. One of the prisoners, Peter Firth, had been accused of murdering the town's popular doctor, Barnard Hughes. Harry needed someone to defend him at a show trial. Hunched, hangdog and potato-faced, a growly bear, a whole sagging geography of disappointments and, of course, an American icon, Matthau as Cobb would discover in himself a saving remnant of Clarence Darrow and pass it on to a Harvard prosecutor, a military court and the hostile citizens of his own home town. After which, in *Against Her Will: An Incident in Baltimore* (1992), he had mysteriously relocated to Maryland, which state he promptly sued to liberate a young Greek widow from a mental hospital where she'd been subject to such psychiatric frauds as insulin-shock and electro-convulsive therapy, and forced to live in a coal bin. Since the state of Maryland in 1944, under a "sovereign immunity" clause of English Common Law, would not permit itself to be sued, we learned something about Thomas à Becket and Henry II as well as Bedlam.

I'd like to think these movies did okay on CBS because there was still an audience out there for courtoom dramas in which the very scruples that distinguish our legal system from Hitler's or Stalin's could be celebrated—instead of a mob in a permanent rage at pettifogging advocates, hair-splitting judges, bleeding-heart social workers, do-good civil libertarians and other professional tear ducts; a gray wall of rant waiting to be written on by rogue cops, samurai militia men and citizen vigilantes. I'd like to think so because Matthau looks like and reminds me of my own uncle, also a lawyer, who willed me his wristwatch. I grew up every other summer in my uncle's narrow Georgetown house, in his breakfast nook, decoding the morning newspapers like I.F. Stone; in his library, reading the great books; in his garden, hearing about his student days at the University of Texas, his bohemian days in New

Orleans with the National Labor Relations Board and his judge advocate days in Tokyo, defending Japanese accused of war crimes; the inside stories on Big Oil, Southern racism, bought congressmen, Drew Pearson, Chiang Kai-shek, and unions in trouble. To borrow an image from geometry, for my uncle—as for Clarence Darrow, Sam Ervin and Thurgood Marshall—the law was a fulcrum, a point of rest between magnitudes. On these magnitudes, the fulcrum imposed a necessary relationship, and a governing principle. The law was likewise balance and proportion. I live now in my own narrow house in Manhattan, and always wear my uncle's wristwatch. Without him, I wouldn't know the time of day.

But probably we watched those TV movies not because we liked balance and proportion; we just liked Walter Matthau. Surfing for an adrenaline fix, we no longer care about the rights of the accused as much as E.G. Marshall or even Harry Hamlin used to. Spending so much time with our heads in sitcoms, where Pillsbury Doughboys male-bond and Wonderbread Barbies look for a safe-sex date and nothing will ever happen in a Chinese restaurant, we are too busy even to be *curious* about the invisible lives of those enigmatic classes who aren't on e-mail and don't have a website, nor about the invisible hand that cuffs them. The only detectives acceptable to the mass audience in the last decade, besides Jessica, have been revivals of retreads: Robert Urich comes back as *Spenser* in several cable movies with several different Susan Silvermans, to track down a runaway teen in Boston's "Combat Zone," and bust the porn-and-prostitution ring that ran off with her; to solve the mysterious murder and castration of a newspaper reporter by Colombian drug-dealers in Wheaton, Massachusetts; to bring to Canadian justice, in surprising Toronto, a cadre of terrorists who assassinate African dignitaries and counterfeit American credit cards. Stefanie Powers and Robert Wagner come back as *Hart to Hart*, their low-cal Nick and Nora impersonation, a bit long in the capped teeth, maybe, for the trademark petfood billing and cooing, but resourceful enough to outwit Stepford citizens of a sinister hicksville like Roddy McDowall and Howard Keel, and to top-hat and soft-shoe their way through a murderous Broadway musical in which Jack the Ripper is a battered wife. Even Jameson Parker and Gerald McRaney return, as *Simon & Simon*, that Odd Couple sibling rivalry, to spend a whole two TV movie hours looking for a missing yacht and a missing mother, while telling cuckold and dental-floss jokes.

Whereas Rob Estes—Rob Estes?—well, when they dug up Mike Hammer for a network movie, he was no longer Stacy Keach, the toughest of chip-on-the-shoulder cookies, but the slick Rob Estes, from *Silk Stalkings*, in pastel Miami instead of mean Manhattan, with Pamela (*Baywatch*) Anderson all wrong as Velda and Dr. Joyce Brothers ridiculous on a skateboard. Give Dick Van Dyke credit for managing three marginal seasons as the senior citizen/doctor-detective in *Diagnosis: Murder*. Bill Cosby didn't even last till Christmas as a retired police forensics pathologist for whom Rita Moreno hardboiled chicken soup.

This leaves *The Rockford Files*. When Jim Garner returned in November 1994 for a projected series of six *Rockford* TV movies, he brought with him Joe Santos as Dennis, his pet cop, and Stuart Margolin as Angel, his pet grievance, and the usual mob connections, for old time's sake, and the Pontiac Firebird, needing some body work. But otherwise, they didn't trust their primal stuff. Of course, Jimbo himself was 66 years old, not an age to fall off cliffs with a pair of gunsels after having been stuffed in a trunk with Joanna Cassidy, the high-priced lawyer he seemed to have married and then divorced since last we saw him, perhaps on the rebound from Kathryn Harrold, the blind psychologist who did him wrong and broke my heart in 1980. So a certain stiff decorum was in order. But you are never too old to scam, which is always what he did best anyway, besides talking his way into worse jams and getting beat up on, which maybe accounted for the lopsided grin, in a formula that varied as seldom as Kabuki theatre or kosher circumcision. Instead of scamming, however, the iconic antidetective in *I Love L.A.* was merely put upon, *afflicted*, as he explains, with "everything but a plague of locusts." After having had enough time off for two separate cycles of cell-regeneration, he was hauled on stage not to act, but to *react*, blankly incredulous, to a world made out of Court TV and tabloid roadkill and plot summaries of leftover *Law & Order* episodes. Bad enough they had to include the Rodney King riots and a killer fire come down from the Hollywood hills; they also threw in the Northridge earthquake. And then, as if afraid our affections were too attentuated to sit still for anything less than *everything*, they were so desperate as to stuff the holes in their heads with knockoffs of the Marilyn Monroe–Joe DiMaggio sob story, with thinly disguised plagiarisms of O.J. and the Menendez brothers and even a nod to the McMartin Preschool case.

No wonder Rockford was disgusted. No wonder he was trying to sell his trailor, intending to leave town forever for some Sunset City where he could play Liar's Poker with Sam Spade and Shane. Asked, "What's wrong with L.A.?" Jimbo replied: "The quality of life." And then, after a pause: "There *isn't* any." For a private eye to have used up L.A. is mythically equivalent to a cowboy's using up West. There's nowhere left to go except Hawaii, where Magnum's all wet, or Deep Space Nine, where they make you wear a uniform. Our heroes have lost interest in us. At least cops have to stay put; only their wives leave.

Mortal man is a broomstick [which] raiseth a mighty Dust
where there was none before; sharing deeply all the while in
the very same pollution he pretends to sweep away.

Jonathan Swift

Members of a secret society with a code of silence, a centurion brotherhood, the thin blue line between solid citizens and savage tribes, cops can fall off wagons; nap in patrol cars; moonlight as bouncers and bodyguards; sleep with a partner, a prostitute, or even a perp; break and enter and search and seize; rough up suspects; carry an extra "throwaway" weapon, strapped to a dainty ankle, in case a bust looks less than righteous; plant evidence; lie on the witness stand; cover for a corrupt colleague; cross dress; eat free doughnuts when they are hungry and their own guns when the mean streets meet their dead end behind eyes that have seen too much. What cops are not permitted to do, at least on television, is burst into song.

From the critical and popular reaction to *Cop Rock* in September 1990, you might imagine Steven Bochco had done to the flatfoot hour what Roseanne Barr had done to the National Anthem: the unspeakable to the unsingable. Maybe three of us disagreed. Why shouldn't cops have a song in their heart? So they come down hard on a crackhouse and the street people segue from mo-fo into a menacing rap. So the mayor of Los Angeles, looking under her twenty pounds of latex a lot like Maggie Thatcher, accepts a bribe and Hello-Dollys on her desktop. So it's gospel music to a judge's ears when a jury delivers a guilty verdict on some pond scum. If the Randy Newman ballads for *Cop Rock*'s pilot were less electric than these showstoppers, they hurt more. Bullied as we've been for years by the drumbeat and piano-roll, rocked, jazzed and Mooged to cue up an emotion the actors otherwise can't quite manage, what's *wrong* with a song-and-dance? Stephen Sondheim does it all the time when he decides he would rather be sung than said. Why not Steven Bochco? Why let commercials have all the fun? How come it never before occurred to anybody else that a police lineup is like a chorus-line audition? Lapsing into the lyrical also seems like an agreeable substitute for interior monologues, which have seldom worked on television. (Even Glenda Jackson embarrassed herself in Eugene O'Neill.) On Broadway, we pay $75 a pop for *The Three-Penny Opera* with Sting. *West Side Story* was almost as mean, and *Sweeney Todd* a whole lot bloodier than *Cop Rock*. Cowboys have been singing at least since *Oklahoma*. In *Evita*, every-body cried for Argentina. Where there's *Hair*, there is also *Grease*. Remember what Handel did to *The Messiah*. On British television, we got *Rock Follies*, *Pennies from Heaven* and *The Singing Detective*. (Bochco claims he'd been thinking about a musical *Hill Street* long before he finally saw Dennis Potter's *Singing Detective*.) On American television, the best we could manage was a *Singing Nun*. Not only would many a talk show and miniseries improve as musicals, but in my opinion *L.A. Law* would have lasted another decade if Gilbert and Sullivan had been available.

But ABC cancelled *Cop Rock* two months into its expensive run—because of the production numbers, each episode cost a third again as much as an ordinary hour of dramatic television—while Bochco was trying to talk Billy Joel into volunteering five new songs. So we can have cops as famous as Elvis (*Kojak* and *Columbo*), cops who taught European intellectuals everything they think they know about American culture (*Starsky and Hutch*), cops who are independently wealthy (Gene Barry in *Burke's Law*), cops with pet cockatoos (Robert Blake in *Baretta*), cops who smoke pipes (Jack Palance in *Bronk*), cops who are also vigilantes (*Nasty Boys* and *The Hat Squad*), cops from other planets (Eric Pierpoint or Maryam d'Abo in *Alien Nation* or *Something Is Out There*), cops who are also psychos (Miguel Ferrer in *Broken Badges* and, possibly,

Fred Dryer in *Hunter*), cops who were really cops before becoming actors who played cops (Dennis Farina in *Crime Story*), cops in helicopters (James Farentino in *Blue Thunder*), pigs on hogs (Broderick Crawford in *Highway Patrol*, Erik Estrada in *CHiPS*), and law enforcement officers who are not only female (Jessica Walters in *Amy Prentiss*, Rachel Ticotin in *Crime and Punishment*, Brenda Vaccaro in *Dear Detective*, Teresa Graves in *Get Christie Love*, Betty Thomas and Mimi Kuzyk in *Hill Street*, Melissa Leo and Isabella Hoffman in *Homicide*, Stepfanie Kramer in *Hunter*, Lindsay Wagner in *Jessie*, Jamie Rose in *Lady Blue*, Kathyrn Harrold in *MacGruder and Loud*, Olivia Brown and Saundra Santiago in *Miami Vice*, Peggy Lipton in *Mod Squad*, Amy Brennerman in *N.Y.P.D. Blue*, Lauren Holly in *Picket Fences*, Angie Dickinson in *Police Woman*, Kate Jackson in *The Rookies*, Mitzi Kapture in *Silk Stalkings*, Heather Locklear in *T.J. Hooker*, and Karen Sillas in *Under Suspicion*), but who can also be counted on to subscribe to *Ms.* magazine (Sharon Gless and Tyne Daly in *Cagney & Lacey*). While female TV cops have to look good in the swimsuit issue, just about any American male, ecto-, endo-or mesomorphic, will do—John Ashton, Lloyd Bridges, Raymond Burr, Carroll O'Connor, Michael Douglas, Johnny Depp, George Dzundza, Peter Falk, Judd Hirsch, Rock Hudson, James Earl Jones, Hal Linden, Tony Lo Bianco, Karl Malden, Lee Marvin, Don Meredith, Pat Morita, Ken Olin, Telly Savalas, William Shatner, Paul Sorvino, Ben Vereen, Clint Walker and Jack Webb. Male plumage is in fact one of the joys of syndicated reruns, transcending vagaries of fashion to approach anthropology or archaeology. Nehru jackets, psychedelic ties, plaid pants and bell bottoms signify, as if in the disco seventies cops were undercover golfers. And *sideburns*...In his social history of fin-de-siècle Vienna, *A Nervous Splendor*, one of Frederic Morton's nice conceits was to use the rising price of sugar (a Sacher torte: *mit Schlag*) as a metaphor for the rising tide of anxiety (twelve-tone music, psychoanalysis, kinky Klimt, blood in the strudel and waltzing jackboots). Think of sideburns as a hairy equivalent of this intellectual confectionary index.

Just don't sing. (On the beat, in the dark, maybe a whistle.) The designated singer on cop shows is the snitch. Not much has been written on this subject, nor will I waste your time with a dilation on the comparative body languages of the snitch on *Night Heat* vs. the snitch on *Miami Vice*. But the snitch is the interface between

CLOPs and RUBBERs (rotten, underworld, blackmail, bestiality, eczema and randomness). Or the O-ring. Or the Mac mouse. I have written elsewhere about what I called the *Tequila Sunrise* paradigm, in which a Michelle Pfeiffer is the go-between, trampoline, surrogate, Chinese finger-puzzle and universal joint permitting Kurt Russell and Mel Gibson to go to bed with each other while pretending that they're not—the same role that Judith Campbell Exner played for Jack Kennedy, Frank Sinatra and Sam Giancana (and Marilyn Monroe played for Joe DiMaggio, Arthur Miller and Norman Mailer, as well as Jack and Bobby). So in the dialectic of law and disorder, snitching makes possible a Gnostic transaction between light and night. More often than not it involves either wearing a wire or copping a plea. Obviously, wire-wearing (a sacrificial goatishness) and plea-bargaining (a trading in futures on the guilt exchange) are forms of erotic bondage. But they are also fractals from which we intuit the bigger picture of chaos theory and its pecking order.

In the pecking law-and-order, cops hate the shamus below them and the brass above. And even more than they resent the brass, politically ambitious prosecutors, grandstanding mayors and busybody city councils, cops despise (on roughly this ascending scale) the FBI, the DEA, the CIA, the vampire media, diplomatic immunity and the Witness Protection Program. Except on *Miami Vice*, know-it-all feds are better dressed and better paid than beat cops or even homicide detectives. Each disinforming and counter-intelligent agency is empowered to throw around its weight and its press clippings and its glamourpuss connections; to seize jurisdiction of unusual cases, snatch exotic suspects from a precinct's custody and, between ritual incantations of "national security," barter a deal for the greater glory of this week's task force, this month's holy war on drugs and Arabs, and next year's wedge of the budget pie. In *Wiseguy*, the Department of Justice got itself a PR break so long as Ken Wahl as Vinnie Terranova believed his under-cover-ups made a difference in the Manichean struggle against organized crime and international drug trafficking; but he went straight to the hospital with a hand-held rocket launcher on finding out that he'd helped engineer a CIA coup. Briefly, Friday nights on Fox, the DEA had its own cinema verité series conveniently called *DEA*, and the hotshots may have been heroes to themselves as they took on the coke-smuggling Corderas of

Ecuador and their swinish German aide de camp, but the rest of us had seen so many cop shows in which federally-mandated drug-busters sold out for bags of laundered money that, in droves, we didn't watch. In the only TV movie ever devoted to investigators for the IRS, *In the Line of Duty: Kidnapped*, Dabney Coleman used his computer to identify rich lawyers with vulnerable young sons he could snatch and ransom.

On cop shows, the Know-It-Alls are also Fuck-Ups. Think how far the FBI has fallen in public esteem from the fifties, with Richard Conte in *I Led Three Lives*, and the sixties and early seventies, with Efrem Zimbalist Jr. in *The FBI* on Garrison State ramparts watch duty against the godless pinkos, organized Italians and radical teenyboppers; to the late eighties, with Robert Loggia in *Mancuso*, bossed by "a combination of Howdy Doody and Machiavelli," furious about Ollie North and Chappaquiddick and ashamed of his own agency for bugging Martin Luther King Jr; to the nineties, with Kyle MacLachlan in *Twin Peaks* talking to fir trees and the Tibetan Book of the Dead, and David Duchovny in *The X-Files*, at least as suspicious of his own superiors as he is of Alien Sperminators. Adumbrate our lower regard for spooks since the sixties and seventies—with Patrick McGoohan in *Secret Agent*, Robert Culp and Bill Cosby in *I Spy*, Robert Vaughn and David McCallum in *The Man from U.N.C.L.E.*, Peter Graves, Barbara Bain and Martin Landau in *Mission: Impossible*, or even Don Adams and Barbara Feldon in *Get Smart*—in the light of what we learned in the eighties from Bill Casey's Iran-Contra sitcom.

(That the FBI should have spent so much time worrying about Dr. King's sex life instead of J. Edgar Hoover's, couldn't find an Abbie Hoffman in front of its computerized nose, and teamed up with a trigger-happy SWAT team at Ruby Ridge and the Alcohol, Tobacco and Firearms fire-bombers at Waco, perhaps contributed to our disenchantment. That the CIA had been opening the mail, tapping the phones and spying on thousands of Americans for years, as well as performing LSD mind-control experiments on human guinea pigs, plotting with the Mafia's help to assassinate foreign leaders, and always the last to know about North Korea invading the South, the British, French and Israelis invading the Suez Canal, Sputnik's launching, missiles in Cuba, a Yom Kippur war, the Ayatollah, and the collapse of the nonprofit police states of Eastern Europe perhaps accounts for our growing suspicion that what the agency's secret sharers and underground men had really been up to in their Langley "wilderness of mirrors" with their covers, fronts, doubles, moles and coded discourse, was writing Norman Mailer novels. While we await the Aldrich Ames miniseries, we can gladly construe the 1994 return of *I Spy* as a TV movie in which Culp and Cosby end up strapped down, back-to-back and naked, in heavy Austro-Hungarian Empire chairs—thus fulfilling the Huck (Jim)–Ishmael (Queequeg)–Natty Bumppo (Chingachgook)–homoerotic–miscegenated psychosexual subtext of the original series back when we still Leslie A. Fiedlered while the Cold War burned. Or we can pay to see the Hollywood version of *Mission: Impossible*, in which the meticulous preparation and split-second timing of the original series, as IMF perfected its weekly sting at the expense of yet another gray little podunk of a foreign country with sex-crazed communists in charge, is jettisoned for a chewing-gum bomb, a laptop computer, whirlybirds, laser lights and a Tom Cruise missile on a one-man rampage to avenge the slaughter of his comrades, all of whom turn out to have been wasted by his own intelligence-agency boss. This movie's self-destructing message: Instead of teamwork, *trust nobody*.)

Compared with the high-tech crimes and misdemeanors at law enforcement's fat-cat level, the mean-street litterbox looks like a day-care center, and our local cops, however occasionally raunchy, bent, excessive or stress-crazed, are avatars of a guardian god. *White people still love cops.* Behind the razor-wired walls and security cameras of our suburban enclaves, inside our triple-locked and computer-coded home entertainment centers, lost in lurid media-scapes of abduction and dismemberment, we rely on them to die for us. As in this amazing country there are cable television channels entirely pledged to food, weather, cartoons and shopping, there is also a cop channel and a police state of mind. It's just that we must customize it for ourselves, as we program our digital five-tray compact-disc players, with a log of listings and a remote control. Somewhere in the past, a wise old head will be teaching his hot-tempered younger partner how to navigate *The Naked City*. Somewhere in the future, the telepaths and cyborgs sort through the postapocalyptic rubble or hack into the data havens of the crimelord matrix. Always in the now, the thin blue line is bleeding and the New Centurions doubt Rome.

Because, as cop shows see it, the big picture is that chaos theory is now in charge. Peace of mind is a losing cause, and so perhaps is a civil society. The consolations of *Columbo* are closing down on us. Peter Falk, in his iconic raincoat, chewing his iconic cigar, had always unriddled, explained and *solved* his cases, more like a private eye than a cop, and more like New York than Los Angeles, in a ceremony as tyrannically stylized as a performance of Cambodian dancers. Almost invariably, the villainous masterminds he'd outsmart—Patrick McGoohan, Robert Vaughn, John Cassavetes, Jack Cassidy, Anthony Andrews etc.—were wealthy or well-born, seigneurial creatures of twisted hubris. Columbo was their natural nemesis: peasant wit versus princely privilege. And if we happened not to be into the prurient details of class animus, we could think of him instead as either the perfect child of Enlightenment rationality, or—so immemorial are the satisfactions of the form—a reincarnation of Hanuman, the red-faced monkey chief of Hindu mythology, the son of the wind god and a nymph, the Ramayana trickster and grammarian who saved Sita from the demon Ravana, about whom Octavio Paz wrote essays and Maxine Hong Kingston wrote a novel. But in the contemporary cop show, villainy is free-floating and entropic, a virus or a conspiracy or a Mongol horde.

Maybe this is why the camera gets jumpier every season—as if on the verge of a nervous breakdown from all it must look at. In *Inside Prime Time*, Todd Gitlin argued that *Hill Street Blues* was really all about "the crisis of liberalism." Certainly it is hard to imagine better role models for the liberalized, sensitized and traumatized eighties man-with-feelings than Frank Furillo and Henry Goldblume, both as alert to the wounds of race and class and gender as a card-carrying member of the ACLU, as conscience-stricken about children, the elderly and homeless as a neophyte social worker, and as injured in their idealism as any bleeding heart private eye (from saintly Marlowe to soft-boiled Rockford) by the brute face of an evil increasingly mindless and random, beyond greed and social science, unto the depraved indifference of drug cartels and drive-by gangbangers. On *Hill Street*, not even our favorite characters were immune to sexual assault or exempt from sudden death, as if *Barney Miller* had gone to Bosnia.

But the crisis of liberalism got its start earlier on TV cop shows—if, in fact, the crisis of liberalism isn't what most of television has been about ever since CBS pulled the plug on Ed Sullivan. It began in 1973, when Joseph Wambaugh's novels were adapted for episodic television, simultaneously, by NBC in the anthology series *Police Story* and by CBS with George Kennedy as Bumper Morgan in *The Blue Knight*. *The Blue Knight* stuck around for only a season, but *Police Story* lasted four years and steadily darkened, like the novels themselves. Wambaugh's L.A. cops in *The New Centurions* had an ugly job to do, but were also creatures of noble compunction, with personal problems that colored their street behavior. Bumper Morgan may have been impatient with bureaucratic regulations and suspects' rights, but he walked his beat with a fatherly hand and a kindly heart. By 1975, however, with the battered children and the severed heads of *The Choirboys*, Wambaugh was feeling rotten, as if Popeye Doyle had written *Catch-22*. Listen to Baxter Slate: "I mean that the weakness of the human race is stupefying and it's not the capacity for evil which astounds young policemen.... Rather it's the mind boggling worthlessness of human beings. There's not enough dignity in mankind for evil and that's the most terrifying thing a policeman learns." Later, he will add: "And if there's no evil there's very likely no goodness. There're only accidents." And Slate is the last of the liberals, who went to Dominican Catholic schools and studied classical literature before becoming a cop and a MacArthur Park "choirboy." Tune in on a nineteen-year veteran of the street wars like Spermwhale Whalen:

> You remember that slut roamed into Sears and had the baby in the restroom?...She cut the cord with her fingernails and just dumped the little toad in the trash can and left it for the janitor to find the next day. And the dicks couldn't prove the baby ever drew breath and she cried all over the courtroom and they couldn't find her guilty of manslaughter or nothin. Anyways some dude from one a these Right to Life groups comes into the station to interview the detectives on how they felt about it and the dicks kissed him off down to the desk officer who happened to be Lard. And Lard says, "You want my opinion, the third generation welfare pig shoulda been sterilized when she turned fourteen so she wouldn't be runnin around foalin in every shithouse in town. Far as crime's concerned she did the taxpayers a favor. Only crime she should be found guilty of is litterbug."

Nobody said this on *Police Story*; it's off any network map of civil discourse. Nobody even said it in the lousy movie Hollywood made out of *The Choirboys*. But the difference between cops on television before Wambaugh and after him is that nobody would even have *thought* it on *Adam 12, Columbo* or *Madigan*, whereas it's possible to imagine Howard Hunter saying something like it on *Hill Street*, and Crockett on *Miami Vice*, or Munch on *Homicide*, or Sipowitz on *NYPD Blue*. Wambaugh would go on to get a little too cute in *The Black Marble*, with a "Big Sewer" cop at a bigtime dog show, dreaming of wounded bunny rabbits and nightingales singing in the raspberry bushes of old mother Russia. And to take his revenge on Hollywood for *The Choirboys*, with *The Glitter Dome*, in which the dream factory was kiddie porn and snuff flicks and mad skaters on a roller rink in the parking lot behind a bowling alley, waltzing themselves to death, and a beach where old people went to sell their gold and wound up with their mouths taped and their throats slit. And to branch out, in *The Golden Orange*, to Reagan country, Orange County, the Southwest capital of white collar crime, with its parvenu bankers and Rolls Royce dealerships, landlocked yachts and "hot mommas" leaving vapor trails of wrinkle cream behind them. He'd also publish true-crime books that made absorbing TV miniseries. But black humor devolving to *disgust* was his distinctive gift to Bochco and the cop shows that came after. Oddly, not till Andre Braugher's Pembleton on *Homicide* would any TV cop avail himself of Wambaugh's only antidote to this disgust, his metaphysical itch—a howling dervish in the shadow of the golden cupola under the onion dome of the Russian Orthodox Church, in *The Black Marble;* the "ritual and mystery and guilt" of Roman Catholicism in *The Glitter Dome;* the temptation in the desert, the parting of the waters and the Easter week resurrection in *The Golden Orange.* (In one of his novels, one of his several ex-seminarian cops tells an old woman, "Life would be unbearable if we didn't have the devil, wouldn't it?" And she replies, "You're absolutely right, Sergeant Welborn. Life would be *hell* without the devil.") But except for holidays, God makes most of His television appearances on Pat Robertson's Family Channel.

And so, in January, 1981, we arrive at down-and-dirty *Hill Street*, hand-held Wambaugh with the Ophuls/Mizoguchi camera constantly in motion, the Robert Altman tracking shots and overlapping dialogue, the John Dos Passos entanglement of out-of-sequence storylines and subplots, the "step-frame" process, the grainy laminated look and cops who *die* even though we *care* about them: all *momentum*. (Plus, of course, Veronica Hamel as Joyce

Davenport, a public defender to sigh for.) According to Gitlin, Daniel J. Travanti's stoic Furillo was an anti-Friday and anti-Kojak who "negotiated truces" in the middle of a meltdown of "the middle-class therapeutic ethos." Institutions responsible for education, health and welfare no longer worked, and neither did cities. *Hill Street*'s "swarming" motion "was the energy of American liberal-middle-class ideology turned on itself, at a loss for direction." At its best, this "first postliberal cop show" could be "positively rhapsodic about the contradictions built into the liberal world view in the early eighties. It not only acknowledged uncertainties but embraced them." To some of us, that "embrace" looked more like a holding on for dear life, even a paralytic seizure—which could explain why, seven months later, everybody too young to vote started watching MTV; and, a year after that, everybody too old to care would be stopping in for a beer with Norm on *Cheers*; and a decade later we voted for Newt's postliberal and posttherapeutic Contract on America.

Except that the recombinant DNA of television, public opinion and popular culture doesn't work that way. So many of us spend so much time watching, it would be equally convenient for psychologists and polemicists alike to believe that the medium's practicioners were, if not the unacknowledged legislators of mankind or the antennae of the race, at least a satellite dish picking up suction from the perforations in our subconscious. But Ronald Reagan, so postliberal he was antediluvian, had already been elected president when *Hill Street* hit the air. The American public could be said to have voted against a "therapeutic ethos"—and the social-worker ideology of the welfare state—before Bochco ever went into his herky-jerky despairing act. The audience got there first, which may be why they wanted a cowboy in the White House. So on the one hand, *Hill Street* was television-a-little-late-as-usual, playing catchup. On the other hand this same television had a mind of its own. As if the gloomy word hadn't reached them, competing dramatic series went on being therapeutic before and after the 1980 election. Each week in a police forensics laboratory, Jack Klugman's *Quincy* persisted in investigating alcoholism, incest, rape, teen suicide and toxic-waste dumping. Every week at the Los Angeles *Tribune*, Ed Asner's *Lou Grant* continued to worry his readers sick about racism, sexism, senile judges, teen gangs and journalistic ethics. Neither *Cagney & Lacey*, than which no series has ever been more devoted to social-worker answers to our infrastructural questions, all the grueling way to A. A. meetings where Christine should have run into Frank, nor *St. Elsewhere*, madcap specialists in stop-gap solutions to medical crisis problems, even got started till two years into the punk reign of Ron and Nancy Vicious. The fact is, TV can't get by for long without some sort of therapeutic ethos; it is not only the flipside of commercial salesmanship but also one of the strongest currents in the narrative stream from Sophocles to the Brothers Grimm, from mystic quests to Kafka's bedbug. Another fact is that writers for *Lou Grant*, like Seth Freeman, *Hill Street*, like Michael Kozoll, *Cagney & Lacey*, like Patricia Green, and *St. Elsewhere*, like Tom Fontana, have their own issues to resolve, which we used to call axes to grind. A third fact is that we watch more than one pro-gram, in as many frames of mind. We are at least as conflicted as the characters we taste-test.

Pervasive menace and nameless dread were, however, gaining on us. As down and dirty as *Hill Street* was, *Miami Vice* was a strobe in the eye. I saw the pilot in late summer of 1984, in a screening room at NBC in Rockefeller Plaza, just as the city fathers of America's only third-world capital had begun to complain about the image they imagined the series would project, but before executive producer Michael Mann got around to issuing any of his Sorbonne Situationist manifestos on the manifold meanings of it all. Of course, there was a story, involving Panamanian shrimpers, Colombian druglords, and fathers and sons. And actors who articulated more or less intelligibly: "Give him an inch and he thinks he's a ruler." And the usual Odd Couple buddy bond relationship between mismatched undercover cops: Sonny Crockett (Don Johnson), a good ol' homegrown boy with an Italian sportscar, a two-day stubble, a live-in sloop, and a pet gator named Elvis, missing a son and mourning a marriage; and Ricardo Tubbs (Philip Michael Thomas), a black dude-dandy come down from New York to avenge his brother's murder, a prince of Caribbean breezes, with gorgeous ringlets. But as much as it may have been about cops, *Vice* seemed more about colors and shapes in violent motion, with the sun hammering down on broken water and palm trees waving like windshield wipers and sleek fishy women lolling on coral-reef dreamscapes. For three minutes I stared at a wheel on Crockett's Ferrari. Not even the steering wheel, just one of the four that roll on the road; I admired a tire. Later on I'd stare at and admire a pier. Toward the end, I was obsessing about a *garage*. The feel was French, like Cocteau on one of his benders, Godard in *Alphaville*, or maybe *Diva*, when the Asian jailbait rollerskates in her Parisian penthouse, or peels an orange in a white Matisse tower: post-Impressionist painterly, and also Brian De Palma, like the *Scarface* remake. At last on television, something to *look* at.

For all its water traffic, dog races, condos, flamingos and jai alai courts, Miami didn't look like Miami; impossibly peach-colored, bruise grey, sleazy puce or stainless steel, it looked like a Cubist Shangri-la. Nor did Crockett and Tubbs look like cops; no belts, all pleats, in Armanis and Versaces, they looked like Italian film directors. Not even their unsmiling boss, Lt. Castillo (Edward James Olmos), looked as if he'd ever visited a police station except in cuffs. With his pocked face, inky eyes, narrow black suit, narrow black tie, narrow black mustache and secret Southeast Asian psychic war wounds, he looked like a sinister umbrella. And murder didn't look like murder, either. Seen through filters of psychedelic lollipop, angled at from ceiling fans or sewerholes, dissolved underwater in montage, superimposed upon in a surreal sandwich of rearview mirrors, revolving doors and hubcaps, cued to songs by Phil Collins, Cyndi Lauper, Lionel Richie, Ted Nugent, the Eagles, the Pointer Sisters, the Fat Boys and the Stones, while G. Gordon Liddy, Roberto Duran and Little Richard lounged around in retina-cooling pastels, murder was postmodern *arty*. When the perpendicular man in a white suit with a hypodermic syringe went up the diagonal white stairs to the cobalt-blue bedroom to dispose of the horizontal woman with the black face, her eyes opened, and the room tilted, and bed spilled into the mirror, which was staring at a rectangle of blank white light. Cut in a switchblade jitter to Crockett and Tubbs and Phil Collins in the Ferrari Spider, as if above it all in a helicopter in Vietnam, looking down on like-wow patterns through a blood-gorged rock dream. No psychobabble on *Vice* about traumatic childhoods and out-of-control cities; whether your mother loved you and your boss didn't; your father abused you and the legal system is bought and paid for; you can't get it up 'cause your sister's a nun—leave all that to *Hill Street*, as busy as a Balzac boardinghouse with compunctions and ambivalences. Of course, Miami cops would bust Miami perps. Murder, however, was *hip*.

By February 1985, twenty million yupscale trendoids were staying home from movies and clubs for their Friday night fix of the gaudy *Vice* amalgam of cop show, music video and car commercial. I called Michael Mann in Burbank. He glibbed me with Eisenstein and Bertolucci and what he said was his program's "almost operatic dialectic." He had signed up playwright Miguel (*Short Eyes*) Pinero to write one episode and star in several more, as the Colombian druglord who had wasted Tubbs's brother. He was chatting up Tom McGuane. So I called Todd Gitlin, in Berkeley. Never mind postliberal; what about postmodern? "It looks astonishing," Gitlin said. "But we get a kind of blankness. One big thing in the new visual culture is dissociation through juxtaposition. Things are just there. Anything belongs with anything else. A cop holds a gun against a blue stucco wall with a strip of chrome off to the right. What does it mean? Anything it wants to mean." When I suggested that *Vice* somehow *felt* like Vietnam, at least the sexdrugs-rock-and-roll Vietnam we carry around in the head from reading Michael Herr and Robert Stone, Gitlin, who gives good sound-bite, was ready for that one, too. His grad students were writing papers on "the iconic figure of the Vietnam vet" on television: "There's a haunted sense. Whatever the war was about it isn't over. Now starting with *Magnum*, the vet is the hero instead of a psychopath. Look at *The A-Team*. We've got loners fighting for the right, but off to the side. In a corrupt age they make their own rules. The system doesn't work so cut corners. Miami's a good place for this, a sort of 'air-lock' zone between us and the brown skins, the heart of darkness."

Well, yes. As a content-junkie, I hadn't failed to notice that Latin America had taken over from Vietnam in the pulp imagination as our pre-eminent third-world hell-on-wheels, with the drug lords as the Viet Cong and the Andes as one big Nose Cone. Not every *Vice* storyline was obsessed with coke-tweezed rug-munchers and the savage cartels that supplied them—there were episodes as well on pimps, prostitutes and pornography; on arms dealers peddling stolen Stinger missiles and Nationalist Chinese generals moving opium out of the Golden Triangle with the help of our elephants and spooks—but most were, with an increasingly baroque filigree of CIA and DEA connivance, of conspiracies of rightwing businessmen, loony paramilitaries and National Security Agency gonzo renegade ex-Marines to smuggle cocaine to pay for arms for Frito Bandito Freedom Fighters who specialized in raping and killing radical nuns. Not only did this seem to happen every third Friday on *Vice*, but one or another version of the same plot, involving drugs and death squads and clandestine agency coverups, also surfaced in half a dozen TV movies and in series shows as various as *Lou Grant, The Equalizer, Shannon's Deal, Cagney & Lacey* and *Law & Order*, as if every executive producer in Burbank had been on the Christic Institute's mailing list. In retrospect, it's amazing that Iran-Contra surprised *anybody*.

But what we seemed to take away from *Vice*, instead, was a generalized paranoia, pretty in pastels. You couldn't trust the government. You couldn't even trust your hero. Sonny Crockett was so far undercover one season, he persuaded himself that he was his own criminal alterego, Sonny Burnett. The thin blue line was a torn net and a leaky sieve. Like the luckless gangster in Doctorow's Dutch Schultz novel, *Billy Bathgate*, even the good guys were falling off the side of the boat, their feet in a tub of cement, down through the glittery corruptions to a bed of slime, singing "Bye Bye Blackbird." Cop shows still did their civic duty—befriending the vulnerable, injured, homeless and bereaved; avenging the innocent and powerless; roughing up the evasive snitch; tough-love sermonizing, as if according to some weekly lesson plan, on the hateful corrosiveness of racism and homophobia; inclusive enough at their station house to welcome every diversity save lawyers—but easy judges were a trial, drug money a temptation, children bearing children who shot children an occasion of despair, and the centurions themselves resented and feared. With a gnostic demiurge rampant and devouring, the cops and the public coarsened.

In 1990, *Law & Order* worked on NBC and *Equal Justice* didn't work on ABC because *Law & Order* belonged to the nineties and *Equal Justice* to the seventies. "Justice," wrote John Milton in the seventeenth century, "in her very essence is all strength and activity; and hath a sword in her hand, to use against all violence and oppression on the earth." This fierce idea of justice as a woman warrior, a terrible angel with a swift sword, accords remarkably well with the current punitive temper. It was seldom to be found in *Equal Justice*, where a big-city district attorney's office was something to which the young and the beautiful were drawn as if to Italy or Broadway. For these fresh out of law school assistant DAs, variously idealistic, opportunistic and horny, the court was a theater and crime was a play and oh, how they longed to perform. Swimming in stress was good for their muscletone. (ABC simultaneously floated a Pony Express series, *The Young Riders*, and it was hard not to translate *Equal Justice* into *The Young Prosecutors*.) While they would stop periodically to think about the politics of law enforcement, they were always in a hurry to get back to the Tinkertoys and Erector Sets of their private lives.

Whereas, on *Law & Order*, the cops who spent the first half-hour trying to figure out who did what to whom, and the prosecutors who spent the next half hour trying to prove it in court, didn't have private lives, or lovable eccentricities, or television "relationships." (Just as well, too; the cast ever since has been a revolving door.) The moral math consumed them. Race, class, money and power made them so edgy that *they never went home*. Lean and mean, all they did was their job. Suddenly the rest of television, seeking to ingratiate instead of scourge, seemed fuzzy. Like *Kojak* and *The Equalizer*, *Law & Order* knew every geometric angle of New York City. It was as if its cameras had been intimate alike with boardrooms and pawn shops, the garment district and the private school, insider trading and the A train, the shadowed streets, the stricken faces and the Deer Park. It was also as though the writers every week tried to improve on the city's tabloids: a Mayflower Madam bust, a Tawana Brawley scam, a Marla Hansen slashing, a Happy Land after-hours arson, a Malcolm X assassination, the bombings of abortion clinics and World Trade Centers, each surprise twisted to a sudden stop at a clever station of the triple cross. It was also as though Michael Moriarty's Ben Stone were Milton's avenging angel, our samurai and Robespierre, until he turned into our Shane. That he'd leave the show, jumping or pushed, was clear in April 1994, when he walked out on a case in Harlem that managed somehow to remind us, all at once, of Yankel Rosenbaum and Gavin Cato in Crown Heights, of the beating of Reginald Denny after the Rodney King verdict in Los Angeles, of white racism, black anti-Semitism and Tom Wolfe's *The Bonfire of the Vanities*. But he didn't actually quit till May, after a witness he had bullied into testifying against the Russian Mafia was gunned down despite promises of police protection: "You stay in this job long enough, and you just don't have any feelings."

On *Law & Order*, our angry angels are capable of behaving badly. They will have to learn, all over again, that means corrupt ends. They also get raped, shot, and dead. Worst of all, they lose the occasional case. Neither *Perry Mason* nor *The Defenders* ever lost a case. For our designated Robespierres, the guardians of civic virtue, to lose in a television courtroom is as unsettling to the audience as the failure of a Pembleton and Bayliss to coerce a confession from Moses Gunn on *Homicide*. Where's the closure? How are we supposed to go on with this hole in us, a wound whose ragged edges crave to heal but can't?

Homicide was a *Hill Street* for Baltimore, so fast-forward we'd often wonder just what hit us, with drive-by wisecracks and percussive mayhem, as if not only the cameras were jumpy, but the actors, the director and executive-producers Barry Levinson and Tom Fontana, too. It started off smart, right after the 1992 Super Bowl, introducing us to the troops—described as "a thin blue line between us and the invasion of Baltimore by terrorists"—and introducing the troops to a strangulation, a disembowelling, an Elmore Leonard joke, a widow who had buried so many husbands for the life insurance that their bodies were all mixed up in no-frills Styrofoam coffins at the cemetery and a theory of crime in Baltimore: It's the fault of all the chromium in Chesapeake Bay, which gets into the crabs, which crabs the poor eat, thus polluting their minds. After which, in spite of being jerked around and pre-empted so often Baltimore might have been Brigadoon, *Homicide* got profound, with an emphasis on "redball" cases—that is, high-profile, bad-publicity cases in which the police commissioner, the mayor and even the governor express a feverish interest, like the mugging and murder of a white female tourist by a black teenager, or the serial-killing of the "Angels of Baltimore." A "redball" requires all the detectives, working overtime and under pressure. It ups the Wambaugh/Bochco ante, the sense of a station house besieged—one of their number, the resident conspiracy theorist, will commit suicide; and half the squad will be gunned down when the police dispatcher sends them to the wrong number on the wrong floor of an apartment building—and of angry, cynical and paranoid cops, hunkered down in an inner-city bunker inside a fundamentalist freakview, like a Trotskyite or Hezbollah sect, lobbing jokes like hand grenades.

Let me zoom in on just one of these redball cases, the mugging-murder, to represent both *Homicide*'s take on race relations in the war against crime, and television's take on yet another straddle-sore social issue: gun control. As the husband of the dead woman, the father of stunned children, Robin Williams is all pain, no punchlines: "I lost my wife, but I joined a club." This club, a "secret society" of the bereaved, meets in police stations and for arraignments, in court rooms for the trial, on streets outside the halls of justice where the magic slate media are eager for a sound-bite, and maybe, too, in some "virtual community" of grief, online to a nightmare absence, whistling in the ether. Williams is under-stood by *Homicide* to be as much a casualty of violence as the wife who is gunned down when she won't relinquish her locket to the mugger. His brand-new "vocation" is waiting, but for what? Explanations? Justice? Forgiveness? To the *Homicide* detectives, he is a wince, a reproach, and an embodiment of everything they can't allow themselves to feel. He wants to hold one of their guns, not to shoot, no bullets, just to get an idea of...what? He can't *locate* his missing wife or his missing manhood. The detectives are equally bothered by the boy, Vaughn Perkins, they've arrested for the crime. What does he mean when he says in a note to Williams, "I had the power, but I forgot who I was"? He's just as enigmatic on becoming a Muslim in prison and confronting the confused husband of his victim: "She's gone—*this* is about me." Is that an apology? Nor is Andre Braugher's Pembleton the only member of the squad to wonder why the death of a tourist is a "redball," while black children are dying every day in Baltimore. *Homicide* seems to have cornered the market for African-Americans on episodic television who have other matters to attend to than serving as examples to white people of how to be better behaved or as metaphors to technicolor our bondage fantasies.

But in one respect, the two hours of Robin Williams on *Homicide* were absolutely typical of entertainment television: they were in favor of gun control. TV, in which we see more guns per week than most civilians will get a real-world glimpse of in a lifetime, has always deplored the culture that dotes and gloats on them while simultaneously glorifying the last resort of take-no-prison-ers. Cop shows—not *even* but *especially*—oppose the promiscuous availability of everything hot and metallic, from a Saturday night special to an assault rifle, as do real-world police chiefs. I can't think of a single continuing series, in the decades since JFK's assas-sination with a mail-order Mannlicher Carcano, that hasn't devoted an episode to death-by-misadventure involving a handgun too readily nearby, or the easy purchase of the sleek weapon that aggrandizes the sociopathic sniper on a rooftop, or a gang-banger turf war in which bystanding grammar-school children end up cut down in the exchange of fire from semiautomatics bought in Florida by thugs and hoodlets. Among the TV movies just as worried, the most moving was *Without Warning: The James Brady Story*, on cable twelve times in the month of June, 1991, even as the U.S. Senate began deliberations on a House bill mandating a seven-day waiting period for handgun purchase; even as *48 Hours* on CBS and *Frontline* on PBS did scary take-outs on the fierce lobbying of the National Rifle Association. We seemed poised as a nation to disenthrall ourselves from the peculiar notion that happiness was a warm barrel and a big bang. *Without Warning*, starring Beau Bridges as President Reagan's press secretary and Joan Allen as his extraordinary wife, Sarah, was a powerful argument. What happened to Brady in front of the Hilton, when John Hinckley decided to impress Jodie Foster, was distinctly un*sporting*. To praise this movie in public, as I did, was to invite an avalanche of abusive mail, some of it even signed. But you've probably seen yourself the N.R.A. commercial on late-night cable with the red-breasted Bambi bashers standing around a saltlick swapping Elizabeth Taylor jokes. They *belonged*, and we could too. Joining the NRA would entitle us to an ID card, a magazine subscription, a windshield decal, a shooter's cap and an "accidental death or dismemberment" insurance policy. It seemed to me—then and now—that if they couldn't bag a Liz Taylor or Jane Fonda, they would settle for wasting a unicorn. The Second Amendment to the Constitution says, in full: "A well-regulated militia being necessary to the security of a free State, the right of the people to keep and bear arms shall not be infringed." The first clause is seldom quoted. The historian Paul Fussell has suggested that if we want to own a gun, we ought also to serve in a real militia, to patrol borders and dig latrines. But that's not what the gun lobby's all about. None other than Robin Williams, in one of his comic monologues, told us what the gun lobby's really all about: "Kill a small animal, drink a lite beer."

The third postliberal, posttherapeutic, postmodern, post-Toasties and pre-Microsoft cop show of the nineties was another Steven Bochco, *NYPD Blue*, which whole cities like Dallas and Syracuse declined to watch on their ABC affiliates in the fall of

1993 for fear that a few harsh words (for instance, *scumbag*) and a few fleeting glimpses of forbidden flesh (a bare bottom, a shapely breast: was that a female nipple?) might diddle the blameless dreams of the cauliflower children who had been dropped in our nests by bumblebees. It's a measure of much that is odd in the national psyche that Bochco should think crotch shots and semi-profanity somehow creative and daring; that ad agencies, network affiliates, blue-nosed pressure groupies and segments of a sullen public should get lathered about images less lurid than the run-of-the-satanic-mill rock video, the low-fat soft porn of ESPN's *Bodyshaping*, or the lingerie spreads in the Sunday *Times Magazine*; and that even those of us who liked the show should neglect to notice for a season or so the coarsening of cop etiquette since *Hill Street*. This callousness was there to see in the pilot in Dennis Franz as Andy Sipowicz, an out-of-control alcoholic who despised equally the lowlifes on the street, the prosecutors and judges who returned them to that street, and himself. Declaring private war on one of these lowlifes, to whom he fed a toupee, Sipowicz was then gunned down in the middle of a cuddle with his regular weekly prostitute. So it was David Caruso's turn as John ("Hey!") Kelly, the red-haired choirboy heart throb and professional Mr. Sensitive, to strong-arm mobsters into coughing up the creep who'd plugged his partner. After which in tit-for-tat, the mob ordered a hit on Kelly by his colleague Amy Brennerman, who turned out also to be his prolly cupcake between divorce proceedings from a lovely uptown lawyer, Sherry Stringfield.

Caruso would take his class resentments with him when he quit Bochco for Hollywood after *NYPD Blue*'s first season, and Stringfield take her perfect complexion to *ER*, and Andy quit the bottle to win the heart of an assistant district attorney, and Jimmy Smits assume the role of Mr. Sensitive, with a dead wife and homing pigeons; and *NYPD Blue* would think out loud about gays and immigrants and drugs and racism. But what this series has been best at week after week is trampling on the weedy rights of suspects, smacking snitches upside their plug uglies, coercing confessions from uppity pimpled perps and, in general, using the badge to open cans of worms. You could almost feel the sigh of relief on *NYPD Blue*, as on *Law & Order*, when the State of New York elected George Pataki governor. With Mario Cuomo gone, and the death penalty back, they could threaten suspects with needles as well as rape. I mean, how many times can you frighten a soft white boy with insinuations of what big black men will do to him in prison, before viewers start to wonder if you aren't yourself a little bent? But lethal injection has pizzazz.

Which is not to say that *NYPD Blue* is pro-capital punishment. Bochco, since *Hill Street*, may have so far embraced the contradictions of the liberal world view and the breakdown of the therapeutic ethos as to disdain due process, but he isn't writing yet for *Commentary*, *National Review* or the *Weekly Standard*. At least on television, cops know enough about death not to root for it as if gas chambers and electric chairs deserved pep rallies. *Law & Order* may have spent most of the fall of 1995 and the spring of 1996 exploiting capital punishment as a bogeyman, but when it concluded the season with a visit to an execution, after which every member of the cast cracked up in different gaudy ways, it was following in a long and honorable tradition of episodic television, from *The Defenders* to *Kojak* to *Midnight Caller* to *In the Heat of the Night*, excepting only *Dragnet*. TV movies have likewise been as soft as Dukakis on an eye-for-an-eye, refusing to cede to any state perfect knowledge in final things. (What else is God for?) As the national bloodlust heated up in the last decade, television seemed to get cooler, even melancholy, about whether "off with their heads" was really a deterrent, whether only poor people paid the ultimate price and whether revenge is good for the soul. In *Dead Man Out* (1989), Danny Glover played a shrink hired to "cure" a mentally-disturbed murderer so the state could then proceed to kill him. Ruben Blades played the inmate into whose disordered mind psychiatry would stick its stubby fingers. The big irony was obvious: Why should the state care if a killer is healthy enough to understand why *he* is being killed, if not for some weirdly projecting guilty conscience on the part of the state itself? A quieter subversion of our social complacency—speaking *sotto voce* in the almost choral iterations of marrow-chilling euphemisms like *process* (for psychiatry) and *issue* (for madness) and *item* (for death)—asked us whether we were prepared to forgive ourselves for penal colonies that were of their nature crazy-making. In *Somebody Has to Shoot the Picture* (1990), photographer Roy Scheider teamed up with reporter Andre Braugher to try to unravel a coverup in time to save the life of death row convict Arliss Howard; they got a story and he got the chair. In *The Shadow of a*

Killer (1992), hero-cop Scott Bakula opposed capital punishment even for a pair of mob-connected enforcers to whose wasting of a fellow police officer he had been the only witness, as a matter of wimpy scruple. In *Live! From Death Row* (1992), TV reporter Joanna Cassidy and her cameraman, on death row for a ratings-grabbing special, were seized as hostages by mass-murderer Bruce Davison for a prime-time show-and-tell from which we emerged more admiring of mass murderers than of the media. In *Last Light* (1993), what the new guard on Death Row, Forest Whitaker, discovered on befriending the affectless convicted killer, Kiefer Sutherland, was a history of abuse in both their childhoods and a violence in himself for which no "hole" will ever be deep enough. In *Witness to the Execution* (1994), as Faye Dunaway in *Network* subsidized terrorists so long as they'd stage their hijackings and kidnappings in front of her cameras, so TV producer Sean Young secured rights to the "live" telecast of an electrocution for her pay-per-view subscription service by promising the governor 30 percent of the merchandising windfall. In *Beyond the Call* (1996), Sissy Spacek, who used to be his girlfriend before he went to Vietnam, forgave David Strathairn for the crimes that landed him on death row because of post-traumatic stress disorder, and also, of course, because she's Sissy. These movies varied in quality from none to considerable, but cumulatively they suggest society itself is bloodthirstier than the television set in front of which we lapse for narrative; and that society, at least on this topic, pays no attention whatever to what TV tells it.

In *Law & Order*, assistant district attorney Jill Hennessey was so appalled by what she saw of lethal injection, she got herself killed in a car crash. In *NYPD Blue*, on the wagon but off the leash, Dennis Franz decided not to execute the slime ball who killed his son. There's that much margin left between a decent sense of limits and the barbaric snarl. But if Andre Braugher ever wakes up from his *Homicide* coma and declares himself in favor of summary justice, I'm moving to New Zealand. Or are there serial killers in New Zealand, too?

There, where the mark was, I plunged my knife in to the hilt.
The blood welled out over her delicate white skin.... With
a shudder I stared at the stony brow and the stark hair and
the cool pale shimmer of the ear. The cold that streamed
from them was deathly and yet it was beautiful, it rang, it
vibrated. It was music! Hadn't I felt this shudder before and
found it at the same time a joy? Hadn't I once caught this
music before? Yes, with Mozart and the Immortals.

Hermann Hesse, *Steppenwolf,* 1927

I don't particularly want to chop up women, but it seems
to work.

Brian De Palma

On television, serial killers are more popular than the Witness Protection Program. For one thing, even in real life, they are almost
always white and male. For another, almost always on television and
surprisingly often in real life too, they stalk women and children.
For a third, it's usually their mother's fault. For a fourth, looking
ordinary like the rest of us, they've got really disgusting stuff going
on all the time in the limbic wastes of their neural net, but also an
elaborate plan—with coded patterns and cunning props and esoteric patter—which makes them scarier and encourages excessive
behavior and overacting on the part of everybody around them, as
well as *noir* production values. I will explain in a minute that the
rest of the culture is just as bonkers on the subject, maybe even
worse than television, but it's worth noting here that the current
attack on TV violence got its noisy start in 1993, when sensitive
members of Congress were freaked out by *Murder in the Heartland,*
the ABC serial-killer miniseries with Tim Roth as Charlie Stark-
weather and Fairuza Balk as Caril Ann Fugate, his Lolita-Raggedy
Ann sidekick, under that big Nebraska sky, inside those grey
Nebraska barns, on their affectless carousel of death, ponying up to
the electric chair as if it were a vibrator or a thrill-ride.

But serial killers were a prime-time staple long before *Murder in*

{166}

the Heartland, and went on obsessively afterwards in spite of the negative publicity. In the last seven years alone, I can recall: *The Penthouse*, from which Robin Givens was lucky to escape, a high-rise defenestration having been the fate of a half dozen other young women too pretty for their own good. And *Donor*, in which Melissa Gilbert, among slit throats and man-eating CAT scans, found herself bobbing for bodies in chemical tanks in the bowels of a major metropolitan hospital. After which in *With a Vengeance*, the same Melissa had no sooner recovered from amnesia than the Northwest Slasher returned to finish his messy job. Just as after *she* finally recovered from alcoholism, Suzanne Somers in *Exclusive* became the latest target of a serial killer, probably Michael Nouri, because he usually is, though in *Psychic* his specialty was tattooed redheads. And *Nightmare in Columbia County*, where Amanda Peterson was so lame-brained as to strike up a penpalship with rapist-killer Christopher Atkins, a psychopathic blue lagoonie. And *When a Stranger Calls Back*, with Carol Kane getting a second chance to nab a serial killer of babysitters who turns out also to be a ventriloquist. And *Falling for You*, in which Jennie Garth really might have guessed that Costas Mandylor liked to pick up baby dolls in singles bars just to hurl them out of skyscrapers. And *Breach of Conduct* where Courtney Thorne-Smith likewise should have known that Peter Coyote was up to something icky in the nuke-proof bunker of his very own military base. Just as, in *Fatal View*, Cynthia Gibb should have known better than to marry a John Stamos who was always talking on his cellular phone to some younger chick who ended up, very dead, in Cynthia's pink pants. Not to mention Jane Seymour in *Memories of Midnight*, wandering around Athens, Venice, and Zagreb, looking as if she'd been hit on the head with a croquet mallet, clueless as to the anti-social behavior of Omar Sharif—although, in *Praying Mantis*, this very same Medicine Woman, pretending to write romance novels, was herself "the Wedding Night Killer," sort of like Pamela Anderson, whose amnesiac dreams in *Snapdragon* of severed arteries and white slavery and tiger cages proved to be so hard on anyone caught napping in her lewd vicinity.

No less than Helen Hunt went undercover, in *The Company of Darkness*, to sleep with and ensnare Steven Weber, a serial killer of little boys. Jean Smart actually played a serial killer in *Overkill: The Aileen Wuornos Story*, and maybe you would, too, if your father beat you, your brother raped you, your lover burned your face with cigarettes and somebody stole your baby. Only her superior muscle-tone enabled Chelsea Field in *Complex of Fear* to elude a ski-masked serial rapist-killer who hung out in the weight room, on the squash court and at the balcony windows of the Woodside Condominiums development as if he had a memership key. In his last television movie before he died of AIDS, *In the Deep Woods*, Anthony Perkins turned out not to be the serial killer, with cigarettes and pliers, of successful young career women, even though he wore the right raincoat for the job. It used to be that we could count on traumatized Vietnam vets as serial killers, but that wouldn't explain *Citizen X*, in which Russian detective Stephen Rea finally cornered Jeffrey DeMunn after he had killed dozens of young women and small children in and around the Rostov-on-Don commuter railway line. Nor, from Great Britain, *Band of Gold*, a serial-serial (that is, a multiple-episode series about multiple murders in series) in which the aggrieved prostitutes of Yorkshire, already the victims of alcoholic parents, abusive husbands, sadistic pimps, bent cops, corrupt pols and mass unemployment, unite to catch their own nemesis by pretending to be, of all things, scrub women—rather as if Thomas Hardy had written a feminist *noir*, a sort of "Upstairs, Downstairs" *Jude the Obscene*.

In a three-part "arc" of *Homicide*, someone was butchering the "angels" of Balitimore—a nurse in an AIDS pediatric clinic, the group leader of a shelter for battered women, etc.—which caused Andre Braugher to have an argument with God. After a hiatus that lasted two decades, *Ed McBain's 87th Precinct* returned to the air in time to solve the ritual murder of young women who all happened to be college track stars. Almost every one of the half-dozen Richard Crenna miniseries about the New York City police detective "Janek" has featured a serial killer, from a specialist in strangling nightclub singers who got his start in surprising Saigon, to a sort of vigilante sanitation-cop who used heroin overdoses to take out the unsightly homeless in Grand Central. Almost every other episode in three seasons of *The X-Files* has featured one variety or other of serial killer, and not necessarily an alien. My personal favorite was the serial-killing translator of medieval Italian poetry who met lonely women on the Internet, asked them out on dates, sat parked with them at night, in big American cars in lonely municipal spaces, suffocated them by secreting a membrane of gastric juices that worked as well as a baggie, and proceeded to feed on their fatty tissue: Vampire liposuction!

Okay, this is where I explain that serial killers are as all-American as cherry pie and tax fraud. From Hollywood: Alfred Hitchcock and Brian De Palma and *Basic Instinct* and *The Silence of the Lambs*. Or, more recently, *Copycat*, in which Sigourney Weaver was a forensic psychologist who could read the minds of serial killers, but had been so traumatized by one of them—a leering Harry Connick Jr., who probably sang at her—that she refused ever again to leave her fancy San Francisco apartment until she was interrupted in her book-writing, pill-popping, brandy-swilling and Internet computer games by police detective Holly Hunter, who needed her help tracking down *another* serial killer who seemed to be, well, a *plagiarist*, copying the golden oldies of the Boston and Hillside Stranglers, Jeffrey Dahmer and Ted Bundy and Son of Sam. Two lurid hours later, almost everybody was almost dead, in a cultural production as slick as a fashion magazine, as glossy as a car commercial and as gaudy and shallow as cyberspace, whose only excuse for being was the eagerness of millions of us to see two of our favorite actresses hanged or shot or turned into jumpsuits. And, from literature, just this decade: Bret Easton Ellis and *American Psycho*, whose commodity-fetishizing Wall Street broker amused himself by making obscene telephone calls to Dalton girls ("I'm a corporate raider. I orchestrate hostile takeovers. What do you think of that?" "Dad, is that you?"), torturing dogs, popping eyes out of the heads of homeless beggars, raping Aspen waitresses with cans of hair spray, nailing Bethany's fingers to a hardwood floor and sodomizing severed heads. Or Joyce Carol Oates and *Zombie*, whose 31-year-old Quentin was so beyond parenting or social work, a garbage sack of junk food and junk ideas, of Taco Bell beef burritos and dark matter in an expanding universe, that abducting and lobotomizing young boys with an icepick to surgically create someone who would love and obey him seemed only natural, like Bosnia and Rwanda and Woody Harrelson and Oliver Stone.

But, of course, the abduction and mutilation and murder of young women and little boys by serial creeps isn't just American; it's *modern*. Take a look at a book that came out from Harvard in 1995, Maria Tatar's *Lustmord: Sexual Murder in Weimar Germany*. She begins with a quote from Robert Musil's high-culture novel,

The Man Without Qualities. The protagonist meditates on local tabloid coverage of a prostitute's murder by a carpenter: "They had expressed their abhorrence of it, but they did not leave off until they had counted thirty-five stabs in the abdomen, and described the long slash from the navel to the sacrum...while the throat showed the marks of throttling." Musil, of course, was feeling bad about Vienna on the eve of World War I. Tatar feels even worse about Weimar, after that war was lost, when everybody seemed to have tabloid tendencies. They were more than just morbidly curious about serial killers and sexual murder (*Lustmord*) in Weimar. In paintings by Otto Dix and Kurt Schwitters, novels by Alfred Döblin and Hermann Hesse, films by Fritz Lang, plays by Frank Wedekind, graphics by George Grosz, they were pathologically obsessive. Dix painted himself as a "Sex Murderer," and smeared the canvas with red handprints. Grosz had himself photographed as Jack the Ripper, among mirrors and masks and dolls. Wedekind starred himself on stage as the Ripper, and cast his wife as one of his victims. Lang gave us Peter Lorre as a child murderer. Doblin somehow managed, in *Karl and Rosa*, to "sexualize" Rosa Luxemburg's assassination into an hysterical masochistic indulgence on *her* part, a self-inflicted martyrdom through exquisite torture. Tatar explores this Weimar kinkiness in elegant and persuasive case studies of Dix, Grosz and Doblin; in sidelong glances at the askew tilt to Friedrich Murnau and Rudolf Schlichter; in historical sketches of the Vampire of Dusseldorf, the Silesian Bluebeard, nineteenth-century *Liebestod* and "the extraordinary artistic investment in representing women" like Eve, Circe, Medusa, Judith and Salome "as creatures of overpowering sexual evil"; with the obligatory references to Weininger and Theweleit, spicy quotes from Marx, Susan Sontag, and Elisabeth Bronfen, and deft flashforwards to Norman Mailer's *The American Dream*, Patrick Susskind's *Perfume* and Hollywood splatter flicks.

Tatar doesn't mention television; at Harvard they probably don't watch it. But anyone who's looked at both TV *and* Picasso's *Demoiselles d'Avignon* (or Klee's *Dogmatic Composition*) is likely to wonder about what she calls "the gender politics of cultural production" and a "modernist project that aestheticizes violence and turns the mutilated female body into an object of fascination and dread." Fragmentation! Disfigurement! Transgressive energy! Emancipation of form from content! How come the artist so often seems to identify with the psychopath, and succeeds, after fancy knife work, in starring *himself* as sacrificial victim and symbolic, reborn phoenix? Bad boys! Dead girls! Chop-chop! Modernism! Why Weimar? Well, damaged men come back from war, less than heroic. What did they find, besides the usual urban pathologies? Women happily whole, at work, and agitating about suffrage. The pathology of *Dolchstoßlegende* ("stabbed-in-the-back") met the fantasy of sexual revenge, as if women and Jews were one big vampire film like *Nosferatu*, as if a corpse itself were a work of art. Not for the first time, though seldom so brilliantly as in Tatar's slender book, fascism and modernism are conjoined; they correspond; they are letters from the same camp, with its weak male-ego boundaries and chimney smoke of human cinder. Why not, then, Hollywood? And certainly Burbank. *Our* culture, right or wrong.

Serial killers were a specialty on the NBC series *Midnight Caller*. One episode caused such a commotion in 1988 that the series returned to think it through all over again in a second show the following season. In this instance the serial killer was an AIDS-infected sociopath. Knowing his own doomed condition, the sociopath went about San Francisco bedding down members of both sexes, careless or callous of the consequences. One of those he bedded down was an ex-girlfriend (Kay Lenz) of "urban folk hero" radio-host Jack Killian (Gary Cole), who rampaged after him. Before filming started on the first episode, gay activists—undestandably worried about a witch hunt of AIDS victims who were already pariahs—protested a script that called for this one-man epidemic to get wasted by one of his victims. Producers agreed to minor changes—Jack visits a leather bar, has his consciousness raised and even saves the sociopath from being blown away—but what we saw on air was a huge fudge. So, as sensitized as Jack himself, they went back to the drawing board the following November; and Lenz would die, with some dignity, in a hospice; and Jack used his nightly sermonette to be angry about "the people getting rich on this disease," the very first television attack on profiteering drug companies in the plague years.

Television's response to AIDS could have been the sorriest chapter in the short history of a medium ever ready to exploit the popular culture's morbid fascination with and panicky paranoia about everything from deviant sexuality to bloody vampires. Instead, it was the medium's finest hour of empathetic witness.

Social Diseases

There was a gleam in Charlotte's eye, maybe devilish, maybe not; and a feather in her black cavalier's hat, and strawberry blonde hair on the shoulders of the black coat that flapped after her like batwings; and she was pushing a wheelchair at top speed, out of the hospital through the back door of the geriatrics ward onto the lawn and into the light; and she seemed altogether a girl out of the history of painting, an angel or witch, between the Middle Ages and the Renaissance, not of our world as she shouted and gasped: "When they had the real plague in the old days, you know what they did? They danced! The good old *danse macabre*!...danced till they dropped!"

Clive with a ruined face rose from the wheelchair: an apparition out of Yeats, a coat upon a stick. He turned an ungainly circle. We saw him from behind a sun. We saw the fillings in his teeth as he grinned and gulped at death. Then he was dispossessed, and Charlotte like a black fan or a black flower opened and spread herself to take his body into her lap, and uniforms came in silence from all sides. And *their* dance was oddly regimental, as if to make a square, a quarantine, around the zero-sum narcissus on the great lawn in the English countryside.

Charlotte (Lizzy McInnerny) was a minor character in the 1987 HBO mini-series *Intimate Contact*—a teen-aged child of the aristocracy; a heroin addict, who contracted AIDS from a dirty needle; a death-junkie who's nanny used to tell her that, no matter how awful she felt, there was always someone worse off; she was at last that someone. The wheelchair, she explained to Clive, "is all part of the Plague Pal service." Clive (Daniel Massey) was a major character in *Intimate Contact*, a middle-aged and once-dynamic Thatcherite and businessman, with a son who had just won a First at Oxford, a daughter almost as smart who was a whiz at photography, a BMW and a big house on manicured grounds in which his handsome sheltered wife Ruth (Claire Bloom) hung between charities like a lovely chandelier. A year and a half before the start of *Intimate Contact*, Clive on a business trip to New York also contracted AIDS: "I poked some dirty little tart when I was too pissed to show good judgment, and now I'm paying for it."

Well, you may say, how convenient: AIDS, but also heterosex. This horror, however, isn't choosy, as we could have guessed from, say, Zimbabwe. And *Intimate Contact*, a thesis movie—the public is ignorant and ignorance can and will be vicious—touched most bases on the diamond of the disease. A gay couple, one of whom was dying as unpleasantly as possible in the same ward as Clive and Charlotte, would teach Ruth how to care for a husband she had hardly known in their glide through a twilit life of gaudy objects and introduce her as well to their sexual underworld, a rough-trade grotto no less fearful and no more savage than the arctic overworlds of Ruth's golf club and Clive's conglomerate. Ruth had also to confront her own subterranean sexuality. Holding herself together "to protect my family" from the dreadful news—"I'm going to disgust you," Clive told her—she was at first wretched, then wilfully composed. But it was a composure of a thousand agitations, of mad molecules spinning in the shape of a porcelain vase. The control was hysterical; the body, an alien text no one had bothered to translate for her.

She was otherwise magnificent, growing up from denial to coping to assertion as the women at her golf club shunned her, the men at Clive's company fired him, and their feverish children put on attitudes to see if they fit their angry emotions. At a tea dance, a TV studio, a charity road race or the twenty-fifth wedding anniversary party to which her guests forgot to come, she was grace in modulation, from a panic that almost routed her to a contempt that seemed to purify her to the tempered steel of the last messy stage of a previously unexamined marriage. Nor was she alone in her excellence. Massey's Clive was mostly disagreeable for the first two hours, his self-pity taking the form of an isolating arrogance. It didn't occur to him that AIDS had happened as well to his family. But something green grew inside as the trunk of him wasted away, a vertical band of color, and it got to his eyes, and he saw beyond himself. In reaching out in the last half of the TV movie to death-junkie Charlotte, he escaped the solitary confinement of the dying. As Charlotte, McInnery scared the breath right out of us; she seemed to belong, if not in a painting, then in a febrile nineteenth-century novel, perishing of TB and meant somehow to embody sick male notions of eros and thanatos. Also riveting was Mark Kingston as the company doctor whose first loyalty was to the company instead of to his patient. If Kingston's guilt abraded him for the better, the story was different for his wife, social-climbing Sylvia Syms, who began as a beast, vacillated, found in qualm some courage, and then was lost forever to all decency. Had *Intimate Contact* concluded with the family's acceptance, it would have been merely worthy. But by persisting past death, through grieving, to the beginnings of renewal, only to end in an abrupt dark corridor in a schoolhouse full of parents who turn on their own children, it told us things we'd rather not know—about failures of character and mass hysteria, loneliness and guilt, tremors, vomiting and incontinence, swellings that burst, bodies that burn, glands, bones and cinders. It also told us something about new communities of the afflicted.

Look at me! I am what AIDS looks like.
Molly Ringwald, *Something to Live For*, 1992

Not bad for television, especially since *Intimate Contact* predated the publication of *And the Band Played On*, the Randy Shilts attack on government and media for ignoring "the gay disease." Nor was this mini-series the first attention prime-time TV had paid to AIDS. Most of us met our first AIDS patient in a 1983 episode of *St. Elsewhere*. In fact, the departure of Mark Harmon as the romantic lead on the NBC hospital show was explained by his having contracted HIV, and we were later told he'd died of it. In NBC's *An Early Frost* in 1985, Ben Gazzara and Gena Rowlands, as Aidan Quinn's parents, faced up to their son's homosexuality, and his sentence of death, eight years before Hollywood finally got around to making a movie on the subject. There was an hour of *The Equalizer*, in 1986, about a child ostracized and abused for his HIV infection; and an hour of *L.A. Law* in 1987 about the mercy killing by a distraught companion of a suffering lover; and the two hours of *Midnight Caller*, already noted; and a 1990 hour of *The Trials of Rosie O'Neill*, about the formation of makeshift communities of the aggrieved and the bereaved.

If we hadn't learned much from Jack Killian, there were other programs. At the end of the ABC docudrama *The Ryan White Story*, as if assigned to stare at the *Wisconsin Death Trip* photo album, we met the real people actors had impersonated for two hours. As in *The Equalizer*, the victim was again a child who *wasn't* gay, a 13-year-old hemophiliac who got tainted blood in a transfusion. Once again, while it would have been nice for a network to face up to our pariahs, what we saw on televison was certainly superior to the indifference of the federal government and the avoidance behavior and/or disinformation in the national press. Lukas Haas, with his Grant Wood adopt-this-orphan look, his star-child self-absorption, his nervous intelligence, fidgety bewilderment and brittle rage, played Ryan White, seeming always to know more than he let on and to be out of phase, in his violent mood swings, from those adults who stood around him like dumb trees. In Kokomo, Indiana, his hemophilia had already excluded him from dangerous sports, like his younger sister's competitive rollerskating. We followed him to the hospital, the respirator, the biopsy, the terror. We saw him shunned by neighbors, and barred from junior high school. We went to court with his mother (Judith Light) and his lawyer (George C. Scott). If the burglarizing of his household on Christmas Eve, the running down of his dog on the street and the bullet through his bedroom window seemed an excessive piling on, nevertheless, taking our heart in his hands, Lukas Haas broke it like a wafer.

Three months later, in April 1989 on CBS, another TV docudrama managed to find another cohort of AIDS victims who happened not to be gay, nor intravenous drug users and not even this time, hemophiliacs. They were babies who got it from their mothers. *Littlest Victims* was the true story of Dr. James Oleske (Tim Matheson), a New Jersey pediatrician who, in 1982, in an inner-city hospital, first suspected AIDS as the cause of impaired immune systems in children, and sought research funding from state and federal agencies that refused to believe him. Predictable as it may have been as a trauma-drama with a kid-friendly test-tube hero, *Littlest Victims* was also considerably more forthright in its criticisms of establishment science than the rest of what circulated, like waste-recycling, in the mainstream media at that time.

Ask gays back then about the coverage and they were, of course, outraged. Where were the stories about on-again off-again funding of medical research, depending on how scared straights were *that* week? Or about an individual's right to privacy vs. the profit motive of the insurance companies? Or about alternative medications, macrobiotic diets, residential discrimation, bureaucratic hostility, exile in Mexico, the grotesque overpricing of AZT and the ethics of placebo testing on people sentenced to death? Instead, we got *Cosmopolitan* and *Newsweek*, like Alphonse and Gaston. *Cosmo* told us in January 1988 that, "There is almost no danger of contracting AIDS through ordinary sexual intercourse." *Newsweek*, that bully pulpit for Masters and Johnson, in a March 21 cover story begged to differ: "AIDS is breaking out. The AIDS virus is now running rampant in the heterosexual community." These were evil buffooneries, like a *People* magazine cover story, also in March, on "AIDS and the Single Woman"—with photographs of twenty-one women, three of them black, and one Latina, as if it didn't matter that female victims of AIDS were 70 percent black and Latina.

But the media were how we thought out loud about our plague years and the cognitive dissonance was killing us. What *Cosmo* published was a sort of Pamper: protective packaging for the sore-of-heart who were straight, white, middle class and "untargeted": "Penile penetration of a well-lubricated vagina" was still safe so long as you stuck to the missionary position, at least in places where *Cosmo* was likely to be read. If heterosexuals in Africa *did* have a problem, *Cosmo* blandly explained it: "Many men in Africa take their women in a brutal way..." This was anthropological and racist nonsense, but typical of the *Cosmo* yuppie worldview, the view from the Cloud Club of the Chrysler Building or the Grill Room of the Four Seasons or the bold type in the glitterati gossip columns, from which you could see neither Africa nor our own third world. If AIDS in California was 91 percent a gay disease, and in Texas 96 percent, in New York City it was the leading cause of death for women between the ages of 18 and 34. Twenty-six percent had contracted the virus from infected men, not infected needles. The number of children with AIDS increased 50 percent from 1986 to 1987. *Ninety* percent of those kids were black or Latino.

After such fiddling, maybe Rome deserved to burn. And *Newsweek* would be there, pouring on oil. ("Not since Hitler's diaries," said one incredulous staffer about the AIDS cover story.) According to Masters and Johnson in *Newsweek*, at least three million Americans were AIDS infected, double the estimate of the U.S. Centers for Disease Control; and 200,000 of the afflicted were non-drug-using heterosexuals—*seven times* the CDC estimates. AIDS was *everywhere:* in the bedroom, the brothel, the blood bank and the dental floss. M & J's survey sample of eight-hundred drug-free heteros, about which *Newsweek* huffed and puffed and blew its own horn, was of course preposterous—a self-selected batch of volunteers arbitrarily confined to four cities, with no follow-up interviews of HIV positives and no accounting for the tendency of people to lie about high-risk hanky panky. Compared with the meticulous testing of millions of blood bank donors and military personnel, M&J might as well have spent a morning polling the first 800 names in Gurley Brown's Rolodex. And what were we to make of a *Wall Street Journal* report that Masters & Johnson, before mongering these fears, had been refused the $500,000 they'd solicited from the American Foundation for AIDS Research to develop an anti-AIDS spermicidal jelly? The same thing we made of the syndicated "Dear Abby" newspaper column publicizing "a disposable, specially treated paper towelette that destroys the AIDS virus on public toilet seats, telephones, restaurant tables, silverware and door knobs." New York City's Board of Education passed out fifty thousand pairs of rubber gloves to protect teachers from their own pupils, and the local cops wore those gloves to break up a demonstration of gays at St. Patrick's Cathedral. (The gays hooted: "Your gloves don't match your boots!")

I mention all this for historical context. Television was speaking up, sympathetically, at a time when other media were either hysterical or dumb, in denial or paranoid, and the rest of us wanted to avoid the topic. Retina-eating cytomegalovirus, lung-choking pneumaocystis carinii, and organ-rotting Kaposi's sarcoma: *ugh*. Hemophilia, anal abrasions, genital herpes, trichomoniasis and Nonoxynol-9: *gross*. Any causal relation between poverty, prostitution, drugs and disease was only mentioned by bleeding hearts whose secret mantra was the *s* word: *socialism!* That we were as a nation ghettoized by race *and* sexual orientation was an unacceptable injury to the self-esteem. Fear and loathing had made a comeback, in a country kinky to begin with about its private parts. (Across the Atlantic, fear of AIDS and hatred of gays and the usual Thatcherite contempt for civil liberties metastasized in 1988 into Clause 28 of the Local Government Bill, passed by both houses of Parliament, forbidding use of public funds "to promote homosexuality" *in any way*. So much for seeing a play like *Breaking the Code* by the Royal Shakespeare, or borrowing a book by Jean Genet from the village library, or looking at David Hockneys at the Tate.)

Unfortunately, how we thought about AIDS would determine social policies that touched us almost everywhere we lived: medicine and the Hippocratic oath; civil liberties and mandatory testing; network television and commercials for condoms. It would determine how we collected blood, administered prisons, licensed marriages, applied for insurance, educated children and looked into our mirrors. It was itself determined by the media, plugged into our fearful sockets. And the media seemed not to care if what they told us was true or not. Because we hadn't tuners and amplifiers to steer through this killer buzz, nor bifocals for a close reading of the facts, nor previous experience or any wise men to help us feel our way, we depended for *all* the weather in our heads on the information environment—conscienceless, retina-eating media conglomerates. That's the context. From big-screen Hollywood, where so many of the living had known so many of the dying, personally, there were big-budget films about murderous babysitters and killer lesbians. But from small-screen Burbank and the far-flung precincts of cable, we got a steady stream of honorable worrywort movies, series episodes and educational specials, doing what TV does best, which is to tell stories about people who are hurting.

The NAMES Project, and its AIDS Memorial Quilt, finally made it to television in the fall of 1989 on HBO. This patchwork of grief had started two years earlier in San Francisco. Designed by friends and loved ones, each panel commemorated a life lost to plague—three feet by six. In *Common Threads*, we walked on runways among ten thousand of these panels, covering fourteen acres of the Ellipse behind the White House in Washington, D.C. We listened to Bobby McFerrin's music and Dustin Hoffman's narration, looked at clips of famous talking heads, from C. Everett Koop to Eddie Murphy, and met five of the victims: a decathalon athelete, a landscape architect, a naval officer, a little-boy hemophiliac, and an IV drug user who was too late kicking his habit. And we read a scroll of dread statistics: fifty-nine thousand Americans so far dead in the decade of the eighties, more than died in Vietnam; one hundred and fifty new deaths every day; one new case every minute. To make a quilt you stitch two layers of fabric together with a soft thickness between them. Quilts have been around for thousands of years, doing duty in Europe, Africa and Asia as cloaks, military doublets, cheap armor, petticoats and bedcovers. The best quilts, patchworks of bright medallions on white muslin with design variations on a Tree of Life, were North American. In the eighteenth and nineteenth centuries quilting was deemed a minor art—minor, of course, because women did it. Sewing machines were thought to have abolished this cunning handicraft. Not so. The AIDS Memorial Quilt is art, and also a comforter—a binding together, for warmth, of color and love and the fabric of memory.

Which is what we continued to see, on television: panel by panel, name by name. Terence McNally's *Andre's Mother*, an eight-minute essay on denial that seemed at the Manhattan Theatre Club in 1988 to float in the mind like a haiku, was distended on public television in 1990 to an hour, with Sada Thompson as the mother who circles around her son's homosexuality and death from AIDS a half-dozen times without ever permitting herself to utter the taboo words, without ever looking his lover in the eye. She is not...uncomprehending; she is devastated, thick with grief. And it is her own behavior as much as Andre's that she wants to avoid: "I don't approve," she says at last; "I can't...It's too terrible a criticism of me." But grief is greedy. It demands, if not meaning and forgiveness, at least extenuation; somebody else to blame. And Andre's lover, Richard Thomas, is just as greedy: for kinship and recognition, and for naming. Andre's death is the ultimate criticism of both of them, a permanent absenting of himself, a silence to fill up with excuses. On the telephone, in a restaurant, at the memorial service, in Central Park with their white balloons, the widow from Dallas who remembers her baby on a beach and the young man who is writing a book on Samuel Barber look for some language to talk about their mutual ghost, an actor who had played Edmund in *King Lear*.

Besides entertainment-and-information specials like *Red, Hot and Blue*, with pop-rockers like k.d. lang, Sinead O'Connor and David Byrne singing Cole Porter while Carrie Fisher, Whoopi Goldberg and Richard Gere schmoozed; the teen-directed rap-and-animation *Talkin' About AIDS*; BRAVO cable's annual month of Sundays devoted to raising funds and awareness, with info-plugs by Eric Bogosian, Geena Davis, Tommy Tune, Jodie Foster, Laura Dern and John Malkovich; and a second year in a row for ABC's two-hour *In A New Light* disease-o-rama with Arsenio Hall and Paula Abdul introducing peptalks and pop tunes by Hulk Hogan, Barry Manilow, Lily Tomlin, Pat Benatar, Dr. Joyce Brothers, Elton John and Assistant Surgeon General Dr. James Curran, there were also AIDS TV movies in the social worker and art therapy modes not merely every season, but what seemed like every several months, teaching us how we should at least *behave* no matter how we actually *felt*: decencies in search of an etiquette of caring. Who knows why? Gay-bashing was on the rise all over the country. (In New York, violence against gays increased by more than 100 percent from 1989 to 1990.) *TV Guide* reported in the spring of 1991 that advertising agencies believed the climate of public opinion had changed, from sympathy to indifference or disgust, and that television ought to find another tune to play. Except on television, most of us seemed to believe that the victims of AIDS deserved it. Just as, except on television, most of us were in favor of the gas chamber and the electric chair.

And yet: *Our Sons*, on ABC in 1991, was really about mothers. Successful businesswoman Julie Andrews thinks she has come to terms with her son's homosexuality. But when Hugh Grant (!) tells her his lover is dying of AIDS, she must master a whole new grammar of emotions. It's one thing to visit Zeljko Ivanek at a hospital and see what Kaposi's sarcoma looks like; it's another at her son's request to fly to Arkansas and bring back the boy's mother. Ann-Margret, a cocktail waitress, decided years ago she no longer had a son. What happened between these very different women was an hydraulic exchange of energies, memories and fears. Of course, this is what television is usually about: relationships. Even public television, as in the "American Playhouse" production that same fall of Craig Lucas' *Longtime Companion*, a sort of *Big Chill* and *Canterbury Tales* for gays, in which a handsome bunch of white guys—including Bruce Davison, Campbell Scott, Patrick Cassidy and Dermot Mulroney—sat around talking and relating and dying, while Mary-Louise Parker watched helplessly. It was actually funny, like Gogol and Beckett.

And yet again...In the 1992 network docudrama *Something to Live For: The Alison Gertz Story*, Molly Ringwald, no longer pretty in pink, cries out to an auditorium full of junior high school students: "Look at me! I am what AIDS looks like." She is 24 years old. She contracted AIDS from a single heterosxual encounter, at age 16. She has been persuaded, after the various hysterias of hospital workups (with orderlies zip-suited as if for a Three Mile Island meltdown), terrified boyfriends (as if she were a Love Canal), self-blaming parents (Lee Grant and Martin Landau), defaulting insurance companies and a grief therapist in the Berkshires, that she has something to contribute to the safe sex campaign and the demystification of a disease demonology. Young, gifted, white, female, innocent of leather bars and IV drugs, upper-middle class and Upper East Side: such unfairness ought never to happen to such a sweetheart. *"No one deserves to have this disease, no one!"* she tells the kids at junior high. And they give her a hug.

For an entirely different glimpse of what AIDS looks like, we could have been watching PBS that summer and seen, on *P.O.V.*, Pat Buchanan's favorite fire hydrant, *Tongues Untied*. *P.O.V.* means "point-of-view," and the point of view of *Tongues Untied* belonged to Marlon Riggs, who seemed to be just about everything Alison Gertz wasn't: an anti-Ringwald, male, black, gay and doubly disdained in straight white America. In his collage of skits, rap, camp, autobiography, newsreel footage, poems, dance and music video, Riggs tried to tell us how he felt before he died. Some of it was funny—a barbershop quartet singing "Baby, Come Out Tonight." Some of it was angry—at straight black activists with no time for gay men, at a gay white subculture with no time for black men and homophobic entertainers like Eddie Murphy. Some of it broke the heart—like listening to Billie Holliday. And ten or so minutes were shocking—even on cable TV, we seldom see full frontal male nudity, or black men kissing each other. Seventeen PBS stations in fifty of the nation's biggest markets refused to air *Tongues Untied*. But what's the point of public television if it refuses to hear the Other in America, speaking in a different anguish?

Just as remarkably, the three-year-old ABC dramatic series *Life Goes On* devoted most of its fourth and final season, in the preeminent family hour of 6 to 7 o'clock Sunday nights, to a step-by-step trailing after of a young AIDS patient on the stations of his cross. As if the hard-working Thatchers, Bill Smitrovich and Patti Lupone, hadn't enough trouble—he'd never be the architect he dreamed of, but has opened a restaurant; their Down's syndrome child, Corky, was unlucky in love but his sweet perseverence should get him through high school—Corky's sister Becca (Kellie Martin) had to pick a boyfriend (Chad Lowe) who happened to be HIV positive. And so, every week that spring of 1993, we got it all: Chad, attacked by skinheads outside the AIDS hospice; Kellie with literal blood on her hands; Bill with his daughter at a clinic, as terrified as she is; Dan Butler, the first "out" gay any of them's ever met, explaining at the hospice that the virus "doesn't care who you sleep with"; brutal bullying at high school and a cowardly attack on Bill's restaurant ("When," asks a female cop, "are we all going to learn we're holding onto the same piece of cloth?"), which the hospice volunteers will clean up after, in time for something like a Last Supper. To be followed by Kellie and Chad finding out whether there's any such thing as safe sex; by Chad's advance to full-blown AIDS; by cancellation of his insurance and his commitment to the county hospital charity ward; all the way to those metaphorical white balloons...A weekly network dramatic series did the very job of education that community school boards in places like New York City were afraid to attempt. This was what hate crimes and gay-bashing looked like. And what being tested for AIDS felt like. And even how traditional families like the Thatchers tried to *be* for one another: a sanctuary and a trampoline.

For how a nontraditional family did the same thing, we had to look no further that summer than to *Silverlake Life: The View from Here* on public television, a video diary so relentlessly alert, so horrifically intimate, so helplessly self-conscious and so passionately unhappy, that they probably gave it the Grand Jury Prize at the 1993 Sundance Festival as a way of defending themselves against it, of warding off the kicks and punches its crazed bravery inflicted on them. While we watch, filmmaker Tom Joslin and his lover of twenty-two years, Mark Massi, die of AIDS. But they have turned a camera on themselves to tape the process. A former student and longtime friend of Tom's, Peter Friedman, edited forty hours of this tape into a memoir of "the walking dead." This camera jumps at every tremor on the faultline of the disease and the relationship. We see them in Los Angeles going to a health food store, a supermarket, the bank, the therapist and the hospital. As if for the first time as well as the last, Tom, Mark and the camera contemplate not only their lesions but Dumpsters and hummingbirds, palm trees and swimming pools, telephone wires and pizza, marathon runners and a high school band. "It's a beautiful day in the neighorhood," says Tom, mimicking Mr. Rogers from his childhood. Mark sings "You Are My Sunshine" but he's also angry that Tom won't take his medication. Rather than go to an auto show they pretend from their porch that they're on a European cruise. For their last Christmas they visit Tom's family in New England—a mother coming to terms with her son; a father still furious; a supportive brother who'll later speak at Tom's funeral. A faith healer, "channeling," speaks in tongues. So, really, do the doctors. There are snippets as well of an earlier film of Tom's, from fifteen years ago, also on public television, when he and Mark were exuberantly young, healthy and full of the post-Stonewall literature of liberation. At the beginning of their film, both were bothered that when they talked into the camera, they couldn't see themselves on the monitor; toward the end they're afraid to turn the camera on. In front of our eyes they shop, bicker, sing, dance and die. Trying to pour Tom's ashes into an urn, Mark spills some: "You're all over the place," he says.

That fall, *And the Band Played On* finally came to pay-cable television, after Hollywood and CBS bailed out. An hour or so into Roger Spottiswode's film adaptation of the angry Randy Shilts best-seller, frustrated on almost every conceivable medical and bureaucratic front, at a conference of the elders of the Food and Drug Administration to think about quality control in the blood supply for hospital transfusions, Don Francis (Matthew Modine) finally lost his temper. "How many dead hemophiliacs do you *need*?" cried the seething young scientist from the Centers for Disease Control in Atlanta. Twenty minutes later, after Dr. Robert

Gallo (Alan Alda) had cut off Don's research funds from the National Institutes for Health because he sent blind samples to the retrovirus people at the Paris Institut Pasteur, Don blew his stack again: "Stop turning a holocaust into an international pissing contest!" In any other movie, either of these outbursts would have signalled a narrative surge towards climax. Like AIDS itself however, this flawed but powerful film—about the disease and how it spread in a decade of indifference, hostility, idiocy and opportunism—was long on devastation and short on resolution. Angry, perplexed, accusatory, *And the Band Played On* was a detective story at the end of which the killer sneered. We tracked this killer from 1977, when Copenhagen reported the first victim, to 1992, when the death toll reached 194,364 American men, women and children, with forty million cases predicted world wide by the turn of the century; from San Francisco, where a Halloween parade turned into one long candlelight memorial mass, to Atlanta, where CDC scientists fought a disease they couldn't understand, much less cure, to Washington, D.C., where Ronald Reagan took plague less seriously than his predecessor, Gerald Ford, had taken swine flu.

There were so many rumors beforehand about the TV movie, we need reminding what we actually saw, versus what we may have heard or feared. The villain of *And the Band Played On* was the Reagan administration, *not* bathhouses, though Gallo of N.I.H., scrambling for a patent and a Nobel Prize, came off as an unprincipled gloryhound. We could have used more on the hysterical media and on the unconscionable insurance and pharmaceutical industries, but the focus was on government and those communities (gays and ghettos) that government considered expendable. As such, with Phil Collins, David Dukes, Richard Gere, Anjelica Huston, Glenne Headly, Swoosie Kurtz, Steve Martin, Ian McKellen, Richard Masur, Saul Rubinek, Charles Martin Smith, and B.D. Wong in supporting roles, it came across as a combination of *The Andromeda Strain*, *The China Syndrome* and Zola's *J'accuse!* At the end, while a scroll rolled—dread statistics, panels of the NAMES quilt, montages of the famous dead from Rock Hudson to Arthur Ashe, from Liberace to Ryan White—Elton John sang again "The Last Song."

There were AIDS activists who objected to one or another emphasis or omission in *And the Band Played On*, whose screenplay, by Arnold Schulman, had already been nibbled on and quacked at by a pondful of left-and-rightwing ducks. And if I'd been an ACT UP urban guerrilla, I'm sure I'd have so much invested in this long-delayed production about my own life and death, to be seen in dozens of reruns by tens of millions, that any movie short of *The Sorrow and the Pity* would amount to an insult. From the street, the mainstream always looks soft and faithless, rounding off distinctive edges. Living the life, you can't see yourself in their cartoons. But that's what TV does to everything—softens, rounds, flattens, inflates and approximates. From such a stereo, we get mostly types. What we wish for in a popular culture is a plenitude of them, sufficiently diversified, to let us intuit from these scattered signs the existence of some complicated truth. The surprise of the last decade has been that so many did show up so often, on television, against the current of the mainstream's fear and loathing, with no conceivable hope of profit. Meaning well, while never enough, is not a crime. And until AIDS, TV had never even meant well when it came to representing gay and lesbian realities. It took television almost fifty years to graduate from fagbashing and pansy jokes to Margarethe Cammermeyer.

Imagine how healthy it would have been, in the Ed Sullivan or even the Mary Tyler Moore years, to see a documentary like *Why Am I Gay? Stories of Coming Out in America*, which came to cable in the summer of 1993. For an hour, what we heard from academics about the biology, psychology and anthropology of sexual preference wasn't nearly as compelling as the on-camera witness of Edgar, a gay Puerto Rican cop from the Bronx, and Susanne and Judith, a middle-aged lesbian couple who started a social mixer for gay teenagers in Houston, and Michael, from Ohio, singing a cappela doo-wop with the Flirtations before AIDS got him. Nor as scary as Ira's Kansas parents who had him committed, as if he'd been stolen and brainwashed by a cult, to the "structured environment" of a born-again halfway house, where guilty sexual sinners study the Bible and keep watch on one another so they won't debauch the local mall. In *Why Am I Gay?* we met friends and families, mostly supportive. We went to concerts, dances, therapy and, of course, the march on Washington, where Susanne and Judith were married and Michael sang. As well as pride, we got some jokes. ("Just because they're lesbians doesn't mean they're profound!") It would be pretty to think this quiet hour might actually change the minds of a Sam Nunn or a Bob Dole on, say, gays in the military. But one supposes that for that to happen, Phil Donahue would have to interview, on camera, Alexander the Great and his noble companions, while they danced naked around Achilles' sepulchre in Troy.

It's not television's fault that it can't talk America into doing or feeling anything America's not already inclined to do or feel. Only the theater has tried harder, with Terence McNally, Tony Kushner, Larry Kramer, Chay Yew and Jonathan Larson. Whereas, from Hollywood, at long last in December, 1993, after the many programs I have so far discussed and almost as many more I haven't, all we got was Jonathan Demme's *Philadelphia*, opening to an overkill of media congratulation, its minor virtues blown up into a Verdi *Aïda* excess. Wishing *Philadelphia* were a good movie didn't make it one, anymore than wearing a red ribbon to the Tom Hanks Oscar party was throwing yourself on the barricades. As in so many anguished films about South Africa, where our hero turns out to be a white lawyer or journalist for whom black suffering is somehow redemptive, so in Hollywood's first big-budget AIDS film, the hero is a black heterosexual turned heroic by the woundedness of a gay white man. In order to sell middle America on sympathy for the stricken, when *Philadelphia* wasn't preachy, it babytalked. And yet middle America is just another stereotype. Middle America has been watching the same TV as everyone else. And on TV, before Tom Hanks, Mark Harmon, Aidan Quinn, Swoosie Kurtz, Ian McKellen, Lukas Haas, Molly Ringwald, Chad Lowe and Kay Lenz had already portrayed the suffering of AIDS. And after Tom Hanks, so would Amy Madigan, Dennis Boutsikaris, Mary-Louise Parker, John Lithgow, Randy Quaid, Linda Hamilton, Eric Stoltz and a dozen other actors less well-known, in TV movies either weepy or outraged, and in TV serials as sure-fire subplots.

On Lifetime cable we got the Roxy and Vinnie Ventola story, *And Then There Was One*—not the best AIDS docudrama but smart and scrupulous, with Madigan and Boutsikaris happily married, blessed with friends, gainfully employed as writers, needing only a child to complete their circuit, looking like winners after six years of trying, at a party videotaping greetings to their very own unborn child, at the hospital videotaping Roxy's triumphant childbirth laugh—except that there's something wrong with baby Miranda, and with her parents too, and between Halloweens and hootenannys, one by one, they'll die. *And Then There Was One* wasn't really interested in *why* Roxy and Vinnie and Miranda got AIDS. More on the movie's mind was how we respond to something so arbitrary. Vinnie had God, Roxy had Vinnie, and maybe they weren't enough. You couldn't talk, write, buy or faith your way out of it. Nobody cares what's *fair*. And something else, an odd spin perhaps peculiar to those of us who try too hard to think about television, also attended my watching of *And Then There Was One*. Not on the screen, but behind the eyes, inside the head, as if the optic nerve were attached to some shadowy place deep down where we can't any longer be sure what's actual, it occurred to me to wonder: Roxy and Vinnie had been real people, with real AIDS. The writing they wrote was comedy. The comedy they wrote was for TV sitcoms—for Norman Lear's *Sunday Dinner*, a miserable short-lived series, and for Lear's *The Powers That Be*, somewhat funnier but also doomed to a quick cancellation. That means they'd contracted to come up with the usual 44 jokes per half-hour, not counting commercial breaks. And while they were being funny on demand, like a fizz machine, they were also trapped in a situation tragedy, as their own time ran out. Liking or disliking something on TV suddenly seemed impudent.

And then on ABC we got *A Place for Annie* with Sissy Spacek as a pediatric nurse who seeks to adopt an abandoned baby who's tested positive for HIV. When the baby's mother, Mary-Louise Parker, reappears wanting her baby back in spite of her vampire look and her fullblown death-sentence AIDS, Sissy will arrange for all of them to live together, along with her loving teenaged son, Jack Noseworthy, and her redoubtable Scots-burr nanny, Joan Plowright. So remarkable is this cast that it will soldier on absorbingly through an uplift script directed in slow-motion, as if AIDS, like almost every other trouble that's ever been noticed on television, were one more burden a white woman bears. On NBC in *Roommates* Bill (Eric Stoltz) is an upper-class Harvard-educated piano-playing neatness freak who eats salads, watches tennis and reads *Moby Dick*. Jim (Randy Quaid) is a working-class pool-playing ex-con who leaves his jacket on the floor and feeds his face with stew from a can. Both Bill and Jim have AIDS, but only one of them is gay. Can you guess which? If social worker Lisa (Elizabeth Peña) had not insisted that they bunk together at the hospice,

Bill would not have discovered that Jim, in spite of his homophobia ("This isn't *my* disease, it's *yours*"), has a heart the size of the Indian subcontinent; Jim would not have known that Bill, contrary to his sissified fastidiousness, is a Minnesota Fats at eightball; and it might never have occurred to any of us that AIDS is a form of socialism, in which distinctions of class dissolve in the solidarity of dying: *The Odd Couple Meets the Plague*. On the other hand, on CBS, in a true-story *My Brother's Keeper*, identical twins both went into the same seminary, both left to teach in public schools on Long Island and both are gay. If only one is HIV-positive, the other is eager to participate in a Johns Hopkins bone-marrow transplant operation that could be life-saving. An insurance company says no, a court says yes, and their mother, Ellen Burstyn, won't talk to either of them, maybe because they're both John Lithgow, in an amazing bravura performance. The difference between this TV movie and most others is that except for mom the entire community rallies round the Johns (teachers, students and parents), as if on Long Island they'd seen so many well-meaning TV AIDS programs, they'd finally got the liberal-humanist message.

There's more. When the hospital shows made their triumphant return to network primetime in 1994, AIDS was all over the place as something to worry about, like incompetence and budget cuts. But enough. By the time I saw the AIDS quilt in person, three years after having seen it on television, in the Winter Garden at the World Financial Center down in the Hong Kong sector of Manhattan, there were more than sixteen thousand panels, and we had just heard that week that the global incidence of AIDS might prove to be triple the previous estimates, and this wasn't nearly as newsworthy to the four daily New York papers as Joey Buttafuoco or Princess Di's bulimia. We may just be on the threshold of an extraordinary burst of creativity, because so much talent under a sentence of death is in such a hurry to say everything at once, as Thucydides, Boccaccio, Defoe, Poe, Dostoyevski, Capek and Camus wrote about the plague; and Dickens, Hugo, Turgenev, Keats, Shelley, Chopin, Debussy, D.H. Lawrence, Robert Louis Stevenson, Kafka, Mann and Ingmar Bergman tried to come to artistic terms with tuberculosis; and Baudelaire, de Maupassant and Ibsen contemplated syphilis; and Tolstoy, Bernanos, Arnold Bennett and Akira Kurosawa were obsessed with cancer. On HBO, the panels had been laid out like a carpet. In the Winter Garden, they were hung up like tents or sails. If you chose, you could read out loud a few of the names yourself, at a lectern with a microphone. As we did so that afternoon, sounding the names of the lost across a ghostly sea of banners, it almost seemed that we were part of a new political protest art, bringing beauty instead of insult into the world, a rite beyond mourning to healing, in colors other than blood—as if from a Navajo sand painting they'd made topgallants, mizzenmasts and mainsails; as if, from a requiem mass, they had somehow imagined pennants, and kites, and caravelles.

The Center for Disease Control and Prevention in Atlanta tells us that by the end of 1995 half a million Americans had been diagnosed with AIDS; and of these, 62 percent were dead. The number of people with HIV is at least twice that. World-wide, the United Nations Joint Program on HIV-AIDS just announced from Paris that an estimated 1,300,000 people already have AIDS, a jump of 25 percent from 1994 to 1995. That 21,000,000 adults now live with HIV. That 42 percent of these adults are women. That another 7,500 are infected every day. That forty million cases are predicted by the year 2,000. When the shameful history of the last twenty years of this century is written, there are likely to be more names on the panels of an AIDS quilt than on any honor roll of the righteous who tried to help. Writers, producers, actors and television executives tried to help. I don't know why Newton Minow's vast wasteland turned into a geography of conscience on this death watch—as if, having sold us so much beer, detergent and death on the installment plan, they decided to market instead tender mercies and saving grace; and I'm sorry so much of it seems to have fallen on deaf ears and hardened hearts, like atrocity footage from a foreign country with the wrong skin color; and I wish more of what they gave us had been as artful as *Angels in America.* But compared to the behaviors of hate radio, tabloid journalism, organized religion, the federal government, big-money science, corporate America and the feverish self-promotions of the beltway wiseguys pedalling away in their blisterpacks on the tricycles of their careers, television's telling stories in the Age of AIDS looks more like ancient Greece, where they knew from pity and terror. Or like the surpassing and mysterious "assault of peace," near the end of Andre Malraux's novel, *The Walnut Trees of Altenburg.* Germans on the front in World War I released a poison gas on their Russian enemy. And then they saw what they had done. And then they converged, like jungle animals on water points, to bear the bodies out of the chaos of a forest "in which the stricken and the dead swarmed like brothers under the blood-stained greatcoats gesticulating in the wind."

AGAINST ABORTION? DON'T HAVE ONE.
California bumper sticker

About abortion, even Granada in England and public television in the United States are not just shy but scared. When Detective Chief Inspector Jane Tennison of Scotland Yard can't choose to abort the unwanted child of a dead-end relationship without feeling so guilty about it that her police work is compromised, the bad vibrations from a hot-button issue have warped dramatic values and character logic as much as they've trashed polite discussion and civil discourse, and no other imaginable woman on entertainment television really has freedom of choice, either.

We first met Helen Mirren's Jane in January 1992, and the *Prime Suspect* in this British miniseries Thursday nights on *Mystery!* seemed to be Jane herself. Although nobody suspected her of having committed the grisly murder, she was presumed guilty by the old-boy network at New Scotland Yard of almost everything else. She only got the high-profile case because a more popular male detective had dropped dead. She had to release the likely killer for lack of evidence. She found that some of this evidence had been suppressed, or tampered with, by members of her own team. She couldn't find a car that only she thought crucial to the case. But most of all, she was guilty of a sex crime: she was a woman. Not only that, but a woman no longer young, nor a glamourpuss; and she smoked too much. On American TV since the eighties, a woman older than Lolita who smokes instead of jogging is automatically either a bad person or else working-class, probably bowls and is therefore dumb. Jane was anything but dumb, of course. It's just that she came home from the Yard at night too preoccupied for her needy boyfriend. Her boss didn't like her. Her resentful underlings didn't take her seriously. Her principal suspect strung her along like a yo-yo, and his girlfriend, the moody and mesmerizing Zoë Wanamaker, seemed to haunt her like some sort of alternative sexuality, an option never exercised. Even Jane's father was mystified by her workaholism; she missed his birthday party to appear on a "Crime Night" TV program. Nor was she ever invited out for a night of boozy bonding with the boys.

Naturally Jane cracked the case, intuiting the emotional algebra behind the crime from an appalling duet of her suspect, singing a song from *Carousel*, and his wiggy mother, singing Elvis. But what was extraordinary about the first *Prime Suspect*, aside from the splendid performance by Royal Shakespeare veteran Mirren, was that Jane *did* neglect her hearth, and any other outlet for a healthy emotional life outside work, and yet this difficult woman was permitted in a script by Lynda LaPlante, directed by Christopher Menaul, to find more than enough satisfaction in her equally difficult job. Over several Thursdays, without one scrap of sermonizing nor any comic strip light bulbs popping off above their heads, the Yard boys learned to respect her, especially her Grand Inquisitorial skills at interrogation. To this scrupulous police work within a thriller frame Granada brought the same remarkable production values it had lavished on *A Very British Coup*. Before our eyes we saw intellectual activity as its own reward, and an equal-opportunity employer. It was feminism at its most subversive. *Men* have always been willing to sacrifice domestic relationships to the higher calling of some exact science. (*Shut up*, we explain to the children: *I'm building a bomb to save the world*.) Jane played the same game.

In Hollywood, they were so surprised that they immediately thought of doing the same thing themselves all over again, merely worse, with Meryl Streep in the lead. (This was greeted with such ridicule, the idea died.) At CBS, Howard Stringer was so impressed, he tried to buy *Prime Suspect* for his network. (When that failed, he launched what he imagined to be its equivalent, a Friday night series called *Under Suspicion*, with big, blonde and distracted Karen Sillas as Rose Phillips—call her either "Phil" or "Philly"—the only female detective in the piggy-cop squad room of a Northwest city where it rained on her cigarettes. James Wolcott, at *The New Yorker*, was obsessed by Sillas: a Norse myth in a miniskirt; a highbrow Barbie Doll; a sex symbol so blankly cryptic that sex itself seemed out of the question; an "anti-babe" who took blondeness to abstraction. I liked her, too, maybe because of a gender-bending subtext: "Phil" could be male; "Philly" was a female horse. More probably because, whether she was bending down from her great height to pick up a clue about sperm or horticulture, or interrogating the shifty-eyed as if they were guilty of Watergate or Pinter, she was a remote as an ice sculpture. By the end of *Under Suspicion*'s single season, only Wolcott and I seemed to be watching.)

In the second *Prime Suspect*, sneaking sex on the sly night off with a fellow Yard detective who happened to be black and trying afterward *not* to reach for a cigarette, Jane had to cope with the combustible politics of race and class as well as gender. In the dug-up garden in a benighted Afro-Caribbean neighborhood in a London as wet as Karen Sillas, cops found the decomposed body of a 17-year-old girl. With both a by-election and a race riot in the offing, Jane had to be supersensitive sorting through skull fragments, pornographic snapshots, Yoruba amulets, fallible memories and the ambiguous images on the videotape of a reggae concert. What once again astonished was the way Helen Mirren *listened*, as if her whole being were an exquisite ear, priestly or psychoanalytic, communicating the sense that intelligence was not only a kind of passionate sonar, but also sexy. By the third *Prime Suspect*, from its stunning opening sequence to a last-minute surprise in its triple-helix plot, Helen Mirren/Jane Tennison had become a heroine of culture. As the camera swam through the lower depths of London vice and the higher reaches of official corruption, even the music was creepy— either wounded and romantic or ominous and dissonant—like the anthem of some drowned republic: Weimar maybe. Somebody was killing our children. Fresh from another ruinous love affair, Jane entered a world of tabloid journalism, corrupt social services, blackmail and coverup, murder and suicide, homophobia and AIDS; of rent boys "on the game" and "punters" who buy and sell them; of gay cabarets, meat-market streets, roof gardens, drag shows and transvestites. Having in one miniseries fought a gender war, and in another saved London from race riots, in this third she took on all the orphans in the burning world, and the riddle, as well, of sexual identity. She also decided to have an abortion.

So this was the Jane with whom we reacquainted ourselves in April 1995, having learned how to play hardball office politics and so gotten herself promoted to Detective Chief Inspector, chewing gum to stop smoking, still single, checking herself in for a D&C. She would emerge to take charge of the case of a missing child, a 14-month-old baby girl named Vicky, leading her now-loyal troops into battle against uncooperative psychiatrists, sleazy porn merchants and the werewolf media. She would ask us to think about everything from Susan Smith to the sale of children on a pedophile exchange. And she would misconceive her entire investigation because, of course, symbolically speaking, *the missing child was her own*. Guilty Jane chased ghosts.

I fell off the double-decker bus. It wasn't just that the fourth *Prime Suspect*, with SWAT teams and hostage crises, out-of-control cops and anal-retentive shrinks, traumatized mothers and abused children, was old news to anyone who had ever watched a network movie-of-the-week. It was more that all of a sudden Jane couldn't function effectively in a job she'd worked so long and hard to get. She'd managed in the previous miniseries to prevail as a detective in spite of getting dumped by a man jealous of her career, in spite of sexism, sabotage and even criminal behavior at her own Scotland Yard, in spite of the scandal of an interracial love affair with a colleague, early pregnancy and advanced nicotine withdrawal. This time out, however, a perfectly legal and straightforward medical procedure threw her into such a gloomy funk that she almost blew the case. And why was this, exactly? Bad faith? False consciousness? Internal contradictions? Unacknowledged mourning? Intimations of infanticide? William Rehnquist?

Little Vicky turned out to have gone missing not because she'd been kidnapped, but because her distraught mother had killed her and dumped the body. An equally distraught, and to me unrecognizable Jane, missed the telltale signs because (apparently, psychologically) she had committed the same crime. The Jane I thought I knew, having made up her mind to abort and then kept an appointment to do so, would have smoked some cigarettes, chewed some gum, drunk some scotch, looked in the mirror and experienced ambivalence afterwards, in the privacy of her own home, but she would also have left these ghosts hung up in a plastic bag in the hall closet while she went off to behave professionally at the Yard. The ghosts would wait there patiently for her return, like every other misgiving in a complicated life.

Perhaps you've noticed that in the real world women who have abortions react as variously afterwards as human beings of all kinds have reacted at all times, in the aftermath of any important choice, across the spectrum—with relief as well as regret. Only on television for the last twenty years have the appropriate and obligatory emotions reduced themselves to uncontrollable grief and incapacitating guilt, and that's if the writers, the studios, the networks and the advertisers will permit an abortion at all. On almost every other social issue from domestic violence to homelessness, from racism to homophobia, television has gotten braver since the fifties. But on abortion, with exceedingly rare network exceptions, it's been in a steady retreat since a pro-choice episode of *The Defenders* in 1963. I mentioned *Maude* in chapter II; her fictitious mid-seventies abortion shortly after a 1973 real world Supreme Court decision made one legal, drew more protest mail than any other episode of any other sitcom on CBS, including *All in the Family*. Those angry letters had a chilling effect on the craven networks. Not another recurring character on series television would abort another fetus until a high school student reluctantly decided to do so over several episodes of *TV 101* in 1989—which several CBS affiliates refused to run. By the time the folks on *Picket Fences* got around to rattling this cage, in 1995, they'd already broken so many other taboos that hardly anyone noticed: David Kelley, being outrageous again. More fuss was made about a similar decision on *The Real World*, but *The Real World* was cable television. Even worse, it was teenybopper MTV. And even so, sponsors jumped ship. Not that the prime-time small screen wasn't rampant with pregnant women, even victims of incest and rape, often affirming their right to choose and usually pretending to think about it. It's just that they invariably decided not to, like Murphy Brown.

To this politic omission, there have been occasional exceptions on dramatic series, not involving recurring characters—episodes of *Cagney & Lacey* in 1985, *The Trials of Rosie O'Neill* in 1990 and *Law & Order* in 1991, all three about protests at abortion clinics turning violent, permitting our heroines and heroes to debate the issue in the pro and con abstract, as if, before *Roe v. Wade*, 2,000 American women hadn't died every year from illegal abortions, whereas, in 1985, only *three* did. Thinking about terrorism was a way of not thinking about the fetus.

Roe v. Wade actually got its own movie on NBC in 1989, with

Holly Hunter as the Supreme Court case and Amy Madigan as her lawyer—the only network TV movie ever devoted entirely to abortion, from which advertisers fled in maddened droves even though it cracked the Nielsen Top 10 in ratings. (This was the same year that many radio stations wouldn't run Susan Sarandon's spots promoting the National Organization of Woman's pro-choice march on Washington.) It was probably odder that Norma McCorvey should show up in the Supreme Court than on network TV. In a democracy, the unlikeliest people, petitioning for redress of grievance, end up changing our lives: a Brown, a Gideon, a Miranda. You'd think a doctor might have sued the State of Texas for its law against abortion. Norma McCorvey sued instead. A carnival barker living in a trailor, a refugee from an abusive marriage barely capable of taking care of herself, and pregnant again in February 1970, McCorvey found herself a young lawyer, Sarah Weddington, who would take her case to the top. By the time the Court ruled in favor of "Jane Roe," she had already gone through a punishing birth and given up the child for adoption.

For the purposes of *Roe v. Wade* the TV movie, Norma McCorvey was called Ellen Russell. She was really, of course, Holly Hunter. Imagine the grinding of teeth in the clenched jaws of the bombers of Florida abortion clinics and the body-snatchers on Long Island. Holly Hunter! Even if *Roe v. Wade* gave almost equal time to fanciful theories of prenatal sentience, how could anybody root against *Raising Arizona, Broadcast News* and *Miss Firecracker*? It would be like rooting against Sally Field in *Norma Rae*, or, for that matter, Henry Fonda in *Gideon's Trumpet*. And Amy Madigan—*Places in the Heart, Field of Dreams*—as Sarah Weddington, who had never been to court before she took on "Roe" as a client...more unfair stacking of the emotional deck, unless you happened to have seen *The Silent Scream*, the anti-abortion agit-prop movie, in which case you needed reminding that the "sanctuary" objectified and depersonalized in this nasty piece of work was also a woman, with her very own right to life.

These heavy weather advisories having been posted, was *Roe v. Wade* any good as a movie? It was very good as a movie. Hunter with her cheap jewelry and torn jeans, sleeping in the back of a flatbed truck, was marvelous: resilient, sarcastic, semi-tough. Madigan was scared ("I feel like the whole Movement's counting on me"), but not so much so as to let the men take over after they hadn't helped with the brief. Nor were the two of them portrayed as flawless heroines: the plaintiff lied to her lawyer; the lawyer was so busy, she forgot when her client's baby was due. Scriptwriter Alison Cross also gave the dialogue some edge; to her awful, self-righteous and un-loving mother, Holly-Ellen-Norma said, "Fold it five ways and stuff it." And producer-director Gregory Hoblit, a veteran of *Hill Street Blues* and *L.A. Law*, chose daringly to give the movie a country-and-western look, sound and feel, a juke-box twang like Holly's own: "I'm pregnant; I'm not *trash*." This struck an important chord. We were being told by a TV movie that abortion rights were a class as well as a gender issue. Even if Sister Sandra and the Supremes went on to change the Court's tune, well-to-do white women could always move to another state, or fly to France for the "contra-gestation" pill. Real-life McCorveys hadn't that option; they cleaned upscale houses for a living.

Not having to answer to advertisers, HBO could be a little braver. So that's where we saw *A Private Matter* in 1994. The recipe seemed typical of network TV movie—a plucky heroine makes a difficult choice that costs her her job and her standing in the community. Though misunderstood by doctors and lawyers and set upon by mosquito media, she will not only prevail, but get to be played by Sissy Spacek in a Joan Micklin Silver production. But *A Private Matter* was about abortion in 1962, before *Roe v. Wade*. The heroine played by Spacek was Sherri Chessen Finkbine, the host of a *Romper Room* children's TV program in Phoenix, Arizona, expecting her third child. From a business trip to Europe, her husband Bob (Aidan Quinn) had returned with what he thought were tranquillizers, but which turned out to be thalidomide. Sissy had to force herself into an all-male discussion on the part of mate and medico as to what to do about this bad news. Deciding reluctantly to abort, she was dismayed to find her name in the newspaper, and to be dismissed from *Romper Room*. And to be sandbagged by a TV interviewer. When the hospital backed out in the face of so much negative publicity, her choices narrowed even more. She flew to Sweden. That's what women who could afford it did, before *Roe v. Wade*. But *A Private Matter* was as much about the landscape and the geography of choice as it was about the law of the land: Surgeons and shrinks, newspaper reporters and TV station managers, husbands and politicians—everybody was telling Sherri Finkbine what to do, and none of them was Sherri Finkbine.

From Lifetime, the cable channel that says it's for women, we'd expect a bit more than network courage. And a bit more is what we got. *Choices of the Heart*, an otherwise interesting 1995 biopic of Margaret Sanger, told us some of what we needed to know about the Irish-American nurse who took on Congress, the Catholic Church, the postal service and Anthony Comstock's Society for the Suppression of Vice; the pamphlet writer, magazine editor, bohemian radical and founding mother of Planned Parenthood; a red-haired angel of choice who went to jail for insisting on the right of women to birth control. Moreover, with Dana Delany from *China Beach* as the young Margaret, sitting around in Greenwich Village in 1914 with Mabel Dodge, John Reed and Emma Goldman, it was possible to believe for two hours that socialism might make a comeback. From Ellen Chesler's splendid biography *Woman of Valor*, however, we know that while the real Sanger may not have been as gorgeous as Delany, she was a lot more complicated than *Choices of the Heart*. In England, for instance, she had an affair with Havelock Ellis, as she would later fool around with H.G. Wells. Like many young socialists, she ended up a registered Republican. And her solution to the dying of so many poor women from self-induced abortions in Lower East Side tenements was not just facts on contraception; she emphatically favored legal medical abortions. Which we wouldn't have known from this movie about her.

Once again, in November of the year of Sanger, *P.O.V.* on public television came partially to the rescue. "Leona's Sister Gerri" told us the dreadful story of a young woman, Gerri Santoro, who died in 1964 from an illegal abortion on the floor of a motel room, and whose gruesome post mortem photograph after its publication in *Ms.* magazine in 1973 became an icon, a pro-choice agitprop equivalent of the fetus in a bottle. Producer-director Jane Gillooly interviewed Gerri's sister, brother, daughters and friends, the room clerk at the motel, the chambermaid who found the bloody body, the cops on the case, the publisher of *Ms.* and the author of the accompanying article. From these interviews, a heartbreaking album of family snapshots and skillfully edited footage of demonstrations for and against abortion, Gillooly gave us the sad life behind the awful symbol, acquainted us with Gerri's no-win situation and the sinister silence that preceded her decision (as well as a second sort of silence that followed in her family after they got the news), and worried out loud about symbolic politics in the media and on the streets. We also heard the contradictory things her grown-up daughters say today about abortion, choice and their mother.

According to every reliable public-opinion poll an overwhelming majority of the American public favors choice, including legal abortions. But so fretted are the raw edges of debate on the subject that television, in all its variety of genres, has decided not to have an opinion—or, like Clarence Thomas at Senate Judiciary hearings on his nomination to the Supreme Court, to keep it a secret. Isn't it odd, to be so brave, as we have seen, on behalf of AIDS victims in the face of public indifference, disapproval and disdain; to be so idealistic, as we shall see, about race relations in this country, even as a distempered public polarizes, and yet to blink unto blindness on an issue so important to the very women television has supported in related campaigns for equal opportunity and pay, against sexual harassment, spousal abuse and acquaintance rape? I wish I lived in a world where no one wanted an abortion, because fool-proof contraception was readily available, and all children anyway were loved and cared for. But I live instead in a world where network television won't even advertise the morning-after pill, and where children themselves are having children—usually by men no longer children, though often closely related to them—for whom moralizing anti-choice ideologues don't have time or money or affection, so busy are they telling Normas and Sherris and even Sandras what to do with their own bodies, and caring more about abstract ideas, like prenatal sentience, than they do about the kids already dying on an installment plan in our imperial cities. Where the Hyde Amendment denies Medicaid funding for abortions for poor women; and the Supreme Court's 1992 ruling in *Planned Parenthood v. Carey* permitted states to impose a whole new set of restrictions on a right we all thought *Roe v. Wade* had guaranteed; and parental notification and consent laws proliferate along with the mandatory waiting period and "counseling" requirements that include a graphic snapshot of a helpless fetus; and health and family-planning clinics are firebombed; and doctors and nurses and receptionists are murdered. We scientize, parsing trimesters. We theologize, counting "souls" like crazy Gogols. We hope for a technological deliverance, like the French pill. We argue about splinters in a Republican

Party platform plank, as if either Bob Dole or Ralph Reed should have any say at all on a woman's right to reproductive freedom. And we look into our media mirrors for some reflection of these hopes and fears, because television news, talk shows, entertainment programs and even its commercials conspire with the clash on the streets of bodies and balloons and sandwich boards and symbols, in competing magics of guerrilla theater and doctored spin, to determine our personal parameters and our national agenda. If television fails to represent our most troubling complications, how are we supposed to imagine ourselves?

Real rap is the only way young black people have of kicking the real knowledge.... We've gotta uncover this mystery of why we are poor and why we're killing each other in the streets. That's got to be uncovered in the music, and if you want rap that's not on the political route there's so many rappers out there you can find somebody who's just rockin' beats. But we gotta use our outlets because this is our only outlet that we can use, almost uncensored, so what else can we do? The classroom ain't getting it done for us, newspapers, the church, none of these are getting the job done.

Ice Cube, 1992

I'm just kind of a dumb dude who never finished the 4th grade. I'm wandering around the streets with my baseball hat on backward and $150 tennis shoes I knocked another kid out to get. I'm looking for real trouble to prove that I am a man. Well, how do I define what a man is? I define what a man is from the rap music I hear.... A man is defined in that culture as a breeder who gets the woman pregnant and then she gets welfare.

Ross Perot to David Frost,
on how young black men really think, 1996

A light and diplomatic bird
Is lenient in my window tree.
A quick dilemma of the leaves
Discloses twist and tact to me.

Gwendolyn Brooks

There was a nice movie moment a half-hour into *The Tuskegee Airmen*, on HBO in August, 1995. Army Air Corps cadets Laurence Fishburne and Cuba Gooding Jr. drop out of the Alabama sky one sun-struck afternoon in 1943, and emergency-land their training wheels on a highway directly in front of a prison chain-gang. The pilots emerge from their cockpits in warrior harness, and remove their Martian goggles. If the good old boy of a guard is startled, his prisoners are amazed: *Black men can fly.* Who, besides maybe Eleanor Roosevelt, would have believed it? Certainly not Christopher McDonald, the Army major who seeks to sabotage their training. Nor John Lithgow, a southern senator determined to make sure they never see combat. Maybe Andre Braugher, as Lieutenant Colonel Benjamin O. Davis, who will show up later on, between episodes of *Homicide*, in North Africa, with a surprisingly hairy head.

Never mind Joe Louis, beating up on Max Schmeling. Or Jesse Owens, at the 1936 Berlin Olympics. Even in a war against Hitler, the last thing a Jim Crow Army in a Jim Crow America really wanted was black men looking down on them. It took most of the war, and a punishing loss of melanin-deprived pilots, for most of the African-American graduates of the Tuskegee training program to get overseas at all. Then it took another bureaucratic hassle to get them out of North Africa, into Italy and Germany, as bomber escorts. And after the war, in which combat pilots of the four squadrons of the 332nd Fighter Group managed to bring back every single bomber they had been assigned to protect, it took another fifty years to get their story on any screen.

The Tuskegee Airmen—directed by Robert Markowitz from a story by one of the original cadets—was a so-so feel-good Guy Movie, in which actors like Fishburne, Gooding, Braugher, Malcolm-Jamal Warner, Courtney Vance, Allen Payne, Mekhi Pfifer and William Earl Ray had obviously enlisted to give something back to their community. So much star power might have overwhelmed a slender and predictable plotline. (You knew these 1995 guys would never have taken any of that 1943 crap.) But they were out to throw a bell curve. The composites they embodied (Hannibal, Cappy, Peoples, Train) wanted to fly. And proved, of course, that they could, sort of like Jackie Robinson, Miles Davis and Toni Morrison. You were encouraged to cheer, as I did, when a bomber pilot from whitebread Texas, with a run on Berlin in his immediate future, *requested* the 332nd as his escort. He knew his stats.

Two thoughts occurred in passing. The first had to do with symbolic resonance. Before any Army air cadets ever arrived in Tuskegee, there was a college in town, on the site of an old slave plantation. Booker T. Washington started the Tuskegee Institute in 1881. While W.E.B. DuBois made an eloquent case against Self-Help Booker, even DuBois's "talented tenth" had to have some college to go to. Tuskegee is where the botanist George Washington Carver worked on his peanuts and sweet potatoes; it's also where the novelists Ralph Ellison and Albert Murray went to school. The resonance was that for more than a century, at Tuskegee, black men had grown wings.

The other thought was about television. We knew most of the actors in *The Tuskegee Airmen* because of TV. In the current climate of a backlash on affirmative action, of fear and loathing of the urban "underclass," of Mike Tyson, Louis Farrakhan and Willie Horton as pin-up bogeymen and welfare queens as voodoo dolls, of hate radio, Aryan militias and the fire-bombing of black churches all over the South—television, where the ad cult meets the melting pot to stipulate a color-blind consumer, may be the only remaining American institution outside of schools that still believes in integration. As much as the novels of Toni Morrison and the plays of August Wilson seek to reimagine the lost history of their aggrieved people, their love and work, their nightmare passage and redemptive music, so has television ever since *Beulah* tried to sing this same song in each of its popular forms: in such sixties sitcoms as *Julia* with Diahann Carroll and *Room 222* with Lloyd Haynes, in seventies sitcoms like *Sanford and Son* and *The Jeffersons*, in eighties sitcoms like *The Cosby Show* and *Frank's Place*, and in nineties sitcoms like *South Central, Roc, Fresh Prince of Bel Air*, with Wil Smith, and *Moesha*, with Brandy Norwood; in variety shows with Flip Wilson, Nat "King" Cole, Lena Horne, Dionne Warwick, Richard Pryor or Whoopi Goldberg; in TV movies like

Howard Beach, Murder in Mississippi, The Court Martial of Jackie Robinson, The Josephine Baker Story, Best Intentions, There Are No Children Here, The Vernon Johns Story, Zooman, Assault at West Point and *Lily in Winter*; in miniseries like Alex Haley's *Roots*, Gloria Naylor's *The Women of Brewster Place*, Sidney Poitier as Thurgood Marshall in *Separate But Equal*, C.C.H. Pounder as a Roxbury mother in *Common Ground, Laurel Avenue* on HBO and *Queen* on CBS; in televised presentations of Broadway and off-Broadway plays like Anna Deavere Smith's *Fires in the Mirror* and George C. Wolfe's *The Colored Museum*, Danny Glover in *A Raisin in the Sun* and Charles S. Dutton in *The Piano Lesson*; in made with TV money feature films like Julie Dash's *Daughters of the Dust* and Matty Rich's *Straight Out of Brooklyn, Native Son* and *Hoop Dreams*; in documentaries like *Eyes on the Prize, Zora Is My Name, Color Adjustment, Malcolm X: Make It Plain, Adam Clayton Powell, Clarence Thomas and Anita Hill, Going Back to T'Town*, Barbara Kopple's *Fallen Champ* and Nicholas Lemann's *The Promised Land*.

And this far from exhaustive list has so far omitted any mention of weekly dramatic series starring James Earl Jones, Louis Gossett Jr., Denzel Washington, Cicely Tyson, Tim Reid, Mario Van Peebles, Richard Roundtree, Ruby Dee, Joe Morton, Carl Lumbly, Billy Dee Williams, S. Epatha Merkerson, Howard E. Rollins Jr., Avery Brooks, Yaphet Kotto, Alfre Woodard, Garrett Morris, Ossie Davis, Roger Mosely, Andre Braugher and Regina Taylor. Or talk-show hosts like Oprah in the afternoon and Arsenio Hall at night. Or Ed Bradley every week on *60 Minutes*, and Bernard Shaw every night on CNN, and Charlayne Hunter-Gault whenever she wants to on public television. To which we ought to add African-American anchors on the local news; rap and hip-hop videos on the various cable music channels; and entire networks, like Fox and UPN, in their color-coded fledgling seasons, during which they would look anywhere for pairs of eyes.

And professional sports: Ken Griffey Jr. and Deion Sanders in commercials for soda pop or breakfast cereal; *Bo Knows Racism*. We may be sure that somewhere late at night, in the rat-warren carrel of a remote academy, a postdoc in American popular culture has already formed a theory and is writing a thesis on pro basketball, than which there's no game more postmodern, all velocity and attitude, so antithetical to reactionary baseball with its slo-mo mosey to a culmination and its rhapsodic hesitations. Most of us have never seen Michael Jordan, Magic Johnson, Charles Barkley and Shaquille O'Neal except on television, and more often in Nike or Rebok commercials than dunking or dribbling. (Before shoes, Bill Russell flacked for Bell Telephone, Willis Reed for Dannon yogurt and Wilt Chamberlain for Brut aftershave.) Yet there are posters of Michael and Shaq in action on the bedroom walls of little boys from Paris to Phnom Penh, as if they were Bogart or Elvis. And they *are*, only bigger. Such a Dream Team. It's impossible, in fact, to imagine American popular culture at all without the seasoning and savor of black genius: without jazz, blues and basketball. *In your face!*

Of course, on the electronic plantation, if our darkies aren't playing basketball we'd prefer that they be funny. And we'd rather not see them at all Thursday nights, when most of the nation sits still for an all-white bloc of NBC sitcoms, until *ER*. Still: As late as 1959, the philosopher Hannah Arendt got herself in trouble with fellow liberals by writing a magazine article—for the socialist quarterly *Dissent*, no less—in favor of mixed marriages. Her fellow liberals felt that raising the spectre of miscegenation played into the hands, and the fantasies, of anti-integration bigots. And yet, by the end of the eighties, on NBC's *In the Heat of the Night*, Carroll O'Connor as chief of police chief in the Southern town of Sparta was conducting a season-long romance with black city councilwoman Denise Nicholas concluding in matrimony, after which they lived together and she wouldn't let him drink gin. Television has come a long way since Ed Sullivan scandalized a third of the country by kissing Pearl Bailey on a Sunday night—and so have the advertising agencies that sponsor it, from an antebellum Rastus for Cream of Wheat and Aunt Jemima for pancake mix to a postmodern Spike Lee for rocket-science sneakers. What we see on TV is a more integrated America than we see almost anywhere else outside the locker rooms of baseball teams or the barracks of a volunteer army: at conclaves, for instance, of law-firm partners or bank vice presidents or college professors; at board meetings of foundation executives, corporation trustees, book publishers and even editors of leftwing magazines; at shop meetings of construction union workers, in roomfuls of *New Yorker* cartoonists, or in sessions of Congress.

Which is not to say that the local TV news, with its nightly line-up of perps and pimps and popinjays, doesn't offer up a different mirror to white Americans of aberrant black behavior, in housing projects in drive-by neighborhoods. Nor is it to say that white and black audiences process the same images in the same way, coming to roughly similar conclusions about, say, the Million Man March, Jesse Jackson, Dennis Rodman, Rodney King and O.J., not to mention Jesse Helms or Pat Buchanan. For that matter, while white Americans were tangled up in our psychic kinks about black sexuality, African-American males tended to have a different take on Clarence Thomas and Anita Hill from African-American females; and younger black females, a different take from older black females; and middle-class blacks, from working class blacks. We should no more expect Cornel West and Sister Souljah to *think* the same thing after watching the same TV than we would expect of Susan Faludi and Orrin Hatch, or Tony Kushner and Tipper Gore, or me and Rupert Murdoch. We each bring to the box our separate embattled selves, a constructed identity that is on the one hand the space in the middle where everything else about us intersects and overlaps (race, gender, faith, socio-economic status, sexual orientation, family obligations, professional associations, friends, enemies and health), and on the other hand what postmodern theorists call "a radically overdetermined site for the contestation of core cultural notions"—that is, whatever gets dumped on us. And even this poor composite is provisional. It *depends*. You got lucky, or a raise. Whereas, last night, I sang a sorrow song.

Some of you men sure do make me tired.
You got a mouthful of gimme, a handful of much obliged.
Bessie Smith

And none of *this* is to say that the prettier picture of race relations we see on television has had *any* measurable effect on those relations in the real American world. On TV cop shows like *Law & Order*, *NYPD Blue* and *Homicide*, S. Epatha Merkerson and James McDaniel are New York lieutenants, to whom the plain-clothes detectives report, and Yaphet Kotto is a Baltimore shift commander. Unless a critic like Robert F. Moss told you so in a magazine article, you wouldn't know that the real world of Baltimore is a city 60 percent black with a police force 33 percent black, where only 18 percent of command-level jobs (from captain up) were held by African-Americans. Nor that in New York's real world, where white cops rioted in 1992 on the steps of City Hall against the policies of our first black mayor, 93 per cent of those officers with a rank of sergeant or higher are white male Anglo. And in none of the dozens of TV cop shows set in Los Angeles from *Dragnet* in 1952 to *High Incident* in 1996, have we ever met a cesspool mind and garbage-mouth like Mark Fuhrman. As for crimes committed, perps pursued and prisons over-populated, entertainment TV actually paints a portrait of big-city mayhem more technicolored than facts warrant, in order to avoid the stereotyping of late-night local news. Moss notes that in Baltimore 90 percent of homicide victims are black, and so are 90 percent of their killers. (His source is *Sun* reporter David Simon, who wrote the book from which the *Homicide* series derived.) But a prime-time audience is no more interested in monochromatic crime scenes than it is in real-world stats on police department staffing and promotions, or how come our public schools are falling down while prison-building is a growth industry.

When William F. Buckley Jr. tells us that "the ratings of Bill Cosby's television show and the sales of his books" prove that race prejudice is a thing of the past in this country, he hasn't been talking to Ice Cube, Rodney King, Cornel West or even to Bill Cosby. He needs a refresher course in the difference between representation and reality. Only by *not* watching TV could we have failed to see representations of dozens of realities significantly different from the middle-class Huxtables in cozy Brooklyn Heights—of, just for starters, Kahlil Kain as the predatory "Zooman" of Bed-Stuy, Tina Lawford and Larenz Tate in South Central between riots, Tim Reid in voodoo New Orleans, James Earl Jones and Vanessa Bell Calloway trying to get some sleep in Seattle, Joe Morton hospitalized in Howard Beach, Mary Alice and Rhonda Stubbins White against the odds in St. Paul, Maya Angelou in the Horner housing projects on Chicago's southside, C.C.H. Pounder in Roxbury, Massachuetts, Natalie Cole in sharecropper Alabama, Curtis McClarin at Exeter, Samuel L. Jackson at West Point and Blair Underwood in Philadelphia, Mississippi.

Buckley could also use a TV refresher course in the sort of history that tells us something else besides what white men did in the daytime. (The behavior of white men at night, after all, accounts for the lustrous spectrum of African-American complexions, from ebony to copper to cinnamon.) He needn't go back beyond the 1950s if he's busy, though there have been several pretty good movies on the Ku Klux Klan from its night-riding heyday during Reconstruction to the second coming of the coneheads in the 1920s, when their grievances were almost as much populist as racist, equally fearful in *Cross of Fire* (NBC) of Carnegies, coloreds, Catholics, DuPonts, Rockefellers, Jews, the robber barons *and* the unwashed immigrant masses, Wall Street *and* godless socialism, "Al Capone and Teapot Dome." And splendid documentaries like Nicholas Lemann's *The Promised Land* (Discovery), on the movement of more than six million blacks in the forties and fifties— the largest single peacetime migration of peoples in recorded history—from the rural South to the urban North, from Mississippi's Delta to Chicago's South Side. Or Vince DiPersio and Bill Guttentag's *Blues Highway* (TBS), covering the same story by following the music from cottonfields, church choirs and juke joints to the dives on Forty-seventh Street where, by mysterious transmutation, hymn chords and Ashanti drums and off-beat West African phrasing ended up in the blues of Blind Lemon Jefferson, Big Bill Broonzy, Bessie Smith and Ma Rainey. And, of course, there's always *Roots*.

But the fifties will do for a start. In 1953, while the Supreme Court was still in session, brooding about segregated schools, there was a dinner party at the White House. The new chief justice, Earl Warren, had been invited, as well as John W. Davis, the former presidential candidate who had argued South Carolina's Jim Crow case before the court. After dinner, Dwight D. Eisenhower took Earl Warren aside, and this is what Ike said about the South: "These aren't bad people. All they're concerned about is to see that their sweet little girls are not required to sit in school alongside some big overgrown Negroes." While this avuncular-kinky-apartheid comment didn't show up in either television miniseries devoted to Thurgood Marshall and *Brown v. the Board of Education*, almost everything else we need to know made the cut. In his 1991 ABC miniseries, *Separate but Equal*, George Stevens Jr., had the star-quality advantage of Sidney Poitier as Marshall, who argued the NAACP Legal Defense Fund case against Clarendon County and Topeka. So what if he didn't look much like Thurgood. Icons look like themselves. Poitier's been making movies for almost fifty years. Not all of them are nifty, but in most he is somehow superior not only to the material but to everyone else, black or white, on the screen, with more pride and reserve, intelligence and control, intensity and grace. To the Supreme Court, whether suffering from stage fright or playing with his model trains, he brought both edge and mischief. He also had accomplished help: Burt Lancaster as John Davis, reading W.E.B. DuBois; Richard Kiley as Earl Warren, diffident, instinctive, shrewd; Damien Leake as Kenneth Clark, playing with those horrific dolls. Behind them like gathering clouds: the parents of children who needed decent schools and buses to get to them, a Southern District judge voting his conscience despite a burning cross, volunteers who researched the briefs and clerks who bullied the Supremes. Trying to be high-minded, commercial TV often sinks into a noble-noodle soup; so much important history and heroic rhetoric and remedial seriousness tastes like Pepto-Bismal. But inside the moral vortex of *Separate but Equal*, there was room for wit, and a surprising avidity for details of process. To be sure, on the ultimate American committee there was a sliding scale of scruple, a clash of personalities, and nine pairs of eyes on the main chance, the good opinion of posterity, the U.S. Constitution and the clock. Nevertheless they reversed themselves, deciding that segregation was *exclusion* and thus unlawful. The King James version of the Bible was also written by a committee. A bunch of ex-sinners put the good news together in the first place.

In *Simple Justice*, an unusual 1993 *American Experience* docudrama based on Richard Kluger's account of the same events, public television had to make do with Peter Francis James instead of Sidney Poitier as Thurgood Marshall, and Pat Hingle instead of Richard Kiley as Chief Justice Warren. But James actually looked like Marshall, and *Simple Justice* went further back in history, to Howard University in the thirties, where Marshall had studied law with Charles Hamilton Houston (James Avery), and both declared war on *Plessy v. Ferguson*. And rather than concentrate on Clarendon, *Simple Justice* also took in Maryland, Texas and, of course, Topeka—which only got its top billing because the court didn't want to look as if it were ganging up on the South. Once again we looked through the eyes of Kenneth Clark (Giancarlo Esposito), and wanted to avert them, as black children playing with his dolls disdained and rejected their own image. Once again, Felix Frankfurter (Sam Gray), as an Austrian immigrant and a Jew, is seen to have been reluctant to cast a deciding vote, which is why he worked so hard for unanimity. And once again, as if perhaps to distract us from glimpsing just how messy compliance would prove to be, the wishy-washy "all deliberate speed" is invoked. "Sometimes," said Thurgood in 1954, "I get so damned tired of trying to save the white man's soul." Imagine how he must have felt in 1991, upon relinquishing his own seat on the court to Clarence Thomas, the pip that squeaked.

So the historical stage is set for everything that won't happen during the rest of the fifties, thereby making the sixties inevitable—everything, that is, to be reported in fourteen hours of *Eyes on the Prize*, the Emmy-winning PBS series on the second American Revolution. The first six hours of *Eyes* retold in interviews, documentary footage and period music, the stirring story of the civil rights movement in the South from 1954, when Marshall won his case against segregated schools, to 1965, when Congress approved the Voting Rights Act. What did this revolution seek? A seat on the bus, a meal in the dime store, a desk in the classroom, a minute in a polling booth, nothing more complicated than the Fourteenth Amendment. And how could such a revolution fail, escalating of necessity from passive resistance to civil disobedience, sometimes choreographed, often improvised, with those anthems and that imagery of sit-ins and freedom-rides, of black preachers and black teachers and fearless children against Klansmen, hoses, bombs and dogs? Eight subsequent hours, in 1990, told another story. Kennedys died and so did Kings. The cameras followed a sea change from Freedom Now to Black Power...from Dr. King's nonviolence and James Meredith's "March Against Fear" to Malcolm X and Stokely Carmichael. This motion was geographical as well as rhetorical, heading north, from the backwoods and bayous to urban wastelands. The music changed too, from gospel to rock. And so did the iconography, from white collars and black business suits to dashikis, berets and guns. See Jesse Jackson in Cicero; Carl Stokes in Cleveland; Muhammad Ali defeating Sonny Liston and refusing the draft; Malcolm gone to Oxford or Egypt, then gunned down in Harlem; Martin opposing war in

Vietnam and murdered in Memphis; teachers on strike against students in New York City; Panthers in Oakland; flames in Watts, and Detroit, and Miami. What started as the shape of moral passion made coherent, a curve in space and time, fell apart. Simultaneous protests, against prejudice at home and war abroad, confused, divided and exhausted everybody. Economic injustice in the north was harder to beat than Jim Crow in the south. The social gospel couldn't compete with a theology of greed.

About Malcolm: for those of you who imagined that Spike Lee's big-screen movie told it all, check out another *American Experience* documentary, less emendation than hypertext on public television in 1994. Lee's *Malcolm X* seemed to me to be three movies—the first a gangster flick in which *The Godfather* met *Guys & Dolls* in Boston and Harlem in the forties; the second a combination of *Birdman of Alcatraz*, *A Nun's Story* and sixties protest; the third, *Bad Day at Black Rock*, *Jesus Christ Superstar* and *Thus Spake Zarathustra*—all of them running around inside a big tent as expansive in its generosity of spirit as a Walt Whitman multitude, containing everyone from Rodney King to Nelson Mandela and everything from the Klan to Mecca. Not just *Gandhi* but also *Lawrence of Arabia*. Against such mythologizing, writer-producer-director Orlando Bagwell in *Malcolm X: Make It Plain* submitted archives. witness, remembrance and journalistic scruple. And while Bagwell supplies material that Lee omitted—on Cassius Clay, on Louis Farrakhan, on pimping, on Malcolm's brothers joining the Nation of Islam before he did, on his guilt feelings about leaving his mother in a mental hospital for twenty-six years—even so Malcolm emerges as a self-made hero of *consciousness*. In front of us, he *thinks*, inventing himself and changing shape. It is an act of language as much as logic. He *articulates* this recreated self. Of all the perspectives—from Alex Haley, Gordon Parks, James Baldwin, Sonia Sanchez, even Peter Goldman and Mike Wallace—the most persuasive was Ossie Davis's: "He was indeed our manhood, our shining black prince...." And he *did* look remarkably like Denzel Washington.

Blackside, the television production company responsible for all fourteen hours of *Eyes on the Prize*, returned with an additional five in 1995, looking back at *America's War on Poverty*. Odd how most of us choose to recall the sixties as a decade of hedonistic self-indulgence, of acid trips and tribal tantrums, as if the disco seventies and the junk-bond eighties were anything to brag about and the GinGrinch nineties a sort of twelve-step recovery program from the excessive behaviors of the bleeding hearts, the ungrateful young and the uppity underclass. Blackside preferred to recall the sixties, like the thirties, as a time when Americans in and out of government felt there should be room for us all at the table. J.F.K. may have read Michael Harrington's *The Other America*. L.B.J. tried to do something about it, installing Sargent Shriver at the Office of Economic Opportunity, declaring a war on poverty from Appalachia to the Deep South, from inner cities to strawberry fields. While Great Society programs made no provision for housing or jobs, they made trouble by insisting on "maximum feasible participation" by the poor. These modest initiatives would be disembowelled not because money ran out in the open wound of Vietnam, but because will ran out in Congress; not because they *didn't* work, but because they *might* have. There were a local political ripple-effects in Mississippi, where Head Start teachers like Marian Wright Edelman got involved in health care and voter registration; and in Newark where poet-playwrights like LeRoi Jones and a United Community Corporation insisted on some social services in exchange for the "eminent domain" destruction of their neighborhoods to make way for a new medical school; and in Kentucky, where the Appalachian Volunteers were arrested for *sedition* when they took on coal-company stripminers; and in California where Governor Ronald Reagan accused young lawyers in the Rural Legal Assistance program of a "socialist" conspiracy with Cesar Chavez and his farmworkers union against the grape and lettuce growers; and in New York City, where welfare mothers took not only to the courts but also to the streets, and cops on horseback rode them down like Cossacks.

And if what happened next still needs particularizing, we could do worse than sit still for a rerun of NBC's 1990 TV movie *Murder in Mississippi*, whose producers probably went to their neighborhood theater to look at Alan Parker's *Mississippi Burning* (1988) and decided, instead, to tell the truth. What Parker did for the 1964 murders of Mickey Schwerner, James Chaney and Andrew Goodman was what he had done for Turkish prisons in *Midnight Express* and for voodoo New Orleans in *Angel Heart*. He stuck his fingers in the Evil Eye. Blacks were lynched, and crosses burned, and the FBI, of all people, did something brave about it. (Imagine a movie about the civil rights movement in which black people don't have names!) Whereas *Murder in Mississippi* was about an unlikely friendship of Chaney (Blair Underwood), black from Meridian, and Schwerner (Tom Hulce), Jewish from Greenwich Village; and Goodman, too (Josh Charles), who joined them too late to appreciate the danger but in time to die at the hands of cops and Klansmen outside Philadelphia in what Bob Moses later called "the season of blood." To make sure we have our memory straight, the movie actually let us look at Porky himself, J. Edgar Hoover, promising on television that summer *not* to protect the voter-project volunteers.

Thinking about those burning crosses and seasons of blood, it occurs to me to wonder why, when the World Trade Center is bombed, and then a federal office building in Oklahoma City, so many editorialists in newspapers and commentators on television tell us so solemnly that terrorism has arrived at last on our pacific shores. To Black America, this isn't exactly news. Of course, definitions of terrorism differ. I'd have thought, for instance, that a welfare "reform" bill that dumped a million children into degrading poverty was, well, terroristic.

Better yet were the two brief seasons of *I'll Fly Away* on NBC, a Falsey-Brand production and a secret history of the American South, from approximately 1958 through the sit-ins and freedom rides of the sixties. With his wife institutionalized after a nervous breakdown, Forrest Bedford (Sam Waterston) was not only a politically ambitious district attorney but also the single father of 6-year-old John Morgan, who felt that everything bad in the world was his fault, 13-year-old Francie (Ashlee Levitch), a contentious tomboy about to be sideswiped by her own biology, and 16-year-old Nathaniel (Jeremy London), equally devoted to some distinctly kinky high-school Greco-Roman wrestling and the sort of blues music he could find only in juke joints in the wrong neighborhood. Naturally, in the two-hour pilot, Forrest would hire a black house keeper, and forget to ask her name. It was Lilly Harper (Regina Taylor). Together, for the next two years, on three different nights, in three different time slots, despite umpteen preemptions and a six-week "hiatus," Forrest and Lilly puzzled out their different meanings as a second civil war heated up. He was the constitutionalist and the guilty liberal, looking for a moral compass. She *was* a moral compass, always swinging true north, after the hesitancies of thought, and then confiding her conclusions to a journal that framed each hour of the series. Between crises with his children and his mistress, an armful of warm litigation named Christina LeKatzis (Kathryn Harrold), Forrest incurred the enmity of the White Citizens Council and lost his race for state attorney general when he prosecuted a white bus driver whose reckless and boozy passage killed black passengers on their way home from a church social. He embodied Albert Camus's working definition of an *intellectual*: "someone whose mind watches itself." But Regina Taylor's amazing Lilly was the defining *intelligence* of the program. Slow-starting, sure-footed, she hadn't been put on this earth just to take care of other people's children; she had a child of her own. Nor had she been put on TV just to teach white folks how to behave decently; she had a self that was other than "domestic," and a future to create. Divided between houses, trying to decide if she ought to move north with a "Cool Papa" music-man (Dorian Harewood), choosing to go to a protest march and sit-in on the courthouse steps, registering against all odds to vote, she was, like Rosa Parks and Fannie Lou Hamer, an existential heroine. By the time high school history teachers all over America discovered its didactic possibilities, NBC had cancelled *I'll Fly Away*. With indifferent ratings, it probably only got a surprise second season because (1) Falsey and Brand had a hit on another network, *Northern Exposure* and (2) all those guilty white liberals in Burbank felt they had to do *something* to show they'd noticed the riots in nearby South Central Los Angeles.

But there was one last surprise: *I'll Fly Away* returned to the air with a two-hour wrap-up TV movie in the fall of 1993, not on NBC but on public television. In *Then and Now*, a gray-haired Lilly Harper, an activist-author and college lecturer, tries to explain to her grandson in Atlanta in 1992 what it had been like in Bryland, Georgia, in 1962. We flashback to the arrival in Bryland of a black teenager from Detroit, who will speak incautiously to a local white woman. What happens to this boy is what happened to Emmett Till, and Lilly's father (Bill Cobbs) knows who did it. And Forrest Bedford, as ever personsifying the crisis of liberal conscience, needs his testimony to prosecute. At last Lilly's father will prove worthy of his daughter. But the Harpers will have to leave town forever. Having told her story, Lilly can't help returning to Bryland in body as well as mind, and we find out what happened

in thirty years to all the children, if not the country. On the Bedford porch, with the last good-bye, Lilly for the first name calls
Forrest by his first name. After which, on Monday nights for the
next nine months, public television reran all thirty-eight episodes
of *I'll Fly Away*. Not every hour was transcendent. In order to give
its characters time to think, the series didn't so much transcend as
it accreted, in layers of scruple and witness. It took Michelangelo a
long time too, from 1533 till 1541, behind the altar on the west wall
of the Sistine Chapel, to finish his *Last Judgment*.

How is it, anyway, that a black woman hired as a nanny for an
upper-class white family is considered a *worker*, while a single
mother struggling under impossible conditions to raise her own
children on welfare is considered a *parasite on society*? In ABC's
1993 TV movie *There Are No Children Here*, based on the nonfiction
book by *Wall Street Journal* reporter Alex Kotlowitz, Oprah Winfrey stars as the welfare mother of two young boys, Mark Lane and
Norman Golden III, who must pick their way like trash collectors
across the minefield rubble of southside Chicago's projects, at
which the cameras stare through the appalled eyes of Goya.
Michael Jordan is also looking down like a semiotic signifier,
though he doesn't seem to notice the yellow gang caps, the school-
yard gunfire, a child in a Dumpster, or the international flight of
capital. From the book, we know that reporter Kotlowitz has seen
to it that one of these boys, a stutterer whose "brain thinks so fast
your mouth just can't keep up," will transfer to private school in
another neighborhood. From the TV movie, his mother will get
the financial help she needs to move out of the Henry Horner projects. What this means, one supposes, is that the rest of us—me,
Bill Buckley, Clarence Thomas—don't really have to worry about
the children who are refugees from violence in the inner city
because there will always be a *Wall Street Journal* reporter and a
TV talk-show hostess to make up for the absence of a civil society.
In her memoir, Mary McCarthy assured us: "People with a bad
conscience always fear the judgment of children." Well, don't you
wish this were true—that Rousseau's idea of a child, or
Wordsworth's, or even Freud's, still applied? "I am determined,"
wrote Charles Lamb two centuries ago, "that my children shall be
brought up in their father's religion, if they can find out what it is."

Old wounds, passionate witness, dreamy retrospection, disgruntled hindsight…Alex Haley, whose TV miniseries *Roots* absorbed

so many millions of Americans without changing how they felt about anything important, confided a sly story to readers of *TV Guide* in 1993. He'd visited a former Alabama slave plantation, the Forks of Cypress, in 1986. Some white folks visiting at the same time claimed to be direct descendants of the Irish planatation master, James Jackson. Haley said "hi." He, too, was a descendant. Col. James Jackson Jr., a Confederate war hero, had been Haley's great-grandfather: "Many of the genteel white folks to whom I've introduced myself as blood kin have been understandably reluctant to face the facts...." Haley's purpose in *TV Guide* was to promote yet another *Roots* spinoff, a six-hour miniseries about his grandmother, called *Queen*. As Queen, a bastard child of Tim Daly and Jasmine Guy, Halle Berry had to grow up as the personal slave of her own half-sister; to sustain the Forks household after Martin Sheen, Paul Winfield and her mother all perished, her father came home from the Civil War minus an arm, and Yankees burned the cotton; to hit the road passing herself off as white and be raped by Victor Garber; to mate with and be abandoned by Dennis Haysbert, a union organizer who'd get lynched; to have a baby almost stolen by religious nuts Sada Thompson and Elizabeth Wilson; to be hired as a maid by kindly Savannah abolitionist George Grizzard; and to be wooed by the widowed ferry boat captain Danny Glover; after which, not counting a scary nervous breakdown, she would give birth to a second son, Simon, who will go to college and sire Alex.

Halle Berry will never be a Cicely Tyson. Except for her hair, she soldiered on unchanged for all six hours, hitting the same two notes of tantrum and yearning, less like Sojourner Truth than Cinderella. But who says a miniseries on black people has to be better than a miniseries on white people? A year later, millions of us spent four nights watching *Scarlett*, with Joanne Whalley-Kilmer, Timothy Dalton, Ann-Margret, Sir John Gielgud, Esther Rolle, Colin Meany, Jean Smart and Sean Bean. Rhett wants a divorce. Ashley drinks. Melanie's dead. Nuns contemplate turning Tara into a convent. Scarlett has not only been kicked out of Charleston for vulgar plumage and bad behavior, but she is also, secretly, pregnant. Nor will our headstrong heroine consent to living in Savannah with her Robillard grandfather, Gielgud, who throws his nightcap at her in a senile snit. Having met some fiddle-faddle O'Hara cousins, among them a gun-running priest, she will flash those eyes, toss that head, stamp that foot, rip that bodice and leave on the next boat for the Old Sod. The miniseries lingered so long in Ireland, for the stately mansions, masked balls, feisty horses and wet sex, they should have called it *Gone with the Potato*. In a bog of blood and beer, Scarlett discovers that the decadent English aristocracy treats Irish peasants worse than the decadent Southern aristocracy treated darkies, with time out for erotic bondage, murder, rebellion, rape, real estate and Druids. Though most critics were unhappy about what Alexandra Ripley and CBS did to Margaret Mitchell and/or David O. Selznick, I didn't give a damn. *Gone with the Wind* was a rubbishy novel somewhat improved by a movie that was insufficiently ashamed of its casual racism and its pathological notion of rape as redemptive. If a spunky Scarlett needed a drizzled Ireland as another lost cause to feel sad about between beddings in a sequel, and another cycle of injustice to travesty, I cry—*Erin-Go-Blarney*. Which it did, for a hoot.

But the publisher of the sequel, the producers of the miniseries and the estate of Margaret Mitchell were so stung by reams of ridicule that they decided to do better the third time around. So the estate hired British novelist Emma Tennant to write a sequel to the sequel, bringing Scarlett home again. And sold the rights to this sequel-sequel to St. Martin's Press for $4.5 million. And Tennant, whose eighteen books include a wicked sendup of Jane Austen, spent two years writing 575 pages of something called *Tara*. Which manuscript she relinquished to St. Martin's on Thanksgiving 1995. And which they hated so much—it must not have been dumb enough—that basically they fired her. This caused a commotion in the better newspapers, which is how I first heard about a clause in the estate's contract with writers. Any writer of any sequel to *Gone With the Wind* is explicitly forbidden from including "acts or references to incest, miscegenation, or sex between two people of the same sex." Isn't this remarkable? Haven't they read Faulkner? Do you suppose it never occurred to Rhett to take ownership advantage of a slave girl? Haven't you wondered whether, hanging in Ashley's closet, there might be Confederate drag? After all their troubles, why shouldn't Scarlett and Melanie seek consolation in each other's arms? Well, then: a restrictive covenant! Think what Donald Barthelme did to Snow White, Robert Coover to Pinocchio, Günter Grass to the Brothers Grimm and Salman Rushdie to Scheherazade, not to mention what Marlowe, Shakespeare, Goethe and Mann did to Dr. Faustus. What an amazing contract and an amazing country, where someone else owns all the rights, deeds, warrants and sanctions to almost anything—corporate logos, gene-splice patents, radio frequencies, website addresses—where, like a Coca-Cola trademark or a Walt Disney mouse, Mitchell's estate has sole ownership of, and a license to franchise, the sex habits of *imaginary beings*. Who says slavery's dead?

It would be wonderful if every representation of the African-American experience were as ferocious among the ambiguities, as angry, funny, dreamy and at war with, and forgiving of, the regnant cliches, as Lorraine Hansberry's *A Raisin in the Sun*. The 1989 *American Playhouse* production of *Raisin*, with Danny Glover and Esther Rolle, was superior to the 1961 film with Sidney Poitier and Ruby Dee in at least one important respect: it restored prescient passages on feminism and African nationalism, and on class and violence, that had somehow been snipped from or abbreviated in the shorter Hollywood and Broadway versions. As Walter Lee's younger sister Beneatha, Kim Yancey obviously embodied Lorraine Hansberry's several younger selves, all of them impatient with any sort of "universalizing" middle-class uplift.

But art is a lot to ask for, in any medium. Like pink people, black folks are willing to put up with bad or mediocre television so long as they seem to be part of the mix. We all need to see some semblance of ourselves in the magic mirror. TV's fairy tale of integration is like Hollywood's fairy tale of assimilation. We prefer *stature*, but we'll settle for *cute*. Even stereotypes encourage us to believe we belong to a stock company, a national repertory theater. As sitcoms go, *The Jeffersons* and *Diff'rent Strokes* may have been a visit to the dentist for a laughing-gas ambush, but were they any more insulting to anybody's intelligence than *The Real McCoys* with Walter Brennan, *Ivan the Terrible* with Lou Jacobi, *Bosom Buddies* with Tom Hanks, or *Punky Brewster* with Soleil Moon Frye? As if Iron Eagle and Darth Vader were Dick Van Dyke, Patty Duke, John Forsythe, Jane Seymour or Robert Urich, television has kept looking for some place safe to put Louis Gossett Jr. and James Earl Jones. Besides playing Fiddler in *Roots* and its two sequels, and supporting roles in *The Nurses* and *East Side, West Side*, Gossett has starred in network series as a private detective–restaurateur, an ex-slave and Yankee Doodle revolutionary dandy (*The Young Rebels*), a chief of cardiology taking on the hospital bureaucrats (*The Lazarus Syndrome*), a professor of anthropology taking on cults and tongs (*Gideon Oliver*), and a science teacher-football coach assigned to bodyguard the crown prince of an alien world called Quadris (*The Power of Matthew Star*). Besides playing Haley himself in *Roots* Jones has appeared in one or another network series as a cop (*Under One Roof*), a police captain-professor of criminology (*Paris*), an ex-cop (*Me and Mom*), and an ex-cop-ex-con-private eye (*Gabriel's Fire*), not to mention commercials for the Bell Atlantic Yellow Pages. The Fox cop show *New York Undercover*, actually shot on the streets of New York, instead of Toronto or Vancouver, has a jumpy camera eye, a heavy breathing rap soundtrack, the usual druggy subplots and the usual buddy-bond of stressed partners, but what makes it unusual is that neither buddy is white. Not only are Malik Yoba black and Michael DeLorenzo Latino, but we see a Harlem more various and surprising than the usual mean streets, sullen tenements, lurid graffiti and ghostly transactions on a crack exchange: an expansiveness of hills, bridges, boulevards, theater marquees and hospital spaces; a vitality of street markets, church socials and playground basketball; a civility of blue-note jazz and genteel stoops and an occasional brother from another planet. If *The Court Martial of Jackie Robinson* was not an especially terrific TV movie, in spite of Andre Braugher and Ruby Dee, it certainly needn't apologize to either big-screen version of the Babe Ruth story, in spite of John Goodman and William Bendix. If, in spite of Lynn Whitfield, Ruben Blades and, of course, Louis Gossett Jr., *The Josephine Baker Story* on cable TV was too much of a Top 40 emotional hits—the 1917 St. Louis race riots; the all-black vaudeville circuit; bare breasts and banana girdle; the Ziegfeld Follies in North Africa; Walter Winchell at the Stork Club, Bob Dylan on a motorbike and commies under the bed—it was at least as interesting as Cornel Wilde bleeding to death on Chopin's piano in *A Song to Remember*, with quadruple the historical overbite and symbolic-bran roughage of Jimmy Stewart and June Allyson in *The Glenn Miller Story*.

By the same tokenism, if we must have a miniseries devoted to Frank Sinatra and co-produced by his own daughter, why not Michael, Jermaine, Marlon, Tino, Jackie, La Toya, Janet and all the other singing and dancing Jehovah's Witnesses in *The Jacksons: An American Dream*, with Angela Bassett as Mama Kath the suffering enabler, Billy Dee Williams as Motown poobah Barry Gordy,

Holly Robinson as Diana Ross, Vanessa Williams as Suzanne de Passe and multiple Gloved One rock concerts, like Nuremberg pep rallies pandering to the polymorphous perversity of the prepubescent? Why not uplift biopics like *The Vernon Johns Story* with James Earl Jones, of course, and his Bach B-minor organ of a voice, as a trouble-making Baptist preacher his black middle-class parishioners fire from Montgomery, Alabama's Dexter Avenue Church, only to end up with Martin Luther King Jr. as his soft-spoken replacement? Or, in *The Ernest Green Story*, Morris Chestnut as the first black to graduate, in 1958, from Central High in Little Rock, Arkansas, with Ossie Davis, C.C.H. Pounder, Avery Brooks and the 101st Airborne looking on, after which he'd go on to Michigan State, Lehman Brothers, the Rockefeller Foundation and the Carter administration, before joining the transition team of another boy from Little Rock, President-elect Bill Clinton? And if desegregation of our public schools was what Supreme Court Justice Benjamin Cardozo once called "a great principle growing into the promise of its logic," then so, according to a lesser principle with a marketing logic, was a 1995 cable-television movie like Showtime's *Solomon & Sheba*, from the Italian homeboy Dino De Laurentis. Jimmy Smits, TV's favorite semi-Hispanic, played ancient Israel's wiseguy Master Builder. And Halle Berry, quite recovered from her harrowing experience as Alex Haley's grandmother, was Her Virgin Majesty Nikaule, who hadn't on her wedding night cut out her evil husband's heart just to give away her kingdom's frankincense to a goatish bunch of Hebrews, not when she could offer up to these imperialists the Cradle of Gold (the lost desert metropolis of Ophir) and her own cuddlesome body. Prior to dark erotic deeds, these two power-trippers spent most of the TV movie crossing sand, pitching tents, comparing notes on cosmology and statecraft, and poeming at each other. Like folk music, the Popular Front, Thurgood and Felix, and the civil rights movement, it was a glorious interlude of Judaeo-Kwanzaa solidarity.

I am not interested in indulging myself in some private, closed exercise of my imagination that fulfills only the obligation of my personal dreams.... It seems to me that the best art is unquestionably political and irrevocably beautiful at the same time.

Toni Morrison

Bill Buckley also needs to meet some ghosts. Among these ghosts, there is surpassing art. For the African-American community, these ghosts are the unappeased, the unwritten and the tumultuous dead, the dream shapes and memory residues of ancestral gods and homelands and a nightmare flashback to collars, mouth-bits and servitude: "the people of the broken necks and fire-cooked blood," as Toni Morrison has written; black boys "hanging from the most beautiful sycamore trees in the world" and "black girls who had lost their ribbons." Whereas, for white Americans, they are the return of the repressed. Television is a ghost machine and centrifuge.

In the 1989 ABC miniseries *The Women of Brewster Place* what's spectral is an impasse; and the white people, all of them, are ghosts. Except in commercials, you can't see them. Oprah Winfrey wanted Gloria Naylor's wonderful novel for her own, bought it to do with as she pleased and starred herself shamelessly as Mattie, who suffers enough to wear out God. The project was shored up with so much prodigal talent—Cicely Tyson, Lynn Whitfield, Lonette McKee, Olivia Cole, Barbara Montgomery, Mary Alice, Paula Kelly and Phyllis Towne Stickney, not to mention Douglas Turner Ward, Moses Gunn and Paul Winfield—that acting magic covers over most of the holes in the miniseries where the novel was full of language magic: of mythic murmur and incantation. On television, Brewster Place is state-of-the-art ghetto, a dead-end block of tenement houses in a nameless city with a Berlin Wall. To the business of this block, which is female consciousness-raising, men were incidental tourists—Ben, the alcoholic handyman, beat upside the head with two-by-fours; C.C., a menacing druggie delinquent; Gene, so threatened in his manhood he turns into a migratory bird; and, of course, Reverend Woods, looking for a lady for the night—the sort of ineffectual, malign or just no-account unreliables whose ubiquity in compositions by black women like Naylor, Alice Walker, Gayl Jones and Ntozake Shange makes an Ishmael Reed go crazy-polemical, as if the bad news from his sisters were somehow counterrevolutionary.

But oh my those women: there's the Christian mammy Mattie, whose ungrateful muderous son skipped bail, causing her to lose her house and hope. And the lovely neurasthenic Ciel, done wrong by Gene, mourning a dead Serena. And Etta Mae, a good-time girl at the end of her bounce. And Cora Lee, a baby-loving welfare mother who's transformed by the bard. (One of her children asks, "Is Shakespeare black?" To which Cora Lee replies, "Not yet, baby, not yet.") And the firebrand middle-class dropout Kiswana, who used to be Melanie before taking her African name, and who wants to start a tenants' association. And the star-crossed lesbian lovers, Lorraine and Theresa, punished beyond any necessary dramatic logic. And inevitably, the blue-haired neighborhood busybody Miss Sophie, at whom Theresa will fling the ingredients of a meatloaf: onions, olives, eggs. What happens to these women is abandonment, destitution, rape (toned down from the novel) and the death of a child who goes after a roach, into its hiding place in a broken light switch with a pair of scissors. As to exorcise, there's a community production of *A Midsummer Night's Dream* (better than the novel) and a block party to raise money for a lawyer to go after the landlord (the novel is better), after which the women attack the spectral wall that seals off Brewster Place from the absentee white world, as triumphantly as the women rose to roust the British tax-collectors in Wole Soyinka's Nigerian memoir *Aké*.

These women are refugees: from fathers and lovers and traumatized pasts. And prisoners: to the Wall, in their cul-de-sac. And subtractions: from the brutal white math, the powerful abstraction on the other side of the Wall, that has systematized every figure and form of social relationship, all the magnitudes of money. In Gloria Naylor's novel they escaped by levitation, a supernatural lift-off of exalted language, a magic carpet of collective aspiration. In Oprah Winfrey's miniseries, directed by Donna Daitch from a teleplay by Karen Hall, they are rescued by luminous performances from Whitfield as Ciel, by Jackee as Etta Mae, by McKee as Lorraine and by Tyson as Kiswana's mother, whose tongue lashing of Robin Givens on the mixed meaning of being black and the antecedents of a proper pride would have been glorious to behold on any stage.

The Women of Brewster Place did well enough in the ratings to inspire a weekly half hour soft-soap series, which languished two dreary months on ABC. It was set mostly in a soul-food restaurant, unfortunately reminding us of just how good *Frank's Place* had been before CBS cancelled its subscription. It starred Oprah again, but without a first-rate supporting cast around her, she seemed incapable of modulating herself anywhere between extremes of Hallelujah! and despair; she must suffer or she would affirm, like a seesaw. And it was written by Earl Hamner of *The Waltons*, instead of Gloria Naylor, who would never have permitted any of her characters to say, "A broken heart doesn't have to be a cold one."

In *Daughters of the Dust,* on public television in 1992, we got as far away from a big-city ghetto as it's possible to go and still imagine you are in America. One of those independent films with low budgets and lofty aspirations that have to be both lucky and good to find a theatrical distributor, *Daughters* had been financed by PBS and an "American Playhouse" which waited happily for it to finish its arthouse run. Till the Gingrich Congress cut funding for public television and the National Endowments, "American Playhouse" specialized in this sort of Johnny Appleseeding of the visual arts, commissioning and creating instead of cannibalizing culture. Except *Daughters* was more than a landscape shrub; it was the Garden of Eden. On the Sea Islands off the coasts of Georgia and South Carolina, from memories of West Africa and a Middle Passage into captivity and servitude, former slaves and their descendants created their own language and civilization. From this language Gullah came words like gumbo and voodoo. And from Julie Dash, the director of *Daughters*, came an evocation of the creation myth of that civilization, an epic poem of exile and migration, in images as regal as Bertolucci's Mandarin Chinese court.

The year is 1902. The Gullah, "the children of those who chose to survive," will be leaving their Sea Islands to go north to places like Harlem. A missionary woman, born there, returns to encourage the migration with her Christian god. A photographer full of bookish chat is a voyeur in these bare ruined choirs. There are watery totems, mythic horses, gold rings, wishbooks and mysterious effigies in glass jars for conjuring in the branches of the talking trees. The men go about their Islamic business, and everybody eats a lot. But, as in *Brewster Place,* remarkable women are the story here: the grandmother of all these Daughters of the Dust, and Yellow Mary back from Cuba; and a victim of rape, the Original Sin; and the child who will grow up to tell us what we are seeing: "I can speak my mind...a full-grown woman." Under their parasols, or in their trees, in song, dance and ritual, these women are the past and the future—magical beings, ghosts and dreams: "Woman is the sweetness of life—that's what I remember."

As white as I am, as European, I was reminded of such gorgeous movies as *Diva* and *Death in Venice,* or Ingmar Bergman on a cheerful day; also Chekhov's *Three Sisters,* and sometimes even *Sunday in the Park with George.* The composed and painterly quality suggested Japanese kabuki, too. But *Daughters of the Dust* had access as well to an altogether different reservoir of sensory images: an African unconscious. Each character in every dazzling tableau was said to represent an Ibo or Yoruban deity. It was as if, through the pointillist camera eye of Julie Dash, we saw back thousands of years, read the mind of an unimaginable past, before Islam, Christianity and monotheism and even sensed the "spice-sweet ginger smell" in Toni Morrison's *Song of Solomon,* the rich scent of the East "and striped tents and the sha-sha-sha of leg bracelets...the way freedom smelled, or justice, or luxury, or vengeance"—a gaudy dream of *female* emancipation.

Whereas our contemporary mind was what Anna Deavere Smith read, down to its fractured fault, in another "American Playhouse" production two years later. Rather than folklore, headlines inspired her *Fires in the Mirror.* On August 19, 1991, a white man, an Hasidic Jew, lost control of a station wagon in the Crown Heights section of Brooklyn, swerved onto the sidewalk, and killed a 7-year-old Caribbean black boy, Gavin Cato. Three hours later, Yankel Rosenbaum, a 29-year-old rabbinical student from Australia, was stabbed to death. Four days of demonstrations were followed by almost two years of recriminations, during which questions were raised about Rosenbaum's medical treatment, a jury surprisingly acquitted a young black man accused of stabbing him, everybody criticized the cops, and the tabloids played up hatred between blacks and Jews. It should be remarked that there are black people in Crown Heights who aren't Caribbean and Jewish people who aren't Hasidic, and most Caribbean blacks and Hasidic Jews didn't hurt anybody. But we are here to talk about art, not journalism. From interviews with scores of neighborhood people, media heavies and noisy clerics, performance artist Smith fashioned a play with nineteen speaking parts, all of which she took herself—from Orthodox rabbis to local black businessmen, from jittery housewives to spooky street kids, from Gavin Cato's mother to Yankel's brother Norman, from the feminist Letty Cottin Pogrebin to the inevitable Al Sharpton.

For the television production, director George C. Wolfe added black-and-white interstitial photographs, and footage from the nightly lycanthropic news. But it was Smith's one-woman show. She played with phones, coffee cups and hair; she put on accents, spectacles and airs. She was pain, bafflement, posture and *shtick*: Which was worse, the Holocaust or the slave passage? Was this a question anybody should be asking? Was there an answer that meant anything? "Bad boys," kosher dishes, James Brown and the colors of the Israeli flag were talked about, as well as David Dinkins, Malcolm X and Adolf Hitler. By juxtaposition, we saw around corners and into recesses. Hate went up like a kite, but also laughter. Like a Lily Tomlin and a Whoopi Goldberg, Smith impersonated. Like the "Camera Eye" and "Newsreel" sections of a John Dos Passos novel, she recapitulated. And like talk-radio, docudrama and meta-history, she hallucinated. *But with a wicked wink.* To the anguish of Crown Heights this exorcist, chameleon and mimic brought her own surpassing generosity. If she could speak in so many tongues, maybe our culture could also hear them. As much as performance art, *Fires in the Mirror* was performing grace.

August Wilson's ghosts showed on CBS, from Broadway, in February 1995, with *The Piano Lesson*. Wilson adapted his own Pulitzer-winning play for television; his longtime collaborator Lloyd Richards once again directed; and Charles S. Dutton recreated his Tony-winning stage role as Boy Willie, a Mississippi sharecropper come north from the Delta in a watermelon truck to seize and sell his sister's piano so that he could buy land of his own. Dutton alone was enough to flabbergast—monomaniacal yet credulous; menacing yet sportive; acrobatic yet muscle-bound and spasm-twitchy; locked down, silted up and stock-still at some sedimentary center yet gathering to explode. But there was, besides, the music. Even for land, would you sell that music?

Such a piano, playing itself when nobody looks. On this piano, a plantation mistress used to tinkle European tunes. For this piano, before the Civil War, slaves were exchanged. Because of this piano, boxcars burned and children grew up fatherless, and men even now fall down wells in the Delta. On this piano, like a mural, has been carved the pageant of a family and a race, an iconography of servitude, a history of the blues. Boy Willie's sister, Alfre Woodard, refuses to sell that past, although she won't *touch* it. But Boy Willie is a man of the future. He may hear the music, even dance to it, but he needs money to buy the acres he's always tilled, and, if he has to, he will steal and sell his soul. While we wait for the ghosts to show up, we learn the stories of Boy Willie's shy and lovelorn buddy, Courtney Vance. Of Carl Gordon, a railroad porter with a gun. Of Lou Myers, a gambling man. And of Tommy Hollis, who has gone up in an elevator, and found Jesus, and proposes marriage to Alfre Woodard because "I need a woman that can fit in my hand." There is a music in these men, of lamentation and exultation.

Years ago in a review of a book by García Márquez, John Updike characterized Latin American Magic Realism as a kind of "surreal fever" that weathered the past "into fabulous shapes in memory without surrendering its fundamental truth." It ought to have occurred to those of us who go to the plays of August Wilson, listen to the music of Ella and Aretha and read the novels of Ralph Ellison, Toni Morrison, John Edgar Wideman, Toni Cade Bambara, Wesley Brown and Alice Walker, that black Americans have been Magic Realists since at least the Middle Passage. From Ellison's *Invisible Man* to Morrison's *Beloved*, out of that wounding, at that piano—such ragtime and shadow play, blues and banshees. When Morrison's *Beloved* inexplicably failed to win either the National Book Award or the National Book Critics Circle fiction prize— though it would later achieve a Pulitzer—a story circulated that the panel of critics had said to one another during their deliberations that they simply didn't *believe* in ghosts. If I were a critic who had voted against *Beloved*, or for that matter, a white American asked to contemplate the history of my country and its never-finished Civil War, I would find it convenient, too, not to believe in ghosts. But those ghosts, including Malcolm and including Martin, have shown up on television, as plain-speaking and prophetic as the clowns in Shakespeare's plays and the angels in Rilke's sonnets. We have seen and heard them on the dream machines in our living rooms. As James Baldwin once explained, "If I am not who you say I am, then you are not who you think you are."

A Choice of Elsewheres

In *Absence*, Peter Handke's fable of identities lost and found, four strangers depart from a nameless city in an unnamed country for a train trip into a twilight zone, fleeing some catastrophe like an earthquake. An old man always scribbling in a notebook, a young woman always looking in a mirror, a soldier whose own mother wouldn't recognize him on the street and a gambler who'd rather be an artist leave behind walls, squares, castles, statues, a monotone humming and the very symbolic Hotel Europa. They follow signs—a rainbow-colored beehive, an ancient sun dial, a peregrine falcon, a diamond-patterned python, egg-shaped pebbles in a helmet and a seed pod fallen from a plane tree like a parachute— through forests and across deserts, to the "wavy and dune-like" plateau of a "chimerical" Ultima Thule, with a sacred cave, a "stalactite grotto" and a "nonstillness" guarded by a salamander. Here their guide abandons them, as the author deserts his book: "My longing is dead. I know it, I know its place in my heart; it's there but dead. So where can I go? And where am I? Do places exist no longer? Have I burned up all the light inside me? Can't I look forward to beauty any longer? Am I then lost? Is it all up with me? Or am I, in my weakness, at my goal?"

Who is this guide? Like Handke, he's a writer, promising images in space, "in the shaping of a story." But also an illusionist. The soldier complains: "He didn't guide me straight into the distance but led me around in a circle with his magic signs, deeper and deeper into a labyrinth." We seem to have gone backwards in time, through geological ages, to the prehistoric childhood of the race and "a geography of the present tense," where "the infant Moses in his basket will float forever in the slowly flowing Nile." We have also gone, like St. John of the Cross or a Sufi lapwing, on the standard mystical quest, hearing voices and seeing visions. We have left a corrupt city and a loveless culture for raptures of the oceanic id. We arrive with a hatful of mushrooms at a perplexing Now. *Where are we?* At a choice of elsewheres.

To get out of their heads, Aztecs munched *teonancatl*, a sacred mushroom. Zaparos drank *ayahuasca*, a hex potion. Mixtecs ate *gi-i-wa* puffballs and the Yurimagua of Peru were partial to an alkaloid exudate of tree fungus very much like belladonna. It used to be for the rest of us that Old Europe, black Africa and an opiated Orient were boutiques into which we wandered with a shopping list—Greek light, German sausage, Russian soul, French sauce, Spanish bull, Zen koans, hearts of darkness, the blood of the lamb, and a double-knuckled antelope humerus from Olduvai Gorge. We'd rub our fuzzy heads against the strange, and see if something kindled. (In Bulgaria, attar of roses; in Patagonia, penguins and Nazis.) Or we got into our cars and drove away, which was about as American as you can get. Watching *Driving Passion: America's Love Affair with the Car*, a four-hour celebration on the TBS superchannel of the Tin Lizzie and the Jeep, the Beetle and the Pimpmobile—a sort of V-8 version of a Walter Benjamin "arcade," if not a Michel Foucault "archaeology"—it occurred to me that my license had long ago lapsed. To motor through a century of piston-popping, from Henry Ford to Yutaka Katayuma, from family farms to soulless suburbs, from Willie Vanderbilt's steam-powered tricycle to Don Johnson's white Testarossa, from *My Mother the Car* to *Knight Rider* and *Stingray*, from drive-in movies to drive-by shootings, was to be reminded of elbow room and Daniel Boone and *The Getaway;* of Bonnie and Clyde, *Lolita* and the Teamsters; of Kerouac's *On the Road* and Updike's Rabbit, who ran away on four wheels, but who'd end up selling Toyotas; of Ken Kesey and his Merry Pranksters, with Tom Wolfe in the back of a Day-Glo bus, on their way "in a wine and bongo time" from Berkeley to a Houston loony bin to Timothy Leary's acid pond at Millbrook where Allen Ginsberg was on troll patrol; of Max Apple's *The Oranging of America*, in which Howard Johnson himself, on the road with a trailer full of ice cream, sought "some secret vibration" of place to tell him where to raise his latest roof, orange as a New Hampshire sunset. Harry Crews wrote a novel in which a guy *ate* a whole car. Harold Robbins wrote *The Betsy*. A character in John Cheever's sad last novel *Oh What a Paradise It Seems* imagined "in a lonely fantasy of nomadism a world where men and women communicated with one another mostly by signal lights and where he proposed marriage because she turned on her parking lights an hour before dusk, disclosing a supple and romantic nature." Not to forget *Thelma & Louise*, in which Geena Davis and Susan Sarandon managed not only to emancipate themselves in a Thunderbird convertible, while listening to B.B. King, Tammy Wynette and the Temptations after blowing up a truck (!), but also to leave behind Ridley Scott's Pop Art gas pumps and honkytonks and to fly by booster rocket to a fabled future, into an ultimate lightness of being in a Great American West, as if Big Sky and Monument Valley were landscapes of the female mind, a gaudy dream of Mother Earth.

Or we used to sit and smoke, contemplating, like Richard Klein in *Cigarettes Are Sublime*, such fellow puff-fish as Moliere, Baudelaire, Mallarmé, Jules Laforgue and Jean-Paul Sartre (as well, of course, as Helen Mirren in *Prime Suspect*, Andre Braugher in *Homicide*, and Vaclav Havel in Prague), listening to Bizet's *Carmen* (set, of course, in a cigarette factory); reading Svevo's great novel about smoking and psychoanalysis, *The Confessions of Zeno*; rerunning in the mind's teary eye movies like *Casablanca*, in which everybody smoked incessantly except Ingrid Bergman; thinking about dandies, prostitutes, Goya, the Galoises Soldier, the Gitanes Gypsy and the humble weed as a source of esthetic satisfaction, an aid to reflexive consciousness, a variety of religious and artistic expression, a tool for managing anxiety, a symbol of sexual and political freedom, a minor god, lyric muse, mystical joy, consolation, sacred and erotic object, parenthesis, prayer and "principle of camaraderie."

But that was before HBO and ESPN and C-SPAN, besides Ralph Nader and the Health Nazis. Now, we watch television. And so, in spite of danger warnings, does everybody else. The French watch reruns of *Magnum*, and complain about Yankee cultural imperialism. The Iranians watch *Baywatch* by satellite relay, driving their mullahs crazy. The Poles love *Dr. Quinn: Medicine Woman*. The

Japanese can't get enough of *ER*. And *Twin Peaks* was briefly all the rage in Budapest. Among gondoliers and shoguns, in puddles of cathedral light, at the feet of Toltec stelae, behind a Veil of Maya in a Himalayan comfort station, everybody is tuning in to *The X-Files*. As the French waitress once advised A.J. Liebling: "A chagrin of love never forgets itself. You must not make bile about it."

The work of television is to establish false contexts and to chronicle the unraveling of existing contexts; finally to establish the context of no-context and to chronicle it....The lie of television has been that there are contexts to which television will grant an access. Since lies last, usually, no more than one generation, television will re-form around the idea that television itself is a context to which television will grant an access.

George W. S. Trow

All week long in Stockholm, after the embassy lunch and the postage stamp with her face on it, before the concert and the banquet, between snowflakes and candleflames and the joy ride in a the Volvo limo behind a police escort to the Great Halls and Grand Ballrooms, the singing waiters and the reindeer steak, in the middle of the trumpets and the madrigals, the black velvet and the silver sceptre and the golden spoons, Toni Morrison was the opposite of blasé. What she did was levitate. A Nobel Prize for Literature will do that for you. It will also do it for those of us who were there, in December 1993, simply to bear witness. I felt proud to be a citizen of whatever country Morrison came from. After her dispossessions and her hauntings, her buttercakes and babyghosts, her blade of blackbirds and graveyard loves, not Doctor Street, no Mercy Hospital and all those maple-syrup men with the long-distance eyes, just look where she was now. That Friday night we stood at banquet tables in Old City Hall, in white tie, ballgowns and trepidation. First, the fanfare sounded. Then, from above us on the gilded balustrade, the processional began. Finally, the winner of the Prize and of our hearts came down the marble steps, on the arm of the King of Sweden, as if from the throne of Sula and Solomon. And at that moment she gave lessons to the noble rot of Europe on what *majesty* really looks like.

But you should have seen her the night before, in the tiny bar of the Grand Hotel, with Fran Lebowitz, the post-Warhol wit. They were talking about the parricide trial of those pretty-boy voids, the Menendez brothers. It turns out that for many months in their separate living rooms, parked in front of their separate Court TVs, kibitzing obsessively on the telephone to each other as if they were color analysts at a Super Bowl or an invasion of Panama, Morrison and Lebowitz had spent each weekday afternoon watching every minute of the first two trials. Like *fans* they'd developed a rooting interest, with fierce opinions on the tennis-bum greedhead cryba-bies themselves (Lyle with his $4,000 toupee and Erik with his wet-dream screenplay), on their alleged abuse as kids (oral, anal, tacks, *cinnamon*), on their bully of a father, Jose (with his purported porn-biz connections), their failure of a mother, Kitty (that pill-head boozehound) and the hair-dos and hemlines and reptilian gleams of their defense attorneys. No detail was too arcane to lack specific gravity and symbolic heft. It was like the shoptalk of immunologists or fly-fishermen.

Several years later, in *The New York Review of Books*, we'd learn that the critic Elizabeth Hardwick had also been watching Court TV, first for the Menendez trials and then for O.J. Simpson's. She had opinions on Jose's mistress, Lyle's Porsche, whether pins had ever been stuck in Erik's genitals and a public avidity for "the old sob story" of family crime and "situational murder" that goes all the way back to classical tragedy. She also thought about herself watching:

> This raging intimacy and emotional attentiveness came about from the extraordinary span of the television coverage. The fanatical hours were not only set aside on Court TV and CNN, specialized channels, but also on the regular stations. The purest measure of demand and urgency came when the vast audience, resting its feet or nodding off a bit in front of the long-established afternoon soap operas, was inter-rupted for the California judicial theater, an offering as slow as the plot clips on *As the World Turns* are quick and efficient.

Back in the early seventies, at a dinner party in Brooklyn Heights, Lionel Trilling decided not to take me seriously because I moon-lighted as a TV critic. I made him calculate the minutes he himself spent every week in front of the box, between essays on Dickens and Freud and Whittaker Chambers. Somehow, Trilling didn't want to count news programs as *watching television*, or Knicks and Yankees games, or late-night reruns of old movies remembered fondly from his youth, although he would grant me *Kojak*, to which he was devoted. I got him up to almost eleven hours a week, averaged over a year, with the occasional moonshot or assassination. When I told this story in print not long after he died, his widow Diana wrote an indignant letter to the editor. Lionel *never*...but he did. He just didn't call it television. Diana herself, every bit as serious as her husband, watched reruns of *M*A*S*H* every night before her eyes gave out.

Did you know that Lionel Trilling was devoted to *Kojak*? Who loves you, baby? Well, for one, *The Liberal Imagination* loves you. And, for another, *Sincerity and Authenticity*.

Americans watch television, *all of us*, even Nobel Laureates and Trillings, except perhaps for William F. Buckley Jr. Bill Buckley claims never to watch the stuff—except *60 Minutes* and, presumably, himself on *Firing Line*. He has never seen, he says, "an episode of *Dallas*, or of *Roseanne*, or *Geraldo*, or of the black lady who is alternately fat and thin, I forget her name." Whereas Kurt Vonnegut, when he isn't writing, which he says he isn't anymore, watches all the time: "I'd shoot pool if I had a table but I don't." Dennis Potter's *The Singing Detective* blew him away. Ken Burns' *Civil War* "is a cultural treasure on the order of a *Mona Lisa*." Vonnegut was just as impressed by the staging of *Hill Street Blues* as he'd been by stream-of-consciousness in literature. Besides: "I would rather have written *Cheers* than anything I *have* written."

Peggy Charren, who gave up running Action for Children's Television to campaign for Bill Clinton in 1992, forsakes the remedial seriousness of public TV and C-Span to watch *The Simpsons*, a program that once made affectionate fun of her. Charren's better at policing herself than Sonny Mehta, the President of the Alfred A. Knopf division of the Random House book-publishing conglomerate. Because of his "addictive personality," Mehta has to ration himself after every Knicks basketball game on cable, or he'd end up "watching anything with any plot at all, all night long." Katha Pollitt, the luminous poet and feminist critic, has recovered from her dependency on *I, Claudius* and *L.A. Law*, but is a secret afternoon consumer of CNN's *Headline News*, as if to trip on juxtaposed despairs. Which is sort of how Charles Kuralt uses TV now that he's retired from CBS. Checking into a hotel anywhere on the road, the first thing this Johnny Appleseed of American decencies does is switch on CNBC and giggle at the hopping up and down of the stock exchange ticker, that superstitious magic. Like Sonny Mehta, Gloria Steinem must ration herself on TV movies: "Two minutes and I'm hooked; I always watch to the very end." She'd been partial to the Canadian TV-newsroom serial *E.N.G.* till it disappeared from Lifetime cable, and will push her pause button to sit still for the occasional *thirtysomething* rerun "even though it seems sort of fifties now." Whereas film critic and social historian Nora Sayre refuses ever to watch *any* movie on television; big screens and dark theaters are part of the experience. On small screens, she favors such serial forms as "*Poldark, Dynasty,* Anita Hill and Watergate." Concert flautist Eugenia Zuckerman finds herself on the treadmill every morning, watching *The Today Show* till it slows her down. She then switches to the American Movie Channel, which so absorbs her that she will stop treading, whereupon she needs her MTV. Susan Brownmiller, the author of *Against Our Will,* finds herself after a visit to Vietnam mysteriously drawn to Japanese and Korean programming, as well as Diane Sawyer and Cher hair-care infomercials. Molly Ivins, the column-writing Mother Courage of Texas journalism and erstwhile leftwing tilt on *60 Minutes,* declares that her all-time favorite TV show, in the cable wastes at 4 AM, is *Working Out for Jesus with Beverly:* "We do arm exercises to Deuteronomy. It's a keeper."

We are talking about busy people. And they are talking about television, which they watch in the parentheses of their opinion-forming, book-writing, music-making and other agitations of the equilibrium. Nor, although we have been told that watching television requires less brain activity than eating a meal and uses fewer calories than *sleeping,* have these exemplary citizens, as a consequence of this shameful activity, dumbed down, gone blind, grown hair on their palms or Uzis in their attics or looted a Savings & Loan. Are we to presume they're better than the rest of us, somehow immune to pop-cult viruses epidemic among the lesser masses? Of course not. They are as easily distracted as the rest of us, as easily pleased, as easily bored, by exactly the same programs, to which, instead of smoking up a black lung or driving themselves to death and distraction, they resort for exactly the same slippery reasons we do. Almost any example would prove it, from Mary Tyler Moore to an NBA play-off game. But let's look at the oddest of balls.

I don't know why people expect art to make sense. They accept the fact that life doesn't make sense.

David Lynch

I didn't much care for *Blue Velvet*, the 1986 movie in which Lynch looked at the fifties as if they were a Rorschach test, and saw nothing but corrupt sexuality. I'm sure there was plenty of corrupt sexuality running around in that low suburban decade, and some of it rubbed off on all of us, but *Blue Velvet*'s wallow in voyeurism and castration anxiety seemed excessive, even unprincipled. We were sentenced for a couple of hours to a juke-box mind, full of Roy Orbison, severed ears and a kind of alchemical torturing of the body of Isabella Rossellini.

But *Twin Peaks*, the Lynch miniseries that debuted on ABC the Sunday after Easter 1990, seemed at first at least as much creepy-fun to stare at—mountains and bridges; sawmills and stags' heads—and lots more interesting to think about. As in *Blue Velvet*'s suburbia, there was a violent/erotic underworld beneath the prosperous surface of this Pacific Northwest township, where "health and industry go hand in hand." But in addition to the corrupt sexuality, Lynch and his "co-creator" Mark Frost had larded in corrupt politics, corrupt capitalism and corrupt psychiatry, not to mention bikers, Swedes, cocaine, pornography and the F.B.I.

So why not spend however many months it took to solve the murder of the Twin Peaks high school homecoming queen, as well as the torture-rape of one of her classmates? Assisting us in sorting out the suspects would be F.B.I. agent Dale Cooper (Kyle MacLachlan) and Sheriff Harry S. Truman (Michael Ontkean). We would serve time in gas stations and country clubs, hospitals and diners, where we'd meet Piper Laurie, Richard Beymer, Joan Chen, Russ Tamblyn and many aerobic young actors we'd never heard of, including James Marshall (a James Dean loner-type) and

Lara Flynn Boyle (everybody's best friend) as star-crossed lovers.

All these people, furtive, lugubrious, sidelong, blankly enigmatic, just plain horny, would lie to us, but that was okay, because the F.B.I. would know they lied. Not only was MacLachlan/Cooper in love with Douglas firs, snowshoe rabbits and cherry pies, but he was also some sort of vatic visionary, a Dick Tracy on acid. He read auras and reported directly into a dictaphone, as if it were a bat-familiar, every minute of his busy days and nights. And Harry Truman actually liked him. Indeed, their parody of the Gilgamesh/Endiku buddy-bonding may have been the most meaningful relationship in the miniseries. Imagine Mailer's *An American Dream* serialized by television instead of *Esquire*. Or: *Mary Hartman, Mary Hartman*, with a teleplay by Céline. Or *Dark Shadows* meets *Mayberry R.F.D.* Or *Falcon Crest* meets *Naked Lunch*. But also Brechtian, sort of, or maybe no? We never thought Lynch and Frost would stab us in our Caesar salad.

It's like sex and it takes time.

Lynch on Twin Peaks

At 10:01 PM, Thursday, April 17, 1990, the phone started like a car alarm. Everybody in the continental United States—my children, my editors and my enemies—wanted to know about the dwarf. What did he *mean*? Why was he talking *backwards*? In Cambridge, Massachusetts, in Madison, Wisconsin, in Berkeley, California, there were *Twin Peaks*-watching parties every Thursday night, after which… semiotics. About the dwarf: what gives? Buñuel was mentioned, and Cocteau, and Fellini.

Jane O'Reilly, one of the founding mothers of seventies feminism, ought not to have been watching TV at all. The author of *The Girl I Left Behind* should have been finishing her book on radical nuns. After the dwarf she went to Central Park, where the dog walkers were very upset about how parents treated children in the Pacific Northwest. Barbara Ehrenreich, America's lone remaining socialist with a sense of humor, rushed home for Thursday's episode: "I left my exercise class after I'd only done *one* leg. I risked *asymmetry*." Ehrenreich hadn't cared about a TV program since *St. Elsewhere*, for which she'd never abandoned an exercise class. She found Cooper's dwarf dream "deeply puzzling." She was sure the casino/brothel was important. From Lynch, she got "some sense that America is the strangest place in the world."

Friday morning, after the brothel and the dwarf, in the bowels of the CBS Broadcast Center on West Fifty-seventh Street, there was a gathering of the Lynched. A graphic artist had imaged a "tree" of *Twin Peaks* relationships: Harry and Josie; Ben and Catherine; Ed, Norma, and Nadine; James, Laura, and Donna; Bobby, Laura, and Shelly; Dr. Jacoby and the Log Lady. (That every other in *TP* was significant is one reason why novelist Bill Sheed gave up after the pilot: "I'm too linear. I was blinded by the number of people who go to bed together.") But how do you compute a soft-shoe dwarf? Friday noon Betsy Pochoda, then book editor of *Entertainment Weekly*, and Andrew Kopkind, the radical journalist, met for lunch. Instead of Lithuania or Earth Day they discussed the dwarf. Pochoda couldn't explain it and didn't want to: "It's a warm bath. I'm on an intellectual and moral vacation." Kopkind was contemptuous of the idea that Leo killed Laura: "Leo's a redder herring than Lenin." That afternoon the editor of *New York* magazine, Ed Kosner, called demanding an explication of the dwarf. Forget the dwarf, I said. What about the Brie?

We told them we were going to give them a two-hour, moody, dark soap-opera murder mystery, set it in a fictional town in the Northwest with an ensemble cast and an edge. And very early on after we delivered the pilot, they said that we'd given them exactly what we said we were going to give them. And that what we'd done was so foreign to their experience that they couldn't presume to tell us how to do it any better or different. Basically, they said, "Guys, you go make the series, and we'll be real anxious to see what it looks like."

Mark Frost, the Collaborator

Lynch, the director of *Eraserhead* (1978), *The Elephant Man* (1980), *Dune* (1984) and *Blue Velvet* (1986), and Frost, a former *Hill Street* story editor, wrote the pilot for their surreal serial in nine days, shot it in twenty-three and came in, with Lynch directing, on time and under budget ($4 million). The rest was all-American hyperbole:

"When *Blue Velvet* Meets *Hill Street Blues*" (*The New York Times*). "The first great drama series of the nineties" (Detroit *Free Press*). "As strange and unsettling a project as any in the medium's history" (*People*). "The first TV masterpiece of the '90s...*Dallas* with an IQ, *Dynasty* without all that lousy acting" (Dallas *Morning News*). "Mayberry RFD Goes Psycho; Pee-Wee's Playhouse Has a Nervous Breakdown" (*Entertainment Weekly*). "Just this side of a godsend...A captivating blend of the existential and the pulpy, the surreal and the neo-real, the grim and the farcical...new age music for the eyes" (Washington *Post*). "Idiosyncratically brilliant, magically bonkers and strangely hypnotic. Couch potatoes across the land may emerge feeling french-fried...Imagine Norman Rockwell possessed by the spirit of Salvador Dali, or *Our Town* written by Kafka" (*Newsweek*). "Like nothing you've ever seen in prime time, or on God's earth. It may be the most hauntingly original work ever done for American TV. The pace is slow and hypnotic, the atmosphere suffused with creepy foreboding, the emotions eerily heightened...the scalding intensity of a nightmare" (*Time*). "It's Lynch's own dark Hobbitland, as unduplicable as moving water" (*GQ*). "Miraculously good. It has both the insidious weirdness of Lynch's best movie work and the weird insidiousness of top-of-the-line TV trash" (*The New Yorker*). "What you might find if you dragged the bottom of Lake Wobegon" (*Connoisseur*).

I do not except myself. I was as excessive as the rest of them. Can I blame me, when even series co-star Ontkean described *TP* as "a Kabuki-style *Peyton Place* on peyote buttons"? Yes, I can. I've been burned before by the firecrackers and smoke bombs of a hype culture. Lynch was more realistic: "I still don't see what the difference is, at all," he told *Rolling Stone*. "To me it's a regular TV show." And his partner Frost was also worried: "The pace of the culture's accelerating all the time. Too much attention is dangerous. Maybe they'll digest us too quickly, spit us out." It's easy to say, in retrospect, that the spit hit the fan in reverse.

Diane, I'm holding in my hand a small box of chocolate bunnies.

F.B.I. Agent Dale Cooper,
to his microcassette recorder

Who's that lady with the log?
We call her the Log Lady.

Exchange between FBI Agent Cooper
and Sheriff Harry S. Truman

There's a sort of evil out there…strange in the woods…a darkness, a presence.

Truman to Cooper,
before a meeting of the Bookhouse Boys

The body of 17-year-old high school homecoming queen Laura Palmer washes ashore, in a plastic bag, near the Twin Peaks sawmill. Before Sheriff Truman can even begin to investigate, there's a second victim of torture and rape. The F.B.I., in the person of Agent Cooper, arrives to run the case. Everyone's suspect: the football quarterback who bays at the moon; the ponytailed trucker who beats up the waitress at the local diner; a Kerouac-reading biker; the landgrabbing owners of the sawmill, the lodge and One-Eyed Jack's; the creepy town shrink who wears cotton swabbing in his ears; crazy Nadine, with her eye-patch and her drapes; maybe even Audrey, the teen vamp with the wonder tongue who will make her play for Cooper after the Norwegians leave town, and about whom Lynch had a saddleshoe fetish; and who knew *anything* about the Log Lady?

In April 1990, I had reason to believe that the letter *R*, dug out by tweezers from under a fingernail on Laura's corpse, would prove to be the serial killer's way of spelling out his name, victim by victim, despite all the *J*'s at which Cooper threw pebbles in his dreamy reenactment of a Tibetan deductive method involving broken bottles and major league baseball measurements, because various Euro-trashies reported this detail from a bootleg Lynch cassette kicking around decadent cineaste circles in Mexico and Bulgaria, on which our killer was identified in the last 18½ minutes, which minutes became briefly as notorious as the missing snippet of Richard Nixon's White House tapes and the long-playing version of Arlo Guthrie's "Alice's Restaurant."

Synopsis omits everything spicy we associate with artifacts of Lynch—sinister fluidities, absurd shocks, deadpan puns, painterly pointillism, rampaging non sequiturs, erotic violence, a warping of light, a moony sense of unconscious randomness, and demonic possession. (Marshall Berman, author of *All That Is Solid Melts Into Air* and the only intellectual I know who admits to enjoying TV almost as much as he enjoys Marx, Freud, and the modernist gangbusters, admitted liking the way *TP* looked through doors "into rooms with doors into still more hidden rooms, the way the shots convey an endless depth...It's a *soft labyrinth*.") Why *does* the deputy sheriff cry at the sight of blood? What about those traffic lights, or the stag's head in the bank vault? "Let me stop you in the hallway," says Cooper to Truman, as, of course, he stops him in the hallway.

Synopsis also omits Angelo Badalamenti's synthesizer compositions: sometimes clueing us in on a shift from musical beds back to the murder case, at other times impersonating wind in the Douglas firs or horns in the mountain fog, as often deliberately subverting the emotions on the screen. Badalamenti and Lynch had conspired before, on *Blue Velvet* and an album of moody Julie Cruise love songs and a theater piece at the Brooklyn Academy of Music called *Industrial Series No. 1,* in which a midget sawed wood, a female acrobat performed half-nude and dozens of broken baby dolls were lowered by wire from a catwalk. "David," explained Wendy Robie, *TP*'s one-eyed Nadine, "loves broken beauty. He loves to see something or somebody that's beautiful and then broken in some way, who still goes on." But David, as of the end of April, had himself directing only the *TP* pilot and the dancing dwarf episode. His attention was wandering.

*We blew up a South Lake Junior High swimming pool. I
was arrested. We made the Salt Lake City and the Boise
papers.... These bombs we were making were pipe bombs
and they would hit the ground and not explode until they
were about eye level....We threw it in the pool so that the
shrapnel would hit the side of the pool. We threw it around
10 o'clock Saturday morning, and the smoke came up
shaped like the pool. This thing rose up just instantly shaped
like a pool. Just for a moment, till the wind blew it away.*

Lynch, on his Idaho boyhood

*The bags had a big zipper, and they'd open the zipper and
shoot water into the bags with big hoses. With the zipper
open and the bags sagging on the pegs, it looked like these big
smiles. I called them the smiling bags of death.*

Lynch on his student days in Philly and
the body bags in the local morgue

Lynch was born in 1946 in Missoula, Montana; grew up all over the
Northwest, where his father was a Forest Service research scientist;
hated high school, in Washington, D.C.; studied art, with some
time out in Austria to look for the expressionist Oskar Kokoschka,
at the Boston Museum School and the Pennsylvania Academy of
Fine Arts, where he fashioned his first film, a 10-second loop of six
heads throwing up and bursting into flames, which got the attention of the American Film Institute under whose auspices at the
AFI Greystroke Mansion in Beverly Hills where he hid out from a
first wife and first child, he completed *Eraserhead*, about a zombie,
his spastic girlfriend, and their mutant child. It's considered auto-
biographical.

He was working for Mel Brooks, who calls him "Jimmy Stewart
from Mars," as a *writer*, when Brooks, on a breathtaking dare after a
single screening of *Eraserhead*, made him director of *Elephant
Man*. It would be the last time Hollywood loved him. *Dune*, the
$40-million bomb which might not have been much better, only

longer, even if Dino De Laurentis hadn't butchered it, sent him back to Bob's Big Boy. After sandworms: the severed ear. He had total control over *Blue Velvet*, which is where after another wife and another child he met his bicoastal inamorata, Isabella Rossellini, who told *The New York Times* that "he's seraphic, blissed. Most people have strange thoughts but they rationalize them. David doesn't translate his images logically, so they remain raw. Whenever I ask him where his ideas come from, he says it's like fishing. He never knows what he's going to catch." According to his daughter, Jennifer, "He loves Reagan. He loves America. He's got a strong go-get-'em attitude when it comes to America's enemies." According to *Newsweek*, "He's fascinated by human organs. When one of his producers underwent a hysterectomy, he made her promise to send him her uterus."

I'd sit at the keyboard and David would sit in a comfy chair and we'd go back and forth. You throw your minds up to the ceiling and they meet somewhere near the light fixtures. The script becomes written by a third party. I can only describe it as a kind of Vulcan mind meld.

Mark Frost

Born in New York in 1954 and raised in Minneapolis and Los Angeles by a family of actors, Frost wrote his first play, for the Guthrie Theater, at age 15, and was a veteran of network TV before he was old enough to drink. Steven Bochco plucked him off the campus of Carnegie Tech, after his junior year, to write episodes of *The Six Million Dollar Man*. From Burbank, he went back to Minneapolis, taking "a six-year vow of poverty" as Guthrie's playwright-in-residence, after which it was documentaries for public television till Bochco sang his siren song again. For three years on *Hill Street* Frost served as a writer, a story editor and an executive story editor. After *Hill Street*, he did the screenplay for an overwrought but interesting voodoo-cult thriller set on the streets of New York, *The Believers*; and then hitched himself to Lynch.

These guys needed a hit. In the four years since they had teamed up, a script on the strange death of Marilyn Monroe, called *The Goddess*, couldn't get financial backing. Their Steve Martin-Martin Short movie, *One Saliva Bubble*, about a Kansas town zapped by X-rays from a military satellite, was cancelled six months into production because of the De Laurentis bankruptcy. And NBC turned thumbs down on their notion for a pilot of *The Laurians*, about a bunch of earth detectives who chase after alien infiltrators. It wasn't really a question of whether Lynch could learn to live with making commercials; nobody was willing to let him try.

There are two things that continue to bother me, not only as an agent of the bureau but as a human being. What really went on between Marilyn Monroe and the Kennedys, and who really pulled the trigger on JFK?

Cooper to Diane

Twin Peaks was full of more inside jokes than any previous network series except for the autistic *St. Elsewhere*. The opening bird "referenced" the robin at the end of *Blue Velvet*. Those flickering lights in the morgue were an accident Lynch liked so much that he wrote them into the script. The roadhouse singer was the same Julie Cruise for whom Lynch and Badalamenti wrote an album. Dead Laura was named for Gene Tierney's character in the 1944 movie, and of course *Lynch's* Laura would also have a double. A countertop jukebox in Norma's diner was supposed to remind us of a William Shatner episode of *The Twilight Zone*. From *Details* magazine we learned that the art on Dr. Jacoby's office walls was actually by Russ Tamblyn. The sheriff was named Harry S. Truman not for the President who dropped the atom bomb but for the sheriff who vanished on Mt. St. Helens. The genuinely obscene Brie routine was just one of Bochco's boys seeing what he could sneak by the Broadcast Standards pecksniffs: "You go so fast they can't track," explained Frost. "And it helps if the guys have their mouths full when they're talking."

While we had no way of knowing in the spring of 1990 that a suddenly overcommited Lynch was so busy off the set—making commercials for Opium perfume, pitching another TV series to Fox, working up a new theatrical release, *Wild at Heart*—that he wouldn't get back to directing another *TP* episode for months, and that neither he nor Frost had had the vaguest idea of where to go next in the Pacific Northwest except to make doughnuts from holes in their heads, I am trying hard to remember what it felt like then, when *Twin Peaks* still had a grip on the imaginations of tens of millions; when a workaholic writer like Linda Wolfe gave in to the oddest compulsion to reread Sherwood Anderson's *Winesburg, Ohio*; when Jane O'Reilly was reminded of the novels of Don DeLillo, like *Libra* and its "theology of secrets"; when Marshall Berman analogized the *look* of the series to F. J. Church and the Hudson River School, and worried a lot about Cooper's going to bed alone (no *wonder* he dreamt of dwarves), as Jerzy Kosinski used to worry about Tubbs in *Miami Vice* not getting as much sex as Crockett; when (I'll admit it) I myself imagined Cooper as a combination of Ludwig Wittgenstein, arriving in Cambridge from Vienna with a clarinet in an old sock and his secret despair in a closet, the philosopher of impasse and cul-de-sac, afraid of open spaces, a prophet of the Unsayable confiding to a taperecorder, "Whereof one cannot speak thereof one must be silent," *and* Michel Foucault, arriving from Paris at a Bay Area leather bar with his blindfold, handcuffs, riding crop, and alligator clips, looking for a "limit-experience" and the indigenous Barthesian *jouissance*. This, of course, was ridiculous. We know now that Lynch was merely moody, more of an Andy Warhol than a Dennis Potter; that *Twin Peaks*, while lovely to look at, had nothing more interesting going on inside the "soft labyrinth" of its pretty little head than the usual vulgarized Freudianism—*Daddy did it!*—after which, as the ratings plunged, little remained for Cooper to do but play chess by mail with avatars of the serial killer "BOB," wait for the arrival of deep-space aliens and confront his own twisted soul in a wilderness of mirrors at the Black Lodge, where Walt Disney met the Egyptian Book of the Dead. So much for American Gothic. But so desperate were we for gorgeous distractions, for music videos of delirious consumerism, for maximum weightless fluidity inside an amniotic baggie of lascivious signifiers and vampire hickeys, that we let ourselves be conned.

This is what happens to TV critics when they look at something new, and to newspapers and magazines wanton to be with it. Because an interesting new book is published at least five or six times every month, book reviewers learn to hoard their adjectives and ecstasies. On television, the odd is downright thrilling. Not to embrace it is to perceive yourself as *finished*, dead to the New, terminal in the enthusiasms. Besides, it's a chance for once to be serious, after Pee-Wee Herman. We used to be able to count on magazines like *Time* as early warning signal systems on radar lookout with their sarcastic popguns for the menacing blip of avant-garde, or anything else alarming to the bourgeoisie. The media today are not to be distinguished from the engines of publicity at RoboCorp, and the ad agencies they hire to fog us, and the Departments of Pop Cult at our major universities with a heavy investment in the attention deficit disorders of the American post-doc, and the rest of what Valéry once called "the delirious professions…all those trades whose main tool is one's opinion of one's self, and whose raw material is the opinion others have of you." Once upon a time, *Twin Peaks* seemed to *matter*—like whether Lucy's baby would be a boy or girl, or Jack Paar would stop crying, or who killed J.R., or if the O.J. Simpson trial told us anything we didn't already know about spousal abuse, celebrity culture, justice for sale, L.A. cops and American racism—and then suddenly it didn't, like the Gulf War.

Root out content. Find the codes and messages. TV offers incredible amounts of psychic data. It opens ancient memories of world birth, it welcomes us into the grid, the network of little buzzing dots that make up the picture pattern. There is light, there is sound. I ask my students, "What more do you want?" Look at the wealth of data concealed in the grid, in the bright packaging, the jingles, the slice-of-life commercials, the products hurtling out of the darkness, the coded messages and endless repetitions, like chants, like mantras. "Coke is it, Coke is it." The medium practically overflows with sacred formulas.

Don DeLillo, *White Noise*

Six years after *TP* went away like *The Lady of Shalott* does anyone care any more outside those cultural studies departments at the odder universities where, between seminars on Indo-European patriarchy and symposia on "Contours of Mother Earth, From George Eliot's Red Deeps to George Sand's Occluded Paths to Willa Cather's Canyons," they still word process monographs on "The Liminality of Laura Palmer: As Body-Bag and Fetish"? Probably not. But *Twin Peaks* does say something about the liminality of television, that portmanteau of thresholds. For instance:

TELEVISION AS RECYCLING

Daddy did it, and so did a serial killer, and maybe the aliens. Lynch found Michael Ontkean from the TV discard pile of *The Rookies*; Peggy Lipton from *Mod Squad* and the even older *John Forsythe Show*; Lara Flynn Boyle after she perished from rough sex in Central Park with Robert Chambers in *The Preppie Murder*; and Ray Wise, the furious father, from *Dallas*, *The Colbys* and *Knots Landing*. Both Richard Beymer and Russ Tamblyn had all but vanished from any screen after *West Side Story*, except for Beymer's four-month run in *Paper Dolls*, a witless ABC series on New York's modeling and cosmetic industry. Miguel Ferrer would graduate after his *Twin Peaks* Jack Webb imitation to the misbegotten cop show *Broken Badges*, the Philadelphia-lawyer series *Shannon's Deal*, and a string of TV menace movies.

For every Debra Winger, who got her show-biz start as Lynda Carter's younger sister in the late-seventies *Wonder Woman* series, there are dozens of Lloyd Bochners and Greg Evigans who will never escape the box, six-inch homunculi forever. That is, for every Clint Eastwood (*Rawhide*), Jodie Foster (*The Courtship of Eddie's Father*), Robin Williams (*Mork & Mindy*), Sharon Stone (*Bay City Blues*), Michael Douglas (*The Streets of San Francisco*), Meryl Streep (*Holocaust*), Warren Beatty (*Dobie Gillis*), Kathleen Turner (*The Doctors*), Tom Hanks (*Bosom Buddies*), Sally Field (*The Flying Nun*), Steve McQueen (*Wanted: Dead Or Alive*), Geena Davis (*Buffalo Bill* and *Sara*), James Dean (*Danger*), Michelle Pfeiffer (*Delta House* and *B.A.D. Cats*), Denzel Washington (*St. Elsewhere*), Mia Farrow (*Peyton Place*), Bob Hoskins (*Pennies From Heaven*), Glenn Close (*Too Far to Go*), Tim Robbins (*St. Elsewhere*) and several generations of the Steve Martin/Billy Crystal/ Eddie Murphy/Dana Carvey *Saturday Night Live* gang, there have been hundreds more, some of them famous and others merely familiar, for whom Lilliput is Habitat—like Lucille Ball, Milton Berle, Elizabeth Montgomery, Robert Urich, Susan Saint James, James Brolin, Kate Jackson, Gary Collins, Meredith Baxter, Robert Conrad, Morgan Fairchild, Michael Landon, Cheryl Ladd, Peter Graves, Barbara Eden and David Janssen. Patty Duke has had one TV show or another for more than thirty years. Ray Walston in spite of a distinguished career on Broadway and the big screen especially in musical comedies, will be remembered as *My Favorite Martian* in the sixties and the *Picket Fences* judge in the nineties, as his buddy Bill Bixby was half *Eddie's Father* and half *Incredible Hulk*. To cancel Raymond Burr they had to kill him. David Hasselhoff bounces back like a Pepsodent Dracula. It's hard to imagine a prime-time season without Valerie Bertinelli or Peter Strauss. Till she got her own series, *Dr. Quinn, Medicine Woman*, Jane Seymour had a miniseries for every season, fall, winter, and spring, just changing the color and cut of her hair. Think how much time we've spent at home with Richard Chamberlain and Jaclyn Smith—Chamberlain, because over the decades he's perfected a *nonplussed* look that works as well in claptrap by James Clavell or Collen McCullough, a blank incredulity equally appropriate to sixteenth-century Japan or twentieth-century Australia, a dumb wonder he wears like a boutonnière in every role from the shogun-on-training-wheels to the sex-starved priest, as if through the pips on his domino we glimpse, rather than God's grace, all the unpleasant randomness in the universe; and Smith, because over decades she becomes not less beautiful but rather more glazed behind increasingly elaborate camera filters, like an Italian miniature or a Russian icon, under coats of shellac and yards of yashmak. Once they even appeared together, in *The Bourne Identity*, with poor Richard obliged to wake up in Robert Ludlum's bed in Paris, half-maimed and half-drowned and more nonplussed than usual because entirely amnesiac, wondering whether he might be the terrorist jackal Carlos.

Then there are those actors so swallowed up by a single television role that they lose their own identities and end up weirdly iconographic, part of the culture's shorthand, as vivid as characters from Dickens, corporate logos, dollar signs or swastikas: Rockford, Columbo, Kojak, Beaver, Fonzie, Hawkeye, Archie Bunker, Ted Baxter, Ralph Kramden, J.R., Mary Richards and Murphy Brown, a Partridge Family or a Brady Bunch. Nor, like radioactive waste, will anyone who has ever been on network television really truly perish. They'll all show up eventually, to be outsmarted by Angela Lansbury on an episode of *Murder, She Wrote*.

And the same goes for the co-creators, executive producers, story editors and directors. If Lynch was new to television, Frost was not. He'd been one of Bochco's boys, like Michael Kozoll, who had written short stories admired by Elizabeth Bowen before ending up in Burbank working on series like *Quincy, McCloud, Switch, Kojak* and *Delvecchio*; Gregory Hoblit, a refugee from the Berkeley Free Speech Movement, who would go on from *Hill Street* to write the pilot of *L.A. Law* and produce *Hooperman*; and Anthony Yerkovich, who would write the pilot for *Miami Vice* and produce *Private Eye*. Bochco himself had paid his dues at *The Name of the Game, McMillan and Wife, Delvecchio* and *Paris*. Running NBC at the time when *Hill Street*, almost by accident, got on the air and struggled through its first season of lousy ratings and multiple Emmy awards, was Fred Silverman, the Dollfuss of daytime and action-adventure shows, who would manage to sell his low cunning to all three networks before lapsing into independent production, and who had wanted a blonde bombshell instead of Joyce Davenport as Daniel J. Travanti's main squeeze on the series, as he had wanted the series itself to be called *The Blue Zoo* instead of *Hill Street*. Stephen J. Cannell has written and produced more shows, from *The Rockford Files* and *The A-Team* to *Sonny Spoon* and *Silk Stalkings* and *The Commish*, than that tireless Energizer Bunny, Aaron Spelling, who even as we babble has prime-time soaps on four different networks. Half the sitcoms of the seventies and eighties, and most of the good ones, were written by James Brooks, Allan Burns and Ed Weinberger, from Grant Tinker's MTM shop before he divorced Mary Tyler Moore to take over NBC from Fred Silverman, which is where he dreamed up *St. Elsewhere*, as "*Hill Street* in a hospital," just as *Magnum* had been "*Rockford* in Hawaii." Barney Rosensweig wasn't always executive producer of *Cagney & Lacey*; he got his start on *Charlie's Angels*. One Diane English hit-series like *Murphy Brown* earned her favored time-slot treatment for three more tries. After their success with *Northern Exposure* on CBS, John Falsey and Joshua Brand, who'd been known as the Doctors of Death when they wrote for *St. Elsewhere*, spread themselves so thin in *I'll Fly Away* on NBC and in *Going to*

Extremes on ABC that they temporarily vanished. James Burrows directs the pilots of almost every new sitcom producers suspect might actually be classy. In *Inside Prime Time*, Gitlin tells us: "Fully half of prime-time television is scripted by only 10 percent of the Writers Guild's 3,000 active members." (One ought to mention that only slightly more than 3 percent of Guild members are African-Americans.) Combine such busy serfdom with prior network commitments to a handful of bankable stars (like Bill Cosby, Michael J. Fox and Ted Danson) and "back end" guarantees to executive producers with a winning track record (Bochco left NBC for one long-term deal with ABC, then left ABC for another long-term deal with CBS), and what you get, Gitlin says, is

> Cronyism, mutual backscratching, behind-the-scenes favors, revolving doors, musical chairs, careers made by falling upward, the "amazing largesse" given to favored members of "the creative community"...The same names may stay in circulation for years, or decades—sometimes because a rare competence will out, but more often because beneath the hell-bent pursuit of the fugitive audience, and the smooth logic of taking the fewest risks, old-boy networks bind this savage business together against its own ignorance and against its centrifugal whirl.

But what you also get is better television. The best dramatic series of the eighties and the nineties, from *Hill Street* to *Homicide*, from *St. Elsewhere* to *Picket Fences*, from *Lou Grant* to *Law & Order*, from *China Beach* to *The X-Files*, are better written, better cast, better shot and more encompassing, more novelistic in their depth of character and breadth of concerns, as well as wittier, than any of the fossil fuels that we remember so fondly from the fifties Golden Age of Television until we actually look at them again in retrospectives at the Museum of Broadcasting; and superior, too, to the general run of contemporary Hollywood's kiss-kiss bang-bang boom-bleeders. As Broadway used to look down on Hollywood, so Hollywood used to look down on TV, a loftiness scarcely credible even in the fifties and sixties, when directors like George Roy Hill, Steven Spielberg, John Frankenheimer, Arthur Penn and Sidney Lumet got their start on television, and an attitude impossible to sustain in the eighties and nineties, when such children of the box as Rob Reiner, Ron Howard, Jim Brooks and Penny Marshall direct most of the handful of Hollywood films that weren't conceived for multiple viewings by 12-year-old boys, and when directors like Frankenheimer, Barry Levinson, Joan Micklin Silver and Robert Altman desert the big screen for the small one whenever they have something interesting to say about prisons, rain forests, urban life, education or the American political process. There is more generosity and intelligence in a single hour of episodic television written by a Bochco, or a Tom Fontana, or a David Kelley, or a John Sacret Young, out of the hundreds of such hours each of them wrote before the inevitable axe, than in all the screenplays combined of Joe Eszterhas and John Milius.

Unfortunately this same recycling also includes those television executives who cancel the show because there is always a worse one waiting, who censor the script as if they could write a memo without a secretary, and who barter and browbeat the "talent" as if they had some—the empty suits and psychic yardgoods salesmen and the shape-shifting, back-stabbing sycophants who fetch for them—fearful every other minute of their conscious day that they will be found out for faking competence and fudging issues and pretending they have interior lives to console them for their many crimes against intelligence and decency; that they'll be jettisoned from the Mother Ship with nothing to market but their stress-related opinion of themselves. These are the people you saw at the July 1996 summit meeting with Bill Clinton, resentful at having to kunckle under and promise three hours of children's programming *every week* on each of their networks. You'll have noticed that in this book I haven't mentioned any network children's programs. ("Kidvid" they call it, as they call the children "mice.") This is because, except for the vagrant *Schoolbreak Special*, there hasn't been any worth praising. These guys are the reason why. If the little people are hungry for meaning, let them eat Cookie Monsters.

TELEVISION AS ACCIDENT AND IMPROVISATION
Hill Street only made it onto the air at NBC because the network was in third place, and only stayed there longer than a season because it collected some Emmys, and there was nothing in the can to replace it. *St. Elsewhere*'s secret was that Mark Tinker was one of its writer-producers, and his father Grant was in charge of the network. ABC killed off *China Beach* to make room for the yuppie prosecutors on *Equal Justice*, and they couldn't even finish a second season. CBS killed off *Lou Grant* because Ed Asner's leftwing opinions on Latin America and militant leadership of the Screen Actors' Guild had

become an embarrassment. It wouldn't have another Top Twenty dramatic series until it brought back *Cagney & Lacey* from the grave after a write-in campaign by devoted viewers. And after cancelling *Cagney & Lacey*, it had to wait three more years till *Northern Exposure* surprised everyone in a summer throwaway slot. Barry Diller, widely known as a programming genius, had only one hit at Fox, *Married...With Children*, and managed to axe *Alien Nation* just as sci-fi turned popular again; that he was long gone to a home-shopping channel by the time *The X-Files* limped through its initial season was a blessing for paranoids and sperm-suckers worldwide. *Mary Tyler Moore* and *M*A*S*H* both tested poorly in focus groups before making the schedule, and fared not much better in the Nielsens in *their* initial seasons. *Cheers* looked at first like a loser. *Seinfeld* took two years to find its deracinated audience. There weren't enough mothers and daughters in America who wanted to understand each other for *My So-Called Life* to make it on ABC, but it's a cult smash in reruns on MTV. *Roots* amazed everybody, and almost immediately thereafter a biopic of Martin Luther King Jr. was a ratings disaster. Why can't Jonathan Winters, than whom only Richard Pryor and Robin Williams are funnier, keep a job, while Jeff Foxworthy has one at two different networks? Try *explaining* Merv Griffin, Pat Sajak, Michael Landon—or even Ted Koppel.

In his collection of essays, *An Urchin in the Storm*, Stephen Jay Gould takes on sociobiologists like E.O. Wilson who would have us believe that the world today is exactly the way it has to be and *ought* to be; that if the people in charge seem mostly male and mostly pale, talk to Darwin about it; that everything from the status of women to the IQ scores of black schoolchildren to the caste system in India is the result of a tyranny of the genes. Gould insists instead that nature is diverse and evolution is messy. Evolution has never been a "ladder" or "chain of being." It is "a ramifying bush with a million branches." Natural selection is sloppy: cost-inefficient. What we see about us, or in the mirror, is as much a consequence of chance, contingency, compromise and quirk as it is the product of necessity or design. Bacteria have been around for three billion years, dolphins have bigger brains than people, and Gould cherishes all of us. Our genes evolve, and so do organisms on a different plateau, and so does an entire species, in fits and starts, for purposes that are often contrary. Some adaptations are dandy, but others are aren't, and a few produce "by-products"—unpredictable problems and utilities and skills—that end up being at least as crucial to the surprised species as a long intestine or a cloven hoof. Our Big Brain, for instance, didn't develop just so we'd feel bad on realizing that we have to die. But our thinking about death shapes much of what we make of our lives. Nature moves as much in a dance, or a in stampede, as it does in lockstep. Besides, we also evolve culturally. If biology constrains us, we are amazingly free to improvise new selves in the interaction or "dialectic" of this genetic architecture with the plasticity of the living environment, to write the next chapter of our own history, and not by accident. We are not beetles. There are blanks in our program.

Is this what happens in Burbank? It would be pretty to think so.

TELEVISION AS CONVERSATION AND COLLECTIVE FANTASY

Critic Robert Lewis Shayon liked to make fun of TV audiences. One of his favorite tropes, quoted by practically everybody, was the Trobriand analogy: "The Trobrianders of New Guinea, as described by the late Bronislaw Malinowski, make no temporal connections between objects. There is a series of beings in their codification of reality, but no becoming. Value for the Trobriander lies not in change, but in sameness, in repeated pattern. His world is comprised of acts that lead nowhere; they are an aggregate of bumps that jerk along, like his speech, repeating the known, maintaining a point, incorporating all time in an undisturbed monotony." William Gibson, in his new novel *Idoru*, is even harder on this case, quoting a "Slitscan" producer on how she sees her audience: "Which is best visualized as a vicious, lazy, profoundly ignorant, perpetually hungry organism craving the warm god-flesh of the anointed. Personally I like to imagine something the size of a baby hippo, the color of a week-old boiled potato, that lives by itself, in the dark, in a double-wide on the outskirts of Tokyo. It's covered with eyes and it sweats constantly. The sweat runs into those eyes and makes them sting. It has no mouth, Laney, no genitals, and can only express its mute extremes of murderous rage and infantile desire by changing the channels on a universal remote. Or by voting in presidential elections."

Well, I have already mentioned Toni Morrison and Lionel Trilling and Gloria Steinem and Kurt Vonnegut and Barbara Ehrenreich and Marshall Berman and Molly Ivins. There is a lot of becoming in that crowd, not much monotony, no laziness or potato-colored hippos. This is our literature speaking, from a recliner. And if we are weary by now of thinking about episodic TV, we might for a moment compare television's performance as a showcase for American literature to Hollywood's. See who does more Arthur Miller, Eugene O'Neill, Tennessee Williams, Wendy Wasserstein, Jon Robin Baitz, Richard Nelson and David Mamet; who has better dramatized John Updike and Harold Brodkey, Willa Cather and Edith Wharton, Thomas Berger and Tom McGuane, not to mention Stephen King. I had my doubts about the three-part public television production of O'Neill's *Strange Interlude*, with Glenda Jackson and Kenneth Branagh floundering in heavy Freuds, and my suspicions about an overmuch of Tennesee Williams, going on so luridly about impotence, castration, cannibalism and rape, but was I supposed to prefer instead Hollywood's version of *The Scarlet Letter*? Whatever possessed Disney? Maybe Cyndi Lauper: "Girls Just Wanna Have Fun." We are almost one hundred and fifty years removed from Hawthorne's gothic clam chowder, and Nate himself was two hundred years removed from the seventeenth-century New England he fantasized about. Since none of us can really be relied upon to imagine a kinky past in white socks and black knickers, why not stick in all the stuff he carelessly omitted, like truculent Algonquins, comely slave girls, lynchings, witch hunts, more violins than Mantovani ever dreamed of, the wet bare bottoms of Demi Moore and Gary Oldman and Robert Duvall, and a happy ending with Hester and Dimmesdale and their demon-child lighting out in a pony cart for Carolina territory. I mean, well, after lots of weather, they are burrowing in the grain bin like a couple of naked moles; Demi wears her scarlet letter like a designer label; Gary's been hanging out in Haight-Ashbury with the Diggers; Robert hangs himself; and the anal-retentive Puritans would have hanged almost everybody else, except that the miffed Algonquins chose that moment to save the day with a convenient massacre. I'll stick with Stephen King's killer clowns.

TELEVISION AS AN IMAGINARY HOMELAND

For one week every three months or so, the folks at *NYPD Blue* show up in the city where the series is ostensibly set, as if for electroshock, to shoot exteriors. They are otherwise stuck on a California soundstage, being lean and mean in a terrarium. Nor are they alone out there. Maybe it didn't matter that *Love & War*, where tabloid riffraff in a downtown bistro munched wisecrack potato chips as translated from the Diane English, and *704 Hauser Street* where a black family moved briefly into Archie Bunker's old house, and even *Murder, She Wrote*, where Jessica spent half of every season teaching on a ridiculously sylvan city college campus, were all confabulated in Left Coast cubbyholes on the San Andreas fault. But what about *The Nanny*, in which Fran Drescher's supposed to be for Queens what Daw Aung San Suu Kyi is for Myanmar, a noisy Joan of Arc? More confounding, what about *Seinfeld*, that cheese doodle of urban fecklessness and penis jokes to which our hero wears a prophylactic smirk? Or *Mad About You* in which Paul Reiser and Helen Hunt seem to float like Peter Pan and Tinkerbell on the air currents above a Neverland Manhattan? Or for God's sake, *Friends*? Don't they require, as they go to movies or eat Chinese, some psoriatic qualm about relationships, bicycle messengers and meta-narrative that only comes from trying like Sisyphus to find an apartment, a lover, a cab, a *zeitgeist*, even an ontology? Shouldn't they wear T-shirts that spell out DEATH BEFORE MELLOW? Shouldn't they be speaking the sarcasm of the damned? How can they manage to be hip, much less postmodern, under a palm tree? Even the TV movies in which they talk about us behind our backs, like *Howard Beach: Making the Case for Murder*, *The Preppie Murder*, *The Mayflower Madam* and *Getting Gotti*, are shot in Toronto. Whatever happened to the imperial city as theater or symphony, as Babel and Sphinx and jumping beans, as a polychrome riot of dynamic capitalism, radical dissent and symbolic significations—Greenwich Village *and* Harlem, Wall Street *and* Hester Street, Madison Avenue *and* the Bowery, Carnegie Hall *and* Little Italy? Whatever happened to *Stage Door*, *Rear Window* and *Breakfast at Tiffany's*? Or for that matter, *Kojak* and *The Equalizer* and *Molly Dodd*? Even *Brooklyn Bridge* was shot in Burbank.

A typical New Yawk crybaby whine: Didn't the mayor's wife, Donna Guiliani, First Lady of Fun City, show up on an afternoon soap, not perhaps quite fresh but certainly game after pushing a little too hard on the perky pedal at the harmonium of her co-anchor command post on the cable TV foodie channel, between interviews of a meat-thermometer salesman and Sprout Man himself, gussied up in green humus, before a symposium on "The Great Fluff-Off" at a festival to flack The Year of the Marshmallow? Is there reason to believe that any TV place is really *real*? Was Mary Tyler Moore's Minneapolis real? Or J. R. Ewing's Dallas? Perry Mason's Denver? *Hill Street* used some Chicago exteriors, but shot itself after dark on not-so-smart L.A. streets. Don't bother looking in Wisconsin for the Rome of *Picket Fences,* where they cope each week with the usual smalltown troubles, like dead bluejays in the mailbox, severed hands in a pickle jar, serial bathers, forced busing, elephant abuse, euthanasia, fetal tissue and abortion, homelessness and Native Americans, AIDS and gay dentists, flying saucers, killer nuns and a murder (by nicotine poisoning) of the teacher dressed up as the Tin Man in a high-school production of *The Wizard of Oz.* The entire cast of *The X-Files* spends nine months of the year in Vancouver, British Columbia. Like used-car commercials in the fifties; like that odd tinny sound of soaps, community access, Food Network natter and public TV pledge weeks; like the muddy soundtracks of war and western B-movie reruns and cotton candy tints of "colorized" gangster semiclassics; like the sullen yak of skinheads and other lower-class losers on the afternoon freak shows; like the wormholes and WIMPs ("Weakly Interacting Massive Particles") of astronomical physics, as if they had been prerecorded in a space lab orbiting Sirius the Dog Star, and some Mandelbrot of fractals, each resembling the other no matter how they are scaled—television is *imaginary space.* And more than ever, it is an imaginary space that contemplates itself, in the late-night Letterman manner and Gary Shandling's *Larry Sanders,* or *Talk Soup* and *Hardcore TV.* Even the critics can't help ourselves. About *Northern Exposure,* I said that first summer: "a vegetarian *Twin Peaks.*" About *Picket Fences*: "David Lynched in Rome, Wisconsin." And: "*Mayberry RFD* Meets the Manson Family Values." Or: *Hill Street Cheese.*

I would like to blame these dislocations on *Miami Vice,* which, as I have explained at inordinate length in the section on cops, is much more about vice than it is much less about Miami, and finally, excessively, most of all about its arty, affectless self. But my need of *Miami Vice* is compositional rather than didactic. It was the TV elsewhere at its gaudy least, a poisoned lollipop of cool, as *Twin Peaks* was the TV elsewhere as its corrupt laziest, a wallow in the perversely polymorphic. But if I were Peter Handke I'd want to guide me to the imaginary and thus oddly temperate Alaskan outback, for a *Northern Exposure* where for four years we found a home instead of a hospital, or a penal colony or a loony bin.

When, in in the middle of *Northern Exposure*'s second season on CBS, Rick came back as a dog, an Eskimo malamute, I felt born again myself. Admirers of the most remarkable series ever to sustain itself on network television will remember Rick as the latest dead body in a long line of Maggie's boyfriends. A space satellite fell on poor Rick in a fraught episode the previous season. Because the satellite fused with his corpse, the folks in Cicely, Alaska, had to bury him in a customized coffin, with the antenna sticking out. The idea of Rick with an antenna was even funnier than the idea of Rick as a dog, no matter how you feel personally about reincarnation—and I'm in favor. But till he malamutated, *Northern Exposure*'s second season was a disappointment. Cicely had been a point in space-time where even Samuel Beckett might have been happy and was likely to be mentioned and quoted, like Leon Trotsky and Susan Sontag, Walt Whitman and Gertrude Stein, Albert Einstein and Krishnamurti. Ed (Darren Burrows), the Indian with the 180-I.Q., had gone to every movie ever made. Maurice (Barry Corbin), the ex-astronaut and real estate tycoon, was intimate with each and every Hemingway cliché. Who can forget the parody of *Twin Peaks*, or Adam Arkin as Sasquatch, a bad-tempered gourmet cook? But in those second season doldrums, *Northern Exposure* seemed suddenly to be looking over its shoulder, as if in doubt of how it got wherever it was. One sure sign of playing too safe was all the attention paid to the sex life of Maggie (Janine Turner), the bush pilot with raging hormones; and Shelly (Cynthia Geary), the 18-year-old former Miss Northwest Passage who shacked up with Holling (John Callum), the 62-year-old French aristocrat tavernkeeper; and even of Chris (John Corbett), the Jungian deejay, *Rolling Stone* mail-order minister, and ex-con/Rimbaud manqué who had seemed the previous season to be picking up quasar transmissions from the plate in Norman Mailer's head. Missing, besides the literary references, was the unpredictability.

But when Rick came back, so did the series, as if in the interim the stately moose had been reading Saul Bellow to refresh the scripts with his twitchy speed-freak patter, half sentimental and half baroque, the mandarin and slangy, the long ironies and the low laughs. Or maybe Mordechai Richler had dropped in to hide from all the Canadians he had offended in *The New Yorker*. Anyway, so long as we had *this* Cicely, who needed a TV New York? In Cicely, our contentious cultures could be counted on to find a common cause. If not a vegetarian *Twin Peaks*, it was at least a *Martian Chronicle* and maybe also a *West Side Story*. See Joel—Rob Morrow as Dr. Flesichmann, shipped off to the Arctic Circle to pay off the government loan that got him through med school—fish his old rabbi out of the cold black waters. See a Catholic priest arrive in Cicely in a Winnebago church-on-wheels, to baptize Shelley's child and Maggie's plane, after a visit to the still, some arm-wrestling and some cribbage, and a friendly disputation on the twelfth-century Albigensian heresy. See the gay wedding, and also the wheelchair Olympics. Who among us was surprised? No one who already believed Chris had a black brother; that Shelley, like a Singing Detective, dreamed in dancing feet; that on the occasion of the thawing of the ice every spring, a mass-neurotic marathon of hairy naked men would rush through the dawn-stricken streets as if they were Pamplona bulls. Or who had already discovered an ice-cube Napoleon. Or had already grinned through so many references to Nietzsche and Sartre, Dante and Buber, Robert Frost and Marcel Proust. Cicely, a town founded by *lesbians*, was a cafeteria community so congenial to the fantastic, so forgiving of eccentricity, so devoted to the principle of reciprocity and so variously populated by artists, prophets, shamans and chefs, that it was either García Márquez Macondo Magical or downright Buddhist. And how could this have happened if Joel hadn't been fishing in the deep deli waters of Darwin, Frazier, Marx, Freud and *Krazy Kat*; if he hadn't brought with him to Alaska the magic Aztec matzos of a Lower East Side, an Upper West Side and the New York Public Library, the beads and blues of a vibrant, federated multiculture, the designer labels of high-modernist art and the vulgar vitality of pop; a madeleine cookie, a pickle and some ribs?

But Joel went native, as if on some Bruce Chatwin aboriginal walkabout along songlines no longer audible to the rest of us. And we were left behind, convalescent: to be *mediated* by lesser Buddhists like Oprah, Geraldo, Tempest, Montel, Maury, Rolanda, Sally, Jenny, Ricki, Kathie and Regis and Alana and George. To be *hortatoried* by beltway unabombers on the chat channels. To be *sally struthered* by "infomercials" on starvation in Africa and real-estate in Florida and the Greatest Hits of Johnny Cash. To be *historectomied* by Herman Wouk, James Michener and Edward Bulwer-Lytton. To be *devolved*, on a Weather Channel where we are asked to fret about Canadian cold fronts and Kansas cyclones and tropical Caribbean storms and mud slides on Mt. Ararat as if we could conceivably care enough to do anything about it; and on PBS or Discovery where we are told just how *other* insects and penguins are, and spoon-billed bee-eaters and adhesive-padded geckos, and mad scientists and Englishmen; and on MTV, where they are *snarling* at us—never mind Chubby Checker: Metallica (with nightmares about trucks and snakes) and Nine-Inch Nails (upset about animal experimentaion) and Pearl Jam (murdering a child) *do not mean us well*—as if music video were the return of the repressed, like Pat Robertson and gay porn. To be *glommed* and *grokked* and cauterized and therapized, from the teary perspectives of Movies of the Week, the pillbox slits of the cop shows, the sniper sights of the feral comedians, and the watery saucers of an ever-empathic Larry King, into one of whose ears and out the other flaps Ross Perot like a maddened fruit bat—and this is to pretend that we aren't being stared at by the pitiless basilisk bloodshot peepers of the Lettermans and Lenos.

We wake up wondering whether Bryant will feel better today. We go to bed knowing Dave doesn't. Such sad clowns, these Lettermans and Lenos. Like birthday balloons, they hang in the air, waiting for children to stone them. Since age 10, all Dave had ever dreamt of was Johnny's late-night job and then they went and gave it to Jay, who sat on a box in a closet to eavesdrop on the NBC suits during their conference-call coin flip. *Guest host*: what an oxymoronic concept. To be the Prince of Our Disorder: what an ambition! One imagines Johnny himself in exile in Malibu, like one of the deposed dictators in *The Autumn of the Patriarch*, playing dominoes in a rest home on a cliff, "poor presidents of nowhere…begging a hello from passing ships." And so Dave, with a matador's cape slung over his shoulders and beetles scuttling at his silver heels, walked out of the Rainbow Room and followed the prow of his big cigar uptown on the Avenue of the Americas to Black Rock where Howard Stringer was waiting with love and money and 11:30. Such mutual neediness makes you weep. Was Dave worth $14 million a year? He seems gnawed by self-doubts ever since his Oscar night fiasco. That's the bitch about being so postmodern, so self-referential, so mediated and ironized, that whatever you say or think comes pre-equipped with quotation marks and asterisks. You are suspicious of your own text.

Such an elsewhere—impossibly heterogeneous, a riot of subjectivities, everything seen at once from everyone's point of view, fractured, fleeting, violent, disposable, fugitive, totalizing, glossy and parodic. While *Northern Exposure*'s grad-school whimsy seemed designed just for me, those millions of younger Americans who sit still each week for *Melrose Place* are so self-consciously ironic, you'd think they were Jorge Luis Borges or Italo Calvino. One might hope to hear, on wandering these randomly postmodern streets, something at least as surprising as the graffiti discovered by the Groucho Marxist historian Eduardo Galeano on the walls of the various Latin American capital cities he has run away from. In Bogotá for instance: "Proletarians of all lands, unite!" (And scrawled underneath in another hand: "FINAL NOTICE.") Or, in Montevideo: "Assist the police. Torture yourself." But just listen to these voices in our TV heads: "If stupid were glue, Dad could wallpaper New Zealand" (*The Parent Hood*). "Doesn't anybody have sex any more? Am I in Ireland here?" (*Double Rush*). "In my town we didn't have dating. You washed your hair every Saturday night and when you were 14, you married your cousin" (*Empty Nest*). "In a world of pork and beans you might be missin' a few gristle cubes" (*Evening Shade*). "Mom, I know this isn't easy for you, but...so what?" (*Phenom*). "Have you ever thought of switching your earring to the heterosexual side of your head?" (*Good Sports*). "The man who said winning isn't everything was a weenie!" (*Backfield in Motion*). "If Jesus was a Jew, why the Spanish name?" (*Politically Incorrect*). Finally, from Larry Gelbart's cable-TV *Mastergate*: "No one else was in a position not to know as much as the President didn't." Besides: "I'm not cleared to have that kind of curiosity."

If Dave himself isn't sure he's there, can the rest of us be blamed for an agnosticism about reality itself? As the cyberpunk novelist Pat Cadigan has warned us: "First you see video. Then you wear video. Then you eat video. Then you *be* video."

*I refuse to be intimidated by reality any more. What is
reality but a collective hunch?*

Lily Tomlin

Tired of hauling itself around, Meat dreams of flying, like a fax.
Gravity sucks. Slugabed in the romper room, tethered to the all-
news War Porn channel, flatlined by the adman/music video consumer grid, home-shopping for friendship in the beer commercials, reading a Heavy Metal comic, "sampling" on the CD
carousel a customized sequence of Sonic Youth, Pussy Galore and
Tom Petty's *Jamming Me*, even crouched in front of our very own
software, as if it were a harpsichord, on-line and downlinked to all
the other ghosts in the machine, jacked in instead of jacking off, we
imagine through the looking glass, *inside where the information is*, a
weightless fourth dimension, some sort of surf's up, maybe a raft
for Huck and Jim. We long for and *intuit* a digitized Xanadu: Lucy
in the Sky with Diamonds.

The ultimate elsewhere may be cyberspace—the future, we are
told, for all news and entertainment programming, for high
finance and low mind games, for self-aggrandizement and paranoid delusions—that datasphere and dreamscape where we are
boats and nets are sails. If I am suspicious, it may be because the
Net began its webby life as an extension of our Pentagon, a military communications option, just as computer technology itself
was a child of nuclear-era military Research and Development,
with a built-in go/no-go, us-them digital discourse. Game theory,
cybernetics and Artificial Intelligence R&D all originated in the
same think tanks as smart bombs and Star Wars. (See *The Closed
World: Computers and the Politics of Discourse in Cold War America*,
by Paul N. Edwards, MIT, 1996). And the sharks circling the software programs and the server systems are the same as those
already grown fat from feeding on the budget of the Defense
Department to stealth our problematic futures, as if our name
were MUD.

Outside certain leftwing chatrooms, I have yet to see anywhere on the World Wide Web as much social conscience as you'd pick up from a Murphy Brown, a Julia Sugarbaker or a Hawkeye wisecrack and the dimmest TV movie on toxic waste or child abuse. And "Netiquette" has a way to go before it gets remotely near the Buddhist reciprocity of Cicely, Alaska—or, for that matter, *Sesame Street*. And television could also teach the Net a lot about treating women as human beings, instead of lavatory walls. (Browsing, I also noticed a nasty joke: What are a super model's four major food groups? Saltines, Diet Coke, Tic-Tacs and heroin.) But e-mail and bulletin boards are neighborly, and "virtual communities" seem to me a wonderful idea, a magic lasso in a seethe of sects. And I *long* for hacker camaraderie. It more resembles the retro-existential humanism of *Northern Exposure* than the Dungeons and Dragons of the Black Lodge in *Twin Peaks* or *Raunchy Redheads—Wall to Wall* on pay-per-view "adult" TV. You will find it on-line at the East Coast ECHO and deeper down in the older West Coast WELL, without the mercenary hassles of America Online, CompuServe or Prodigy. The WELL throws an annual picnic, where digitheads can f2f. ECHOES meet every other Monday night at the Art Bar in downtown Manhattan, and for tea at the Starbucks on Astor Place, and for jolly-up special excursions to New York's cemeteries and through New York's underground tunnels, as if in search of not only fellowship and edification, but also Beauty's Beast. Vienna! Weimar! Left Bank! North Beach! Maybe there's a *where* there, after all. So, if I can't smoke, drink or drive, and prime time makes me violently ill, I might as well space out, before Bill Gates owns all of it.

News From Nowhere

Listen to the Israeli sociologists Daniel Dayan and Elihu Katz, in *Media Events*:

> Routine, nighttime viewing positions the tired viewer in front of a range of recuperative choices—among channels, among programs, among products. It addresses him as a family member, consumer, sensation seeker, and sometimes as an information user, in the apolitical living room. Evening television tells family members, first, that they want to feel comfortable with one another at home, and, second, that they wish to be amused by the antics and crimes of familiar story characters who are typically remote from their world. It tells them that they have a "right" to be entertained any time at their own choosing, and that they have freedom of choice among channels and genres. It invites them to consider the advertised products and the dreams or needs these fulfill.

Dayan and Katz examined a handful of TV "spectacles" that interrupted this routine. They looked at JFK's state funeral, the royal wedding of Charles and Di, the visit to Israel of Anwar el-Sadat, Watergate and the 1989 velvet revolutions in Eastern Europe—as ceremonies of integration, celebration and reconciliation; as "shamanic events," with a sometimes surprising "transformative dimension"; as anthropological "scripts" of contest, conquest and coronation; as "sacred performances," like Seders or Thanksgiving; as symbolic enactments of rites of passage, newly proposed paradigms, "deep play" and "framing"; as "social dramas" and "redressive assemblies" and even "liturgies" of a civic religion. What they reported, in a prose remarkably graceful for a media studies monograph, was that audiences "read" these media events in a number of ways their producers had never imagined, often ignoring the "supertext" entirely. (And sometimes the event itself is hijacked from the medium, as in Chicago 1968 or Munich 1972.)

Our critical theorists call such staged occasions-of-state "hegemonic manipulations." But critical theorists, while sounding shrewd, are often wrong. Eugene Goodheart, for instance, told us some years ago that "The apocalypse may be the dominant media trope of our time; its endless replay has inured us to the real suffering it might entail. We repeatedly witness the assassination of Kennedy, the mushroom cloud over Hiroshima, the disintegration of the *Challenger* space shuttle in the sky. Repetition wears away the pain. It also perfects the image of our experience of it. By isolating the event and repeating it, its content, its horror, evaporates. What we have before us is its form and rhythm. The event becomes esthetic and the effect upon us anesthetic. The phenomenon is called kitsch." Goodheart defines kitsch as "a term for art of little value or an art that is meretricious, a misleading, ingratiating semblance of the real thing.…Ordinary kitsch covers over reality with the appearance of art: it appeals to the desire for the pleasant and harmonious. But there is also a kitsch of death; an estheticizing of experience."

This sounds shrewd. Except that I know people, and so do you, who have to leave the room whenever there's a rocket lift-off on television, because that *Challenger* launch with the teacher inside is burned on their mind's own retina. How often must we burst into tears at a film clip from the death camps, before media theorists admit that what goes on in our image-filled heads is something more, or something other, than aesthetic? It's not the mushroom cloud that breaks the heart in this atomic age; it's home movies of the radiation-deformed children of Hiroshima and Nagasaki. When we have forgotten almost everything else about the Vietnam war, Americans will remember a single snapshot of a little girl and her baby brother burning alive in napalm. And no matter how many times we saw the Rodney King videotape in reruns, we weren't "inured" to his real suffering; the horror never evaporated; to no one did it become "form and rhythm"—except to those Simi Valley jurors who acquitted the cops. And that tape was replayed endlessly for those jurors *in slow motion*, as if to stone them. They weren't watching it in real time. It became for them a kind of self-hypnosis, after which they voted as you'd expect from a bedroom community of cops with Ronald Reagan's presidential library just down their yellow brick road.

To me, the amazing thing about television apocalypse tropes is that they continue to worry and wound, to sting and scald, over the passing of time and beyond the flow of so many different and competing images; that we believe them at all, much less cling to their clarity and efficacy in a snowstorm of obliterating counter-messages we have learned from disillusioning experience to be wary of or ironic about, if not to disbelieve entirely—of commercials for Edsels; of dire predictions by dismal economists and damned evangelists; of spangled hype for new movies that insult the intelligence of nine-year-olds; of drumrolls and trumpet fanfare for miniskirts, maxipads, designer water, Ritalin, minoxidil, A. Testoni gazelle-skin loafers and Ralph Lauren pajama chaps. Long after mercifully forgetting anything we were ever told about the New Math, the Scardsale diet, Rogaine or swine flu, we will cherish a 30-second snippet of a man in shirtsleeves holding up a column of Red Army tanks in Tiananmen Square.

Dayan and Katz take greater care. Of its nature, they observe, television "privileges the home," making it a "public space," evoking a climate of "intense reflexivity." On television, we have better access to spectacles than those who attend them. Neither power nor money entitles anyone to a better seat than ours in the living room. Rather than an "impoverished" or "deviant" sensation, this "not being there," *while nonetheless seeing everything*, has the quality of "an altogether *different* experience"—capable of reorganizing space, time, geography and history in our heads, suggesting relationships that are contractual rather than hegemonic, collapsing pre-rehearsed consensus, pointing to latent conflicts and inviting previously unthinkable solutions.

This seems to me to apply as much to the punitive serial drama and the socializing sitcom and the TV movie in its therapeutic mode as it does to a packaged "special" or a surprise verdict on Court TV. Whatever's on show, from wherever in the world, we are always present, and will be even more so with three all-news cable services and five hundred boutique channels to choose among, floating by in a bucket-seat in a zeppelin that's superior to the fixed positions of all the official participants, with multiple views of the action in close-up and tracking shot, in intimate focus or broad scan, a livelier sense of duration and scale, and an IV-feed of raw data and expert chitchat, as if we were not only accustomed but *entitled* to the whole picture, to all the pictures all of the time, on royal whim.

Beyond surfing, this whimsical elsewhere suggests a new epistemology of *zoom*, and we are *zoomers*. To zoom is to sample, but not necessarily to engage or believe. A zoomer is to the late twentieth century what a "browser" or "flaneur" was to the late nineteenth. Now listen to Peter Fritzsche in *Reading Berlin 1900*:

> But surely the most awe-inspiring aspect of the great cities in the industrial epoch was their restless, fugitive quality....More than anything else, the machinery and the social relations of industrial development reworked the looks of cities to the point of unfamiliarity. They did so not simply by tearing down medieval walls or by adding immense factories and settling thousands of new laborers, although these were undeniably dramatic events, but by sustaining this activity over time. Neither industrial progress nor commercial activity were geared to preserve the physical character or the social makeup of urban space. As a result, the nineteenth century city was less of a new creation and more of an incalculable, ongoing process. Victorian London, Second Empire Paris, and Wilhelmine Berlin were no longer best described by sturdy four-cornered nouns referring to old squares and new buildings but by a more tentative vocabulary that denoted movement, surprise, and discontinuity. The industrial city was distinctive as much for the everyday experience of unfamiliarity and flux as for the infiltration of smoke-stacks and proletarians.

And where would we "read" (or *zoom*) this discontinuous text and new urban space? In handbills and maps, instruction manuals and advertising labels, regulations and prohibitions, street signs and streetcar schedules, Expressionist poems and modern novels. But, most of all, in newspapers. In the liberal ideal world of the nineteenth century, newspapers were supposed to be "grand institutions of public enlightenment," as liberal idealists hoped television would become in the twentieth. But in the sketches, stories, line drawings, "fleeting reportage" and feuilletons of big-city newspapers like *Berliner Morgenpost*, as on television, what we got was something other. The modern city was fabricated, even falsified, by commodifying the news as a disposable consumer item and by sensationalizing its most fantastic characteristics:

Not only was the present increasingly experienced as brand new, completely different from even the recent past, but it was itself doomed to be merely transitory. Fashions, fads, and all ideas of the moment were thus typically modern creatures, bursting into the scene with great energy before falling into disuse, persisting for a while as ruins, then disappearing again. It followed that any attempt to capture the essence of the age had to focus on these occasionals, which Baudelaire described as "le transitoire, le fugitif, le contingent." To track the merely transitory was to represent the enduring spirit of the age.

Ceaseless mutability, "inner urbanization," intellectual virtuosity with moral emptiness, heightened sensual activity but emotional indifference, "layering, piling, rolling, pushing" and "blur," Dickens and Dos Passos, Döblin and Joyce, Picasso and Braque—well, we had heard it before and would hear it again. (Writing created the role of the historian; reading undermined the authority of the elders; print made possible the Protestant Reformation and the rise of science; cities caused alienation and newspapers; and newspapers caused European nationalism and modernism.) Yet readers of newspapers, like watchers of television, pick and choose; glance at, pore over, peruse and zoom; read headlines, seek sports scores, consult classifieds, in whatever order or its reverse, nonsequentially; want entertaining, need information, and maybe a job or apartment; fold up, pass on, or toss away: "Newspapers tell stories, and they also wrap fish and make paper hats. Insofar as reading is an individual act of 'poaching,' in the words of Michel de Certeau, it might be hazardous to suggest that any sort of text worked on readers, and through readers, on metropolitan experience in common, knowable ways." What a caution. And what a mosaic (of "occasionals"!). If newspapers are what Fritzsche calls a "Word City," television is an Image Megapolis, an Imaginary Capital. This Realm of Signs is every place we've ever been, or thought we were, and every traumatizing trope we brought back like a virus.

*There is a division of labor in the ranks of the powerful. The
army, paramilitary organizations and hired assassins
concern themselves with social contradictions and the class
struggle. Civilians are responsible for speeches.*

Eduardo Galeano, *The Book of Embraces*

Imagine a father and son in China in July, 1991. On our first afternoon in Beijing, we are wowed. The Temple of Heaven intends to
wow. You have seen it showing off—the Four Gates, the Round
Altar, the Imperial Vault and the Hall of Prayer for Good Harvests—in *The Last Emperor*. Ming Mandarins were in charge of the
fifteenth century and they knew it. On their way from the Temple
of Heaven to the Forbidden City, they wore the winter solstice like
a wristwatch. From the white marble, glazed tiles, compass points,
echo walls, royal dragons and elephant chariots, the visitor intuits
gongs and incense. Under a silk tent, we construe the sacred
tablets. We are necromancers, numerologists, and multiples of
nine. And then by bike we flee, as if from Agamemnon's Tomb, to
Tiananmen Square. And the logo of Chairman Mao. And the
dreadful residue of TV memory. Already, just minutes into the
vertigo of Asia and this hit-and-run on an ancient culture that
invented the wheel barrow and the kite, we are seeing ghosts.

I know. I've already used Dayan and Katz to explain that television has turned all of us into Ming Mandarins, above it all with an
imperial perspective, as if a helicopter were our dragon—to whom
no cities are forbidden, for whom the heavens are a peepshow. But
indulge me on China.

When I was at Berkeley—a yesteryear of Golden Doors and
August Personages of Jade—I took Joseph Levenson's course in
classical Chinese civilization and even fancied myself a Taoist. In
San Francisco, in the sixties, Kenneth Rexroth made me read Su
Tung-p'o, Ly You, Li Ch'ing Chao and *The Dream of the Red Chamber*. Twenty years later, I was even asked to write a preface for the
fiftieth anniversary edition of André Malraux's *Man's Fate*. Never
mind that the closest Malraux ever got to the Chinese Revolution

was a 1925 Hong Kong general strike. That's closer than I got. And his Shanghai novel asked the hardest question in a bad-news century: How to die with dignity, having acted with meaning, in the absence of God, on behalf of others?

About the time I was rethinking Malraux, my son Andrew was studying Chinese at the University of Michigan. He asked for an extra year to perfect his Mandarin at the Stanford language school in Taipei. Godspeed, I said, signing a check with secret glee. One of us had to get it right. And so he disappeared for four years into an Asia I could only imagine—of rice paddies, honky-tonks and opium dens; of unfinished novels, student protest movements, romantic fiascos and red stars over golden Buddhas. He would return to attend graduate school—at Berkeley, of course.

Connected by telephone to opposite sides of the continent, my son and I watched Tiananmen on television together when it seemed that the Mandate was about to be returned from Heaven. "I played frisbee in Tiananmen Square," Andrew told me as we stared at a satellite relay. The night before, I had called to alert him to Charles Kuralt, having the time of his life on a Beijing street corner. We felt sorry for ourselves, left out of it. Later, we'd felt sorry for Zhao, kicked out of it. Later still, when the lights went out all over American television, and China vanished from the nightly news, we'd feel sorry for Dan Rather, unplugged. Once upon a time I rooted for my son's *teams,* at places like Ann Arbor; now I root for his countries. But as this "live" television chased the pages of Malraux right out of my head, so it supplanted Andrew's own live memories. When at last, two years later, we found ourselves together in a subdued Middle Kingdom, we filtered everything we saw through the recorded images of another intelligence, like a preemptive template. We were jacked into the fiber-optic nerve of an omnipresent Super Awareness.

That image of a solitary figure holding up a line of advancing tanks belongs of course in the permanent television memory palace in everybody's head, with Jack Ruby's gunning down of Lee Harvey Oswald in Dallas and the slo-mo mosey to nowhere of O.J.'s white Ford Bronco. What we saw on TV from Tiananmen was the exact opposite of the Red Guards in their earlier, convulsive Oedipal rage. Instead of despoiling, these students, at one of history's greatest sit-ins, *ennobled.* This was what nonviolent civil disobedience could be—passionate, resolute, disciplined, even puckish. When they had finished facing down the army on Saturday's deadline to disperse, they escorted truckloads of soldiers on Shuangzhing to the *bathroom*. Remember that moment in the Russian Revolution when Cossacks winked at the workers? And then the workers ducked under the bellies of motionless Cossack horses? That trip to the bathroom seemed to me the Chinese Army's wink. And I hadn't been the only one to think so.

The Sunday after that Saturday deadline, to our amazement, Charles Kuralt returned from history-making Beijing to television-making CBS, on West Fifty-seventh Street, and he was flying high in the studio. "Empty hands!" he said. They were changing the world with empty hands. I accused him of "lacking objectivity." He laughed at me. He had never been so moved. A Chagall angel, he seemed to float. Thinking of another revolution, Malraux once wrote of Saint-Just: "He wanted to live inside history as holy men live inside their faith...to be confounded with the Republic as saints lose themselves in God." No one less like Saint-Just than Charles Kuralt is imaginable, but he seemed nevertheless to have lost himself in freedom, to be exalted on behalf of all of us. But then they killed the children and workers, and President Wonderbread stamped his foot, and Kuralt was speechless, and when I should have stayed home, watching the tanks, I marched in protest from one Manhattan river to the other, from the People's Republic consulate to Dag Hammarskjöld Plaza, and then hurried home to see if we'd made the local news. This was because my son couldn't. He had planned to leave immediately for China. When their revolution failed, he fell off a bicycle, broke his clavicle and concussed himself. While he was bedridden in Berkeley, the blood bath went on without him. So much for fluency in Mandarin. Maybe he's history-prone. Having since gone into cyberspace, he must be a Taoist.

All this has happened before, as Jonathan Spence reports in *The Gate of Heavenly Peace* and as I explained to Kuralt and Rather, at CBS, on the Sunday after the Sunday after the Saturday of the deadline. In front of the gate where my son played frisbee, before there had been that ad for Mao, they killed students in 1919 and then killed some more in 1926, after which the ones they hadn't killed would make the Revolution of 1949 whose old men were now killing children again. Looking at 1926 from the point of view of a rickshaw-puller, the poet Wen Yiduo wrote:

Please, sir, just let me catch a breath, those things there, can't you see those pitch-dark things, some are headless, others hobbling, they frighten me, they just keep waving their white banners and calling out...Ah, they are still holding their meetings, still not behaving properly! See there, whose children are those, they're hardly adolescents, are they?...By tomorrow the city of Beijing will be full of ghosts.

Kuralt and Rather listened politely. On West 57th Street, I often feel like a Nick Carraway seed on the cinnamon bun of all these Gatsbys, so much less *vivid* than they. And those of us who opinionize promiscuously about television for the print media have made anchor-bashing one of our specialties. See the Super Starry Frequent Flyers off like Icarus by Magic Slate to the bare ruined choirs: Brokaw in safari jacket, Rather in combat fatigues, Jennings in designer dreads, standing down, body-miked, parenthetical and anticlimactic in Sarajevo, Mogadishu or Port au Prince, after the aborted deadlines, real-time suspense, exotic locale, uniforms, whirlybirds. Hadn't they gone heavily armed to Haiti, with satellite telephones and nightscopes? Hadn't they wasted our weekend waiting for Jimmy Carter and Raoul Cedras to do something about the rain delay in the war-making? Unlike the rest of us, didn't they already know that C-130 paratroop transports were airborne from Fort Bragg to the Caribbean? Couldn't they have guessed that Bill Clinton in his Oval office media command module, was just minutes away from seizing control of the TV screen like Max Headroom? Depending on what Max said, the marquee names of American broadcast journalism might be back again stateside in time for O.J. Simpson's lift-off and maybe even the mass suicide, in Switzerland, of gun-running lettuce-fetishists on short orders from their solar temple. What really goes on behind the anguished eyes of the resolute anchorhead at crunchtime? *Nobody knows.* It sometimes seems to me that Jennings is secretly thinking about Book III of *A Guide for the Perplexed,* in which Maimonides allegorized the Biblical story of the Chariot. And Rather is probably pissed that Jennings has twice as many drones at ABC to call on as Dan does at Tischful-thinking CBS. At least Brokaw knows he will get to go to the Olympics.

But if Kuralt and Rather haven't read Wen Yiduo or Su Tung-p'o, they have certainly read Malraux. They subscribe, moreover, to journals like *The New York Review* and *The Nation,* as well as the slick newsweeklies. Before joining CBS, they had worked for newspapers, in North Carolina and Texas. Before becoming anchors in New York, they had done time in the burn wards of a flaming world, covering coups and assassinations. (Naturally, the best and brightest end up in New York; network news divisions differ from major-player law firms or investment houses only in pariculars of routine.) Anyone seeing them chat about China that Sunday morning would realize that *reporting* was still their junkie adrenaline rush. And not only were the images they sent back from Beijing more compelling than any story to appear in a broadsheet the following day, but their extemporized captions to those snapshots had a passion and lucidity that need not apologize to the editor of any newspaper, magazine or paperback quickie pecked on a hotel laptop by the ambulance chasers of the dailies and glossies. Which ought not to surprise us. Kuralt *listens* better than most of us talk, writes more gracefully than any op-ed page, and consults a moral compass altogether missing from the beltway/syndication toolkit. Rather's always been more comfortable out of doors where the weather is, like Afghanistan, than worrying in a studio behind a powdered anchorface about his smile, his sweater or his Chung. If the upward logic of careers in electronic journalism converge on anchordom (a glorified isolation booth), then the upward logic of careers in print journalism converge on punditry (a glorified thumb-sucking). Personally, I would rather watch a Rather pump up the teleological significance of a farm-state primary exit poll, a Brokaw feel bad about Oklahoma City or a Jennings scowl skeptically at the latest rhetoric from the Middle East than read Abe Rosenthal on why we should be bombing Libya or George Will attacking *Friends* for smutty-mindedness (while quoting the sitcom's smuttiest lines). That Ink People look down on Pixels, even wildly overpraising movies like *Network* and *Broadcast News*, is especially risible when you see these Inkies simultaneously scrambling for a barstool on Charlie Rose's show or a bully pulpit at CNN, the better to beef up their lecture fees. That television should instead romanticize newspapers—while making savage fun of itself—is equally risible, but also sadder, like an abused wife refusing to press charges.

Never mind the eye-witless local news, a lost cause and a penny-dreadful from the beginnings of television, bubbleheads ("If it bleeds, it leads") pandering to potatoheads (lip-readers of the Murdoch and supermarket tabloids), whose secret purpose has always been to assure us that we're safer at home with a warm machine than we'd be outside in a cold world where rivers rise, planes drop out of the sky and savage tribes stalk chicken littles on the street. "How do you feel?" they ask the wounded and bereaved. It is a sincere question. Having lost their knack for feeling anything at all, they seek a clue. *How* do you feel? In Don DeLillo's *Mao II*, the former Moonie Karen has made a cult of TV news—"lost in the dusty light, observing some survivor of a national news disaster...the lonely fuselage smoking in a field," she is able "to study the face and shade into it at the same time, even sneak a half second ahead, inferring the strange, dazed grin or gesturing hand, which made her seem involved not just in the coverage but in the terror that came blowing through the fog." Karen believes everything that the rest of us are sick of: "pain, ecstasy, dog food, all the seraphic matter, the baby bliss that falls from the air."

But network news was supposed to be, and used to be, different. In all of journalism, who was more impossibly romantic than, say, Edward R. Murrow? Every guild or chivalric order, avant-garde or guerrilla band, even a revolutionary vanguard, needs its tragic hero. The role requires courage and style, valor and grace. But there should also be a wound, a shadow on the splendor, something self-destructive as well as emblematic. Murrow was that kind of hero for broadcast journalists. Emerging from radio into CBS television, he grasped the new medium's power to modify the way a nation thinks about itself, then watched helplessly as TV pawned that power to the ad agencies, and smoked himself to death. He even *looked* like Albert Camus, the Shadow Man hero of postwar French literature—Bogart with a microphone. In an *American Masters* documentary, on *PBS* of course in 1990, we were reminded that Murrow went on too many World War II bombing missions. That he had been stunned when they opened the gates at Buchenwald. That he cared so much about words he often forgot to look at the camera. That he made up *See It Now* as he went along, forever over budget. That after his famous demolition job on Joe McCarthy, Alcoa dropped its sponsorship of *See It Now* and William Paley, the Tsar of all the Children of the Eye, turned against his best-known reporter, bumping the program from the prime-time schedule. That in his last few years at CBS before he resigned in 1961, there were many more *Person to Person* interviews with the likes of Marilyn Monroe than there had ever been documentaries like *Harvest of Shame*, on the plight of migrant farmworkers.

Nevertheless, who would you want instead as the star in your epic romance of journalism? A Walter Lippmann—who happened to forget he was Jewish, from the rise of Hitler through the the discovery of the death camps and even after? A Woodward and Bernstein—who forgot, after the movie with Redford and Hoffman, how to be police reporters and even how to cite a checkable source? A Morton Kondracke or Robert Novak, collecting thousands of dollars from the Republican Party for advising its governors on ways to get reelected? A George Will, who ghostwrote speeches for Jesse Helms and Ronald Reagan? It's not Murrow's fault the "boys" he nurtured at CBS, like Sevareid, Collingwood and Schoenbrun, are gone and dead; that even the youngest, Kur-alt, got so fed up with network news he quit a multimillion-dollar contract, loving honor rather more. (Although it *is*, partially, Murrow's fault that they were all of them boys.) Nor is it his fault that four decades after he took on Joe McCarthy, there hasn't been anything else as courageous on television except the Bill Moyers *Frontline* expose on "the secret government" of our intelligence agencies. "To be a hero," wrote Simone Weil, "one must give an order to oneself." That's not where the orders come from these days. Instead of courage, we've got demographics.

But Murrow's story is bigger than TV, and bigger than journalism. In every institution of our society, there have always been brilliant young men who find surrogate fathers, as Murrow found Paley. For awhile in this relationship of privilege and protection, the young men imagine they can go on being brilliant, on their own terms, forever, immune to the bottom-line logic of a corporate culture which, for its own reasons, has surrounded and preserved them in paternalistic blubber. But in these institutions, we are not at all fathers and sons; we are landlords and tenants, owners and pets. It shouldn't surprise the brilliant young men, and yet it always surprises the brilliant young men, when the party's over and the pets are put to sleep.

Journalism just talks a loftier game. From decades of experience at *The New York Times* (from which one escapes, as if from the Communist Party or the Catholic Church, by jumping over a wall), CBS (where nervous affiliates are always telling the news division how to do its job), the old weekly *Life* (before it died for

People's sins), inside Conde Nast's bat cave and the cryogenic sperm deposit vaults of public television—not to mention time served in penance at such margins as *The Nation*, Pacifica and National Public Radio—I assure you that all big-time news organizations are alike, equally unhappy families, at which paranoia, repression, Oedipal revolt, ulcers and the gripe are as common as colds and salt. Each is a controlled environment like Disneyland, and deserves a satiric novel like Norman Rush's *Mating*, as if West Forty-third and West Fifty-seventh streets were sand dunes in Botswana, and either the executive editor or the executive producer had ordained in the no-smoking cubicles a utopian Tsau, with windmills, rondavels, boomslangs, dung carts, abacus lessons, ceramic death masks, "militant nostalgia," "Anti-Imperialist Lamentations," a Mother Committee and an ostrich farm. But deep down in its inferiority complex, television doesn't feel that way. Like the Republican Party, it remembers, mourns, and mimics a mythic past when reporters were private eyes and cowboys, rather than blow-dried performing seals tethered to a TelePrompTer.

On his way to Diego's, Jeffrey discovers a woman harmed by information excess. All the symptoms are present: bleeding from the nose and ears, vomiting, deliriously disconnected speech, apparent disorientation, and the desire to touch everything.

Ted Mooney

Consider the Fall 1995 network season. If not Mary Tyler Moore in *New York News* as the publisher of a feisty tabloid that hounds down stories on prisons, sweatshops, the Chinese Mafia and cross-dressing deputy police commissioners, it was Mariel Hemingway in *Central Park West* as the editor of a Conde Nastie sort of slick whose table of contents included John-John softball and helicopter sex. Or it was David Allen Grier, an African-American college professor signing on in *The Preston Episodes* as house grammarian at a gossip magazine called *Stuff*. Or the newly divorced and hyperkinetic Tea Leoni reduced, in *The Naked Truth*, from Pulitzer-winning photojournalism to a supermaket tabloid called the *Comet*. Or Debra Messing shacking up, in *Ned and Stacey*, with ad-agency junior executive Thomas Haden Church while supposedly writing for the *Village Voice*, which was almost as likely as Lori Loughlin, a leftwing obit writer for the *Times*, falling for the rightwing Hoboken police detective Tony Danza, in *Hudson Street*. But not as preposterous as D.W. Sweeney, a *Strange Luck* photojournalist, spending more time playing French tickle and Spanish fly with his seductive editor, Pamela Gidley, than he did falling down and burning up on the fraught job.

None of this was quite as wish-fulfilling as a 1989 TV movie, *Money, Power, Murder*, in which the syndicated New York *Daily News* sports columnist Mike Lupica imagined himself as a investigative reporter, played by Kevin Dobson, who was so much tougher than tar and nicotine that, after wandering the rainy waterfront at night and drinking beer from a wet paper bag and stopping to ask a black-and-bluesy street musician to play "Tenderly" on his saxophone, he not only solved the disappearance of a network anchor-bitch, exposed a fraudulent TV evangelist, and tracked down a serial killer with an icepick, but also got to sleep with Blythe Danner.

Now, in thirty-five years of meeting deadlines for newspapers and magazines, none of this has ever happened to me, not a single Chinese mafioso or cross-dressing deputy police commissioner, no sex in helicopters, and especially (alas) not Blythe Danner. Although television has been making newspaper series since the dawn of the medium—*Police Reporter* in 1948, *The Front Page* in 1949, *Big Town* and *I Cover Times Square* in 1950, *Byline, Foreign Intrigue* and *Front Page Detective* in 1951—they almost never get it right, and when they do, they cancel it (*Lou Grant*, a series that worried more about the ethics of news gathering than most journalism schools). In sitcoms and melodramas, Betty Furness, Harry Guardino, Suzanne Pleshette, Lloyd Bridges, Debbie Reynolds, Dabney Coleman, Celeste Holm, Edmund Lowe, Jamie Lee Curtis, Raymond Burr, Shirley MacLaine, Gig Young, Darren McGavin, Nancy Olson, Robert Urich, Shelley Hack, Richard Crenna, Susan Anton, Tim Matheson, Bernadette Peters and Gary Merrill have all played editors and reporters and columnists. But who remembers *Blue Light, Bridges to Cross, Deadline to Action, Gibbsville, Glit-*

ter, Good Time Harry, Hot Shots, Honestly Celeste, Jack and Mike, The Insiders, Kingston: Confidential, Kolchak, Maggie Briggs, The Reporter, The Roaring Twenties, Saints and Sinners, Shirley's World or *Stop Susan Williams?* The superhero assisted in his superheroics by Bruce Lee's Cato was only a *Green Hornet* at night; during daylight hours, he edited the *Daily Sentinel*. Need I mention Perry White, Lois Lane, Clark Kent and their *Daily Planet? Hard Copy*, with Michael Murphy and Wendy Crewson as crime reporters for the L.A. *Morning Post*, lasted only five months on CBS in 1987. *Capital News*, a David Milch production in which Helen Slater and William Russ pretended to work for the *Washington Post*, lasted four episodes on ABC in 1990. Fictitious New York newspapers have been called *Bulletin, Examiner, Express, Globe, Herald, Record* and the *Illustrated Press*. In *The Name of the Game*, media mogul Gene Barry, *People* editor Tony Franciosa and *Crime* reporter Robert Stack all spent quality time with Susan Saint James before she married Rock Hudson's *McMillan*. From *The Odd Couple*, in which he played a sports columnist, Jack Klugman could live forever on residuals, not even counting several seasons of *Quincy*. But his sports-columnizing on *Slap Maxwell* did nothing for Dabney Coleman's career, despite some of the wackiest one-liners in the anals of sitcom: "tears are for ballerinas"; "as serious as beavers in a pantry"; "love don't make the buttercups shine"; "gone like meat on the side of a boat"; and "dead as a walnut."

TV wants print journalism to be more thrilling than any newspaper or magazine ever can be if it has to meet a deadline, just as TV needs cops to shoot more people than the drug cartels, and private eyes who do something else besides industrial espionage and divorce work. In real life, Blythe Danner and Susan Saint James actually married *television* executives.

I'm the local stringer for Ceres Datacom network. I hold citizenship in it, though legally speaking it's sometimes more convenient to be treated as wholly owned depreciable hardware. Our life is information—even money is information. Our money and our life are one and the same.

Bruce Sterling, *Schismatrix*

To be sure, network news producers begin each working day with a careful read of the *New York Times*, the *Washington Post* and the *Wall Street Journal*. But so do the editors of *Time* and *Newsweek*, with a reverence hard to distinguish from an inferiority complex. And so, in their differing ideological bunkers, do the editors of *The Nation*, *The New Republic*, *National Review* and the *Weekly Standard*, with a skepticism hard to distinguish from paranoia. Less remarked is the subversive fact that newsrooms at the *Times* and *Post* are also constantly monitoring CNN. What no one seems to have noticed is that hardly anyone in the national news-gathering business begins his or her working day by reading the *other* 1,700 daily newspapers in the United States. This is because they can get a better take on the rest of the world from the nightly network news with Jennings, Brokaw or Rather. One wearies of hearing that a printed transcript of each network's half-hour evening news wouldn't fill the front page of a *New York Times*. We don't have to read the front page of the *Times*. We scan it instead, in search of the piece of the mosaic that pertains to our personal agenda, then dive inside. Whereas television news, at least before the every-half-hour waste-recycling of the all-news cable channels, was a format insisting on its own sequence. And if you must look at a front-page transcript, seek out something rather more typical of American print journalism, like the Keene, N.H., *Sentinel*, or the San Antonio, Texas, *Light*, or, for the lightest of reading, *USA Today*.

There is a reason the TV version of *USA Today* was laughed off the air and out of syndication in the fall of 1988. No matter how bad we might have felt about television news, we felt even worse about not getting any news at all, especially if, as in New York, we had to stay up until 2 AM not to get it. On Friday, September 16, at 2:17 AM, I learned that for one million bucks, 17 per cent of the American public would throw their pets off a cliff. Of course, this "public" consisted only of those respondents to a poll in *USA Today* (The Newspaper) that asked, "What Would *You* Do For a Million Dollars?" We weren't told if the pets in question were cats, dogs, parakeets, goldfish or iguanas. Nor whether readers *volunteered* to throw their pets off a cliff, or the old heave-ho was a sinister option suggested by the newspaper. Nor whether readers of *USA Today*, as a group, loved pets less than did readers of, say, *Architectural Digest*.

Besides the bad science of the weird sample, there was this larger philosophical problem. Like its print parent, for which it was a frenzied commercial, *USA Today: The Television Show* relied a lot on polls. Polls inquire into our feelings. Feelings are squirmy and inchoate. Asked about and quantified, soft feeling becomes hard fact, without any action. Suddenly, on television, our clouds of anger, unction and blank uneasiness are colored in by a sort of electronic crayon. Innocent of behavior, *we* are the news. This gets us into Bohr and Heisenberg and Wittgenstein, where nobody wants to go, especially at two in the morning. But I do wish somebody would tell Jane Pauley and Stone Phillips at NBC's *Dateline* that their polls—one remembers in particular their asking us, before we knew that Susan Smith had murdered her own kids, if *we* would leave our children in a car with a stranger—are approximately as newsworthy as the ferocious questions Barbara Walters lobbed at Michael Jackson.

But there I was on Monday/Tuesday of the first week of *USA Today: The Television Show*, when I should have been in bed. Edie, Robin, Kenneth and Bill spent more time talking to Brian Bosworth of the Seattle Seahawks than they did, in a presidential election year, to the mineral Dukakis and the vegetable Bush. There was a "cover story" on love, with sound bites from a psychologist and an anthropologist; a visit to the Nieman-Marcus catalogue to look at pianos you could walk on; a featurette on Russians and baseball; "snapshots" about church membership in America and postage stamps in Japan; a weather map impossible to comprehend, and a warning not to invest in gold mines over the telephone. The Tuesday/Wednesday "cover story" was about nose jobs and tummy tucks, with sound bites from a sociologist and the fitness editor of an unnamed magazine, followed by a featurette on how our ambassadors are trained to behave in the company of terrorists (run a roadblock, tell the truth!), two minutes on volunteer firefighters, a very old story about backbiting in the broadcast booth at ABC's *Monday Night Football*, Brooke Shields on Calvin Klein, Yoko Ono talking back to Albert Goldman, a "smokeless" cigarette from R.J. Reynolds that tasted like "burning socks," "snapshots" on limousine sales and the salaries of NFL officials, telephone numbers to call if you wanted major league baseball in Buffalo, and how a doodle on a cocktail napkin became the Fido Dido "attitude" and fashion craze. I missed Wednesday/Thursday, but the "cover story" on Thursday/Friday asked the pertinent question, "Are You Better Off Than Your Parents Were?" and answered with...a poll! No hard facts; merely spongy feelings. Meanwhile, between "snapshots" on how many of us fish and what we wanted in a hotel (cleanliness, location, price), Edie, Robin, Kenneth and Bill talked to Hurricane Gilbert, Elton John, an Olympic boxer who did a Muhammad Ali impression and the new Iranian ambassador to the United Nations, who had already been interviewed at length on Ted Koppel's *Nightline*.

In case you missed them in late September, 1988, the front-page stories in *The New York Times* and the lead stories on the CBS, ABC, and NBC evening-news programs were, on Tuesday, radon, Burma, drought, Kurds, Gorbachev, Dukakis, Jesse Jackson, Bess Myerson, air piracy and acid rain. On Wednesday: Reagan at the U.N., devastation in Jamaica, nuclear waste, George Bush, Yasir Arafat, savings-and-loan bailouts and the gold-filled Peruvian tomb of a pre-Inca warrior-priest, his wives, his servants and his favorite dog. On Friday: Gilbert in Texas, Gilbert and Dukakis, a slump in the housing market, a comeback for Detroit cars with front-wheel drive, peace talks in Nicaragua, identity crisis in South Korea and salmonella in Grade A eggs.

Well, of course, the *Times* and the networks were uptight and anal-retentive and not in the least postmodern, pregenital or polymorphous perverse. *USA Today* producer Steve Friedman had seen the future, and it was $45-million worth of *filler* dressed up as a gigantic pinball or slot machine, in the middle of what looked like an airport departure lounge—Big Brotherly monitors and wanton graphics, distended bars of color and broken bars of music, falling dominoes and boring cylinders, trapdoors and whirlpools—

through which the yupscale anchorpeople wandered as hungry for meaning as nomadic goats. And when Edie, Robin, Kenneth and Bill did stay put, they were not permitted a desk to hide behind. They didn't know what to do with their elbows or knees; their arms and legs hung out like software in a Dali. On the spin of their grins, they swivelled into dread and game-show: PacMan! Fido Dido!

USA Today has been a tremendous success as a national newspaper but it wasn't good enough for national television. Maybe the network entertainment divisions keep trying for a good newspaper or magazine series to compensate for the disappearance of good newspapers and magazines wherever we really live. In the very same fall of 1995 when all those TV shows started, *George* made its first appearance—282 pages of it, 175 of them ads—as a bimonthly "post-partisan" magazine devoted to the "lifestyle" of politics, with Cindy Crawford on its cover and inside, next to a horoscope, Lamar Alexander on his favorite vegetable and Beatle, Julia Roberts feeling bad about Haiti, and Madonna promising us that if she were President, she'd pay teachers more than movie stars and let Roman Polanski back in the country. As if we weren't already afflicted with a *New Yorker* gone Hollywood and a *Vanity Fair* that psychobabbled, this glossy triumph of the kind of journalism that postures in front of experience rather than engaging it, that looks in its cynical opportunism for an angle, a spin or a *take* instead of consulting points of principle, that strikes attitudes like matches the better to admire its own inside wiseguy profile, made *Crossfire* and *The Capital Gang* and *The McLaughlin Report* look like Plato's Symposium. Meanwhile, Philadelphia, Baltimore and Dallas all lost daily papers. In Detroit the only news was published by scabs. (Ben Bagdikian tells us in *The Media Monopoly* that in 1946, 80 percent of our daily newspapers were independently owned; by 1989, 80 percent were owned by corporate chains.) In Los Angeles, the Times-Mirror Company was not so busy Soviet purging its own payroll that it hadn't time to snuff out *New York Newsday*.

Full disclosure: I wrote a column for *New York Newsday* every Thursday for seven years, on the politics of culture. They abolished this column in one of their many face-lift redesigns, but the "tabloid in the tutu" remained my paper of choice until the draconian word came down. "I do not exist," said Murray Kempton on that Black Friday in the newsroom; "I *have* to write." Kempton, a 77-year-old combination of Plutarch and Miss Lonelyhearts, had been writing for one or another New York paper for half a century. I had been reading him since I was 12, and Adlai first lost to Ike, back when there were nine dailies in the Wormy Apple. Now there are three, two of them owned by tycoon union-busters who seem less interested in our city than in their grandiose real-estate and media-empire ambitions. *Newsday*, where Kempton's column appeared four times a week, found out bottom lines are also flat. The brand-new chief executive at the Times-Mirror parent company pulled its plug minutes after coming over to the world of journalism from a world of microwave popcorn and breakfast sugarbombs. The 10-year-old tabloid with a social conscience was close to breaking even, and would even have made a profit in a year or two, but was judged unlikely ever to achieve what the corporate heavies now deem "an appropriate rate of return"—15 to 17 percent. Tough love and tough darts. Kempton would pedal away on his notorious bicycle, to be published only on Long Island; and the rest of us were left behind with the taste of aspirin in our mouths. Remember when they cancelled *Mary Tyler Moore? M*A*S*H? Cagney & Lacey? China Beach?* Like that. What did we lose, besides five hundred book reviews a year, quality reporting on everything from World Trade Center bombings to Gulf War atrocities to ethnic cleansing, and the most aggressive coverage of city politics in New York history? We lost the strongest stable of columnists since the old *New York World*, including two who were openly gay, and our only newspaper page for children and high-school students (in English *and* Spanish). We were merely diminished in heart and jumping beans.

In the final analysis, it doesn't bother anyone very much
that politics be democratic so long as the economy is not.
Eduardo Galeano, *The Book of Embraces*

But instead of sentimentalizing the loss of yet another newspaper in a cutthroat corporate economy, why not sentimentalize the loss of a publishing house? Five years before the bottomliners strangled *Newsday*, they purged Pantheon. Most people don't care who publishes a book, anymore than we care which network broadcasts a program. We want to know who wrote it and what it's about. How it came into being as a physical object in a store somewhere is one of those mysteries we haven't time for, like bread or roses or electricity. Someone, though, must look at a manuscript, decide the culture needs it, take a chance, edit copy, set type, design jackets, cut down trees, *publish*. And those of us who review books as well as those of us who write them had known for a long time that nobody published better than Pantheon. Theirs were handsome books, often difficult, always surprising, from all over the world. Launched in 1942 by refugees from Hitler, Pantheon brought us writers like Boris Pasternak, Jean-Paul Sartre, Gunnar Myrdal, Carl Jung and Guiseppe di Lampedusa, plus Studs Terkel, George Kennan and Art Spiegelman.

Until March 1990 Pantheon was also our preeminent mainstream publisher of social criticism by the likes of Ralph Nader, Barry Commoner, Todd Gitlin and Noam Chomsky. Under the Random House corporate umbrella, Pantheon had been encouraged to discover dissident writers. But this was before the Newhouse media conglomerate bought that umbrella and turned it into a boot. Even as heads were rolling at Newhouse magazines like *The New Yorker*, *Vanity Fair*, *Self*, *Glamour* and *Vogue*, André Schiffrin, the head of Pantheon for thirty years, was forced to resign because he wouldn't cut his list of books by two-thirds nor "broaden his focus." In other words, fewer Chomskys and more generic best-sellers along the lines of *How I Lost Weight, Found God, Smart-Bombed Ragheads and Changed My Sexual Preference in the Bermuda Triangle*. All six of Pantheon's senior editors also quit in protest. And three hundred and fifty writers, editors and friends showed up on a picketline in front of Random House in Manhattan, including Terkel, Kurt Vonnegut, Mary Gordon, E.P. Thompson and Barbara Ehrenreich. Many more, among them Joyce Carol Oates, William Styron, Nadine Gordimer, Arthur Miller, Jessica Mitford, Robert Stone, Maxine Hong Kingston and Elie Wiesel, signed a protest petition. The culture had been wounded.

Pantheon had lately been losing money. So, of course, have our schools, our symphony orchestras and our space program. Alberto Vitale, the new bibliocidal Random House chairman who spoke of books as "units," like boxes of pretzels or spray cans of deodorant, wanted to manufacture fewer varieties in greater numbers, maximizing profit and minimizing risk for the $10-billion Newhouse empire. Apparently talking about communism's collapse, Vitale told the press: "Look at what happened to the countries that considered 'bottom-line' the most obscene expression in their vocabulary." So much for those of us so naive as to imagine that the velvet revolutions of 1989—the disintegration before our eyes of the non-profit police states of Eastern Europe—had been about something grander than cost-efficiency, as well as those of us so romantic as to think of books as "uniques" instead of "units." Vitale would go on to sue Joan Collins for failing to deliver an acceptable best-seller, in spite of a $3-million Swifty Lazar contract specifying that she didn't really have to write it by herself. Famously, he lost in court and on Court TV.

In an America where downsizing labor to maximize profit is considered not only necessary but mysteriously *desirable*, and maybe even a *value*—unlike, say, insuring adequate prenatal care to reduce our infant mortality rate, or immunizing inner-city children against contagious diseases—and where the stock exchange panics every time employment *increases*, there is no reason to feel any sorrier for *Newsday* columnists and Pantheon editors than for air traffic controllers, tugboat captains, steel and garment workers, "adjunct" college professors for whom there will never be tenure, obsolete engineers and whole battalions of the "reserve army of the unemployed" mustered out of our tough-love co-prosperity sphere by "replacement workers" who line up to scab in every labor dispute, by "temps" who will work without health insurance or pension benefits, and by job flight to Jakarta and Taegu.

But we should at least understand that what's happened to TV news in the last decade is just another leprous face of what's happened to every other business in the country. So long as the three networks divided up the ad dollar pie among them, they could afford to carry (and to brag about) elite news divisions capable of competing with elite newspapers. Along came cable, Fox, mini-networks like UPN and WB, Blockbuster videos and the World Wide Web, and—surprise!—stockholders were upset at the size of their quarterly dividends. Nor could these stockholders even be sure who owned *them* at the end of another frantic day of buying and selling and merging.

Before we blame, we should first see if we can't excuse.
G.C. Lichtenberg

It is the purpose of elite media like ABC, CBS, NBC, *The New York Times*, *The Los Angeles Times*, *Newsweek* and *Time* to capture those demographic segments of the many splendored population most passionately desired by advertisers. Corporate America will then pay these elite media for the privilege of talking to this affluent profligate audience. In the Darwinian buinsess environment of the Reagan gerontocracy, during which the media themselves were corporatized, it should be no surprise at all that "news" was suddenly asked to become a "profit center." (And not only on television. Did you know that, with the eager approval of the editors, the *restaurant* critic for *The New York Times* can run up American Express and Visa bills of $125,000 a year, not counting taxis? Eating! Nesting! Styles!) Since the business of television had always been to profit from our distraction, it was only natural to try to turn TV news into a giddier distraction than the regularly scheduled distraction, like a hit of crack:

> *Live from the Al Rashid in downtown Baghdad, Luke Skywalker & the Tracers! From palmy Dhahran: the Wild Weasels of the 35th Tactical Fighter Wing and Raytheon's own anti-missile Patriot missile! From a columbarium at the Pentagon: Pac-Man and Nintendo briefings! On the screen, in-your-face, by remote control: a 'round-the-clock high-tech fuzz-grunge telethon, in weird green cyberspace; a seamless web of SCUD alerts bounced off starfish satellites; color analysis and instant replay by doctors of spin and former Mideast terrorists and Avis rent-a-generals; glitterdome commercials for smart bombs, dumb Arabs and sudden death in overtime!*

Wave goodbye to Walter Cronkite, who took off his glasses to shed a tear on reporting the death of John F. Kennedy, and who told his millions of viewers at the Democratic convention in 1968, after looking at the police riot on the streets of Chicago, "I want to pack my bags and get out of this town." Say hello instead to gaudy spectaculars like revolution in Iran ("America Held Hostage"), Gulf

Wars ("Desert Storm"), World Trade Centers and Oklahoma Cities ("Terrorism Comes to America"), O.J., TWA 800, even hurricanes and Olympics, prepackaged as if for home video and CD-ROM, with thumb-in-the-eye graphics and mood music to cue the rising gorge. Wave goodbye as well to reporters telling us whatever it is they actually know, whether or not they have a picture of it. Say hello to "photo ops" by appointment, "staged news" and computer-simulated "re-creations" of events so contrary as to have occurred while the cameras weren't watching. (How long ago did ABC tell us that diplomat Felix Bloch was a spy, supporting its story with a black-and-white videotape purporting to depict a briefcase swap between Bloch and a Soviet intelligence agent, when what we really saw was two employees of ABC News "simulating" such a swap, tarted up electronically to look like FBI surveillance. Is Felix Bloch in jail yet? No. But he's unemployed.) Wave goodbye to cost-inefficient TV documentary units, inconvenient and overly fastidious scruples about ratings-hyping prurience, over-aged (and therefore over-paid) DuPont/Columbia baton-winning correspondents, and bureaus in most of the rest of the world. (ABC is down to eight, including Beijing; NBC is down to seven, including Mexico City; CBS is down to four, with Tom Fenton left alone to cover England, Russia and all of Euorpe and Bob Simon in splendid solitiude all over Africa and the Middle East. CNN maintains twenty bureaus, including Rio, Nairobi, Amman, New Delhi and Bangkok, but except during wars, only 400,000 people watch CNN, which is roughly the circulation of a magazine like the *Atlantic*.) Say hello, instead, to "infotainment," to movie-star and rock-musician kissy-poo profiles on the primetime magazines, and checkbook trash journalism in its Michael Jackson stormcloud mode in syndication, with the Berserkers from *Hard Copy* and *Current Affair* and *Inside Edition* descending on Neverland to buy the ever-changing stories of Michael's maids, chauffeurs, gardeners and bodyguards, not to mention the media-savvy lawyers, gloryhound private detectives and yo-yo flacks who brokered the sale of cooked data when they weren't leaking illegal wiretaps and stolen depositions. Goodbye, trying hard and meaning well; hello, fire alarms, car bombs, beaver shots and giggles.

Actually I'd be a whole lot happier and the American public better-informed if respectable journalism, print or electronic, were half as energetic and ingenious at tracking down important stories about education, the economy and the environment as the trashy tabloids, print and electronic, are in their pursuit of Michael Jackson, Lorena Bobbitt and Susan Smith. In a modern age when information is a commodity for sale, only the deepest of pockets will end up owning it unless we learn to roll with the spin and duck the sucker punch. Since mainstream journalism is also big business, this means that its yeomen and serfs must think against their own class and wallet interests. It would be nice if every broadcast journalist had a rolodex that included the telephone number of Susan Faludi as well as Henry Kissinger, of Henry Louis Gates as well as Alan Simpson, of just about anybody who isn't male and pale and well-connected. The trouble is not, as James Fallows and others argue, that the media are too cynical about public institutions—having been lied to about everything from U-2 overflights to Castro and the Mafia, from the Gulf of Tonkin to Chappaquiddick, from Watergate to Iran-Contra, from S&L to BCCI, who should believe whom?—but that media tend to be cynical about the wrong things, as if politics were all performance art and no policy, like the novel *Primary Colors*.

It works the other way, too. Those of us who are cynical about the media are also cynical about the wrong media things—about the lecture fees of a Sam Donaldson or a Cokie Roberts; about a Kathie Lee Gifford and her sweat shop; about a Henry Kissinger as a consultant for ABC News, before he became a member of the CBS board of directors, deploring to Peter Jennings the student occupation of Tiananmen Square without telling anyone that his private consulting group had a number of lucrative business contracts riding on the current Chinese government. Like television itself, we tend to personalize whatever bothers us, which means the nearest familiar and therefore automatically contemptible face. It seems never to occur to us that greed modifies behavior more than television does. To be sure, our journalism has mutated, from an older and feistier idea of a craft or trade, into a "profession" that is more like an entitlement—as if our indentured servitude to a bureaucracy with its own pomp, protocols, p.r. flacks, foreign policy, official secrets, beanies and anthems somehow guaranteed white collar civil-service perks like summer homes, Cycladic vacations, Jungian analysis, engraved invitations to Truman Capote's parties and private schools for our sensitive children. Once upon a time, when our fingernails were dirty, we knew the romance of ink, and lived in the high-school printshop, and could read type upside down, and the belching machines seemed somehow to connect brain and word, muscle and idea, hot lead and cool thought. But that was before we got into the information-commodity racket, where we have more in common with the class interests of a Michael Eisner, a Bill Gates or Ivan Boesky than we do with the papermakers or deliverymen. After which our biggest story became ourselves, at the Century Club, the Cosmopolitan and Bohemian Grove, at Kay Graham's or Elaine's or the masked ball charity scam—Alex Solzhenitsyn and Oscar de la Renta and Leona Helmsley invite you to Feel Bad About the Boat People at the Museum of Modern Art—and we weren't really crossing a picket line if we phoned in our copy to the computer, with plenty of time leftover to make it to Yankee Stadium or RFK, where avatars like Boss Steinbrenner and Edward Bennett Williams were waiting to lift us up by our epaulets and our stock portfolios to a sky box to consort with, and be leaked upon by, the Glad Hand and the Big Fix. And you can't tell the pearls from the swine.

The thing that astonished him was that cats should have two holes cut in their coats exactly at the place where their eyes were.

G.C. Lichtenberg

But if conflict-of-interest is something to worry about in reporters, it's even more worrisome in corporations, where it combines with collusion—the ugly underside of "synergy" in this era of metasta-sizing mergers and monopolies—to pave gardens into parking lots. It wasn't ABC's *20/20* journalists who settled the Philip Morris suit; it was Cap Cities. It wasn't the *60 Minutes* journalists who killed another anti-smoking segment; it was the CBS legal depart-ment on behalf of Larry Tisch, on the eve of his profitable sale of the network to Westinghouse. How likely is *Time* magazine to sav-age a big-budget Warner Brothers movie? Will *TV Guide*, which happens to be owned by Rupert Murdoch, ever be genuinely nasty to a series on Fox television, which also happens to be owned by Rupert Murdoch? As we speak, Bill Gates at Microsoft has been buying up everything from Michael Kinsley to the Hermitage, and beating Murdoch to the punch with a second all-news cable channel (in cahoots with NBC), and devising ways to punish Netscape for daring to let people into cyberspace without his seignorial permission, and we're making it easier for him in Congress to own the rest of us. Big media are big business, and the only business they are bigly in is turning a profit, not reporting news. Windows 95, General Electric and Mickey Mouse want us to do as we are told, and only exactly what we are told. In all the hours of NBC's 1996 Summer Olympics coverage, did you hear anybody on air mention that restaurant owners in Atlanta poured chlorine bleach in their trash containers to keep vagrants from fishing for scraps? That many of Atlanta's homeless were shipped out of town, with one-way bus tickets? That the city government, besides outlawing panhandling, evicted a thousand tenants and razed a public housing development to make room for the very Centennial Park and Olympic Village that got terror-bombed? Murrow and Kuralt would not have missed this story.

Six stallions, say, I can afford,
Is not their strength my property?
I tear along, a sporting lord,
As if their legs belonged to me.

Goethe, *Faust*

Mirabile dictu: RCA sold out NBC and its nine TV stations, seven regional sports networks and a serious interest in twelve cable outlets, to a General Electric that also had to think about aircraft engines, diesel and electric trains, nuclear-reactor turbines, satellite systems, long-distance telephone lines, plastics, appliance and insurance companies, and financial and medical services. Having sold out to Cap Cities, ABC, with its eighteen TV stations and twenty-one radio stations, then saw itself further accessorized when Cap Cities sold out to Disney, with its movie studios, its home video production facilities, its three music companies, two publishing houses and eleven newspapers, a dozen magazines, two cable channels, countless theme parks, resorts and retirement communities and a professional ice hockey team. Bill Paley sold out CBS and its fourteen TV stations, eighteen AM radio stations, twenty-one FM radio stations and its country-music cable channel, to Larry Tisch of Loews, who sold out to a Westinghouse which, in addition to its own "Group W" TV stations and satellite distributorship, has also diversified into wireless communications and security systems, refrigeration and waste disposal, nuclear-power plants, nuclear reactors for submarines and aircraft carriers. Not content with stealing professional football and many affiliates from CBS, Rupert Murdoch has entered into a direct-broadcast satellite service with MCI Communications, which will extend his global surveillance reach to all five continents and synergize nicely with his ownership of more than one hundred newspapers in Australia, five in England and one (to be kind, since it's the *Post*) in New York, his major TV network (Fox), his major movie studio (Twentieth-Century Fox), his major book publisher (Harper-Collins), a couple of record companies and *TV Guide* and the *Weekly Standard*. Even Ted Turner—who wanted CBS before Larry bought it out from under him—sold out CNN, TBS, TNT, the Atlanta Braves, the Atlanta Hawks, the Goodwill Games, the New Line Cinema and the Cartoon Network, to Time Warner, which already had a movie studio, a couple of television production companies, two premium-cable channels, part of *E!*, part of Comedy Central and all of Sega, five book-publishing companies, twenty-three magazines, Six Flags and DC Comics. John Malone at Telecommunications Inc. shakes his dubious head and dickers with Bell Atlantic while holding on to the pipes and the wires that feed cable television into more than 45 percent of the country's homes, plus slices of Discovery, Showtime and the Learning Channel, even as Viacom, a competing cable giant and the owner of Paramount, as well as Lifetime, Nickelodeon, MTV, Simon & Schuster, Madison Square Garden and the Rangers and the Knicks, gets so nervous that Sumner Redstone fires Frank Biondi, who goes to work for Edgar Bronfman Jr., whose Seagram's whisky conglomerate bought the MCA Hollywood talent agency. We pretend not to notice that Wells Fargo International Trust is the single biggest institutional shareholder in GE, third-largest in Disney, fourth largest in Time Warner, fifth-largest in Cap Cities, and seventh-largest in CBS. And we'd rather not even think about AT&T, GTE, Sprint, Pacific Telesis, Ameritech or NYNEX.

On the one hand, the military-industrial-entertainment complex resembles a huge vat of Franz Anton Mesmer's "magnetized water," around which, in the dark days before the French Revolution, the comely and the credulous hooked thumbs, into which they plunged fishing poles, and out of which they pulled dollops of curative for their "disequilibrium," while staring into mirrors and listening to a glass harmonica. On the other hand, it mimics the hard-wired and compulsive behaviors of the perpetual-motion clock bug in Kobe Abe's *The Ark Sakura*, eating as it eliminates; thriving on a diet of its own feces; circling always to face the sun.

Such works are like mirrors; if an ape peers in, no apostle will look out.

G.C. Lichtenberg

I'm almost done, a Nowhere Man. I've made a case for television in spite of knowing that the people who create it rely on formula, the people in charge are only in it for the money and the people who watch will grab or reject the meanings they want no matter what I argue. And those meanings, bent, folded, spindled and mutilated however they may be by the commercial venues that unleash them on us, are themselves secondhand, borrowed from a broader popular culture which—let's face it—is where we go to talk to and agree with one another, to simplify ourselves, to find our herd. It's like going to the Automat to buy an emotion. It is real enough, but maybe stale. Or thrilling, but cheap. And the payoffs are predictable. And the repetitions are a bummer. Whereas truly great art is where we go alone to complicate ourselves. Inside its solitude, we take on contours, textures and perspectives, and are transfigured. I actually *believe* that ten minutes of a Mozart piano sonata improves abstract brain activity.

But, of course, you can't ordain great art. It waits in ambush. At least television has asked us to spend a night as a volunteer in a homeless shelter, to work with AIDS patients in a hospice, to stop lynchings and troop trains, save a whale and walk in the virtual shoes of school teachers and physical therapists. While it may not be that "grand institution of public enlightenment" the nineteenth-century liberals hoped for with newspapers, over and over again it has sought to represent the most powerless among us. Over and over again it has encouraged us to imagine not only the world as it is, outside our comfort zones, but the world as it might be if we turned our empathy into citizenship and action. How is it, I'm wondering , that our politics and culture got so *mean* while television was asking us night after night to be *nicer* to women, children, minorities, immigrants, poor people, sick people and strangers? One short answer would be that we have failed to heed its humane agenda because we've shut down in self-defense against the falsified urgencies of the commodity culture and the Realm of Signs; that after so many commercials for too much of everything, we are agnostic about all of it; cool in our genes. An even shorter answer borrows (gasp!) from Karl Marx, written when he was very young: "Since money, as the existing and active concept of value, confounds and exchanges everything, it is the universal *confusion and transposition* of all things, the inverted world, the confusion and transposition of all natural and human qualities."

In other words, like a sound bite (and maybe even an apocaplyptic trope): If money is the only way we keep score, every other human relation is corrupted.

A NOTE ABOUT THE TYPE

This edition of John Leonard's *Smoke and Mirrors* is the first book set in the typeface Abrams Augereau, designed by George Abrams in 1996 and named for 16th century French typographer Antione Augereau. It is an *Old Style* type based on the designs of Augereau's student Claude Garamond.